Monergism or Synergism

Monergism or Synergism

Is Salvation Cooperative or the Work of God Alone?

DANIEL KIRKPATRICK

Foreword by Nigel G. Wright

PICKWICK *Publications* · Eugene, Oregon

MONERGISM OR SYNERGISM
Is Salvation Cooperative or the Work of God Alone?

Copyright © 2018 Daniel Kirkpatrick. All rights reserved. Except for brief quotations in critical publications or reviews, no part of this book may be reproduced in any manner without prior written permission from the publisher. Write: Permissions, Wipf and Stock Publishers, 199 W. 8th Ave., Suite 3, Eugene, OR 97401.

Pickwick Publications
An Imprint of Wipf and Stock Publishers
199 W. 8th Ave., Suite 3
Eugene, OR 97401

www.wipfandstock.com

PAPERBACK ISBN: 978-1-5326-3010-1
HARDCOVER ISBN: 978-1-5326-3012-5
EBOOK ISBN: 978-1-5326-3011-8

Cataloguing-in-Publication data:

Names: Kirkpatrick, Daniel, author. | Wright, Nigel G., foreword.

Title: Monergism or synergism : is salvation cooperative or the work of God alone? / Daniel Kirkpatrick ; foreword by Nigel G. Wright.

Description: Eugene, OR : Pickwick Publications, 2018 | Includes bibliographical references and index.

Identifiers: ISBN 978-1-5326-3010-1 (paperback) | ISBN 978-1-5326-3012-5 (hardcover) | ISBN 978-1-5326-3011-8 (ebook)

Subjects: LCSH: Predestination. | Free will and determinism.| Providence and government of God. | God—Omniscience. |

Classification: BT810.2 .K56 2018 (print) | BT810.2 .K56 (ebook)

Manufactured in the U.S.A.   JANUARY 9, 2018

For Dr. Matthew Bryan Kirkpatrick and Aurora Kirkpatrick

Contents

Foreword by Nigel G. Wright | ix

Preface | xi

Introduction | xiii

Chapter 1   An Introduction to Monergism and Synergism | 1

Chapter 2   The Aspect of Election | 54

Chapter 3   The Aspect of Regeneration | 85

Chapter 4   The Aspect of Conversion | 129

Chapter 5   The Aspect of Justification in the Monergistic Protestant Tradition | 164

Chapter 6   The Aspect of Justification in Roman Catholicism | 198

Chapter 7   A Constructive Defense of Monergistic Soteriology | 251

Bibliography | 275

Index | 289

Foreword

ONE OF THE MOST perennial debates among Christians has surrounded a complex of doctrines that includes election, predestination, human depravity, and free will. For short these have often been called "the doctrines of grace," even if the debates themselves have often been conducted with a singular lack of grace. Perhaps this is attributable to the strong passions that attach to the desire to give the glory for human salvation to God alone. An implicit issue in the controversies that have sometimes emerged has been that of the human will: to what extent is the human will acted upon by the divine will and what role is it to be assigned in the appropriation of human salvation? Does the will fall into line with what God has irresistibly decided antecedently to any movement on our own part, or does the divine will make itself dependent on a human movement towards God, however much that may be assisted by prevenient grace? As the debates continue and finer and finer points are refined, so it can be seen that concessions can be made on both sides, but at the same time there remains an unresolved tension between the two perspectives. In this closely argued volume Dr. Daniel Kirkpatrick chooses to make the monergism/synergism distinction the lens through which the wider territory is to be explored, thus bringing into the foreground what might previously have been thought of as a subsidiary concern. By careful distinguishing of the various ingredients of the debate around monergism he casts new light on old issues and brings to the surface some questions that might reinvigorate them.

It is a legitimate concern today that many who hold the faith today do so for emotional rather than doctrinal reasons. There is everything to be said for emotion, for feeling deeply our love for God and for God's purposes. But without the buttressing that comes from carefully thought through theological constructs, emotion alone remains vulnerable to being tossed around or even dispelled, especially when it confronts powerful intellectual forces against which it is not armored. This book presents us with an emerging theologian who instinctively and by virtue of extensive training knows how to think theologically. This does not mean this is a book without passion—far from it. It is replete with theological passion and conviction. It would be foolish to imagine that it speaks the last word on a topic over which the Last Word probably awaits the Last Day. Yet just as it itself enters into a world of discourse that precedes it, so it is likely to help those who read it enter into the discourse that will succeed it, to their enrichment. This is not to say that it will always command agreement, but even while contesting some issues it ought to be possible for writer and readers to agree, fully and graciously, that "salvation comes from the Lord." This book could be considered a reflection on that simple but profound statement.

Dr. Nigel G. Wright
Principal Emeritus, Spurgeon's College London

Preface

THE CONCLUSIONS OF THIS project ended in the opposite direction from where it began. From 2004–2006, while a Master of Divinity student at Southwestern Baptist Theological Seminary in Fort Worth, TX, I became aware of what I thought was a superior alternative to the Calvinism and Arminianism debate that I wrestled with for years. That alternative was synergism.

Having believed all my life that salvation required a human response of freely expressed faith (and seeing nothing in Calvinism that adequately affirmed such), I was left with the alternative of Arminianism. Such a view radically opposed the *New Calvinism* movement adopted by my peers, yet there were some features of Arminianism which I still could not readily accept. This led me to question whether I was being too general in my conclusions on the issue. For me, it boiled down to whether one had a role in salvation or not. I was troubled with any thought of God determining salvation apart from any human choice. Having read Norman Geisler's *Systematic Theology* and Roger Olson's *The Mosaic of Christian Belief*, I became aware of an aspect of soteriology I never before heard of—the issue of monergism and synergism.

Monergism is the belief that the work of salvation is by God alone. Naturally, I opposed such a view. Salvation requires a human response! A person must believe through real, genuine faith in order to be saved. Next, I read of synergism—the belief that salvation is a work between God and a human. This, I believed, was the superior view given that it accounts for human faith. I wrote on this subject extensively in seminary, even winning the prestigious Walter Thomas Conner Memorial Award for excellence in theological contribution from Southwestern Baptist Theological Seminary on this subject.

PREFACE

After graduation, as I planned on pursuing PhD work, my view began to change. If salvation is synergistic (meaning a work between God and a human), what *work* does the human do? My answer (as is the answer often given) was faith. But is faith a work? Naturally, I opposed such a notion. If faith is not a work which effects salvation, does monergism have any credibility? In other words, is there a way salvation can be by grace through faith and not through works without succumbing to fatalism (or entirely removing the role of the individual believer)? Further reading into the claims of monergists revealed that this (by and large) is precisely their claim. Salvation can entail genuine human faith while not making that faith a work. With this change of perspective, I set out to explore this issue at length.

This book is a revision of my PhD dissertation carried out under the keen supervision of Dr. Nigel Wright (Principal Emeritus at Spurgeon's College, London England). His scholarship is equaled only to his patience in dealing with all the challenges of supervising an American for a British PhD. The differences between our common language and culture have been both fun and funny (especially in his notes that I am writing in "Texas English" as opposed to "English English"). He is more than I could have ever asked for in a doctoral supervisor, and I am forever grateful for his investment in my life and ministry.

It is impossible to thank those who sacrificed the most to see this degree through to completion, namely my family. I am blessed to be married to the most beautiful, loving, and sacrificial woman I could ever imagine. My wife, Michelle Kirkpatrick, has supported me through more than ten years of higher education, sacrificing much in order to make this a reality. My children, Caedmon Matthew, Anna Grace, and Tess Joy Kirkpatrick have sacrificed many weekends with daddy so that I could write. You will forever have my love. I also wish to thank the wonderful people at First Baptist Church of Pampa, TX who supported me greatly. You will always be my "home church." I also wish to thank my parents, Reed and Chris Kirkpatrick, who have supported me from day one in pursuing a PhD. My gratitude for their love, support, and investment in my life can never be adequately expressed.

Finally, I wish to give all glory and honor to God who has first and foremost saved me by His grace apart from any work of my own as well as giving me the opportunity to pursue this degree. I pray that this study would be used for His glory.

This project is dedicated to my beloved brother, the late Dr. Matthew Bryan Kirkpatrick, and to my beloved child, the late Aurora Kirkpatrick, for whom I am most grateful that salvation is based upon the grace of almighty God and not by human works. We will meet, and meet again.

Introduction

EVERY MAJOR, ORTHODOX CHRISTIAN tradition affirms Jesus Christ as the Savior of human souls. Be they Catholic or Protestant, or more narrowly Reformed or non-Reformed traditions, every major biblically orthodox Christian party denies that people are saved by self-driven effort. Rejecting any notions of Pelagianism or Semi-Pelagianism, the Christian community has affirmed with the Apostle Paul, "For by grace you have been saved through faith. And this is not your own doing; it is the gift of God, not a result of works, so that no one may boast" (Eph 2:8–9, ESV).

However, if salvation is all of grace and not of human works, what role does the human have in salvation? Here one is faced with two options. Salvation could be a cooperative endeavor between God and human agents whereby God does his part and humans do theirs. When combined together, the result is salvation. This view is called *synergism* (the belief that salvation is a cooperative work between God and humans). The other alternative is the belief that God alone saves without human causation. This belief (called monergism) claims salvation is entirely the work of God alone and does not require human cooperation.

Ephesians 2:8–9 is but one of many verses which reflects this difficult tension. Salvation is by God's grace and not human works, yet the human must be involved in some way ("you have been saved *through faith*"). If salvation does not occur without the human's activity of faith, is this not synergism? Yet salvation comes from God and not human works. Does this not point towards monergism?

While having biblical roots, the tensions of monergism and synergism came to prominence during the Reformation period. The strong monergistic teachings of Luther and Calvin (along with their followers) led to

INTRODUCTION

accusations of fatalism while synergists were accused of being Semi-Pelagian. The same accusations are made today, and one is often forced to take sides on the monergism and synergism issue.

This book seeks to address this issue in detail. By allowing synergists and monergists to speak evenly, this study attempts to discern which party most consistently and accurately defends their stance that salvation is by God's grace and not by human works.

This study assumes that one cannot properly address the question of monergistic or synergistic salvation without an exploration of each aspect of salvation. Said another way, it is too general to ask if salvation is monergistic or synergistic given that salvation has many components. Further progress will be made in the debate when one examines the parts that make up the whole. In so doing, one will be able to appreciate better the unique features of each aspect of salvation and understand more clearly the roles of God and the human.

In so doing, it becomes imperative to have a clear understanding of the word "works." Again, no biblically orthodox Christian tradition affirms that one is saved by human works, yet the matter at hand is whether salvation is monergistic (the work of God alone) or synergistic (the work between God and a human). While synergists (it will be shown) affirm that salvation is a cooperative work between God and a human, they also claim that salvation is not by works. This, therefore, requires a clear understanding of what one means by the word "works."

Chapter 1 intends to define the word "works" in a way satisfactorily to all parties through an exploration of causation. Building upon Aristotle's theory of causation, this book will understand work as it relates to cause and effect. When a source (the efficient cause) does an activity that causes an effect (the instrumental cause), one may properly understand such action as a work. However, when the efficient cause works through an agency which itself does not cause an effect, one may properly understand such an action not as a work but as simple instrumentality. This means that an exploration of each aspect of salvation is required with particular attention to the roles of both the divine and human agents. If the activity done by an agent causes an effect, it may rightly be assumed to be a work. However, if an agent works simply by means of an activity which itself does not cause an effect, such an action need not be considered a work.

Chapter 1 addresses the issue of monergism and synergism while defining key definitions (such as "works") and other pertinent issues. Chapters 2–6 explore the various aspects of salvation with particular attention to efficient cause and instrumentality. Primarily the traditions to be explored are the Reformed (or Calvinists) and non-Reformed (or Wesleyans/Arminians).

INTRODUCTION

However, as will be shown in chapters 5–6, there is not significant disagreement concerning the doctrine of justification and synergism between these two camps. Instead, the greater controversy over monergistic/synergistic justification involves Protestants as a whole with the Roman Catholic Church. These two traditions will have their views presented, and a formal evaluation will be found in chapter 6.

Chapter 7 seeks to address common accusations against monergism (particularly the concern raised above on whether monergism is fatalistic). There, synergists will speak their concerns against the monergistic tradition to see if monergism can respond adequately.

While each reader is encouraged to form his or her own view of whether salvation is monergistic or synergistic, this study concludes that monergists (as opposed to synergists) best and most consistently articulate their message that salvation is all of grace and not of human works. The hope is that this book will continue dialogue on this subject in a thoughtful manner amongst the various Christian traditions.

Chapter 1

An Introduction to Monergism and Synergism

HISTORICAL SURVEY OF THE PROBLEM

WHO DOES THE WORK of salvation in the perspectives of Christian theology? If God does all the work of salvation, then what is to be said of the will and role of a believer? However, if humankind does the work of salvation, then what is to be said of one's natural ability, the effects of sin, and the power of God? Is the activity of humankind grace driven effort or effort driven grace? All of these questions share a central concern: is salvation monergistic (meaning a work solely performed by God alone) or synergistic (a work shared between God and an individual)?

These questions have been of interest and argument even from biblical times. Spanning twenty-one centuries of the Christian church, one finds a diachronic development in thought on the worker (or workers) of salvation. One may question if a solution to this issue is possible. However, in order to propose a new solution to these questions, a short survey must be done to prove that such a tension exists as well as a brief overview of how such a tension has sought to be resolved. While space and focus do not permit an exhaustive examination of the history of monergism and synergism, a brief examination will show the existence of tension, development of the issue, and historical attempts at resolution while also enabling one to consider if other options may be available.

Monergism or Synergism

Biblical Tensions

While the notions of monergism and synergism are found in various traditions throughout church history, the tensions that source this disagreement are rooted in each camp's interpretation of Scripture. Indeed, one could go so far as to say that the tensions themselves are sourced (not just in the interpreters but) in the Scriptures themselves. Whether Reformed or Arminian, Roman Catholic or Protestant, or even Augustinian or Pelagian, none of these parties would dispute that there must be some type of action on the part of an individual in order for salvation to occur. But what is the nature of this action? That has become the source of conflict, yet as one turns to the Scripture for insight, one finds that things are not without tension.

One may see such tensions beginning early in the Old Testament with the covenant made with Abraham (beginning in Gen 12). Many see this covenant being the means through which God would bring salvation.[1] According to Genesis 12:1–3, God was the initiator of the covenant made with Abraham (or Abram) whereby some affirm that God's initiative came prior to Abraham's response.[2] Most scholars affirm that God narrowed his redemptive plan to be through one man and one nation in order to bring about the redemption of the whole world.[3] So far, there is little disagreement between parties.

However, the covenant God made with Abraham required a response. The covenant is something that Abraham and his descendants (i.e., Israel) should "keep" (according to Gen 17:10), and the sign of such reciprocity of the covenant was circumcision. While most agree that God's choice is the basis for the covenant, it must be received by faith accompanied by the sign of circumcision (Gen 15:6, see also Rom. 4:3).[4] As William Dyrness states:

> And while the covenant was unconditional in the sense that God would never forget his promises and leave himself without a witness—that is, those who would respond in faith to these

---

1. Waltke, *An Old Testament Theology*, 306–7, 314–17.

2. See Klein, *The New Chosen People*, 29, who (from a non-Reformed perspective) states that God chose Abraham by the sheer grace and unmerited choice.

3. Bartholomew and Goheen, *The Drama of Scripture*, 55.

4. There is debate as to whether it was *just* Judaism (or even Judaism) that had made pre-requisites for salvation/justification through "works" of the law. Some suggest that it was Gentile Christians who imposed this pre-requisite upon themselves in light of their elementary understandings of the Torah. See Ziesler, *Pauline Christianity*, 106. Nevertheless, there appears to be a later misunderstanding during the time of the Apostle Paul that the covenant to be God's people was through works of the law rather than by faith which is, as has been shown, not the original design.

AN INTRODUCTION TO MONERGISM AND SYNERGISM

promises—the continuance of each individual in the blessings of these promises was contingent upon their response in faith.[5]

Dyrness goes on to say that keeping the covenant in faith was something that Israel failed to do. God's election required a response, but Israel failed to respond (positively) by repeatedly turning away. As such, God promised that He would institute a new covenant, one that succeeds where Israel failed (Jer 31:31–34). It would be a law written on the heart, providing a knowledge that all people (from the least to the greatest) can know. It will be for everyone, inclusive of a wider community of God's chosen people. Finally, this covenant will include the forgiveness of sin dealt with once and for all.[6] However, this new covenant will (like the first) need to be received in faith.

Tensions are already formed (as will be shown below) as to the relationship between divine election and human faith in this short Old Testament survey. Faith as expressed through outward means like circumcision (to say nothing of other ceremonial rites such as dietary laws and sacrifices) may be considered as works which must be performed to maintain covenant status. Yet is faith, then, a work?

One then turns to the New Testament to find similar issues. It is hardly beyond question that Jesus' original audience (and one might broaden this assumption to include many within first-century Judaism) viewed salvation to be something which they were personally responsible for in action.

Having witnessed Jesus' most public demonstration of his divine power at that point in his ministry, the participants of Jesus' feeding of the five thousand sought him again the next day, not, as Jesus would say, because of the signs they saw but, rather, because they ate of the loaves and were filled. Seeing that the people were in need of a lasting bread which would satisfy the famished soul, Jesus said, "Do not work for the food that perishes, but (work) for the food that endures for eternal life, which the Son of Man will give you" (John 6:27).

Was Jesus telling his followers that the bread that He provides was something to be worked for (ἐργάζεσθε) by them? This would seem to be their understanding given their response in the following verse: "What shall *we do*, so that *we may work* the works of God?" (NASB, emphasis added). As the original audience was Jewish, some claim the original audience understood such "works" to be that of "works of the Law" leading to eternal life.[7] However, what is one to make of such "works of the law" that can work

---

5. Dyrness, *Themes in Old Testament Theology*, 118.

6. Ibid., 122–23.

7. Beasley-Murray, *John*, 91. Notice, however, that Beasley-Murray understands

for eternal life? Given the nature of Jesus' reply, it would depend upon the nature of belief (v. 36).

Similarly, one recalls Christianity's first converts on the day of Pentecost. After Peter's presentation of the Gospel (recorded in Acts 2), the people responded with a desperate plea: "Brothers, what should *we do*?" (emphasis added). Peter's response for what they must do included a fourfold conversion experience: repent, be baptized, be forgiven, and receive the Holy Spirit. Two things are noteworthy here. First, a response of some type to the Gospel on the part of the hearer is required. In other words, Peter might have prefaced his statement with, "There is something you can *do*." Second, this response includes a variety of aspects (both active and passive) by and on the responder.[8]

One will also recall the Roman jailer's similar question during Paul and Silas' imprisonment in Acts 16:30: "[W]hat must *I do* to be saved?" (emphasis added). Obviously, there was an understanding in first-century thought (both in Judaism and Hellenistic thought) that one must *do* something in order to be saved. Paul's response to the jailer answers what he must do: "Believe on the Lord Jesus, and you will be saved, you and your household" (v. 31).

However, despite the continual biblical testimony that humankind must do *something* in order to be saved, one finds elsewhere that they cannot do *anything* in order to be saved. After completing the various requirements as set forth by Jewish law, the rich young ruler asked what else he must do to inherit eternal life. Jesus replied that he must sell his goods to the poor and follow him. One would expect that this *doing* on behalf of the rich young ruler would then be enough to be saved; however, as he refused, Jesus responded that it is easier for a camel to enter through the eye of a needle than for the rich to inherit the kingdom of God. Being alarmed that such doing was not enough, Jesus was asked, "Then who can be saved?" Jesus responded, "For mortals (Gk. "ἀνθρώποις") it is impossible, but for God all things (particularly salvation) are possible."[9]

---

such "works" as a response of faith contrary to the prevalent Jewish understanding.

8. See Polhill, *Acts*, 116. He notes that these four "ingredients" (as he calls them) are a pattern throughout Luke-Acts describing conversion. Pohill cites Luke 24:47; Acts 3:19; 5:31 to show the connection of forgiveness of sins with repentance and Acts 10:43, 13:38–41 and 26:18 as examples where repentance, forgiveness and faith are connected on 117. Though he does not include faith as an "ingredient" (perhaps mistakenly) of conversion (perhaps so as not to confuse faith as the cause of conversion but as an act of conversion), he no doubt sees the role of faith in conversion. These aspects will be developed and explored below.

9. See Hagner, *Matthew 14–28*, 561–62 for a good defense of the meaning of Jesus' statement that salvation by human works is impossible.

AN INTRODUCTION TO MONERGISM AND SYNERGISM

Likewise, one recalls Paul's teaching to the Ephesians: "For by grace you have been saved through faith, and this is not your own doing; it is the gift of God—not the result of works, so that no one may boast" (2:8–9). While the precise meaning of "works" (be they any efforts on behalf of humankind or works of the law which exclude Gentiles) has been a source of debate in modern Pauline studies, one can see that, for Paul, salvation is by God's grace which comes through humankind's faith. One will also note the contrast between faith and works in these verses. Yet what is the precise nature of the relationship between faith and works? To that question, one must turn to church history.

Tensions in the Early Church

The Scriptures set in place a tension between who does what in salvation. From the short survey above, one can see how salvation included actions both from God and humankind, but does this interaction favor cooperation? Is there interdependency, a co-working relationship that transpires in salvation?

Some within the early church believed so. Much of the early church's theological developments centered on Christological and Trinitarian matters. Still, attention to the nature of salvation came to be of crucial significance in the fourth and fifth centuries due to the rise of Pelagianism.

In the late fourth century, the anthropology of St. Augustine of Hippo came to prominence. Humans, he believed, were not only unable to save themselves; they were incapable of making the initial steps towards God to bring about such salvation. Augustine said, "[T]he soul must be purified (from sin) that it may have power to perceive that light (i.e., God), and to rest in it when it is perceived."[10] Regeneration was entirely necessary, and such regeneration is only possible through the monergistic acts of God (by means of baptism), according to Augustine.[11]

In reaction to what Pelagius (an uprising teacher in Rome) saw as demeaning pessimism of humanity and a lack of responsible living in Augustinian teaching, the British monk promulgated a system whereby humanity is free in their will and responsibility.[12] Therein, Pelagius believed that humankind is not constrained to act in accordance with any immoral

---

10. Augustine, *On Christian Doctrine*, 1.10, 525.

11. Shedd, *A History of Christian Doctrine*, 38, 41. For a full treatment on Augustine's view of the will and ability in salvation, see 35–54. For Augustine's view of baptismal regeneration, see "On Forgiveness of Sins, and Baptism," in *Augustin*, 1.23, 23–24.

12. Kelly, *Early Christian Doctrines*, 357.

nature. Rather, each person is responsible for one's own sins making the sin of Adam that which applies only to the historic Adam.[13] In his fifth letter to Demetrias, Pelagius wrote:

> Many people out of ignorance claim that man is not truly good because he is capable of doing evil. In saying this they are denying the perfect goodness of God's creation. In fact man is truly good for the very reason these people say he is not: that he has freedom to choose good or evil. Within the heart of man there is no overwhelming compulsion to act in one way or the other.[14]

Humans, believed Pelagius, are capable of obeying the law of God by their own free will (thereby also being able to resist evil by one's own initiative), and performing enough merits to justify themselves for their salvation.[15] As such, it can be said that Pelagius argued for a monergistic position, though the sole worker of salvation in his view would be that of humankind.

A significant development was made in the early church at the Council of Carthage in AD 417 regarding the workers of salvation. Largely due to the influential writings of Augustine, the bishops at Carthage canonized the following statement:

> [T]hat the grace of justification is given to us only that we might be able more readily by grace to perform what we were commanded to do through our free will; as if when grace was not given, although not easily, yet nevertheless we could even without grace fulfil the divine commandments, let him be anathema.[16]

As such, Pelagianism was condemned as heresy. A human-based monergism, they agreed, was impossible given the effects of sin on the human will.

Augustinian monergism, however, did not settle the controversy. In South Gaul, many still found Augustine's predestinarian theology to be nothing more than mere fatalism. Some, such as Prosper of Aquitaine, felt that, while Pelagius did err in claiming that humankind, in their natural state, can choose the good, such rejection of this claim does not assume the

13. In Pelagius, *Pelagius's Commentary*, 92, Pelagius states in reference to Rom 5:12 that Adam's sin spreads through the world by example or pattern, not through inherent depravity. Should individuals choose to sin in the likeness of Adam, that individual will likewise die.

14. Pelagius, *The Letters of Pelagius*, 5.

15. Kelly, *Early Christian Doctrines*, 358–60.

16. See "The Council of Carthage" in Ayer, *A Source Book for Ancient Church History*, 465.

usurping of the human will by God. While humankind cannot bring about their own salvation, humankind is still able to bring about the initial movements of faith (albeit by an assisting grace of God).[17]

This new breed of teaching would eventually be known as Semi-Pelagianism (a rather mocking term coined during the seventeenth century), though at the time the followers of this view were called Massilians (or *reliquiæ Pelagianorum* according to Prosper). Augustine encountered the works of John Cassian shortly before his death and responded accordingly. After distinguishing this sect from the strictly Pelagian camp, Augustine writes in *A Treatise on the Predestination of the Saints* that not only the increase of one's faith but the very beginnings of faith, rest in God as a gift. As such, the beginnings of salvation rest in God and not in oneself contrary to the Massilian position.[18] Moreover, though the Massilians did not deny the importance of grace, Augustine stressed the priority of grace in the faith of Christians. For Augustine, God does not supplement faith which begins first in the person but rather authors and perfects one's faith.[19] Though Augustine would not live to see the fullness of the controversy that would ensue from these writings, the strong responses against it by Vincent of Lérins and others would necessitate an official response by the Church.

The Council of Orange convened in AD 529 to respond to the problem of whether God's grace restored humankind to a point of natural ability. Twenty-five canons were passed (mostly in favor of Augustinian teaching), and Semi-Pelagianism was condemned as heresy. Canon five illustrates this rejection:

> If anyone says that not only the increase of faith but also its beginning and the very desire for faith, by which we believe in Him who justifies the ungodly and come to the regeneration of holy baptism—if anyone says this belongs to us by nature and not by a gift of grace, that is, by the inspiration of the Holy Spirit

---

17. Kelly, *Early Christian Doctrines*, 370–71. This falls short of what may be understood as *prevenient grace*. For Semi-Pelagianism, humankind was able to cooperate with and show faith in God by natural will apart from any overcoming work by God on the individual's sin. This contrasts the later understandings of prevenient grace where God overcomes the full effects of sin thereby enabling cooperation. Prosper Tyro of Aquitaine's work *The Call of All Nations* was both a response to Augustinianism and to the question: why, if God wills all to be saved, are some not saved? Prosper's response to this question is that the fault lies with the human who did not take the initiative to approach God. For an overview of this, see Cunningham, "The Call of All Nations," 204–7.

18. Augustine, "A Treatise on the Predestination of the Saints" in *Augustin*, 1.1–1.4, 497–499.

19. Ibid., 1.3–1.7, 499–501.

amending our will and turning it from unbelief to faith and from godlessness to godliness, it is proof that he is opposed to the teaching of the Apostles . . . [20]

As one can see, Semi-Pelagianism was condemned as heresy not because it held to synergism but because it believed that humankind was still able to make the first movements in faith toward God. Sin does more than leave an individual weakened or impaired, the bishops declared. They are in need of God to overcome the incapacitating effects of sin in their lives.

Perspectives of Grace and Merit in Thomas Aquinas

The Pelagian and Semi-Pelagian controversies led the church to reemphasize salvation as a gift (as opposed to a reward) for believers. In the church's development of soteriology, sin had to be understood as affecting the whole of the human will rendering him or her incapable of achieving salvation (like some merit-based reward). Salvation is an act of God's grace.

However, the medieval church continued to view and label salvation in terms of merits. This can be seen well in the theology of Thomas Aquinas. In order to be accepted by God, there had to be a *gratia gratum faciens*, or a "grace which makes pleasing" (understood as something within the believer whereby God rewards the inherent value of one's actions).[21] In his *Treatise on the Sacraments*, Aquinas said that there was a twofold efficient cause by which a believer receives grace. There was the *principal* cause whereby only God (being the divine nature) is the source of grace and allows participants to experience his grace, and an *instrumental* cause through which the grace from the *principal* is conferred to the participant through the *instrument* of the sacraments.[22] This, according to Aquinas, was the work of the individual who participated in the merits of the sacraments as well as the work of God who conferred the grace.

Naturally, the question arises—what if enough merit has not been acquired during this lifetime? Aquinas was prepared with an answer. Using Proverbs 10:12, John 11:26, and 2 Maccabees 12:46 for textual support, Aquinas proposed the doctrine of purgatory. In order to absolve any remaining sin and satisfaction, an individual will suffer in this region of hell

---

20. "The Council of Orange" in Leith, *Creeds of the Church*, 39.

21. Cunliffe-Jones, *A History of Christian Doctrine*, 275–76, and Gilson, *The Christian Philosophy*, 345–46. See also this development in Gabriel Biel by Oberman, *The Harvest of Medieval Theology*, 135–39.

22. Aquinas, *Summa Theologica*, III, q. 62, a. 1.

until purged (hence the name) from sin to the point of perfection (similar to the refinement process of gold).[23]

The Reformation Debate to Present

One can see quickly how the acquisition of salvation through merits (albeit they are not rewards but grace gifts) could lead to abuses. The purchasing of indulgences, the power of relics, the exaggerated requirements for penance, and the unaccountable authority of the popes led to abuses that even some in the Roman Catholic Church considered unacceptable.[24]

However, it was not solely the abuses of the church that concerned Martin Luther (Professor of Bible at the University of Wittenberg). Such works of penance, the adoration of relics, and the purchasing of indulgences can be done by any person, even the wicked, he believed.[25] What was needed was a return to the Scriptures (*sola scriptura*) which would reveal *sola gratia* (by grace alone) by *sola fide* (solely by faith) for the grounds of justification. In contrast to the cooperative salvation views of Dutch Catholic theologian Desiderius Erasmus, Luther, in 1525 wrote, "There is nothing else that leads to the grace of God, or eternal salvation, but the word and work of God—grace, or the Spirit, being that very life to which the word and work of God lead us."[26]

As Luther wrote against Erasmus concerning the nature and ability of the depraved human will, Calvin similarly wrote against Albert Pighius (another Dutch Catholic theologian) that humankind is morally and in all other ways incapable of cooperating with God in salvation and is in no way responsible for one's salvation with his treatise on the human will, *The Bondage and Liberation of the Will*.[27]

Though the Protestant Reformation significantly changed the course of human history, it did not settle the issue of who does the work of salvation. Jonathan Edwards entered the debate with John Locke in the eighteenth century with *The Freedom of the Will*.[28] Benjamin Breckinridge

---

23. Ibid., Appendix II, q. 1—a. 1.

24. Consider the abuses of indulgences by John Tetzel and the lavish lifestyle and lack of spiritual guidance by Pope Leo X. See González, *A History of Christian Thought*, 20–21, 26–27. A more robust and thorough examination of Aquinas and medieval theology is reserved for chapter 6.

25. Luther, *On Christian Liberty*, 4–5.

26. Luther, *The Bondage of the Will*, IV. i, 139.

27. See Calvin, *The Bondage and Liberation of the Will*, xiii–xxi.

28. See Edwards, *The Freedom of the Will*, 2–5, though the rest of the work is Edwards's wider response.

Warfield sharply criticized the views of the nineteenth-century Methodist theologian John Miley concerning the same topic.[29] Likewise, no one will find any shortages of literature concerning the role of humankind and God in salvation in the twentieth and twenty-first centuries as well.

Considerations

History has attempted to address who does the work of salvation through a variety of means. In addressing the issue, there have been significant developments in thought giving rise to new considerations. First, the longstanding tradition in the Christian faith since the time of Augustine affirms the depraving effects of sin. The majority of Christian scholarship (particularly with regards to monergism and synergism) has worked on the presupposition that salvation cannot be Pelagian (human-monergism) or Semi-Pelagian given that these views do not faithfully reflect the teachings of Scripture (as well as Christian orthodoxy) regarding the effects of sin and human ability.

Second, history has shown that there needs to be prevenient grace in the life of a sinner. Given that Pelagianism and Semi-Pelagianism are non-tenable options to the majority of Western and Eastern Christians, a grace must be extended to the sinner to overcome the effects of sin. However, as this survey has shown, there have been disagreements as to the extent and effects of this grace.

Third, there is a reaction throughout history against salvation being solely the work of God given that some claim it does not respect the human will. With accusations that monergism is equivalent to fatalism, a satisfactory explanation must be given by proponents of monergism on how the human will is involved in monergistic salvation. On the other hand, however, history is also replete with arguments for salvation being by the grace and work of God whereby humankind's efforts are superfluous. How salvation can involve the human being without becoming fatalistic, Pelagian, or Semi-Pelagian has been a persisting tension.

Fourth, there has been no shortage of attempts to explain how the human will is involved in monergistic (or synergistic) salvation. The majority of attempts to determine if salvation is synergistic or monergistic explore the notion of ability. In other words, it has been debated for centuries that salvation is synergistic or monergistic largely based upon the ability of humankind and the grace extended by God. This approach has not led to any satisfactory agreement (if such is indeed possible).

---

29. Warfield, *Benjamin B. Warfield*, 308.

Lastly, a new approach is necessary. It is unlikely that a continuation of the same practices will yield any significantly new results. To assume that salvation (as a whole) is monergistic or synergistic makes assumptions upon the very nature of salvation. Is one in a position to say whether salvation is monergistic or synergistic without defining and examining the nature of salvation as well as the source and roles of the respective parties involved? Moreover, to assume that monergism is fatalistic or does not involve the activity or will of the individual involved (as is the accusations of some[30]) may not accurately reflect the views of monergists. Indeed, it is possible for monergists to give full support for the active involvement of the individual involved. Finally, the assumptions of some monergists must likewise be questioned. Does synergism have a part to play in salvation? Should all forms of synergism be dismissed? Likewise, does synergism necessarily imply Semi-Pelagianism as some have suggested?[31]

It is the intent of this study to examine and clarify these issues. In light of this historical survey and the considerations it has laid forth, one must examine the claims of theologians and traditions that have gone before. In so doing, one might be in a position to make additional considerations and conclusions that will clarify the role that an individual has in salvation.

THE SIGNIFICANCE OF SYNERGISM AND MONERGISM

One may ask whether such an exploration of the agent(s) of salvation is necessary. After all, if the end result of salvation is the same, does it make a difference who the agent(s) is/are? However, the issue on who does what in salvation does not simply affect soteriological theory.

Those who advocate synergism typically highly (though not ultimately) value the freedom of every person's will. These synergists believe that God has given each person a will that is capable of making decisions as seems right to him or her and that God does not impose his will on the will He gave to humankind.[32] This is to say that God presents an offer of salvation

---

30. See Geisler, *Systematic Theology*, 192 who says that Calvinists (here referring to monergists) believe "humans are completely passive" with regards to their salvation in all ways outside of sanctification.

31. See, for example, White, *The Potter's Freedom*, 103–4.

32. Generalities are made here given that not all synergists are unanimous on all matters. Moreover, synergism takes different forms depending upon which tradition of the Christian faith is being referred to. Still, this statement is generally true and is found predominantly in the Arminian and non-Calvinistic evangelical traditions. See for example Lemke, "A Biblical and Theological Critique," 114.

whereby it is in the freedom and responsibility of each individual whether to accept or reject this offer of salvation. God, they say, does not force his will upon the non-compliant, for, as Norman Geisler, a self-proclaimed synergist states, "Forced love is rape, and God is not a divine rapist!"[33] This severe accusation against monergism calls the monergists' view of the character of God into question, showing the significance of this issue beyond mere soteriological theory.

While many synergists are quick to state that free will is not the highest value in their line of thinking, they too believe that synergism is necessary in order to preserve the good nature of God. Roger Olson (another synergist) claims that if God was the one who controlled all things (including salvation) to the extent as to remove human freedom, He would be responsible for both sin and evil as well.[34] As such, to a synergist, the issue of who does the work of salvation carries significant implications to the nature of God especially if not all people will be saved.

Likewise, those who advocate monergism typically value God's sovereignty over all things (including salvation). For a monergist, the natural human will is incapable of any good thing of eternal or salvific value. This view is based upon the traditional Reformed position of *total depravity* and built upon the Anti-Pelagian writings of Augustine. Therein, humankind is completely incapable of contributing anything besides sin to one's salvation whereby neither the work nor the credit can belong (in part or in full) to humankind. Salvation (in its entirety) is the work of God alone, they claim.[35] As such, for a monergist to claim that salvation is in any way a part of an individual's doing is to diminish the work of God and to credit humankind with a work they are incapable of doing.[36]

As one can see, the implications for being either for or against monergism/synergism will affect one's method and belief in a variety of things. Because the issue of monergism and synergism is not resolved, further work needs to be done on the issue incorporating a different methodology. Are there more critiques that can be made about synergism and monergism rather than analysis of human wills? Is claiming salvation to be the work of either God alone or both human-and-God making too broad of a statement? Is salvation a thing unto itself, or is it a mosaic composed of individual elements that make the full picture? It is these needs that this study seeks to address.

33. Geisler, "God Knows All Things," 69.
34. Olson, *Arminian Theology*, 97–114.
35. White, *The Potter's Freedom*, 92–105.
36. Calvin, *The Bondage and Liberation of the Will*, 199–200.

AN INTRODUCTION TO MONERGISM AND SYNERGISM

THE ASPECTS OF SALVATION

As stated above, one must ask whether salvation is simple or complex by its biblical account. In other words, is salvation a whole unit by itself or is it composed of several aspects that make up the whole? This would depend upon whether one considers the terms commonly associated with salvation to be symbolic or actual. It will also depend upon whether one views salvation to be a solitary act or whether multiple things occur.

To assume that salvation occurs is to assume that there is something or someone that an individual needs to be saved from. It is also to assume that there is a savior of some type that performs the saving act. If the savior performs one specific act, then it would be appropriate to conceive of the salvation as a solitary aspect in itself. However, if the savior provides salvation from numerous things (or if the salvation brought about not a solitary effect but had multiple effects), then it would be appropriate to say that the salvation is aspectual (meaning *having various aspects*) leaving one in a position to examine the various parts that make up the whole.

While various religions (though not all) have concepts of saviors and salvation, the Christian tradition finds its Savior in Jesus Christ through his death and resurrection. This is seen in, perhaps, the most famous verses in all of the Christian Scriptures, John 3:16–17: "For God so loved the world that he gave his only Son, so that everyone who believes in him may not perish but may have eternal life. Indeed, God did not send the Son into the world to condemn the world, but in order that the world might be saved through him."

But what did Jesus come to save the world from? This, without question, has brought forth a variety of perspectives. Rudolf Bultmann (as well as most advocates for Existential Theology) viewed salvation as authentic human existence. For Bultmann, "If the death and resurrection of Jesus are asserted as redemptive acts, in the sense of cosmic events which affect humankind in general so that the individual can rely upon them, this is not the meaning of Jesus—neither sin nor forgiveness is really taken seriously."[37] Rather, salvation (according to Bultmann) is the forgiveness of God expressed through the word of Jesus that God forgives humankind their sin. Those that receive this word (*kerygma*) in faith have freedom in thought, character, and circumstances, not constrained in a humanity that is bound by concrete determinism.[38]

---

37. Bultmann, *Jesus and the Word*, 213.
38. Ibid., 217–219. See also Bultmann, *Jesus Christ and Mythology*, 70–72.

Likewise, Liberation Theology perceives of the salvation found in Jesus Christ to be that of political, racial, or gender liberation. Central to this view is the concept of justice. As God has identified Himself in history with those who are oppressed (Israelites in Egypt, Jesus and women, etc.) and has brought about liberation and validation of worth, salvation should be seen in terms of liberation from oppression and the enactment of justice. Liberation theologian Gustavo Gutierrez writes:

> [S]alvation embraces all men and the whole man; the liberating action of Christ—made man in this history and not in a history marginal to the real life of man—is at the heart of the historical current of humanity; the struggle for a just society is in its own right very much a part of salvation history.[39]

However, most within Reformed and Arminian Christianity, matched with Catholicism (with their respective monergists and synergists—which is the focus of this study) has viewed salvation in different terms.[40] One of the primary necessities for salvation is the problem of sin.[41] While space and focus do not permit one to develop each of these points (though they will be examined in their respective chapters), it can be said in summary that both monergists and synergists believe that sin affects humanity in a variety of ways. Sin causes inherited corruption and natural inability to understand spiritual truth (Rom 8:7–8, Eph 2:3, 1 Cor 2:14, 2 Cor 4:4). Sin also brings guilt and estrangement before God (Rom 5:12–16). It brings separation from God not in a positional sense but in a relational sense (Acts 17:27). Sin is said to bring enslavement (John 8:34, Rom 6). Not only that, but humanity is also said to need salvation from Satan (John 8:44, Acts 10:38, 1 John 5:19). While this does not need to imply an adherence to the Ransom View of the atonement as proposed by Origen and Gustav Aulén, it does take seriously the power of Satan over those who are unbelievers and the necessity of Christ's death which can liberate and redeem. Finally, there is an element

---

39. Gutierrez, *A Theology of Liberation*, 168.

40. When speaking of the aspectual nature throughout this study, what is not meant is the various ways just discussed that relate to social or cultural issues. Trevor Hart makes this observation. While he himself condones such interpretations of salvation in light of one's social contexts, he also observes that there must be some boundaries. One should not use the various aspects of salvation as a "selection box" simply to fit one's needs in one's community apart from the whole biblical narrative of God's redemption. See Hart, "Redemption and Fall," 190. Scripture itself must provide the distinct elements that comprise God's salvation in Christ. The aspects to be surveyed here are not intended to be various cultural or social metaphors; rather, they relate to the plight that resulted from sin as will be shown below.

41. See the section below on "The Meaning of Salvation"

whereby an individual needs salvation from death (Rom 5:14–21, 6:23, Jas 1:15).[42]

From this simple survey, one can see that there have been prominent traditions (particularly monergism and synergism) which see the need for a multi-faceted salvation. As humankind has been faced with many enemies which they have not been able to master, they are in need of a salvation that covers the multiple facets of their needs. It is in consideration of these needs that one may look to the work of Jesus Christ.

What one finds is that the effects of Jesus' death and resurrection addressed these various needs according to both monergists and synergists. That is to say, the salvation that is found in Jesus Christ is composed of various aspects that are not just mere names for the same thing. As an effect of sin, humans stand before God as those who are guilty. This is the very thing that justification (in the classical sense) addresses. One also finds that humankind was enslaved to sin and Satan which is what the aspect of redemption addresses. Given that death is an enemy which humankind cannot master, the aspect of union with Christ (which includes an element of resurrection) addresses this very thing. As the effects of sin are aspectual, so salvation is aspectual. Given humankind's complex dilemma, God gives a complex salvation. This, as will be argued, does not mean that Christ only addresses the issue of guilt in salvation. Rather, the believer is blessed with benefits beyond the fulfilment of his faults.[43]

It is necessary, then, for salvation to be examined in light of the parts that make up the whole. Without such an examination, little progress will be made towards this debate. The Scriptures present various aspects of salvation which include (in no specific order): conversion, justification, election, reconciliation, regeneration, and sanctification. Each of these terms, while having definite relationships, is distinct in their own right. As such, no generalities should be made about salvation as such (especially with regards to monergism and synergism) without an examination of the respective parts.[44] However, this does raise the problem of an *ordo salutis*.

---

42. Again, these views are accepted by both monergists and synergists. Examples of synergists holding these views include: Picirilli, *Grace, Faith, and Free Will*, 152 (quoting Arminius, *Works*, III:178); and Walls and Dongell, *Why I Am Not a Calvinist*, 67–72. Examples of monergists holding these views include: Sproul, *What Is Reformed Theology?*, 118–30; and Horton, *For Calvinism*, 40–48.

43. Again, these views are expressed by both monergists and synergists as will be shown throughout this study. The point that is trying to be made here is that salvation is complex by its nature, and that complexity needs to be thoroughly explored for progress to be made in the monergism and synergism debate.

44. Commenting on Calvin's discourse on union with Christ in *Institutes*, II.XVI. XIX, Crampton rightly observes for Calvin (and arguably the Arminian and Catholic

Monergism or Synergism

AN ORDO SALUTIS?

It is not the intent of this study to argue for a particular *ordo salutis* (ordering of salvation's aspects). However, it *is* the intent of this study to examine the parts of salvation that make up the whole in order better to understand what light such an analysis sheds upon monergism or synergism. When one examines the parts, one finds how each part (or aspect) relates to others. In many cases, the parts cannot be separated entirely from the other aspects lest one try to divide that which cannot be divided. There is a relation between the aspects that binds the whole together. As such, no attempt is made to sever ties which should not be broken. Hence, no rigid *ordo salutis* is argued for here.[45]

This is not to claim, however, that there is no *ordo salutis*. Some critics object to ordering the aspects of salvation for a variety of reasons. Some claim that no order is explicitly taught in Scripture. In other words, no biblical author had the intent to present a multi-tiered order and progression in salvation. One must concede on this point despite the failed attempts of many to point to a single verse (most often Romans 8:29–30 which does not appear to be Paul's intention, nor encompassing of all the aspects of salvation) for an *ordo salutis*.

Claiming, though, that no *ordo salutis* is *explicitly* taught in Scripture does not mean that such an order (both logical and in some cases temporal) might not legitimately be derived from Scripture. That is to say, while one can concede to the point that no single verse can be used to support an ordering of the aspects, one can find specific teachings on which aspects precede and follow others, as will be shown.

One might object to an *ordo salutis* claiming that such an order automatically breaks into pieces what should be seen as a unitary process.[46] However, looking at the aspects of salvation and trying to understand them

---

traditions), "Salvation, then, is not to be considered as many distinct acts of redemption. Rather it is to be viewed as distinctly aspects of a single act, temporally worked out in an orderly fashion, with the doctrine of the believer's union with Christ underlying them and binding them together" (*What Calvin Says*, 72). As such, while the aspects should not be separated from one another, if one were to ask what binds the parts that make up the whole, union with Christ would be a most appropriate answer.

45. Conner gives a helpful observation on this issue. He says that one may make distinctions in God's saving acts but that distinctions can be pressed too far. He states that God does not justify at one moment and then regenerate in another. They are simply ways of regarding the saving act of God in a multi-faceted salvation. One is not complete without the other. See *Christian Doctrine*, 200–201.

46. Ferguson observes this in "Ordo Salutis" in *New Dictionary of Theology*, 480–81, s. v. *ordo salutis*.

in their proper order is not to deny that salvation is a unitary process but that it has distinguishable features or aspects to it. By examining the parts, one does not have to lose the whole.

Nevertheless, it is not the purpose of this study to argue for the existence of or the particular *ordo salutis*. The reason this becomes an issue in this study is that this author is faced with the difficult task of presenting the aspects of salvation for examination. While the aspects of salvation are related, they are distinct. Should one try to categorize the aspects into the camps/categories which seem to share the most similarities, then one severs the relationship (and in some cases the interdependency) of the related aspects. The question then becomes: should one try to analyze the aspects of salvation in light of their similarities and differences in order to gain a better understanding of their nature thereby potentially severing necessary ties or by an *ordo salutis*? The first option is advocated here given that an examination of the parts does not necessitate a loss of the whole. This study will contend that in examining each aspect individually, progress is made in the monergism and synergism debate.

The aspects of salvation will be considered in two categories—the *passive* monergistic aspects and the *active* monergistic aspects. While the definitions of these categories are given in the course of the study, it must be said, once again, that salvation is composed of aspects which have a dependence upon one another from both the active and passive categories.

PERTINENT DEFINITIONS

Aspect will be defined as: *A part or feature of a whole.*

Aspectual will be used adjectivally as: *of or related to an aspect.*

Active will be defined as: *Involving action performed by an individual believer.*

Efficient Cause will be defined as: *the agent who brings about a change.*[47]

Instrumental Cause will be defined as: *A secondary cause that produces the effect which owes its efficacy to the efficient cause.*[48]

---

47. Aristotle, *Metaphysics*, V.2.

48. This definition is that which comes from Thomistic philosophy and in agreement with Aristotelian Philosophy as mentioned above. See Aquinas, *Summa Theologica*, I q. 45, a. 6. See Gilson, *The Christian Philosophy*, 183; Aristotle, *Metaphysics*, V.2, 753 where, speaking of instrumentality, he says, "The same is true of all the means that intervene before the end, when something else has put the process in motion."

Instrumental Means/Instrumentality will be defined as: *the agency or vessel through which the efficient cause works.*[49]

Monergism will be defined as: *The belief that salvation (or a particular aspect of salvation) is entirely the work of God alone.*[50]

Monergist will be defined as: *One who holds to the belief of monergism.*

Passive will be defined as: *Involving action performed upon an individual by God.*

Prevenient grace will be defined as: *The enabling and assisting ability granted by God to humankind that overcomes the effects of sin to the sinful human will in order to allow a person to respond freely to salvation.*[51]

Response will be defined as: *The action taken by an individual after an action/event has occurred concerning him or her.*

Synergism will be defined as: *The belief that salvation (or a particular aspect of salvation) is the result of the cooperative efforts of both God and humankind.*[52]

---

49. This term, slightly different from the one above it though it can include it, refers more broadly to how the efficient cause works. It can include any causality where the instrument produces the given outcome through the efficient cause but is not limited to it. This view was held by Aquinas and is made clear by this statement: "I answer that, There is a twofold efficient agency–namely, the principal and the instrumental. Now the principal efficient cause of man's salvation is God. But since Christ's humanity is the 'instrument of the Godhead,' as stated above (Q. 43, A. 2), therefore all Christ's actions and sufferings operate instrumentally in virtue of his Godhead for the salvation of men. Consequently, then, Christ's Passion accomplishes man's salvation efficiently" (Aquinas, *Summa Theologica*, III, q. 48, a. 6). Note that immediately following this reply, Aquinas follows it up with a second reply that the passion of Christ will not have any effect unless it comes into contact with an individual which comes by means of faith *and* the sacraments of faith. Instrumentality (or instrumental means) refers more broadly to the agency by which the efficient cause works and does not necessitate that the agency is a human instrumental cause that leads to the given effect. To anticipate further discussion, the monergist tradition would affirm agency in justification (namely that it is *by faith*); however, they would not view this as an instrumental cause because of their belief that faith is not the cause of justification though it be a means to receiving it.

50. This is the definition, or a variation thereof, used by and preferred by monergists. It is also, at times, called "operating grace" (as opposed to cooperating grace). See also Demarest, *The Cross and Salvation*, 66 who says, "Operating grace is God working new life in the unregenerate without their cooperation." See also Sproul, *What Is Reformed Theology?*, 184. This definition is agreed to by synergists and those within the Arminian cam See Olson, *The Mosaic of Christian Belief*, 277.

51. See Olson, *Arminian Theology*, 35.

52. This is the definition, or a variation thereof, used by and preferred by synergists. See Olson, *The Mosaic of Christian Belief*, 277 where he says, "Synergism is any belief

AN INTRODUCTION TO MONERGISM AND SYNERGISM

Synergist will be defined as: *One who holds to the belief of synergism.*

Work will be defined as: *Any activity done by an individual that causes a specific effect, outcome, accomplishment, or wage.*

EFFICIENT CAUSE AND INSTRUMENTALITY

Understanding the precise nature of causation will be critical in this study. The Philosophy of Causation has produced numerous conceptions of cause and effect (though some may claim a connection between cause and effect is merely theoretical rather than actual);[53] however, assuming that there is a connection between cause and effect, one can distinguish the efficient cause from the instrumental means.

While Aristotle's traditional *Four Causes* have had their critics, Aristotle (though he built upon his predecessors) developed four helpful ways of explaining how something is what it is and was influential in developing a view of causation that dealt with the material and immaterial.[54] Traditionally, the four causes are the *material* cause, the *formal* cause, the *efficient* cause, and the *final* cause. The material cause refers to the material that composes the change (like silver for a ring). The formal cause is the form or pattern of what a thing is to be (for example, a circular object made of precious metal designed to fit on a finger is what it is to be a ring). The efficient cause refers to the agent bringing about a change to the object which is changed (in this case a metal worker or jeweler). Finally, the final cause is the end product (*telos*) or final aim which states what the action is for (jewelry can be said to have the aim of beautification).[55]

---

that salvation is a cooperative project and process in which God is the superior partner and the human person being saved is the inferior but nevertheless crucial partner." See also Geisler, *Systematic Theology*, 3:136. Another term often used for synergism is "cooperation."

53. It is sometimes argued that David Hume argued that there can be an effect without a cause (see "Causation" in *The Encyclopedia of Philosophy*. However Hume denied such an accusation in *The Letters of David Hume*, I.187. To clarify, Aristotle's theory of causation is not four separate causes, *per se*, as much as four different ways of examining the nature of how something came to be.

54. In fact, Aristotle took the implications of causation and applied them to perception of proper sensibles in *De Anima*, III.1. See Charles, *Aristotle on Meaning and Essence*, 115–16. In the area of causation, Aristotle is exploring the notion of "*aitia*" (the Greek term which loosely translates to "cause" in English). His concern was with first principles which applies to more things than the natural sciences to include a wider discussion of causes and results. See also Code, "Aristotle's Logic and Metaphysics," 49.

55. Aristotle's philosophy of causation may be found in his *Physics*, II.3 and *Metaphysics*, V.2, specifically here in Aristotle, *The Basic Works of Aristotle*, 752.

Monergism or Synergism

As one Aristotelian scholar aptly notes, "It will be noted that of Aristotle's four causes, only two, the efficient and the final, answer to the natural meaning of "cause" in English. This is because we think of cause as that which is both necessary and sufficient to produce a certain effect."[56] Indeed, that is the fundamental concern. How are things as they are? There must be a source bringing about a change (the efficient cause—or *principal* cause according to Aquinas), and there must be the goal of bringing about a change (the final cause).[57] It is these two causes that will be the focus here though the nature of this study warrants greater attention to be given to the efficient cause.[58]

It is the fourth cause (that is—the final cause), where Aristotle addresses the issue of agency. In developing his final cause, he states:

> The same is true of all the means that intervene before the end, when something else has put the process in motion, as e.g. thinning or purging or drugs or instruments intervene before health is reached; for all these are for the sake of the end, though they differ from one another in that some are instruments and others are actions.[59]

The idea is that the efficient cause works through an instrumental cause as a means to arrive at the final cause. This is not unlike Aquinas's view. Aquinas held to the principal cause who was the source of effecting the change. In the soteriological sense, God is the efficient cause who is the

---

56. Ross, *Aristotle*, 75. This would take place in the evolution of the philosophy of causation. For an overview of this, see Schmaltz, "Introduction to Efficient Causation," 3–19.

57. Aristotle himself did not view the four causes as four *separate* causes but rather four different ways of looking at something's beginnings. After giving a description of his four causes, he states, "These, then, are practically all the senses in which causes are spoken of, and as they are spoken of in several senses it follows both that there are several causes of the same thing" (*Metaphysics*, V.2, 753). Hence, this study sees no absolute necessity to explore in detail each of these four causes but only the ways of looking at a cause that are helpful to the discussion.

58. While it would be worthwhile to develop a lengthy response to the final cause of soteriology, it will be affirmed here that the final cause agreed to by both monergists and synergists in Protestant and Catholic circles alike is the salvation of humankind to the glory of God. The final cause, or the effect, will be examined below, however, in the section entitled "The Meaning of Salvation."

59. Aristotle, *Metaphysics*, V.2, 753. In Aristotle, however, when the implications of each of the four causes are carried out, there will be a need for instrumentality. The point here is that when Aristotle defined his four causes, it was in the fourth cause where he expounded upon instrumentality.

cause of and reason for all things coming into being, yet He works through (human) agency.[60]

However, does that mean that all instrumentality is itself a contributing cause? Said another way, must all instrumentality stemming from the efficient cause be, itself, an instrumental *cause*? Does all instrumentality cause the effect to some degree? Naturally, the instrumental cause could not cause anything apart from the efficient cause; however, if the efficient cause worked using an instrument, does not the instrument itself help (to some degree) cause the effect?

One might use the example of medication. If an individual is sick and she goes to see her doctor, one may think of the doctor as the efficient cause and medicine as the instrumental cause. The doctor injects the patient with a shot leading to a final cause of wellness for the patient. In this example, the physician is the efficient cause (because it was through the doctor that the action began to bring about a given change). He or she worked through an instrument (in this case a shot). The outcome is the wellness of the patient. However, what caused the wellness of the patient? One could say the doctor, yet one could also say the medicine in the syringe. The syringe, in and of itself, would not provide the effect wellness without a principal (or efficient) cause (the physician). As such, the physician is the efficient cause. Yet did not this efficient cause work through an instrument (the medicine in the syringe), and did not this medicine cure the patient? Absolutely. Can one say that the medicine healed the patient? Yes. That is because it is the instrumental cause.

However, this alone does not address the fullness of how the patient was made well. There is more to the instrumentality than just a syringe. Did the patient give consent for the physician to give her a shot? Was she conscious and rational enough to make that decision, or was she unconscious

---

60. The validity of this claim and an exploration of the efficient cause in Roman Catholic theology awaits a latter chapter; however, this was the Thomist view. See Gilson, *The Christian Philosophy*, 179–183. See also Pasnau, *Thomas Aquinas on Human Nature*, 203–6. There Pasnau observes the Thomist theory of causation particularly with regards to inclination and the final cause (or end). A saw is forcibly moved by a carpenter, but other things move naturally (like fire spreading). Regarding human nature and causation, Aquinas believed God delegated causal authority to his creatures. The ends are specified by God, but they achieve their specific end. Thus, much of the instrumentality in Aquinas (and as one will see in Roman Catholic Theology as a whole) is instrumental causation rather than strictly agency. To be clear, Aquinas believed God was the *actus purus*, the Unmoved Mover. He himself does not change, and as such is always the First Cause and not the effect. In causation, contrary to Aristotle, Aquinas believed God to be the efficient, formal, material, and final cause. See Burkhill, *The Evolution of Christian Thought*, 189. This, however, does not account for the instrumental cause, which will be shown belongs to the activity of the human according to Aquinas.

and the inoculation was given passively upon the individual? Would the physician have the authority to give said injection to the patient without her consent? Are there certain conditions where the physician would have the right and authority to inject the patient without her consent (again, perhaps the patient was unconscious or another person was able to give consent on behalf of the patient)?

To anticipate further discussion, this relates to whether the instrumentality is active or passive. This does not necessarily mean that the instrument itself must be active or passive (medication, in this sense, would not thought to be either); rather, it highlights what Aristotle himself observed about the uniqueness of moral agents, that is people with a will and soul.[61] It is one thing to talk about how the divine and human relationship correspond yet another thing to speak of a carpenter using tools to build a house, for one set is comprised of rational powers on both sides whereas the other is not. As it comes to instrumentality in salvation, does a human (a rational being) have a role in the effect of salvation? As said above, salvation must be looked at aspectually. As shown in the example of medication above, one's ability plays a significant role in instrumentality (whether as passive or active).[62]

However, the question was raised above whether all instrumentality must be a contributing cause that leads to the effect or if there is the possibility for the efficient cause to work through a means and the means through which it worked not be a contributing cause that leads to the effect.

In the medical example given above, the medication (assuming it was given by the efficient cause of the physician) could rightly be understood as an instrumental cause. The medication *caused* the patient to be well. One can see how the instrumental cause, in this case, was a contributing cause that led to the effect of wellness.[63] Does that mean that all instrumentality is a contributing cause that leads to the effect?

Consider this example. Person A decides to call Person B on the telephone. The telephone is the means through which communication is passed through. Should the telephone be viewed as a contributing cause? It would

---

61. Aristotle's discussion of this can be found in his treatise on the subject, *De Anima* (*On the Soul*), particularly Book II, and as it relates to causation see *De Anima*, III.9–12. Aristotle talks about the faculties in the animal kingdom that are present and capable of movement thereby exploring how the mind and will (which is far different from inanimate objects) relates to movement and causation.

62. For Aristotle's view of active and passive powers in causation (with a particular example of medication on a patient), see *On Generation And Corruption*, 324b15–20 in *Basic Works*.

63. For Aristotle's treatment of instrumental causation (though he refers to it as a last mover or last agent that affects and also is affected), see *On Generation and Corruption*, 324a25–b in *Basic Works*.

AN INTRODUCTION TO MONERGISM AND SYNERGISM

be difficult to understand how telephones cause in themselves communication albeit the means through which individuals communicate. Though the instrument for agency is necessary, it does not mean that it causes a particular action for (in this case) it is the means through which another agent works rather than a source of contribution.

Suppose a person had a pail of water that he wanted to pour into another pail some distance away. Between the two pails of water was a pipe capable of carrying the water directly into the second pail. The man (efficient cause) pours the water through the pipe (instrumental means) which leads to the effect of the second pail being filled with water. The instrument through which the efficient cause worked through was not a contributing cause to the second pail being filled with water albeit a necessary cause through which the effect would not have occurred.

The point here is that instrumentality is essential in the cause/effect relationship. Without some instrumentality, a cause would not lead to an effect. However, that instrumentality does not itself have to be a contributing cause, albeit an essential ingredient for the effect to occur, as each of these traditions would affirm.[64]

---

64. Aquinas held to this view and discusses it in his doctrine of creation. He states "It happens, however, that something participates the proper action of another, not by its own power, but instrumentally, inasmuch as it acts by the power of another; as air can heat and ignite by the power of fire. And so some have supposed that although creation is the proper act of the universal cause, still some inferior cause acting by the power of the first cause, can create... But such a thing cannot be, because the secondary instrumental cause does not participate the action of the superior cause, except inasmuch as by something proper to itself it acts dispositively to the effect of the principal agent. If therefore it effects nothing, according to what is proper to itself, it is used to no purpose; nor would there be any need of certain instruments for certain actions" (*Summa Theologica*, I, q. 45, a. 5). In another helpful observation on this matter, Aquinas observes the notion of human sin. Adam, said Aquinas, can be viewed as the principal cause of sin, but his sin is transmitted to his offspring instrumentally through procreation. The instrument did not cause the sin albeit the way in which the efficient cause leads to an effect. See ibid., I/II, q. 83, a. 1. Again, this does not suppose that instrumentality cannot be a contributing cause, for Aquinas held to instrumental causation as well. The point to note is that for Aquinas (and the other traditions in this study), all instrumental causes are instrumental means, but not all instrumental means are instrumental causes. That is to say just because there is agency involved does not mean that the agency is a cause that leads to the effect. That instrumentality does not have to be an instrumental cause that leads to an effect, see Ehring, "Contemporary Efficient Causation," 302–3 and Schmaltz, "Efficient Causation From Suárez to Descartes," 144–45. Norman Geisler (who will serve here as a representative of the Protestant synergism tradition) also affirms this as it relates to human free will. He gives the illustration of Adam's temptation (and subsequent Fall in the Garden). Adam's sin, says Geisler, is the fault of Adam alone. He was the efficient cause, yet Satan served as an instrumental means in this. Satan, Geisler is clear to state, did not cause Adam's sin; however, he was instrumental in it through temptation. See Geisler, *Systematic*

When applied to soteriology, one may pose the question whether justification (for example) is caused by faith or comes by means of faith. Especially as this study deals with the divine and human relationship, one must consider whether the actions of a human cause a given aspect to occur or are merely a means through which the efficient cause (i.e., God) works. Would faith be a work which is done by an individual which causes justification, or is an individual's faith a tool in the hands of God to bring about justification? If in the agency the instrument is a contributing cause which brings forth through its actions the effect, it may be thought of in Aristotelian Causation an *intermediary cause*. The first cause is the efficient cause, and if there is a secondary cause which deals with the agency through which the efficient cause works, and the agency itself is involved in causing the effect, it is an instrumental cause.[65] Regarding monergism and synergism, there are a variety of perspectives on the efficient cause (or causes) of salvation and precisely what the human's role is in instrumentality. How one understands the instrumental means will reflect how one views the principal cause (and *vice versa*).

DEFINING WORK—A COMMON CONSENSUS

In exploring monergism and synergism, it must be made clear how the activity of an individual constitutes a *work*. In many cases (as will be shown), synergists embrace the term "work"; after all, their view is that one works together with God. However, one should go beyond the mere instances where the word "work" is used and look at the underlying reason of why such an activity constitutes a work. While monergists affirm the activity of individuals in salvation, they claim this is not a work of anyone but God. Why is such the case? How does one distinguish between an activity and a work?

As one begins to understand the meaning of *work*, it will be important to understand not what work *is* but what work *does*. The reason why is because the different types of works which an individual could do are many (belief, sacraments, charity, etc.). It is not as though one can define in a simple definition all the works which the various traditions believe one must do. Rather, one should look for what the work does.

Theology, 3:90–93. As will be discussed below, Calvin did speak of instrumental causation; however, he saw faith not as an activity which merits righteousness but an instrument by which one receives righteousness (*Institutes*, III.XI.VII and III.XVIII.VIII); see Lane, *Justification by Faith in Catholic-Protestant Dialogue*, 22.

65. Tuozzo, "Aristotle and the Discovery of Efficient Causation," 27–28, 31–38.

Here it becomes important to understand work as it relates to the efficient cause and instrumentality discussed above. The efficient cause does some type of action which effects a certain end. The efficient cause (and at times the instrumentality) is a contributing cause which produces a given outcome.

This is not unlike how monergists and synergists address the notion of work. Arminian synergists, for example, refer to work as "efficacy" and activity that is "meritorious" to the contrast of grace which is a free gift.[66] Another speaks of works as that which leads to a wage for duty performed (such are contrasted against grace as well).[67] Still, it was Arminius who often substituted "cause" for "work." In speaking upon the operations of God, Arminius consistently refers to work as that which effects a given outcome. In this example, Arminius speaks of God effecting by his own work his incentives towards sinful individuals.[68] Using Arminius's example, God is the cause who effects a given outcome; however, in the place of efficient cause, the term "work" is used which effects a given outcome (not unlike what was shown above in the section on causation). Norman Geisler (though not identifying himself as an Arminian yet holding to a synergism similar to theirs), writes in this regard, "[A] meritorious work (is that which is) necessary for God to give us salvation," and this, he contrasts with faith which is an activity of an individual that does not obtain salvation.[69] As such, the Arminian tradition views work as that which effects a given outcome, merits a certain goal, and contrasts notions of grace and gifts.[70]

In the Roman Catholic tradition, works are likewise defined. As Aquinas was no doubt familiar with Aristotle's philosophy of causation (quoting him on various occasions), he developed his own view of causation that reflects the causation of Aristotle defined above. For Aquinas, the efficient cause (which he called the "principal cause") does an activity that leads to

---

66. Olson, *Arminian Theology*, 161, 165.
67. Geisler, *Systematic Theology*, 3:265.
68. Arminius, *The Works of James Arminius*, Art. XXIII, 3:263.
69. Geisler, *Chosen But Free*, 198.
70. Another term used to describe what works do is "obligate." That is, if a person did some kind of activity that would merit or earn something, such as salvation, one would be obligated to give that person what he or she deserved. Arminian scholar. F. Leroy Forlines addresses this in *Classical Arminianism*, 130. John Wesley held to a similar view. For him, works are that which are done to effect and merit a given outcome leading one to boasting. Pertaining to salvation, he contrasted works with grace through faith, for by the gift of God, freely given and undeserved, is the means through which one is saved, believed Wesley. See Wesley, "Salvation by Faith" in *The Essential Works of John Wesley*, 210–11.

an effect. The activity coming from the efficient cause is called, by Aquinas, a work. He states:

> Whenever one is said to act through another, this preposition *through* points out, in what is covered by it, some cause or principle of that act. But since action is a means between the agent and the thing done, sometimes that which is covered by the preposition *through* is the cause of the action, as proceeding from the agent; and in that case it is the cause of why the agent acts, whether it be a final cause or a formal cause, whether it be effective or motive. It is a final cause when we say, for instance, that the artisan works through love of gain. It is a formal cause when we say that he works through his art. It is a motive cause when we say that he works through the command of another. Sometimes, however, that which is covered by this preposition *through* is the cause of the action regarded as terminated in the thing done; as, for instance, when we say, the artisan acts through the mallet, for this does not mean that the mallet is the cause why the artisan acts, but that it is the cause why the thing made proceeds from the artisan, and that it has even this effect from the artisan.[71]

This lengthy quote serves a helpful purpose. First, it shows his view of instrumentality discussed above. For Aquinas, the agency "sometimes" is a cause of action (implying there are times when it is not; consider also that Aquinas did not view the mallet in the hands of the artisan as a cause which obligates the efficient cause to work). Second, it shows his differing perspectives of causation comparable to Aristotle. However, and important to the point here, the activity of the formal cause is defined as "work." Notice that the work of the formal cause leads to a given outcome (in this case art).

Scores of examples could be given to show how Aquinas used *work* as that which is the cause of a given effect.[72] As will be shown more in the chapter on Roman Catholic justification, Aquinas held to a view of increasing merit. By doing works of justice, humans merit the heavenly kingdom.[73]

---

71. Aquinas, *Summa Theologica*, I, q. 36, a. 3; italics original.

72. In *Summa Theologica*, III, q. 49, a. 3, Christ's satisfaction is that which works an effect of people's incorporation to him. Also here, Aquinas said Christ's passion works its effect through the agency of faith, charity, and the sacraments. The activity of work leads to an effect. In III, q. 66, a. 12, the blood of Christ and the inward operation of the Spirit (called baptisms) produce the effect of water baptism. Here, he expressly calls operation a cause which leads to an effect. Aquinas's view of work and causation was built upon Aristotle's philosophy of causation.

73. Ibid., III, q. 49, a.5. For the full treatment of this issue, see the chapter on Roman Catholic justification.

AN INTRODUCTION TO MONERGISM AND SYNERGISM

Conversely, expounding upon Romans 4:4, Aquinas said that working leads one to receiving his reward and due according to the debt that his labor entailed.[74] This can be seen well in this statement:

> I answer that, A living thing, by dying, ceases to have vital operations: for which reason, by a kind of metaphor, a thing is said to be deadened when it is hindered from producing its proper effect or operation. Now the effect of virtuous works, which are done in charity, is to bring man to eternal life; and this is hindered by a subsequent mortal sin, inasmuch as it takes away grace. Wherefore deeds done in charity are said to be deadened by a subsequent mortal sin. Reply to Objection 1: Just as sinful deeds pass as to the act but remain as to guilt, so deeds done in charity, after passing, as to the act, remain as to merit, in so far as they are acceptable to God. It is in this respect that they are deadened, inasmuch as man is hindered from receiving his reward. Reply to Objection 2: There is no injustice in withdrawing the reward from him who has deserved it, if he has made himself unworthy by his subsequent fault, since at times a man justly forfeits through his own fault, even that which he has already received.[75]

Passing over the Thomist understanding of justification in order to understand how he defines *work*, here one may see that by dying, operations cease and so do the effects. The effects were caused by "virtuous works" (done in charity) which have the result of bringing someone to eternal life. As one does these works, one receives a reward. If mortal sin prevents one from fulfilling these actions, one forfeits the reward. The cause and effect relationship, the relation between activity and reward, and increase of merit found here and elsewhere in Aquinas must be properly understood (and will be explored in a subsequent chapter); however, as one attempts to understand Aquinas's use of *work*, one sees how it is an activity which effects and leads to a given outcome.

The Roman Catholic Church in its official publications has defined *work* in a similar way. As mentioned above, the best way to understand how a tradition understands work is to look at how they use the word *work* (and its synonyms).[76] In the Catholic tradition, one may observe how work

---

74. Ibid., III, q. 49, a.6.
75. Ibid., III, q. 89, a. 4.
76. In the examples given here, Aquinas, Trent, and the Catechism of the Catholic Church do not expressly define the word "work." One must then observe how the term is used by them to arrive at their definition.

is used as that which contributes to an effect. From the *Catechism of the Catholic Church*:

> "It is clear therefore that, in the supremely wise arrangement of God, sacred Tradition, Sacred Scripture and the Magisterium of the Church are so connected and associated that one of them cannot stand without the others. Working together, each in its own way, under the action of the one Holy Spirit, they all contribute effectively to the salvation of souls."[77]

Here, sacred tradition, Scripture, and the Magisterium work together to contribute effectively to the salvation of souls. By observing how the concept of work is used, the actions of these parties contribute to and effect a given outcome (in this case salvation of souls).[78]

In fact, the *Catechism* consistently uses the term *work* as that which leads to a given effect. In §307, it states that God enables people to be causes that complete the work of creation in their own way. In §308, it states:

> God is the first cause who operates in and through secondary causes: "For God is at work in you, both to will and to work for his good pleasure." Far from diminishing the creature's dignity, this truth enhances it. Drawn from nothingness by God's power, wisdom and goodness, it can do nothing if it is cut off from its origin, for "without a Creator the creature vanishes." Still less can a creature attain its ultimate end without the help of God's grace.[79]

Here, one can see the first (or efficient) cause which operates (or is "at work") in the secondary causes (creatures) who can do nothing on their own. Again, work is related to the cause/effect relationship.

In §337–388, creation is said to be the work of God. God is the one who works, and his work (carried out instrumentally) leads to the effect of creation. In §394, Satan does works that have the consequence of leading people to disobedience before God. In §649, the work of the Holy Trinity leads to the effect of the resurrection of Christ. As such, works are that which contribute to a certain end.[80]

---

77. *Dei Verbum* as quoted in *Catechism of the Catholic Church*, § 95.

78. No attempt here is made to comment on or critique their given view. Rather, here the concern is understanding how the term "work" is used.

79. *Catechism of the Catholic Church*, § 308.

80. More examples could be given. For example, in ibid., §1473, works of mercy and charity (as well as others) leads to the putting off of the "old man" and putting on the "new man." In §1724, by the working of the Word of Christ, one bears fruit. Here, work produces an outcome (spiritual fruit).

Also in the *Catechism*, works lead to rewards. Notice this from the following discourse on the final judgment: "The New Testament speaks of judgment primarily in its aspect of the final encounter with Christ in his second coming, but also repeatedly affirms that each will be rewarded immediately after death in accordance with his works and faith."[81] Likewise, "In every circumstance, each one of us should hope, with the grace of God, to persevere "to the end" and to obtain the joy of heaven, as God's eternal reward for the good works accomplished with the grace of Christ."[82] Grace driven works lead to a reward. The cause and effect relationship is evident, but here special consideration is given to the outcome of the good works, namely a reward. Conversely, the *Catechism* also states in §679 that at the final judgment, those who rejected the grace gift of God and depended upon their own works will receive what is due to him or her (namely condemnation).

In a practical sense, the *Catechism* also defines work in terms of human occupation. In one's employment, it states "A just wage is the legitimate fruit of work. To refuse or withhold it can be a grave injustice."[83] In §1940, it states: "Solidarity is manifested in the first place by the distribution of goods and remuneration for work."[84] While context determines meaning, one can see how even reference to work in one's occupation brings forth wages and remuneration which is compatible with what is shown above.

The Council of Trent, likewise, defined work in a similar light. First, one will notice that Canon I contrasts human works and the grace of God, for a gift is not earned through works. Furthermore, Canon twenty-four states: "If anyone says that justice once received is neither preserved nor increased in the sight of God by good works, but that the works themselves are no more than the effects and signs of the justification obtained, and not also a cause of its increase: let him be anathema."[85] Here, works increase and are the cause of justice. While this concept will be developed further in its corresponding chapter, one may see (in an attempt to define *work*) that works are actions that lead to a given increase.

In line with the *Catechism* (though Trent preceded it), Canon twenty-six states:

---

81. Ibid., § 1021.
82. Ibid., §1821.
83. Ibid., § 2434.
84. Ibid., § 1940.
85. Council of Trent, "Decree on Justification," can. 24, in Tanner, *Decrees of the Ecumenical Councils*, 680.

> If anyone says that the just ought not, in return for good works wrought in God, to expect and hope for an eternal reward from God through his mercy and the merit of Jesus Christ, if by acting rightly and keeping the divine commandments they persevere to the end: let him be anathema.[86]

Here, works lead to recompense. No comment or critique is necessary here other than the observation that works are that which cause a given outcome and (in some cases) lead to a reward or wage. This is also seen in Canon XXXII which anathematizes anyone who would claim that good works are the good merits of God alone and not the human as well. It also states that through these good works, an increase of grace and merit is attained.

In sum, one may conclude that there is a strong and consistent understanding in Roman Catholic theology that works are the activity which effect a given outcome, indebt or obligate another party, and lead to a given reward in a way not unlike the Arminian tradition described above.

The monergistic tradition defines work in a similar light. In fact, it would be central to the Protestant Reformation. While a more through discourse on this subject will be given later, it may rightly be said that much of Luther's concern over the doctrine of justification was because he defined *work* in a similar way as the Catholic Church. It was because Luther understood *works* to be that which produces a given effect that he vehemently rejected justification by works. To believe in justification by works would be to believe that human activities effect justification, something Luther rejected wholeheartedly.[87] For Luther, justification had to be by grace.[88] Yet this, properly understood, shows how Luther understood *works* in the same way as Catholics. Works would effect merit.[89] They would be the basis for receiving something from God. Only the works of Christ could effect salvation

---

86. Ibid., "On Justification," can. 26, 680.

87. Luther had a lengthy discourse with Erasmus on this subject and is quoted as saying, "For the Kingdom is not being prepared, but has been prepared, while the sons of the Kingdom are being prepared, not preparing the Kingdom; that is to say, the Kingdom merits the sons, not the sons the Kingdom" (Luther, *On the Bondage of the Will*, 213). He likewise said, "None of them could do anything but perform works of law, and works of law do not justify; and if they do not justify, they prove their doers ungodly and leave them in this condition; and the ungodly are guilty and deserving of the wrath of God" (ibid., 302).

88. Luther contrasts the work or achievement of a human with the gift of God in Luther, ibid., 104. It was on the subject of human works effecting salvation that Luther wrote so vehemently against Erasmus, claiming that Erasmus had committed the "truly unforgiveable sin" by calling Christians to become "reckless workers" and not considering if such activity is possible for "obtaining eternal salvation" (ibid., 116).

89. Ibid., 211–14.

AN INTRODUCTION TO MONERGISM AND SYNERGISM

for humankind. Humanity, however, cannot produce works satisfactorily to effect justification meaning that justification is because of grace through means of faith in Christ.[90] For Luther, one may (in vain) try to bring good works before God trying to effect justification from them, but to do so is folly and contrary to the Word of God.[91] One commentator of Luther states that human merit and ability is necessary for the justification of humankind in Luther's theology; however, this merit is something that humanity itself could not provide. Through Christ (the fully human and fully divine Man), this merit was gained and is now freely provided to humankind.[92]

John Calvin likewise understood works to be the activity which leads to a reward. Calvin said,

> Yet those good works which he (God) has bestowed upon us the Lord calls "ours," and testifies they not only were acceptable to him but also will have their reward . . . Good works, then, are pleasing to God and are not unfruitful for their doers. But they receive by way of reward the most ample benefits of God . . .[93]

To further show how Calvin understood works, he claimed that not only are there eternal rewards in heaven due to good works but that eternal life itself was the reward of good works.[94] Naturally, one should not separate this statement from the rest of his doctrines and writings, and as to what works bring forth this type of effect is reserved for a later section. The point is simply that for Calvin, and other monergists, works are activities done that produce, merit, and/or effect an outcome.

Again, how Calvin understands the role of good works in relation to justification (and other matters) must await further analysis. The point here is that, for Calvin, works lead to a reward. They are the activity which causes a particular effect. The following quote may prove helpful:

> If there had been only one gift of the Spirit, it would have been absurd of Paul (in Gal 3:2) to call the Spirit the "effect of faith," since he is its Author and cause. But because he proclaims the gifts with which God adorns his church and brings it to perfection by continual increase of faith, it is no wonder if he ascribes to faith those things which prepare us to receive them![95]

90. Luther, "The Freedom of the Christian," 282–83. For more on Luther's thought on this, see Ebeling, *Luther*, 150–53.
91. Gerrish, *Grace and Reason*, 76–78.
92. Cunningham, *The Reformers*, 104.
93. Calvin, *Institutes*, III.XV.III.
94. Ibid., III.XV.III, III.XVIII.IV. See also Lane, *Justification by Faith*, 36–37.
95. Calvin, *Institutes*, III.II.XXXIII. See also Hunter, *The Teaching of Calvin*, 113.

In this section dealing with the Word of God through the Holy Spirit, Calvin claims that the Spirit of God is not the "effect of faith" but rather the cause of faith. In this section, Calvin claims God is the initiator of faith, and the Spirit's work entails increasing one's faith until the believer enters into the Kingdom of Heaven. Faith is not the cause of the Spirit but the Spirit the cause of faith. The Spirit, then, works through the means of faith (instrumentally) to sanctify the church.

That work can be defined in the cause/effect relationship is also attested to by modern monergists as well. Like Calvin and others before him, Michael Horton speaks of "effectual calling." Effectual calling, according to Horton and other monergists, is the application of the Holy Spirit's work when all that Christ has done on the cross is applied through one's union with Him by faith.[96] The fact that this calling was "effective" (that is carrying out a particular effect by the work of the Spirit) distinguishes it from the "general call" which is the presentation of the Gospel but not the application of salvation. In this sense, the work of the Spirit effects a given outcome through his own work of instrumentality.[97]

Charles Hodge makes this observation: "There are two conditions necessary for the production of a given effect. The one is that the cause should have the requisite efficiency; and the other, that the object on which its acts should have the requisite susceptibility."[98] As this fell within Hodge's treatise on soteriology, he observes how humankind cannot be the efficient cause given their depraved condition and thus cannot work or do further activity to produce the effect of salvation; God, however, can. This, again, is reflective of the monergists' understanding of work. The activity of the efficient cause produces an effect which can rightly be understood as a work. Because monergists believe salvation is the work of God alone, they believe God is the efficient cause who does the work leading to the effect of salvation.

While one may be tempted to explore in depth the nature of all of these claims, there was one overarching purpose in this survey—namely, to see if the major traditions that will be explored in this work all understand the meaning of work in a similar way. It is concluded that though the precise works, activities, causes, and means are all unique to each respective tradition, they all understand and use works in a similar way. Work, for Catholics, Arminians, and Reformed monergists, relates to the cause and effect relationship. Work is that which is productive. It is the cause that leads

---

96. Horton, *For Calvinism*, 101. Calvin spoke of effectual calling in *Institutes*, III.XXIV.VIII.

97. See Hoekema, *Saved By Grace*, 80–92.

98. Hodge, *Systematic Theology*, 472.

AN INTRODUCTION TO MONERGISM AND SYNERGISM

to an effect. It is that which merits, achieves, acquires, attains, produces, and requires rewarding or repayment. The respective chapters dealing with the aspects of salvation will make clear that these various traditions use work in a comparable way, but such grounds need to be established at the outset.

Yet it is not only these various traditions that define work in this way but the Scriptures themselves.[99] Repeatedly, the Scriptures teach that the act of creation was and is the work of God (Gen 2:3, Ps 8:3, 102:25 et al.). God's speaking of things into existence constituted the action (or work) which produced the result of creation. Without the cause of the work of speaking, the effect of creation would not be brought about. Likewise, the work of Solomon and the Israelites to produce a temple can rightly be understood to be the actions performed by these individuals in order to produce a certain goal (the completion of the temple) without which the goal would not be reached.

With this common understanding established, it may be concluded that activity which is productive in the sense of causing an effect is a work. To this, all these traditions agree. What is also important to note is that though a tradition may not use the word "work" at times, if the activity at hand is the cause which leads to an effect, it is nonetheless a work regardless if the term is ascribed.

CONTRASTS OF WORKS AND GRACE

Each of the respective traditions to be examined also share a common understanding of grace.[100] Again, as this study will be doing comparative analysis, it is important that one compares and contrasts like subject to like subject. As there was a common understanding of work, there is likewise a common understanding of grace between the traditions.

Arminius defined grace in this way:

> Grace is a certain adjunct of goodness and love, by which is signified that God is affected to communicate his own good and to

---

99. This is not to presuppose here that all references to causation are *monergistic*. As is shown in this same paragraph, the same goes for human activity as well. When one works, an outcome is present. This is basic logic meant to serve the purpose of giving a definition of the word *work*.

100. To be clear, not all of these traditions share a common understanding of faith, a matter which is central to the thesis of this study. Some traditions accuse the others of saying that the activity of faith for some is faithfulness in a given activity which causes a particular effect. All of these matters will be discussed in their respective sections. Here, it is to be affirmed that each tradition understands not only works but grace in similar ways, though faith is understood differently.

33

love the creatures, not through merit or debt, not by any cause impelling from without, nor that something may be added to God himself, but that it may be well with him on whom the good is bestowed and who is beloved, which may also receive the name of "liberality."[101]

For Arminius, one is bestowed with goodness and love by God not because of merit, debt, or any other act of causation other than the benevolence of God. Charles Finney said, "Grace is favor. The word is often used in the Bible to signify a free gift. The grace of God is the favor of God."[102] Naturally, for the Arminians (and other traditions as well), there are different types of grace, but as a whole grace is defined in a similar way throughout as the unmerited blessings of God.[103] Because of this definition, there is a clear contrast in Arminian theology between grace and works (though this tradition, like the others, does not deny the importance and essentiality of works in salvation).[104]

This is not unlike the Roman Catholic position. The *Catechism of the Catholic Church* defines grace as "[F]avor, the *free and underserved help* that God gives us to respond to his call to become children of God, adoptive sons, partakers of the divine nature and of eternal life."[105] It goes on to define grace as "[T]he gratuitous gift that God makes to us of his own life."[106] It distinguishes grace and gifts from merit, which is the *"recompense owed"* for work.[107] In the *Joint Declaration on the Doctrine of Justification*, the Roman Catholic Church affirmed that salvation must include works but the basis of it is grace.[108]

Finally, the Reformed understand grace in similar ways mentioned above. Calvin saw justification as a result of God's grace through means of faith which contrasts a self-justification view (though true justification is not without works).[109] John Owen, reflective of the Reformed Puritans, saw a contrast between grace (the free gifts) and works which merit.[110] James P.

101. Arminius, "Disputation XX," in *The Works of James Arminius*, 2:36.

102. Finney, *Revivals of Religion*, 471. Finney goes on to contrast grace through faith with works in 487.

103. Oden, *The Transforming Power of Grace*, 15.

104. Olson, *Arminian Theology*, 161–78.

105. *Catechism of the Catholic Church*, §1996; italics original.

106. Ibid., §1999.

107. Ibid., §2006.

108. *Joint Declaration on the Doctrine of Justification*, 17, 19, 25.

109. Calvin, *Institutes*, III.XVI.I. See also Lane, *Justification by Faith*, 19, 22, 28 and Warfield, *Calvin and Augustine*, 293–94.

110. Owen, "The Doctrine of Justification by Faith," 356–63.

Boyce states, "[N]ot only are men not saved by works alone, but not even by works combined with grace. Justification cannot arise, therefore, from the good works of men . . . Something entirely outside of man must constitute the basis of justification."[111]

Again, this does not account for the different types of graces found within these traditions (such as prevenient grace, internal grace, sacramental grace, sanctifying grace, and more), nor does it account for the instrumentality of such grace. The point here is to show that each tradition believes salvation is by grace, and the means through which one receives this is through faith.

The significance of this is that salvation is attributed to grace and not works.[112] That does not exclude works for any of these traditions. All would affirm that humans have some role to play in the process, even going so far as to say an essential role. However, none of these traditions would affirm a human-based monergism or even a form of synergism that says their works are what saves them in whole or in part. Why, then, is there such disagreement? That is what this study wishes to explore.

LEXICAL MEANING OF GRACE, FAITH, AND WORKS

As this study seeks to determine which of these traditions bests articulates their message of salvation by grace through faith, a lexical examination is in order to carry out such comparative analysis.[113] In latter sections, the various types of grace and works will be defined (as mentioned above). Here, the goal is to provide a general framework from Scripture of the meaning and roles of grace, faith, and works. The debate between these traditions largely resides in New Testament texts, but it is certainly not limited to it. As such, both Old and New Testaments will be observed.

Grace

The Old Testament root word for "grace" is חן. חן typically is translated as "grace" or "favor" (though it can also mean charm or popularity).[114] As a

111. Boyce, *Abstract of Systematic Theology*, 398.

112. Whether each view truly holds to such view or can withstand criticisms to the contrary will be explored throughout this study.

113. For the sake of focus, there will not be any explicit interaction with the New Perspective on Paul. This survey will assume, as far as the Protestant positions are concerned, a traditional perspective.

114. Koehler and Baumgartner, *The Hebrew and Aramaic Lexicon of the Old Testament* [HALOT], s. v. חן.

verb, it is translated as "to favor someone," "to make gracious," or "to have compassion," and as an adjective it means "gracious."[115] It is said about the חן root, "Generally, these words are descriptive of beneficent actions that are freely offered or received and contribute to the well-being of another or to the health of an ongoing relationship. It is active kindness or generosity exhibited particularly toward those in need."[116]

The New Testament word for "grace" is χάρις. Though like חן it can also mean attractiveness or charm (as the English word "charisma" comes from this word), in the soteriological sense it means "favor," "gracious deed," "gift," "benefaction," "help," and "good will."[117] The verb form (χαριτόω) means "to cause to be the recipient of a benefit, *bestow favor on, favor highly, bless.*"[118] Particularly in Pauline usage, one commentator says, "The linguistic starting-point is the sense of "making glad by gifts," of showing free unmerited grace."[119] Grace, in this sense, contrasts works. As one commentator put it, "The ideas "of grace (*kata charin*)" and "as debt (*kata opheilēma*)," i.e., a reward for work accomplished, are mutually exclusive (as shown in Rom 4:2, 25).[120]

This reflects the claims of the traditions which will be observed, and as comparative analysis is carried out, it will be this understanding by which it will be determined who bests articulates salvation by grace.

Faith

While it will be important to consult the chapters of conversion and justification on this matter to see how each tradition articulates faith in that context, a biblical examination of the term will be given to serve as a basis for comparison.

---

115. Ibid.,, s. v. חנן and חנון; and Brown, Driver, and Briggs, *A Hebrew and English Lexicon of the Old Testament* [BDB], s.v. חנן and חנון.

116. VanGemeren, *New International Dictionary of Old Testament Theology and Exegesis* [NIDOTTE], vol. 2, s.v. חנן. This word is typically found when someone finds favor in the eyes of someone else, such as Gen 6:8, Ruth 2:10, and Esth 2:17. In each case, the recipient was shown this favor and did not do acts to earn it. See also Zemek, *A Biblical Theology*, 112–13.

117. Bauer, *A Greek-English Lexicon of the New Testament* [BDAG], s.v. χάρις.

118. Ibid., s.v. χαριτόω; italics original.

119. Kittel, *Theological Dictionary of the New Testament* [TDNT], vol. 9 Φ–Ω, s.v. χάρις, 394.

120. Brown, *The New International Dictionary of New Testament Theology*, vol. 2, s.v. "Grace," 120. See also Zemek, *A Biblical Theology*, 115–16.

AN INTRODUCTION TO MONERGISM AND SYNERGISM

The Hebrew verb אמן is the word used for this concept. Commonly occurring in the Hifil stem, this verb means "to regard something as trustworthy," "to believe in," and "to have trust in."[121] This is the word used in Genesis 15:6 with the covenant God made with Abraham (and is utilized in Gal 3 and Rom 4). It is also used in Habakkuk 2:4 ("the righteous shall live by his faith"), quoted in Rom 1:17, Gal 3:11, and Heb 10:38. Corresponding to this is the noun אמונה. Translated, it means "steadfastness," "trustworthiness," and "faithfulness."[122] Naturally, this would relate to one's faithfulness to the covenant which appears to go beyond what the verb form suggests (of belief and trust to action and results). One should be cautious, though, of basing too much on a word study without understanding how entry into that covenant was made in the first place as well as imposing New Testament concepts upon the Old Testament. One commentator states, "The language of faith/belief (*pistis, pisteuō*), which is of central importance in the NT, does not hold a position of similar importance in the OT. The difference, however, is perhaps more one of terminology than of basic outlook."[123] The author states the reasoning for such is that even in the New Testament, trust and fear correspond to (and are used in a sense of) moral obedience. This deals with the issue of faith as a belief and faithfulness in works. How closely should those be divided? This study will explore such; however, in the Old Testament, one should observe that the concept of belief and trust is closely related with obedience.[124] The relation between the two is where the tensions between monergism and synergism typically arises.

Πιστεύω is the New Testament verb used in this regard, and it is defined as "to consider something to be true and therefore worthy of one's trust, *believe*," and "to entrust oneself to an entity in complete confidence, *believe (in), trust*, with implication of total commitment to the one who is trusted."[125] Like אמונה in the Old Testament, the noun form πίστις means

---

121. HALOT, s.v. אמן. It is the Hifil stem that fosters the idea being dealt with here rather than the Qal stem which means "confirm" or "support." See also BDB, s.v. אמן which translates this in the Hifil as "stand firm" "trust," and "believe."

122. Ibid., s.v. אמונה. BDB translates this as "firmness," "steadfastness," "fidelity."

123. NIDOTTE, s.v. אמן.

124. It would also be helpful for the reader to observe the meaning of xjb which means "confidence" (HALOT, s.v. בטח) and "trust" (BDB s.v. בטח). This is that which, in relationship to God, trusts and finds security in the favour and blessing of Yahweh (see NIDOTTE, s.v. בטח. The point to note here is that while there is faithfulness to the covenant expected, there is an initial belief, trust, and faith in a particular object (in the soteriological sense, God).

125. BDAG, s.v. πιστεύω; italics original. To reiterate, context determines final meaning, and this section assumes the traditional understanding, rather than the New Perspective on Paul's understanding, of terms.

"faithfulness," "reliability," "fidelity," and "commitment" (referring not to belief itself but action based upon belief to something such as a covenant); however, it can also mean a "state of believing on the basis of the reliability of the one trusted, *trust, confidence, faith.*"[126] One commentator states, "[T]he primary sense of πιστεύειν in specifically Christian usage is acceptance of the kerygma about Christ."[127] This same commentator goes on to say in reference to Paul's understanding of πίστις and πιστεύω, "For Paul, too, πίστις is always "faith in . . . " This is why πίστις and ὁμολογία belong together . . . In (πίστις) the believer turns away from himself and confesses Jesus Christ as his Lord, which also means confession that all he is and has he is and has through what God has done in Christ."[128] Again, there is a relationship between them, but one should distinguish between faith as belief and faithfulness as commitment.

Work

The two verbs in Hebrew commonly used to convey the idea of "to work" are פעל and פָּעַל. עשׂה is translated as to "make," "commit," "prepare," and is used with human and the divine subjects.[129] Important to the discussion here, one commentator states about this word, "Closely tied to this is the fact that Yahweh effects deliverance/salvation for his people and brings prosperity (Num 23:23, Isa 26:12). His works of salvation are his alone, not created by his people."[130] This fits the concept mentioned above that work is that activity which produces, effects, and leads to a given outcome. In fact, the noun form פעל and its cognates (פְּעֻלָּה) mean "deed," "accomplishment," "reward," and "wage."[131] The idea is that they are the effect (or product of) the activity of עשׂה. פעל means to "work," "toil," "create," "to give effect to," "to acquire," and "to complete."[132] One notices that it is this activity which gives effect, acquires, and brings something to completion showing that the

---

126. BDAG, s.v. πίστις; italics original.

127. TDNT, vol. 6, s. v. πιστεύω, 208.

128. Ibid., vol. 6, s.v. πιστεύω, 217.

129. HALOT, s.v. פעל. Examples of this are to make metal in a furnace (Isa 44:12), to create things (even the wicked for the day of trouble—Prov 16:4), and to accomplish or achieve (Ps 11:3—used here as a "what can the righteous do to accomplish/achieve").

130. NIDOTTE, s.v. פעל.

131. HALOT, s.v. פעל and פְּעֻלָּה. See Isa 1:31; 45:9, Deut 31:11, Jer 22:13, et al.

132. Ibid., s.v. עשׂה. See BDB עשׂה. This is the verb found 18 times in Genesis 1–5 "to create." One notices that this activity is that which produces an outcome or is the cause of an effect.

traditions that will be described in this study have a view of "work" which is compatible with that of the Old Testament.

Looking into the New Testament, the verb most commonly used for work is ἐργάζομαι. Translated, it means to "work," "accomplish," and "carry out."[133] It is that activity which is productive, bringing about a particular end. The noun form ἔργον may describe the activity at hand (the work itself) but also "[T]hat which is brought into being by work, *product, undertaking, work*."[134] While no attempt will be made here to define Pauline phrases such as "works of the law" or what "works" meant to the first-century audience, what may be affirmed is that work is that which produces a given effect.

Context determines meaning, and it would not be wise for one to make generalities about the meaning of these words without seeing how they are used in the Biblical narrative. What this section attempted to do was show how grace, faith, and works can be used. It was observed in the section above that each tradition to be explored attempts to articulate salvation by grace through faith (belief, trusts) and not by or because of works (acts which cause an effect). It can be affirmed that the traditions to be explored not only use similar vernacular but also base their understandings in a way similar to the biblical definitions. Whether each tradition can consistently maintain this will be explored throughout this study.

FAITH AS A WORK OR INSTRUMENT

The question now becomes whether faith is itself a work which causes, earns, or gives effect to salvation or whether it is an instrument by which God works. Naturally, this is central to the thesis of this study and cannot be covered at length here (though it will be explored throughout). What can be accomplished at this point is the claims of the three traditions which will be explored on this matter matched with biblical survey to see if these traditions have firm biblical support.

It may be said upfront that all traditions explored here claim that faith is not a work.[135] Arminius said:

> Faith is the instrumental cause, or act, by which we apprehend Christ proposed to us by God for a propitiation and for

---

133. BDAG, s.v. ἐργάζομαι. See 1 Cor 4:12, Luke 6:5, 2 Thess 3:8, Eph 4:28, Rom 2:10, et al.

134. Ibid., s.v. ἔργον; italics original.

135. Again, whether each tradition can uphold this claim is another issue. It must be noted that to claim one thing is not necessarily to hold consistently to one thing. One must not look at what is claimed only but how a tradition constructs their view.

righteousness, according to the command and promise of the gospel . . . That faith and works concur together to justification, is a thing impossible. Faith is not correctly denominated the formal cause of justification.[136]

Wesley, likewise, said, "Faith is imputed for righteousness to every believer; namely, faith in the righteousness of Christ . . . For by that expression I mean neither more nor less, than that we are justified by faith, not by works."[137] Faith, for Wesley, was an instrument (not a work) through which salvation came. He also states:

> I cannot describe the nature of this faith better than in the words of our own Church: "The only instrument of salvation" (whereof justification is one branch) "is faith; that is, a sure trust and confidence that God both hath and will forgive our sins, that he hath accepted us again into His favor, for the merits of Christ's death and passion . . ."[138]

Roman Catholics are in agreement as well viewing faith not as a work activity. They claim, "By grace alone, in faith in Christ's saving work and not because of any merit on our part, we are accepted by God and receive the Holy Spirit, who renews our hearts while equipping and calling us to good works."[139] Aquinas said,

> But if we suppose, as indeed it is a truth of faith, that the beginning of faith is in us from God, the first act must flow from grace; and thus it cannot be meritorious of the first grace. Therefore man is justified by faith, not as though man, by believing, were to merit justification, but that, he believes, whilst he is being justified; inasmuch as a movement of faith is required for the justification of the ungodly, as stated above.[140]

Frequently affirming that faith is the gift of God, the Catholic Church states that faith is an essential activity to be performed by an individual, but

---

136. Arminius, "Disputation XLVIII On Justification," in *The Works of James Arminius*, 2:84. At this point, not much will be made of "instrumental *cause*" as Arminius qualified this with "act." The point here is that he sees a difference between faith as an instrument and works which cause.

137. Wesley, "The Lord our Righteousness," II.10, in *The Complete Sermons*, 103. See also "Satan's Devices," II.2, 232. This is not to say for Wesley (or other Arminians) that one is saved by a faith that does not have works, something he expressly denied in "Upon Our Lord's Sermon on the Mount, Discourse Thirteen," 180–84.

138. Wesley, "Justification by Faith," IV.3, in *The Complete Sermons*, 23.

139. *Joint Declaration*, 15.

140. Aquinas, *Summa Theologica*, I/II, q. 114, a. 5.

because God was the giver of this gift it is all of grace and not a meritorious work.[141] Vatican II said, "The followers of Christ, called by God not for their achievements but in accordance with his plan and his grace, and justified in the lord Jesus, by their baptism in faith have been truly made children of God and sharers in the divine nature, and are therefore really made holy."[142] Faith (expressed in baptism) justifies, and this is not (in their view) an achievement which made them children of God but an act of grace. Hans Küng, likewise, states, "Thus faith, as far as cooperari is concerned, means simultaneously nothing and everything for justification. Nothing, insofar as even it does not produce justification and is neither an achievement nor a good work. Rather, faith wants God to work on itself."[143]

The Reformed have also likewise affirmed that the activity of faith is itself not a work. For Calvin, justification does not stand without works; however, faith, he would claim, is not a work (though faith and works "must cleave together").[144] Luther, likewise, saw a difference between the act of faith and the act of works, for justification is by faith and not works (though faith without works is not truly faith).[145] Timothy George, commenting on the fact that Luther saw the necessity for works to accompany faith, said:

> At the same time, Luther was careful to guard against the temptation to consider faith itself a meritorious work. Properly

141. Whether the claim (found in Catholicism as well as Arminianism) that because first graces are due to God that subsequent meriting and effecting activities on the part of a believer should not be called *works* will be examined and challenged in later chapters. See also *Joint Declaration*, 19, 30–31. For an excellent examination of the role of faith in Catholic theology (with special attention to historic creeds), see Brantl, *Catholicism*, 151–65.

142. *Vatican Council II*, "Lumen Gentium" 5.40, 157.

143. Küng, *Justification*, 266.

144. Calvin, *Institutes*, III.XVI.II. See also Walker, *John Calvin*, 414–15. Moreover, as one has put it, "The imputation of Christ's righteousness (for Calvin), correctly understood, is to be regarded as, in the order of nature, preceding *both* remission and acceptance, —and as being the ground or basis, or the meritorious or impulsive cause of these *two* results, —that to which God has a respect when in any instance he pardons and accepts a sinner" (Cunningham, *The Reformers*, 404). Here, in Calvin's thought, the imputation of Christ precedes acceptance (and remission) making it the basis for one's salvation. The act of faith itself did not merit or cause the result but was the by-product of the cause (namely, the effect). Still, faith must express itself in works and be expression of the heart as opposed to a mere intellectual exercise (*Institutes* I.V.IX and III.VI.IV). See Bouwsma, *John Calvin*, 159–60 and Warfield, *Calvin and Augustine*, 137–39. This does not mean that Calvin advocated for a faith (*fides*) without intellect (*cognitio*). See Muller, *The Unaccommodated Calvin*, 162–63.

145. Luther, *On Christian Liberty*, 8–15. See also Schaff, "The Formula of Concord," 3:116, Art. III.III, "We believe, also, teach, and confess that Faith alone is the means and instrument whereby we lay hold on Christ the Saviour."

speaking, faith itself does not justify; it is, so to speak, the receptive organ of justification. It does not cause grace to be, but merely comes conscious of something already in existence.[146]

The same goes for modern Reformed exegetes. Faith is a necessary condition for salvation, but that is different from saying that faith sufficiently satisfies the demands of God's justice.[147] It is also stated in chapter 11 of the Westminster Catechism, "Faith, thus receiving and resting on Christ and His righteousness, is the alone instrument of justification: yet is it not alone in the person justified, but is ever accompanied with all other saving graces, and is no dead faith, but works by love."[148] Faith is an instrument but not the cause of justification; however, faith must have works accompanying it.

But do these traditions have firm biblical support for affirming faith as an activity but not a work? Consider Romans 3:21–23: "But now, apart from law, the righteousness of God has been disclosed, and is attested by the law and the prophets, the righteousness of God through faith in Jesus Christ for all who believe. For there is no distinction, since all have sinned and fall short of the glory of God." While the fullness of these verses cannot be unpacked here, what can be explored is the meaning of "through faith in Jesus Christ for all who believe." This expresses agency. As James D. G. Dunn notes, "Expressed as an antithesis to "works of the law" (3:20), it is clearly intended to denote *the basis of a relationship which is not dependent on ritual acts, but is direct and immediate, a relying on the risen Christ rather than a resting on the law.*"[149] Here, faith is relying on Christ and contrasts works and ritualistic activity. Commenting on this text, George E. Ladd states, "Thus while the *ground of* justification is the death of Christ, the *means* by which

---

146. George, *Theology of the Reformers*, 71.

147. Sproul, *What Is Reformed Theology?*, 166. See also Horton, "Traditional Reformed View," 86–90. See also the Lutheran World Federation in *Joint Declaration on the Doctrine of Justification*, 30 where they say "*Both* are concerned to make it clear that . . . human beings cannot . . . cast a sideways glance at their own endeavours . . . But a response is not a 'work'" (italics and ellipsis original as it is quoting "The Condemnations of the Reformation Era: Do They Still Divide?") The point there is that this tradition sees a difference between a response and a work. Warfield, in *The Person and Work of Christ*, 558 states, "Our faith itself, though it be the bond of our union with Christ through which we receive all his blessings, is not our saviour . . . Nothing that we are and nothing that we can do enters in the slightest measure into the ground of our acceptance with God. Jesus did it all."

148. Bordwine, *A Guide to the Westminster Confession of Faith and Larger Catechism*, 78.

149. Dunn, *Romans 1–8*, 178; italics original.

justification becomes efficacious to the individual is faith ... Faith is the means by which the work of Christ is personally appropriated."[150]

Claiming that the apostle Paul would not have considered himself to be enunciating a novel idea of justification by faith, Leon Morris observes an Old Testament precedent of the role of faith in the people of God. God's mercy, and not their works, was the basis for Israel's acceptance in the Old Testament (as shown in Isaiah 55), and this served as supportive background for Paul's exposition of justification by means of faith in Romans 9 (and his other writings).[151] In Romans 4:5, it states: "But to one who without works trusts him who justifies the ungodly, such faith is reckoned as righteousness." Here, God is accounting individuals righteous who trust (πιστεύοντι) the Justifier and show faith (ἡ πίστις) despite a lack of works. This has led one commentator to say concerning this passage, "But faith is not a "meritorious work. It is simply giving God the credit of speaking the truth in the gospel about Christ. It is Christ's shed blood, and that alone, which is the procuring cause of God's declaring an ungodly man righteous ... Our faith is simply the instrumental condition."[152]

Through exegetical survey primarily of the Pauline epistles (though not exclusive to them), B. A. Gerrish and Gordon H. Clark respectively observe the meanings of the *pistis* and *pisteuein* words as "belief," and "to trust." Belief can have a secular as well as sacred connotation as it can mean the intellectual assent to particular claims. To trust, however, implies a moral element which must lead to some action.[153] Faith, without trust, is no faith at all; however, if the object of faith is God (a belief in who He is and what He has done matched with a trust and reliance upon this), it stands to reason that this act is not a work but an act of agency which would lead to work.[154]

Paul Tillich also helpfully defined faith as "ultimate concern."[155] It is considered *ultimate* given that it mandates total surrender, and it is *concern* because it is a matter unto an individual. He, therefore, distinguishes between the *fides qua creditor* (the instrument of faith through which one believes in that which is ultimate) and the *fides quae creditor* (the object of

---

150. See Ladd, *A Theology of the New Testament*, 490; italics original.

151. Morris, *The Apostolic Preaching of the Cross*, 263–66, 274–76.

152. Newell, *Romans*, 105.

153. Clark, *Faith and Saving Faith*, 28–35, 95–106; Gerrish, *Saving and Secular Faith*, 2–5, 34–40.

154. Machen, *What is Faith?*, 172–76.

155. Tillich, *Dynamics of Faith*, 1, 4.

faith/the ultimate).[156] For Tillich, faith is an instrument through which one connects with God and his benefits, it is something that finds its source in the individual believer, and it is directed toward the divine.

This appears to be consistent when the occurrences of faith and works are mentioned together in biblical passages. In Ephesians 2:8–9, it states, "[Y]ou have been saved *through* faith" (ἐστεσεςῳσμένοι διὰ πίστεως emphasis added). The διὰ preposition before the genitive shows *means* in this case. It is through means of faith that one is saved.[157] As Donald Guthrie observes through exposition of John 3:16–17, "Thus faith is the means by which people are inaugurated into the new community, seen as a family."[158] This means faith leads one to salvation but is not a work that achieves salvation. Upon exposition of the letter of James, Ralph P. Martin (in particular observation of James 2) claims that works validate the genuineness of the faith which saved but do not cause salvation in their own right.[159]

While more survey could be done, it would not be necessitated by the traditions to be studied here. All, as said above, deny faith as a work and see it instead as an activity of instrumentation. The goal of this study, then, is to see which tradition best articulates salvation by grace through means of faith and not by works.

ACTIVE AND PASSIVE INSTRUMENTALITY

Such faith, however, is indeed compatible with the passive aspects of salvation. While a believer exercises genuine faith in God, salvation, as has been said, is aspectual. Not every aspect of salvation is dependent upon an active response from the believer. God not only has the prerogative but also the sole ability to perform certain acts upon his creation. This is due, as will be explored further, to his roles as Justifier and Elector. As there are none in all humanity who hold these offices (in the soteriological sense), there is no action on their part in this aspect. This is not to diminish or lessen the importance of the activity of the believer; it is still vitally important to the

---

156. Ibid., 10. This does not mean that faith itself is the ultimate. Rather, one should, according to Tillich, understand this ultimate to be God himself.

157. Robertson, *Word Pictures in the New Testament*, 4:524–525. Robertson claims that *touto* does not refer to *pisteōs* in this section possibly on grounds to prove that faith itself is not a work but a gift of God. However, such is not necessary for even faith is a gift from God. See Clark, *Ephesians*, 73–74. Both, however, confirm that faith is itself not a work. To see the Pauline view of justification by faith and not by works in Galatians, see Smith, *The Life and Letters of St. Paul*, 200–206.

158. See Guthrie, *New Testament Theology*, 582.

159. Martin, *James*, 99.

whole of salvation. However, God works certain aspects of salvation in his own right, exercising his sovereignty over his creation.

As such, there is a secondary instrumental means with regards to passive monergistic salvation—namely the working of God, which would rightly be understood as an instrumental cause.[160] That is to say that God (or more precisely his will) is still the efficient cause, but the means by which the individual receives benefits from the efficient cause is through God's working alone. The passive aspects of salvation which will be explored (election, regeneration, and conversion[161]) certainly relate to faith; however, these are acts that by their definition and nature require them to be acts performed solely by God and through God. While faith relates to the aspects, the action is performed passively upon the individual whereby active results will follow.

THE MEANING OF SALVATION

One more critical term must be defined. If this study seeks to determine which tradition best defines *salvation* by grace through faith and not by works, one must understand what these traditions mean by salvation. While much of this study will explore the *cause* (that is the *works* and *worker(s)* of salvation), one must not neglect the *effect*, which is salvation. But what do these traditions mean by salvation?

A helpful preliminary observation to make on this front is that salvation (in each of these traditions) is viewed aspectually as stated above. If one is analyzing the aspect of justification, for example, one might say that salvation (in this sense) refers to one's right relationship with God. If election is the aspect in view, one might say salvation refers to how one becomes a chosen member of the people of God. In each respective chapter, each tradition will present its meaning of the given aspect thereby clarifying what

---

160. Again, this will be shown more clearly in an examination of each aspect. Still, for a general reference to this, see Sproul, *What Is Reformed Theology?*, 185–87.

161. These three are chosen based upon the prevalence of these aspects in synergism and the need to contrast them. There is a fourth common passive monergistic aspect of *redemption* that will not be discussed here given that most synergists do not argue for synergistic redemption. However, this aspect would also show well how there are passive aspects in salvation. Given that redemption is a slave market term and that those who are enslaved have no freedom or rights of their own, they are totally dependent upon the working of God to set them free. See Marshall, "Redemption," in *New Dictionary of Theology*.

they mean by salvation; however, it would be helpful to see if any of these traditions give a broad definition of salvation.[162]

As mentioned above on the section "The Aspects of Salvation," God provides a complex salvation to a complex problem. Salvation, for each of these traditions, relates to the multiple effects of sin in humanity. While the Catholic Church holds to different types of sin (mortal and venial sins) it still gives a general definition of sin: "Sin is an utterance, a deed, or a desire contrary to the eternal law . . . It is an offense against God. It rises up against God in a disobedience contrary to the obedience of God."[163] There are a variety of consequences to sin according to the Catholic Church, but salvation is God's activity of overcoming such sin.

This is perhaps best seen through §457–460 of the *Catechism* dealing with the incarnation of Christ. It states:

> The Word became flesh for us in order to save us by reconciling us with God, who "loved us and sent his Son to be the expiation for our sins": "the Father has sent his Son as the Saviour of the world", and "he was revealed to take away sins" . . . The Word became flesh so that thus we might know God's love (here citing 1 John 4:9 and John 3:16). The Word became flesh to be our model of holiness (here citing Matthew 11:29 and John 14:6) . . . The Word became flesh to make us "partakers of the divine nature", "For this is why the Word became man, and the Son of God became the Son of man: so that man, by entering into communion with the Word and thus receiving divine sonship, might become a son of God." "For the Son of God became man so that we might become God." "The only-begotten Son of God, wanting to make us sharers in his divinity, assumed our nature, so that he, made man, might make men gods."[164]

Again, by salvation, the Catholic Church refers to the undoing of the effects of sin that lead one to experience reconciliation, fellowship, forgiveness, adoption, and justification (to name a few). That many responses are given for the work of the incarnate Christ shows again how these traditions (and why this study) view salvation aspectually.

Synergistic Arminians and Reformed monergists, both being Protestants in the traditional sense, differ more on the cause of salvation rather than the effect (though one finds that these traditions share similar views

---

162. The definitions of salvation provided here should not be separated from how each tradition defines each given aspect.

163. *Catechism of the Catholic Church*, §1871.

164. Ibid., §457–460. See also §55 where salvation is related to receiving eternal life (because sin caused death) and §161 where justification is mentioned.

AN INTRODUCTION TO MONERGISM AND SYNERGISM

with the Catholic tradition).[165] Like the Roman Catholics, both of these traditions understand salvation as the undoing of the multiple effects of sin.

Arminius defined salvation this way:

> The vocation or calling to the communion of Christ and its benefits, is the gracious act of God, by which, through the word and His Spirit, he calls forth sinful men, subject to condemnation and placed under the dominion of sin, from the condition of natural life, and out of the defilements and corruptions of this world, to obtain a supernatural life in Christ through repentance and faith, that they may be united in him, as their head destined and ordained by God, and may enjoy the participation of his benefits, to the glory of God and to their own salvation.[166]

For Arminius, "sinful men" stood condemned and under sin's dominion, being defiled and corrupt; however, through the work of Christ applied in repentance and faith, one has union with Christ, eternal life, and enjoyment of the benefits of God. Arminian scholar Thomas C. Oden, likewise states, "To be saved is to be delivered from bondage, brought into freedom, rescued from death, given a new lease on life. That which is reclaimed by God's saving action is life—abundant life, eternal life, life in the Spirit."[167] Like the Catholics, what sin did salvation undid (though one could and should argue that salvation did more than just undo the effects of sin).

The Reformed, likewise, view salvation in these ways. Calvin said,

> All that we have hitherto said of Christ leads to this one result, that condemned, dead, and lost in ourselves, we must in him seek righteousness, deliverance, life and salvation, as we are taught by the celebrated words of Peter, "Neither is there salvation in any other: for there is none other name under heaven given among men whereby we must be saved" (Acts 4:12).[168]

---

165. As stated elsewhere in this study, Arminians, like Arminius himself, view themselves as Reformed in the strict sense of coming out of the Protestant Reformation and coming out of Reformed (as opposed to Lutheran) Protestantism.

166. Arminius, "Disputation XLII On the Vocation of Sinful Men to Christ, and to a Participation of Salvation in Him" in *The Works of James Arminius*, 2:74. It is worth noting that the next sentence in this section defines God as the efficient cause of salvation.

167. Oden, *Life in the Spirit*, 80.

168. Calvin, *Institutes*, II.XVI.I. See also the rest of that chapter and II.XVII. In book 2 of the *Institutes*, Calvin expounds upon the doctrine of Christ (person and work), and in Book 3 he turns to the application of this grace. In these sections, however, Calvin gives a helpful summation of what Christ accomplished for salvation making this a close reflection of what Calvin (and his followers) understood salvation to be.

While this is not, strictly speaking, a definition supplied by Calvin, it at least shows what salvation did. The condemned and lost were (by the work of Christ) able to seek righteousness in Him, finding deliverance and life. That which sin did, the work of Christ overcame leading to newness of life and union with the divine. A. A. Hodge states that the essential parts that make the whole of salvation are regeneration, justification, sanctification, resurrection, and glorification.[169] This is something that monergists (and Arminians and Catholics) would agree to, but one should notice how this relates to the effects of sin and the work of Christ for salvation in overcoming these effects.

Salvation, then, is the effect of the work of Christ. It is that which overcomes the depraving effects of sin. Because sin (as mentioned above) led to a complex problem, the salvation found in Christ accomplishes multiple effects. Of this the three traditions here are agreed, though they construe their formulation of the cause of salvation differently.

With that said, one should be clear that salvation has a past, present, and future component of which none of these traditions deny. While some of the tension in this matter relates to the progressive nature of justification in Roman Catholicism (contrary to many in the Protestant position), what can be affirmed is that all of these traditions understand salvation having a past, present, and future dynamic, though they construe it differently.

Traditionally, the past, present, and future dynamics of salvation are election and atonement (past), conversion, regeneration, justification, and sanctification (present), and glorification (future). While each tradition (as will be shown) defines these aspects very differently, none of them are denied. Salvation is both an event and process, the effect of Christ's work on the cross.[170] That is to say, the Scriptures speak not only of the "saved" but those who are "being saved" (see Acts 2:47, 1 Cor 1:18, 15:2, and 2 Cor 2:15).

The literature examined in this study appertaining to monergism and synergism in salvation will deal in some way with the past, present, and future dynamics of salvation. The aspect to be examined will determine which time dynamic is in view. What should be made clear, though, is that the

---

169. Hodge, *Evangelical Theology*, 204.

170. See Fiddes, *Past Event and Present Salvation*, 14–34. For a Catholic perspective on this, see Sungenis, *Not By Faith Alone*, 294–95. For a synergistic perspective, see Moody, *The Word of Truth*, 311–13. For the Reformed view, see Demarest, *The Cross and Salvation*, 35–36. As a side note, some people place conversion in the "past" category referring to the event of their salvation; others put it in the present because it took place during one's lifetime. Moody, mentioned here, would be an example of this, 311.

AN INTRODUCTION TO MONERGISM AND SYNERGISM

traditions to be examined affirm not only the aspectual nature of salvation but the temporal nature of salvation as well.

THE USE OF SYNERGISM IN THE NEW TESTAMENT

This study will also bear in mind the following exegetical survey as it relates to synergism. The Greek verb συνεργέω appears 5 times in the Greek New Testament. Συνεργέω means, "to engage in cooperative endeavor, *work together with, assist, help.*"[171] It should be noted, however, that not in any of these five occurrences does συνεργέω refer to a non-believer cooperating with or working together with God in order to be saved. This can be seen by examining these five usages below.

Romans 8:28 refers to the eschatological plans of God causing all things to lead to a good which God has purposed.[172] It says nothing of synergism as it relates to salvation. 1 Corinthians 16:15–16 refer to assisting the household of Stephanas and others who are in the Lord's work. This reference, too, will not be applicable in this study of soteriological synergism because it does not refer to any of the aspects of salvation.

Textual criticism issues aside, Mark 16:20 refers to the Lord aiding the activity of the disciples as they carry out the task of evangelism. The Lord is working with the disciples, giving them all that they need, as they carry out the work of sharing the Gospel. It is important to note that this is not to say that the Lord is cooperating with the unbelievers towards salvation but with the believers who are sharing the word about salvation. The same is true for 2 Corinthians 6:1–2 where Paul speaks of those who are already saved carrying out the full implications of their conversion in faithful service.

One of the usages of συνεργέω used to support soteriological synergism is James 2:22.[173] Therein, James states, "You see that faith was working with his (Abraham's) works, and as a result of the works, faith was perfected." Several things are noteworthy here. First, the context here (as well as throughout the New Testament) does not support that the "works" are repentance and faith. Indeed, James is analyzing the relationship between faith and works whereby the standard definition of synergism (as described above) does not stand. Second, James, here, is dispelling the thought that one can separate a lifestyle of faith and a lifestyle of works. Referring to Abraham who had the faith and evidenced it by works, the believer in Christ

---

171. BDAG, s.v. συνεργέω; italics original.
172. See Dunn, *Romans 1–8*, 481.
173. See, Sungenis, *Not by Faith Alone*, 152.

is to have a faith that *works* (or lives a life of obedience).¹⁷⁴ Finally, notice how it was the faith of Abraham working together with his works that leads to a perfected faith. This was not a divine and human cooperation that effected salvation but the faith of a man who demonstrated the validity of his faith by works.¹⁷⁵

The noun form συνεργός appears thirteen times in the Greek New Testament. It is translated as, "[Pertaining] to working together with, *helping, helper, fellow-worker*."¹⁷⁶ Like the verb form, there is not a single reference to a non-believer working together with God in order to be saved. Twelve out of the thirteen uses of the noun refer to the fellow workers who partner with the apostles in the work of evangelism and ministry.¹⁷⁷ They are those who are already saved and carry out the important work of ministry. Notice that in all twelve of these instances, there is no divine agent. That is not to say that the Lord is not involved in supplying them all that they need or that He too is not at work in the redemption process. Rather, these twelve instances say nothing about God cooperating with a non-believer to bring about salvation.

The only occurrence of a divine agent with συνεργός is 1 Corinthians 3:9, "For we are God's fellow workers; you are God's field, God's building." It is worth noting that neither Arminius, Wesley, Finney, Olson, Aquinas, Trent, or the *Catechism* (in addition to the majority of modern Arminian and Catholic scholars) ever use this verse in support of synergism for salvation. To be clear, many use this verse as support for the synergistic activity between God and people for the task of evangelism or some other use.¹⁷⁸ Still, such omission should be an indicator that this verse does not support soteriological synergism.

That does not mean that there is not synergism advocated in this text. This verse affirms that those who perform the Lord's work are dependent upon the work of the Lord. Their work is assisted by the work of God in carrying out God's redemptive plan.¹⁷⁹ This synergism, however, is not ef-

---

174. Martin, *James*, 48, 93; see full discussion in 82–101.

175. See Dibelius, *James*, 163.

176. BDAG, s.v. συνεργός; italics original.

177. Rom 16:3, 9, 21; 2 Cor 1:24, 8:23; Phil 2:25, 4:3; Col 4:11; 1 Thess 3:2; Phlm 1, 24; 3 John 8.

178. For evangelism, see Russell, "Synergism in the New Testament," 14–17, for Aquinas's view of cause and effect see *Summa Theologica*, III, q. 72, a. 11, for subduing the earth see *Catechism of the Catholic Church*, §307. Again, these are not references to soteriological synergism.

179. Grosheide, *Commentary on the First Epistle to the Corinthians*, 82–83. See also Clark, *First Corinthians*, 62–63.

fecting salvation but, rather, evangelism. Their work is sharing the Gospel, not saving. God is the One who saves, but he uses laborers who will be his witnesses.[180]

Some may claim that though συνεργός and its cognates do not refer to soteriological synergism, the idea is taught in Philippians 2:12–13 where it states: "So then, my beloved, just as you have always obeyed, not as in my presence only, but now much more in my absence, work out (κατεργάζεσθε) your salvation with fear and trembling; for it is God who is at work (ἐνεργῶν) in you, both to will and to work (ἐνεργεῖν) for *his* good pleasure." Thomas Oden calls this text the "locus classicus" for which he (and other synergists) develop their theology of cooperating grace. He states that this text supports the belief that the will gives free consent to divine will which is necessary for salvation to occur (thereby implying that the "work out" which individuals are to do is exercise the will in faith).[181]

John Wesley, expounding upon this text, claims that God first works in an individual through prevenient grace allowing an individual to work out that salvation (yet to come) by willing and showing faith. Because of God's initial work, individuals can work with God in this regard by faith to effect salvation.[182]

Gerald F. Hawthorne, however, observes that Paul is not referring to the individual soul who must activate salvation. Instead, Paul is referring to the entire church which has grown spiritually ill and must become healthy and active again.[183] In other words, these individuals are already converted and justified, hence the command to "work out your salvation" (a salvation they already possess which has a beginning in a moment in time, realized in the present, and is to be carried out in the future). Claiming that a work of faith effects salvation might have further negative implications as will be shown.

This survey of συνεργέω and συνεργός has shown that there is no direct biblical reference of synergism as a cooperative work between God and an individual that effects salvation in the New Testament. This is not an effort to obscure objectivity or form preliminary biases towards one side; rather, a survey of the word group is in order as one makes preliminary observations about this issue.

---

180. Lockwood, *1 Corinthians*, 111–114.

181. Oden, *The Transforming Power of Grace*, 53.

182. Wesley, "On Working out Our Own Salvation," in *The Essential Works of John Wesley*, 323–30.

183. Hawthorne, *Philippians*, 98.

VARIANT POSITIONS AMONGST MONERGISTS AND SYNERGISTS

A brief word of clarification is in order regarding the variant positions of monergists and synergists. As monergists and synergists typically (though not always) view salvation in light of its aspects, one will find someone being a monergist on one aspect and a synergist on another. This is found amongst all three of the traditions which will be examined here.

In Aquinas's view of the principal agent (i.e., efficient cause), God is the sole worker of the interior sacramental effect. He states this is the case because God is the only one who can enter human souls and effect the grace of the sacraments.[184] However, in sanctifying grace (related to the doctrine of justification), Aquinas was thoroughly synergistic.[185]

Augustine, heavily monergistic in certain respects (such as election),[186] was synergistic in other aspects (such as justification).[187] Wesley, a devout synergist, spoke of justification as "the work of God, and not of man."[188] Luther wholeheartedly rejected synergism that leads to salvation, but he embraced synergism in the saved (namely, God and the Christian working together to preach, show mercy to the poor, and comfort the afflicted).[189] Reformed monergist Anthony Hoekema nevertheless defined conversion as "the work of God and man."[190] Sanctification, in all three of these traditions, is viewed synergistically.[191]

---

184. Aquinas, *Summa Theologica*, III q. 64, a. 1.

185. Ibid., I/II q. 111, a. 1.

186. Augustine, "Against Two Letters of the Pelagians" in *Augustin*, 5.2.15, 398.

187. Augustine, "A Treaties on the Grace of Christ, And On Original Sin" in *Augustin*, 5.1.55, 236. See also "On Forgiveness of Sins, and Baptism" in ibid., 5.2.6, 46 where Augustine says "God does not work our salvation in us as if he were working in insensate stones, or in creatures in whom nature has placed neither reason nor will." To see both monergism and synergism together in Augustine, see "On Grace and Free Will" in *Augustin*, ch. 33, 5:457–458. To be clear, it would be anachronistic to call Augustine "Reformed." Here, the reader would do well to observe what is stated elsewhere that monergism does not suppose full adherence to all points of Luther, Calvin, or Calvinism.

188. Wesley, "Upon Our Lord's Sermon on the Mount, Discourse 9" n. 22, in *The Complete Sermons*, 166.

189. Luther, *On the Bondage of the Will*, 289.

190. Hoekema, *Saved by Grace*, 114–15.

191. See Geisler, *Systematic Theology*, 3:192 who affirms (from his synergistic perspective) how even Calvinists (i.e., monergists) view sanctification as synergistic. Wayne Grudem, from the monergistic perspective, claims, "Sanctification is a progressive work of God and man . . . " (*Systematic Theology*, 746). More examples could be given. The point here is that sanctification is not an area of major disagreement when

AN INTRODUCTION TO MONERGISM AND SYNERGISM

The point to all of this is that because analysis of monergism and synergism is often looked at aspectually, one person may be a monergist in one regard and a synergist in another. Typically, traditions fall on one side of the issue or another, though there are certainly exceptions to this case. As such, it will be necessary to look at each aspect individually to see if the synergistic or monergistic side best articulates salvation by grace.

THESIS AND METHODS USED

This book will examine each aspect of salvation in light of the claims set forth by monergists and synergists. In examining the strengths and weaknesses of both views, new conclusions will be made in light of new methodology.

This book will use comparative analysis between a particular synergistic tradition and the monergistic position. When referring to a "synergistic" tradition or a "monergistic" tradition, this author respects that there are variances in these traditions. There is a variety of perspectives within each respective tradition (both synergistic and monergistic), and where significant areas of disagreement are discovered within a given tradition it shall be noted. However, this study will attempt to provide a general yet thorough analysis of each respective tradition whereby they may be compared and contrasted to one another.

Through analysis of each respective aspect of salvation and comparative analysis between synergists and monergists, this study will argue that, on balance, the monergist articulation of salvation by grace through faith and not works is the more coherent account.

---

it comes to synergism unless the view entails progressive justification (which will be discussed below).

Chapter 2

The Aspect of Election

THE UNDERLYING ISSUE

ARMINIAN SCHOLAR F. LEROY Forlines writes, "While Arminians and Calvinists share much common ground, there are major points of difference. Nothing calls attention to that difference like a study of decrees and election."[1] Indeed, it would be difficult for any student of theology to miss the gulf that separates the two parties of Arminianism and Calvinism, especially when it becomes a matter of unconditional election or conditional election.[2]

Calvinists who follow such traditional statements as the *Canons of Dort* and the *Westminster Confession of Faith* hold to unconditional election whereby God chooses certain persons to special favor (particularly for some to be recipients of eternal life and blessing, though it includes certain factors as service and offices as well) in an *absolute* or *unconditional* way where his choices are entirely of Himself and in no way depend upon the actions of the recipients.[3] Consider Calvinist scholar Michael Horton who states: "Out of his lavish grace, the Father chose out of the fallen race a people from every race to be redeemed through his Son and united to his Son by his Spirit. This determination was made in eternity, apart from anything foreseen in the believer."[4] Arminians who follow the teachings of Jacob Arminius, on the other hand, consider election to be *conditional*. Roger Olson (an Arminian scholar) states, "Election is simply God's foreknowledge of who will

---

1. Forlines, *Classical Arminianism*, 35.
2. Ibid., 35, 46.
3. Erickson, *Christian Theology*, 929–30.
4. Horton, *For Calvinism*, 15, see also 53–79.

freely receive this grace unto salvation."[5] In other words, God chooses those whom He foreknows will respond in faith. The *condition* of election, they would say, is faith. Norman Geisler, on conditional election, states, "Salvation (is) both chosen by God and chosen by us (by faith)."[6]

This tension between conditional and unconditional election has caused, as already mentioned, a significant divide between Protestants, and there has been no shortage of debates covering vast issues of freedom of the will, the timelessness of God and decrees, the knowledge and benevolence of God, and more. Nevertheless, as Forlines noted, there is no unity of perspective within the Protestant tradition concerning the aspect of election.

Is it possible, though, that there may be another way to examine the tension in the doctrine of election? While much is to be said of the aforementioned methodologies, might one consider how monergism or synergism plays a role in the doctrine of election? Should monergism or synergism find a role in the doctrine of election, it is possible for new developments of thought to be formed.

TOWARDS A DEFINITION OF ELECTION

It is not so much the definition as derived from Hebrew and Greek lexicons of the term *divine election* that has caused division in theological circles. As will be shown, Arminians and Calvinists find common ground on the definition of election but find division in the way election is applied and construed systematically.[7]

Election in the Old Testament

Old Testament Survey

While the definitions of and debate concerning election in most modern theologies revolve around election in Christ in the New Testament, the concept of election is also found in the Old Testament. There is a surprising amount of agreement between monergists and synergists regarding election in the Old Testament; however, there are also major variances as will be shown.

5. Olson, *Against Calvinism*, 129.
6. Geisler, *Chosen But Free*, 40.
7. For a word study on election from a non-Reformed theology perspective, see Olson, *Getting the Gospel Right*, 276–90. For a word study on election from more of a Reformed position, see Garrett, *Systematic Theology*, 2:472–81.

Monergism or Synergism

The Hebrew verb in the Old Testament for election/choice is בחר, being employed one hundred-seventy times. The *Hebrew and Aramaic Lexicon of the Old Testament* states that (while there are certain instances where בחר can mean "to examine") in the Qal stem, the verb predominately means "to choose."[8] The subject and antecedent of the verb, naturally, varies thereby giving further implications which will be considered in the biblical survey below; however, the basic definition of בחר is "to choose" or "to select" as also affirmed by *The Hebrew and English Lexicon of the Old Testament*.[9]

While there are many proposals as to the differing types of election, for the sake of focus, this study will emphasize three: election of a people, election of service, and election of means.[10] It will be through this survey that one may see how בחר is used and if any inferences can be made.

Election of People

Both monergists and synergists agree that, in the Old Testament, God elects a people for his own pleasure.[11] Observe how the election of people for God's

---

8. Koehler and Baumgartner, HALOT, s.v. בחר.

9. Brown, Driver, and Briggs, *A Hebrew and English Lexicon of the Old Testament*, s.v. בחר. Hereafter BDAG.

10. These three types are built upon Demarest's, *The Cross and Salvation*, 118–35. There are many other types of election found in Scripture that our outside of the present focus of soteriology. Garrett provides others such as: election to responsibility (Rom 11:17–24), election for Gentile believers to receive Abrahamic blessings (Gal 3:28–29), election to Praise God for his grace and glory (Eph 1:6–14), and others (*Systematic Theology*, 478–79). Garrett shows how each of these choices finds its efficient cause in God thereby supporting the claims of the monergists. Karl Barth held to a novel perspective with regards to election in that Christ is both the electing God and the elected man (*Church Dogmatics* II.2), 3. An analysis and critique of Barth's doctrine of election would require far more space than can be provided here. His approach to election, however, will not be used given that his approach arguably holds to universalism, lacks significant biblical support, and ignores significant biblical testimony on the doctrine of election. See Crisp, "The Letter and the Spirit," 53–67 and Packer "The Way of Salvation Part III," 3–11 who cites Barth as one who leaned in a universalistic direction (4). Of course, possible universalism in Barth is a matter of great debate given that Barth himself never committed himself on the issue. Nevertheless, these are side issues given the focus of the present study, and Barth's doctrine of election will not be treated for the purpose of focus. Even still, one should note that in Barth's doctrine of election, God is still the efficient cause of election and salvation in the electing of Jesus Christ. See *Church Dogmatics*, II.2. 123–24. See also McGrath, *Iustitia Dei*, 402 who notes that God elects humans unilaterally without cooperation from the individual according to Barth's doctrine.

11. See also Arminian scholar Klein, *The New Chosen People*, 28–33 and monergistic scholar Garrett, *Systematic Theology*, 472–74.

THE ASPECT OF ELECTION

own pleasure began in Genesis 1—2 with the creation of the first people, Adam and Eve. It should be noted early on that the basis of creation and the choice to be brought into existence was not based upon personal worth or foreseen merit given that Adam and Eve did not yet exist and that God was under no obligation to create, a factor that is agreed to by monergists and synergists.[12] God (who exists eternally and is outside of creation) must be content and fully God in Himself. Thomas Aquinas likewise believed that all things (excluding God) come into existence from God's intention to communicate his goodness generally to all creatures and particularly to human beings.[13] Again, God did not create out of a *need* for worship or fellowship, but out of a non-necessitated *desire*. his choice (בחר) of human beings to be made in the *imago Dei* (as opposed to all other objects of creation) is also based out of God's choice given that all objects of creation were considered good (Gen 1:31).[14]

The calling of Abram from the land of Ur to begin the covenant people of God is critical in understanding God's election of people. Genesis 12—13, 15, 17, and 22 all speak of God's choosing (בחר) of Abram and the covenant blessings to be given to his descendants. God is the electing initiator in this covenant (15:18, 17:7) as He was with the covenants with Noah, Moses, and David.[15]

Election to Service

There is no significant disagreement between monergists and synergists regarding election to service (that is—that God chooses individuals to perform certain duties or tasks that carry out his will).[16] Adam and Eve were chosen by God to be fruitful and multiply, to fill the earth and subdue it, and rule over the other creatures that roam the earth (Gen 1:28). Moses was chosen by God to be the leader of the exodus from Egypt (Exod 3:10) while his brother Aaron was chosen for priestly service (1 Sam 2:28). God chose

---

12. These are statements even Geisler, a synergist, agrees to (as would most synergists). Given God's actuality and simplicity (and other essential aspects of God's nature), God is not dependent upon other things to exist. Rather, he created for his pleasure (what Geisler says was a desire to receive worship), Geisler, *Systematic Theology*, 2:30–31, 438. For a monergistic perspective affirming the same, see Grudem, *Systematic Theology*, 271. This is a general consensus between both parties.

13. Aquinas, *Summa Theologica* I, q. 47, a. 1.

14. See Hoekema, *Created in God's Image*, 11, 66.

15. Dyrness, *Themes in Old Testament Theology*, 116–24 (particularly 117).

16. See Klein, *The New Chosen People*, 27–28 for a synergistic perspective and monergist Demarest, *Cross and Salvation*, 118–19.

the Levites to be the priests who would minister before Him (1 Chr 15:2). Moreover, God chose Pharaoh, an unwilling agent, to service as one who would resist Moses' warnings and pursue the Israelites with overwhelming odds in his favor so that God might demonstrate his power as the Deliverer of Israel (Exod 9:16, see also Rom 9:17). The list could go on.

Election of Means

A final area of examination regarding election will be the election of means. The election of means refers to the agency by which salvation will occur. In other words, God (and God alone) determines the perimeters and conditions of salvation. He will be the one who determines the channels by which He will extend mercy and grace.

In the Old Testament, both monergists and synergists agree that God's election of means was the covenant made with Abraham.[17] As Genesis 12:3 states: "I will bless those who bless you, and the one who curses you I will curse; and in you all the families of the earth shall be blessed." Likewise, God chose the sign of this covenant as circumcision (Gen 17:11). This is not to exclude the means of faith in the Old Testament people of God. While there were certain markers which identified the Old Testament people of God, entry into this covenant was by faith (Gen 15:6, Rom 4:16–17, Gal 3:8–9, Heb 11:8).[18] God is the one who set the perimeters of his choice of people *and* the means by which they become (and stay?) God's covenant people. These are all areas which monergists and synergists agree.

Where Monergists and Synergists Divide

While there is much to be agreed on in the Old Testament concerning election, monergists and synergists do not find common ground on all issues. Regarding election of people as shown above, monergists stress that election does not have to do with foreseen faith (which sharply contrasts Olson's definition of election as those whom God foresaw would believe).[19] As said

---

17. Klein, *The New Chosen People*, 33–35 and Waltke, *An Old Testament Theology*, 290.

18. Whether this should be understood as faith (belief) or faithfulness (obedience) is debated. See Wright, *Justification*, 104–5. This position assumes the traditional perspective.

19. In other words, for monergists there is an Old Testament precedent that election is not based upon foreseen faith or faithfulness that carries into the New Testament teaching on election in Christ.

THE ASPECT OF ELECTION

in Genesis 17:8:"And I *will* give to you, and to your offspring after you, the land where you are now an alien, all the land of Canaan, for a perpetual holding; and I *will* be their God" (emphasis added). Monergists emphasize that "I will give" and "I will be" are more than future tense verbs; they are promises of God expressed to those whom He has chosen that will come to pass because of his faithfulness to what He has chosen.[20] They are expressions of certainty. God *will be* their God just as they *will be* his people. While the covenant involves a reciprocity with keeping the sign of the covenant (i.e., circumcision, Gen 17:10–14), God's covenant people were still the *chosen* despite their lack of faithfulness (as evidenced by the Assyrian and Babylonian captivities).[21] As such, the choosing of Israel was based upon God's choice and not upon foreseen merit given that the nation of Israel (called an "obstinate people" in Exod 32:9) failed to uphold covenant expectations (according to monergists).[22] Thus the election of the Old Testament people of God, according to monergists, found its source in God through the means of his choice.

Regarding election of persons (which is to be distinguished from election of people in the more corporate sense), monergists see more than mere election of certain persons towards service. Monergists see the election of individuals coming into *salvific* effect after the Fall of Adam into sin.[23] While the promises of disobedience in Eden were death, God chose to spare Adam and Eve from immediate death and clothe their nakedness (Gen 3:21). That is to say, God chose to spare Adam and Eve from his immediate wrath, something that will not be true of all persons after Genesis 2. The choice to show such grace, again, was based upon God and not the individual (as shown by Adam's disobedience). God chose one of Abraham's offspring to be the recipient of divine promises (Isaac over Ishmael in Gen 17 and 21). This was not just the corporate election of Israelites over Edomites, monergists contend; it was the choice of an individual blessing on a personal subject, namely the person of Isaac. This continued through Isaac's descendants with the unnatural choice of the second born (Jacob) over the firstborn (Esau). Romans 9:10 affirms this to monergists.[24] The prophet Jeremiah was

---

20. See Dyrness, *Themes in Old Testament Theology*, 125.

21. In other words, though Israel failed to uphold covenant expectations, God continued his salvific covenant promises because he is faithful to what he has chosen. See Bartholomew and Goheen, *The Drama of Scripture*, 123 and Grenz, *Theology for the Community of God*, 453.

22. Demarest, *The Cross and Salvation*, 120.

23. The following points are built upon an outline supplied in Demarest, *The Cross and Salvation*, 121–24.

24. Polhill, *Paul and His Letters*, 294.

also chosen by God for both salvation and service in Jeremiah 1:5, monergists claim.²⁵ As such, with the election of persons in the Old Testament, God is the elector, and certain members of humankind are the recipients of that election to something that includes (but is not limited to) service.

A further area of disagreement regards the ordering of covenant and election. It is important that one not equate בחר (election) with ברית (covenant) for so doing causes numerous theological and practical problems.²⁶ Still, what one may do is bring consideration to how בחר and ברית relate. Synergist Thomas Oden writes:

> In the Old Testament, sacrifice was regarded as mercifully instituted by God as an expression of covenant, enabling the wayward people to draw near to God (Lev 17:11). It was not merely a rational invention of human ingenuity or social identification. Rather, the sacrificial system was a divinely provided means of enabling the approach of sinners to God.²⁷

While synergists (such as Oden and others) may admit that God's choice in establishing a covenant relationship with Israel is of God's grace and not because of human invention or doing, would they consider that those who are in a covenant relationship with God are, in fact, those that are saved and have a right relationship with God to the exclusion of others and not on the basis of foreseen activity (including faith)? This issue will be considered further below.

---

25. See Demarest, *The Cross and Salvation*, 123 where he argues that election to salvation and election to service are supplementary and complementary rather than contradictory and exclusive, particularly in the example of Jeremiah.

26. Reformed theologian Herman Bavinck observes the following: "[T]he two (covenant and election) do differ in that in election humans are strictly passive but in the covenant of grace they also play an active role. Election only and without qualification states who are elect and will infallibly obtain salvation; the covenant of grace describes the road by which these elect people will attain their destiny. The covenant of grace is the channel by which the stream of election flows toward eternity" (Bavinck, *Reformed Dogmatics*, 3:229). See also Venema, "Covenant and Election," 83. This is also not to overlook the obvious difference between בחר and ברית in that the former is a verb and the other is a noun. There are noun and verb forms to both, but for the sake of uniformity it has been opted to keep them the same. Practically speaking, the Reformed churches in the Netherlands at the turn of the nineteenth and twentieth centuries had major fractions due to the equating of בחר and ברית as those who received the sign of the covenant (baptism) often "fell away" from the faith (assuming non-election). Questions thence arose as to their salvation. See Venema, "Covenant and Election," 70. In recognition of the numerous and irreconcilable difficulties, no attempt will be made to equate the two.

27. Oden, *The Word of Life*, 365.

Election in the New Testament

The basic verb form for election or choice in the Greek New Testament is ἐκλέγομαι, appearing 1,586 times and the basic noun form is ἐκλεκτός, appearing 1,588 times. The *Greek-English Lexicon of the New Testament and Other Early Christian Literature* (BDAG) defines ἐκλέγομαι as "to choose (for oneself), to select someone/something for oneself" and ἐκλεκτός as "pertaining to being selected, chosen, to being especially distinguished."[28] Arminians and Calvinists have found common ground in defining these two words as "to choose" and "choice," though there is disagreement in how one should construct these theologically. Nevertheless, there is common ground, and this must be explored.

Election of People

Just as Arminians and Calvinists have found common ground in the Old Testament concerning an election of people, so there is (to an extent) in the New Testament as well. In this case, however, the chosen people of God are not ethnic Israel but the *church*.[29] The church, however, does not merely fall into the purposes and promises of God haphazardly; rather, they were chosen by God to be his people (see also Titus 1:1, Heb 4:9, 1 Pet 2:9–10).[30] Galatians 3 is agreed to by monergists and synergists as identifying the entry point into this covenant (namely by faith in Christ and not by natural lineage thereby allowing Gentile believers to be included in the chosen people of God, namely the church).[31]

Election to Service

There is also agreement on both sides regarding election to service. Both would affirm the election of Jesus as the Messiah. Through the Old Testament prophets, it was foretold of one "servant" who would be chosen by

---

28. Bauer, BDAG, s.v. ἐκλέγομαι and ἐκλεκτός.

29. This is not to affirm *Replacement Theology* which would say that the church replaces Israel. Rather, it is to affirm that through salvation in Christ, the church is the fulfilment of the Old Testament initiatives. For an example of an Arminian who affirms this, see Klein, *The New Chosen People of God*, 211. For a Calvinist who affirms this, see Demarest, *The Cross and Salvation*, 121. This is a standard affirmation from both parties.

30. This is an aspect that Arminians agree to. See Grenz, *Theology for the Community of God*, 452–53 and Cottrell, "Conditional Election," 54–55.

31. Ziesler, *Pauline Christianity*, 66.

God to save his people (Isa 42:1, 49:1, 5, see also Matt 12:18).³² Jesus would say that the purpose of his coming into the world was for the crucifixion and atonement (John 12:27). Naturally this relates to God's choice in sending his son into the world to save it (John 3:16). One can note with regards to election to service the choice of God for some to be disciples and apostles (Luke 6:13, John 6:70, 1 Cor 1:1), pastors, teachers and evangelists (Eph 4:11), and priests that offer up spiritual sacrifices (1 Pet 2:5). These are not the issues over which Arminians and Calvinists divide.

Election of Means

The New Testament shows God's election of means of salvation as faith in Jesus Christ to both monergists and synergists. Those who will not perish are those who believe in the One, Jesus Christ, who was sent (John 3:16). It was God who determined who would be justified and by how, namely toward those who place faith in Jesus whom God displayed as an atoning sacrifice (Rom 3:24–26).³³ The means of reconciliation and a right standing before God are found in God's eternal plans available only through the instrumental means of faith in Jesus Christ (Eph 2:8–9, 14–22).³⁴

Where Monergists and Synergists Divide

While a more lengthy analysis of where Arminians and Calvinists divide will be provided below, regarding New Testament texts, there are numerous places in which the two parties hold to different views.

What monergists want to make clear is a precedent to which the Arminian camp does not hold. Regarding election of a people, monergists emphasize that it was on the basis of God's choice that the church was chosen as the people of God.³⁵ God chose the church to the exclusion of all others. As God was not required to save the Gentiles (or even create the church for that matter), it had to be a matter of choice. If the basis of the election was the will of God, then, according to monergists, the basis for the choice cannot be faith (albeit the means of entry into it for believers).³⁶

---

32. See Arminians Walls and Dongell, *Why I Am Not a Calvinist*, 76 and Cottrell, "Conditional Election," 52. For Calvinist, see Demarest, *The Cross and Salvation*, 118.

33. Chafer, *Systematic Theology*, 3:102–3.

34. See Stott, *The Cross of Christ*, 192–203. This statement is also agreed to by synergists. See Olson, *Against Calvinism*, 130–31.

35. Grudem, *Systematic Theology*, 670–71.

36. Demarest, *The Cross and Salvation*, 132.

While Calvinists may affirm with Arminians that the New Testament teaches election of individuals for service, they also wish to affirm individual salvation for the elect.[37] While God's universal and corporate love for the whole world is mentioned in John 3:16, monergists see God's choice of certain persons to eternal life is shown two chapters later in 5:21 where it states: "Indeed, just as the Father raises the dead and gives them life, so also the Son gives life to whomever he wishes."[38] Using analogous language, Jesus speaks of his flock (the church) which consists of sheep whom the Father has specifically given to him (John 10:29). These "sheep" (i.e., the chosen believers) hear his voice as their own Shepherd and follow him while those who are not his sheep (i.e., not chosen believers) will not respond to his voice (John 10:16, 26).[39]

SYNERGISTS' PERSPECTIVE OF ELECTION

While Calvinists and Arminians have found agreement on a simple definition of election (namely "to choose"), the affirmations of Calvinists are things which Arminians do not wish to hold. Should one examine how the Arminian camp (hereafter synergists) constructs their doctrine of election synergistically, one may find an underlying root cause as the source of the tension that oftentimes goes ignored.

It is interesting to note where many synergists categorize their doctrine of election. Jacob Arminius, for example, treated the issue of election in the overall section of predestination, even to the point of not using the word *election* though addressing the very issue.[40] Arminius states:

> The second precise and absolute decree of God, is that in which he decreed to receive into favor those who repent and believe, and, in Christ, for his sake and through Him, to effect the salvation of such penitents and believers as persevered to the end;

---

37. One should note, however, that certain Wesleyans during the time of Wesley held to an election of "some persons," though they affirmed Christ died for all. Wesley was tolerant of this position, though he did not personally endorse it. See Tyerman, *The Life and Times*, 2:145.

38. White, *The Potter's Freedom*, 192–95. See also Yarbrough, "Divine Election," 1:50–51.

39. This does refer to the inclusion of the Gentiles into God's people (namely the corporate election); see Beasley-Murray, *John*, 171.

40. This is not to say he did not use the term election but rather that he treats the matter of election under predestination without so using the term almost to imply that predestination and election were the same.

but to leave in sin, and under wrath, all impenitent persons and unbelievers, and to damn them as aliens from Christ.

The third Divine decree is that by which God decreed to administer in a sufficient and efficacious manner the means which were necessary for repentance and faith; and to have such administration instituted (1.) according to the Divine Wisdom, by which God knows what is proper and becoming both to his mercy and his severity, and (2.) according to Divine Justice, by which He is prepared to adopt whatever his wisdom may prescribe and put it in execution.

> To these succeeds the fourth decree, by which God decreed to save and damn certain particular persons. This decree has its foundation in the foreknowledge of God, by which he knew from all eternity those individuals who would, through his preventing grace, believe, and, through his subsequent grace would persevere, according to the before described administration of those means which are suitable and proper for conversion and faith; and, by which foreknowledge, he likewise knew those who would not believe and persevere.[41]

Many things are noteworthy here. First, Arminius did affirm certain eternal decrees from God as a means to understand predestination and election (a factor that will be explored further below).[42] Second, according to the second decree that Arminius holds to, God decreed that there be two types of people—those who repent, believe, and *persevere* to the end and those who refuse to believe. In other words, continued faithfulness (perseverance) is required on the part of the believer. Notice that Arminius did not state that God decrees who will repent, believe, and persevere and who will refuse to believe. Rather, he believed that God decreed that there be two paths which individuals could pursue. Third, Arminius believed that God decreed that there be a "means" for salvation (namely repentance and faith) which easily fits the *election of means* category described above. Lastly, according to Arminius's fourth sentiment, God does not elect individuals unto salvation, but He foreknows those who will respond in repentance and faith and who will choose not to believe and persevere.

The great founder of Methodism, John Wesley, closely followed Arminius's thought. Wesley too believed in eternal divine decrees, though like

---

41. Arminius, *The Works of James Arminius*, 185.

42. See Lane, *A Concise History of Christian Thought*, 183. One should note that though Arminius held to divine decrees, he did *not* hold to the Supralapsarian concept of God's decrees (namely where God decreed the disobedience of Adam and Eve and the "fall" of humankind.) See Wynkoop, *Foundations of Wesleyan-Arminian Theology*, 51.

Arminius he believed that the decree of election is conditioned by God on faith. He thus says, "[A]ll true believers are in Scripture termed *elect*."[43]

Arminians who have followed Arminius's and Wesley's teachings share the same perspective.[44] Consider Arminian scholar William W. Klein who says, "To exercise faith in Christ is to enter into his body and become one of the 'chosen ones.'"[45] Consider also Roger Olson who says, "Through faith, a person enters into Christ, that is, into his church and thereby becomes 'elect.'" Norman Geisler (though he does not call himself an Arminian) says, "There is no contradiction in God knowingly predetermining and predeterminately knowing from all eternity precisely what we would do with our free acts. For God *determined* that moral creatures would do things *freely* . . . What is forced is not free, and what is free is not forced."[46]

So what is the basis of this election? C. Gordon Olson states that it is foreseen faith.[47] Election, he says, is conditioned upon faith, and that faith which unites them to the Elect One (Christ) is foreseen by God thereby allowing them to enter into the corporate election of the church. Any sense of individual election to salvation must, he claims, be understood as the individual's free choice to be united to Christ by faith and enter into the corporate elect body, the church.[48]

It is in this line of thinking that one understands Roger Olson's definition that "Election is simply God's foreknowledge of who will freely receive this grace unto salvation."[49] Notice the inseparable link to the Arminian/synergist position between election and foreknowledge (so much so that some, like Roger Olson, appear to equate the two).[50] Norman Geisler also

43. Wesley, *Calvinism Calmly Considered*, 23, emphasis original.

44. See Pfeiffer, *Anti-Calvinism*, 162–73 where he defines election as a divine decree.

45. Klein, *The New Chosen People*, 265.

46. Geisler, *Chosen But Free*, 55. Emphasis his. While Geisler does not call himself and Arminian, his theology is certainly indicative of it. See White, *The Potter's Freedom*.

47. Olson, *Getting the Gospel Right*, 283. This was the claim of Arminius as well in *Works*, I, 254. See also Lake, "'Jacob Arminius's Contribution," 238. Notice there Lake poses the question of why some come to saving faith and others do not if all are covered equally with prevenient grace. He admits Arminius does not provide a clear answer.

48. Olson, *Getting the Gospel Right*, 283.

49. Olson, *Against Calvinism*, 129. See also Arminius, "My Own Sentiments on Predestination," in *The Works of James Arminius*, 1:185, and Clarke, *The Ground of Election*, 90.

50. For Arminius, because election was *in Christ*, one's election (or predestination) did not occur until the beginning of the new covenant. Because Christ served as prophet, priest, and king, restoring humanity back in favor with God, the new covenant is founded upon these realities. Predestination (or divine election) does not occur before the foundations of the world but after the new covenant was established (per Rom 8:30). See Arminius, "Disputation XIV."

holds to this inseparable link, almost equating foreknowledge with predestination/election. Geisler, affirming that God is an eternal being outside of time, knows all things eternally, and in this knowledge he does not foreordain anything that *later* occurs to Him (even going so far as to say that God does not foreordain anything from his vantage point); rather, God foreknows what humans will do freely.[51] With this in mind, one may see the timeline of election according to Arminians. The past aspect has to do with God's foreknowledge of who will respond with repentance and faith. The present tense is the moment in which the individual responds with repentance and faith to Christ thereby *becoming* the elect (in a moment in time). The future aspect is glorification of the elect (though some such as Arminius and Wesley would say that this is also conditioned upon continued faithfulness, though it is not mandatory to hold to this position).

It is with this background clearly in view that one sees how synergism plays a role. God is the agent who chooses, but humankind must also choose God. God's work is in receiving all who will do their work of receiving Him. John Wesley, in his treatise, *Calvinism Calmly Considered*, wrote:

> If it be, I must ask again, "What do you mean by God's 'having the whole glory?'" Do you mean, "His doing the whole work, without any concurrence on man's part?" If so, your assertion is, "If man do at all 'work together with God,' in 'working out his own salvation,' then God does not do the whole work, without man's 'working together with Him.'" Most true, most sure: But cannot you see, how God nevertheless may have all the glory? Why, the very power to "work together with Him" was from God.[52]

What act requires such working together (synergism)? Wesley's context was election. The individual believes in God, and God elects that person. Dale Moody, speaking of salvation and predestination, thinks it is only right to consider predestination in Christ (i.e., election) to be synergistic. Moody states that God foreknows who will respond in faith, and citing Romans 8:38 as a proof-text (that God "cooperates for good with those who love God and are called according to his purpose"), he claims that such cooperation (of faith on the part of the believer and salvation on the part of God) is synergism.[53]

---

51. Geisler, "God Knows All Things," 73. See also Klein, *The New Chosen People*, 30–32.

52. Wesley, *Calvinism Calmly Considered*, 22–23. See also Forlines, *Classical Arminianism*, 46.

53. Moody, *The Word of Truth*, 341–42.

In Norman Geisler's work on election, entitled *Chosen But Free*, he likewise speaks of synergism in this regard. He says, "God's grace works synergistically on free will. That is, it must be received to be effective. There are no conditions for giving grace, but there is one condition for receiving it—faith."[54] Roger Olson, using Wesley for support, says, "This power to work together with God for salvation (which is all God's doing) is simply the calling, enlightening, enabling grace that God implants in a human heart because of his love and because of the work of Christ."[55] In other words, through prevenient (preceding) grace, God enables individuals to work together with Him to believe in Christ and thus be amongst the elect.

F. Leroy Forlines defines what is meant by synergistic: "Active participation in faith by the believer means that it (a God-given enablement to believe) must be synergistic . . . Faith is a human act by divine enablement and therefore cannot be monergistic."[56] Roger Olson likewise affirms that synergism is the human exercise of good will to God, and with regards to election it is one's response of faith in God for salvation.[57]

It is this belief, called *conditional election*, that has caused the rift between Arminians and Calvinists and makes Michael Horton's definition of election (again, "Out of his lavish grace, the Father chose out of the fallen race a people from every race to be redeemed through his Son and united to his Son by his Spirit. This determination was made in eternity, apart from anything foreseen in the believer"[58]) unacceptable.

Arminians claim that one of the primary reasons they hold to conditional election is that they believe it preserves the omni-benevolence of God. For God to be a God worthy of worship, he must be a good God who loves everyone. While he may be just in punishing all sinners and not opening a single way for salvation for anyone, he (according to Arminians), would not be thought of as a loving God. If, however, God loves his fallen creation, he may grant them an opportunity to respond to his love and accept him (by free volition in faith) as their Savior. Because the responsibility (or better termed

---

54. Geisler, *Chosen But Free*, 242.

55. Olson, *Against Calvinism*, 129; parentheses his.

56. Forlines, *Classical Arminianism*, 24.

57. Olson, *Arminian Theology*, 18, 185. It is worthwhile to note that not all Arminians believe in synergism, though most do. Robert E. Picirilli would be such an example. While some of his conclusions appear to have cooperative/synergistic tendencies, he is at least mindful to note that this is not synergism. He writes, "Salvation is *wholly the gracious work of God*, thus yielding no credit or merit to man. There is no room for 'synergism' (the view that God and man work together to accomplish salvation)" (*Grace, Faith, Free Will*, 36; emphasis his).

58. Horton, *For Calvinism*, 15; see also 53–79.

conditionality) is up to humans to accept or reject the offer of forgiveness, God, then, can be said to be an omni-benevolent God who truly loves his fallen creation and deserving of worship from his creatures because He has given each person an opportunity to respond to his salvific grace.[59]

In conclusion, the following points must be noted. First, there are many within the Arminian/synergistic party that hold to divine decrees as a means to understand election. Second, election is related (and oftentimes equated) to foreknowledge of future events. Third, election is conditioned upon faith. Fourth, while election was foreknown in the past, it becomes active in time. Fifth, faith is what makes election synergistic. Sixth, it is necessary to hold to conditional election to preserve God's omni-benevolence and/or universal love for the fallen world.

MONERGISTS' PERSPECTIVE ON ELECTION

Election and the Divine Decrees

Monergists categorize election oftentimes under the main heading (or in association with) the divine decrees. The Westminster Shorter Catechism Q. 7 states, "The decrees of God are, his eternal purpose, according to the counsel of his will, whereby, for his own glory, he hath fore-ordained whatsoever comes to pass." Likewise, Augustus H. Strong defines the decrees of God as: "[T]hat eternal plan by which God has rendered certain all the events of the universe, past present, and future."[60] Many (if not most) monergists and synergists agree that election is a decree of God as has already been shown.[61]

---

59. Olson, *Against Calvinism*, 102–35, Geisler, *Chosen But Free*, 137–39.

60. Strong, *Systematic Theology*, 1.4.3.1, 353.

61. See Berkhof, *Systematic Theology*, 100, 109, 113–14 where he places election as an aspect of predestination which is under the broader category of the decrees of God. See also the discussion in the following paragraphs. See also John Feinberg and Norman Geisler in *Predestination and Free Will*. Feinberg (a monergist) and Geisler (a synergist) both agree that God is omniscient in all things that pertain to the future, controls every detail in creation, predetermines every event, and that God's election of saints comes from eternity past and will be certain (45). Naturally they disagree on details concerning the conditions of election and determinism and the place of free will. The point being made here is that monergists and synergists can agree on the fact that God has determined certain events (including election) to be from eternity past even if one wishes to stray from the definitions of the Westminster Shorter Catechism and Augustus Strong in that every detail is foreordained. Thomas Oden would be an example of an Arminian synergist who would not hold to election as a divine decree as outlined here. See *The Word of Life*, 376. Nevertheless, Arminius, as shown above, held to the divine decrees, though not in a supralapsarian way.

While one may disagree with the Westminster Catechism and others of a strongly Reformed perspective with regards to the *extent* of pre-determinism and predestination, some monergists and synergists have found common ground in that there are decrees set in place by God before the foundation of the world that will necessarily transpire (including in some cases even election). Naturally, the means to election, or the definition of election itself, would vary greatly. However, even John Wesley (a notable synergist) believed (as mentioned above) that God establishes eternal decrees that will be certain, even in election. In his mind, God elects persons to eternal happiness based upon the condition of faith being exercised.[62]

Though there may be agreement between monergists and synergists that divine decrees exist and that election falls in that category, divine decrees must be explained by monergists through biblical survey, and support must be supplied to show how election falls within the divine decrees. With this point in place, one will be able to determine if election shares similar characteristics as do the other monergistic divine decrees.

The Monergists' Biblical Portrayal of Divine Decrees

While not being exact synonyms, terms related to the divine decrees of God are: purpose, counsel, foreknowledge, foreordination, will, predestination, and election.[63] As one searches the Scriptures that speak of God's eternal plans, will, and foreordination, one finds these terms surfacing whereby certain conclusions on the nature of divine decrees can be made.

First, monergists see that the divine decrees are founded in God.[64] While stressing that the source may not be in the personhood of God, *per se*, it becomes clear that God is the source (whether it be of his will, mind, pleasure, plans, etc.) of these decrees. Psalm 139:16 states that the days of one's life were already written in the "books" (i.e., plans) of God. Job likewise concurs with a similar statement: "Since their days are determined, and the number of their months is known to you, and you have appointed the bounds that they cannot pass" (Job 14:5). One can notice from these verses that the divine decrees are founded in God, whether it be in his plans, determination, or will.

62. Wesley, *Calvinism Calmly Considered*, 87–88.

63. Berkhof, *Systematic Theology*, 101–2; Strong, *Systematic Theology*, 1.4.3.1a 353, Chafer, "Biblical Theism," 138. See also Carson *Divine Sovereignty and Human Responsibility*, 27–30 showing how God is the efficient (or as he terms "ultimate personal cause") cause throughout the Scriptures with specific examples given with regards to divine decrees.

64. Berkhof, *Systematic Theology*, 103–4, Calvin, *Concerning the Eternal Predestination of God*, 58.

Monergists claim further examples that divine decrees are founded in God by exploring the orchestration of certain events that were planned and determined by God. This includes such events as the crucifixion of Christ (Acts 2:23), the volitional sin of Herod, Pilate, the Gentiles, and the people of Israel (Acts 4:28), and the betrayal of Judas (Ps 41:9/John 13:18, John 17:12, et.al.)[65]

Referring to election, the Book of Ephesians begins with the statement: "He chose us in Him before the foundation of the world, that we would be holy and blameless before Him. In love He predestined us to adoption as sons through Jesus Christ to Himself, according to the kind intention of His will" (Eph 1:4–5, NASB). Here, the monergist views Paul as saying that salvation (particularly the aspect of election) is found in the eternal and gracious will of God from which He decreed before anything came into being.[66] As such, not only can one see how God is the source of this divine decree but that election itself is a divine decree.[67]

A second major factor in the divine decrees (including election) according to monergists is that they are eternal. 2 Timothy states that Christ "saved us (i.e., believers in Christ) and called us with a holy calling, not according to our works but according to his own purpose and grace. This grace was given to us in Christ Jesus before the ages began" (2 Tim 1:9). In this pastoral epistle, monergists see Paul assuring Timothy that, despite the opposition from the Ephesians, his salvation and calling are certain as God's choice of him in this role has existed before creation and time.[68] The first person plural noun shows to monergists that eternal election is not limited only to Timothy but embracive of all who are in Christ's salvation. As such, to the monergist, there is a past, present, and future aspect to salvation. Justification and sanctification, it is claimed, fall within the present while glorification awaits believers in the future; however, the past aspect entails divine election that is caused by divine power alone. This passage out of 2 Timothy (along with other Pauline cross-references) support this to members of this tradition.[69]

65. Grudem, *Systematic Theology*, 332–33.

66. Vaughan, *The Letter to the Ephesians*, 12–14.

67. It need not concern the reader at this moment whether one should think of election in terms of supralapsarianism, infralapsarian, or sublapsarian. Regardless of how one orders and arranges the decrees of election, creation, permitting the fall, and the provision of redemption, both Reformed and Arminian scholars generally hold to God being the source of divine decrees and that election is itself a divine decree. See Garrett, *Systematic Theology*, 487–88.

68. Mounce, *Pastoral Epistles*, 483.

69. Clark, *The Pastoral Epistles*, 133–34. Clark (as a Reformed philosopher and not biblical scholar *per se*) contributes to the discussion by offering a monergistic perspective rather than biblical exegesis, though his exegesis is not without some merit.

THE ASPECT OF ELECTION

A third characteristic of divine decrees that monergists wish to point out is that they are efficacious. The decrees are efficacious in that what God has determined will be accomplished (Ps 33:22, Prov 19:21, Isa 46:10, Luke 18:31). Again, this (like the previous two) is something that monergists and synergists rarely argue. As James P. Boyce said regarding the efficacy of God's decrees, "But that God is thus active, sometimes, as in his gracious influences upon men, is held as firmly by Arminians as Calvinists. In all such gracious acts, both parties claim that he is both merciful and just."[70]

A final characteristic in the divine decrees (including election) is that they are unconditional.[71] By this statement, it is meant that the decree is not dependent upon or conditional on anything but God. Berkhof notes, though, that the execution of the decree may require an instrumental means or depend upon certain conditions, but the conditions of that decree are included in the decree.[72] As one observes the passage from 2 Timothy as well as Ephesians 1 (while also recalling the numerous passages referring to the divine decrees such as Eph 3:10–11, Prov 3:19, 1 Pet 1:2 et al.), the monergist finds that God (as the source of the decrees) whose decrees are effective are also not dependent upon its object. Creation was a decree from God that came into being apart from any conditions on creation. The choice of Abraham's descendants was unconditional (see also Rom 9:11).[73] Likewise, Paul's doctrine of election for salvation is based upon divine purpose and grace and not foreseen human merit and worth (according to monergists).[74] It is worth noting that though monergists and synergists disagree greatly regarding unconditional election,

---

Berkhof makes an important observation regarding the eternality of divine decrees. The divine decree is eternal because its roots stem from the eternal God. In that there is no succession of moments in God. Moreover, because the decrees lie entirely in the eternal God, the decrees are eternal as well. See Berkhof, *Systematic Theology*, 104. This is not to state that there is not a temporal execution of the decrees. Rather, the decree is in God who is outside of time but executes the decrees within time.

70. Boyce, *Abstract of Systematic Theology*, 123.

71. Hodge, *Systematic Theology*, 1:540. Disagreement between monergists and synergists is prevalent with regards to this.

72. Berkhof, *Systematic Theology*, 105, Shedd, *Dogmatic Theology*, 1:404–5, and Chafer, *Biblical Theism*, 144–47.

73. Dunn, *Romans 9–16*, 542–43, 548–49. Synergist Norman Geisler states that the election of Abraham was dependent upon Abraham "heeding God's call (where he) journeyed to the land of Canaan with his wife (Sarah) and nephew (Lot)" (*A Popular Survey of the Old Testament*, 46). However, even those synergists that see election as conditional in that it requires a response also see that the basis for the election was not based upon foreseen merit or intrinsic worth. Naturally this will be developed in subsequent chapters.

74. Horton, *For Calvinism*, 55–56. See also Guthrie, *The Pastoral Epistles*, 129.

there is agreement in this last point between both parties that election is not dependent upon foreseen merit or inherent worth.[75]

What is significant to point out at this point is that there are many areas of agreement between monergists and synergists regarding divine decrees. A notable Arminian scholar, Robert E. Picirilli, has found many points of agreement between these two parties regarding the decrees. He is quoted as saying that divine decrees are:

- "Founded in the Divine wisdom"
- "A simple unity (that is, one plan)"
- "All-embracing, including whatever comes to pass, whether free or necessary, good or evil"
- "Eternal . . . 'God does nothing in time, which He has not decreed to do from all eternity.'" (quoting Arminius)
- "Immutable"
- "Unconditional, in that nothing outside God can 'condition' His decisions"
- "Incapable of being overturned . . . that is, they are always successful."[76]

Unconditional Election

Monergists will affirm that election is unconditional in the sense that God's election happened in eternity past *and* without foreseen merit or faith. Likely, the first notable theologian to affirm that election was in eternity past without foreseen merit or faith was Augustine of Hippo. Referencing John 15:16, Augustine affirmed the sinfulness of humankind, the inability for one to choose God, and how individuals were chosen before the foundation of the world not on the basis of foreknown faith or good works but by his gracious choice.[77] Consider the *Westminster Confession of Faith*, 3.5 that states:

> Those of mankind that are predestinated unto life, God, before the foundation of the world was laid, according to his eternal and immutable purpose, and the secret counsel and good pleasure of his will, hath chosen in Christ, unto everlasting glory, out of his free grace and love alone, without any foresight of

75. Olson, *Against Calvinism*, 128–29 who also quotes John Wesley stating the same claim.

76. Picirilli, *Grace, Faith, Free Will*, 44.

77. Augustine, "Tractate LXXXVI.2," in *Homilies on the Gospel of John*, 353.

THE ASPECT OF ELECTION

faith or good works, or perseverance in either of them, or any other thing in the creature, as conditions, or causes moving him thereunto; and all to the praise of his glorious grace.

While no monergist, including Augustine, or monergistic confession like the *Westminster Confession of Faith*, would deny the involvement or importance of faith, they would affirm that God from eternity past chose individuals for blessing apart from foreseen faith or obedience.[78]

What is the basis for this conclusion? After all, Romans 8:29 states: "For those whom he foreknew he also predestined to be conformed to the image of his Son." Does not God foreknow and then predestine? Michael Horton thinks not. For Horton, and other monergists, to foreknow means more than "to know beforehand" or mere knowledge. "Foreknow" means to know personally, in loving affection.[79] Horton notes that Romans 8:29 says it is "those" whom God foreknew, not "that" which God foreknew. He writes, "It is not that God foreknew our decision (as the meaning of this text), but that he foreknew those whom he predestined . . . If no one can believe apart from God's regenerating grace, then God could never have foreseen someone believing apart from his prior decision to give that person saving faith."[80]

Referring to the same Romans 8:29 text, Greg Welty observes that the text does not mention *faith* but *people*. God, here, is said to know *people* not foreseen works or faith.[81] Moreover, Welty also addresses the claim that synergists often make that conditional election preserves the omni-benevolence and universal love of God. Welty concludes that the Arminian camp does not escape the very problem they are trying to avoid, for, by their own admission, the God who has foreknowledge willfully creates at least some who will never come to faith. Why would He deliberately create them knowing they would never come to faith? Welty admits he has no answer, but the fact that he does not have an answer, he claims, does not mean that he should abandon the doctrine of divine omniscience (just as those who cannot explain why God elects some unconditionally and not others cannot explain the reasoning but nevertheless do not abandon the doctrine).[82]

A final matter that monergists wish to affirm is that holding to unconditional election maintains the consistency of the other divine decrees. That

---

78. See also Sproul, *What Is Reformed Theology?*, 144–45.
79. Horton, *For Calvinism*, 58.
80. Ibid.
81. Welty, "Election and Calling," 231. Welty also provides a lengthy exegesis against proof texts that synergists/Arminians often us to support conditional election.
82. Ibid., 230.

is to say, like the other divine decrees, they are made without foreseen faith or obedience. To make one of the divine decrees conditional is to go against the system that, they claim, Scripture presents regarding the decrees.[83]

THE EFFICIENT CAUSE OF ELECTION

It is not the intent of this study to provide an exhaustive rebuttal of all matters relating to election. Rather, it is the primary objective to show why monergists believe election is monergistic and why synergists believe election is synergistic. From there one may be in a better position to explore new insights as to which side can best support their views biblically and logically. Having given a brief overview of both positions, one must now consider the main issue of efficient cause.

Synergists' View of Efficient Cause

One must be aware that there are a variety of perspectives within the synergistic camp on the efficient cause of election. Ultimately, most believe that God is the efficient cause of salvation. Consider Roger Olson when he says, "Arminians . . . hold a form of evangelical synergism that sees grace as the efficient cause of salvation and calls faith the sole instrumental cause of salvation, to the exclusion of human merits."[84] This follows the Aristotelian model that was proposed in chapter 1.

Olson, therefore, follows Arminius's own teachings on the subject. As shown above, Arminius held to four divine decrees. The language of these shows that the source of the decrees is God (that is—his will, pleasure, and plan). For Arminius, the reason why election exists is because God chose for it to be so.

Norman Geisler comes close to saying something similar, though his wording almost confuses faith *and* God as the efficient causes of election. He states, "God is the unconditional source of the election, and that election is done with full foreknowledge of all things . . . [T]he elect will freely choose to believe. Election is not *based on* or dependent on foreknowledge. Rather, it is merely *in accord with* it."[85] Geisler comes close to saying that the efficient cause of election is synergistic, for God, being the unconditional source of election (meaning God had no conditions in *giving* the salvation)

---

83. Berkhof, *Systematic Theology*, 105.
84. Olson, *Arminian Theology*, 95.
85. Geisler, *Chosen But Free*, 69; emphasis his.

still foreknows who will freely choose this source, and while election is not based on foreseen faith, it is in "accord" with it. Simply said, faith is in accord with God in the source of election.[86] While the language is unclear with regards to the efficient cause, this study will assume that Geisler means that God is, indeed, the sole efficient cause and that Arminians/synergists claim that God is the efficient cause as a whole.

Monergists' View of Efficient Cause

Monergists unequivocally affirm that the efficient cause of election is God. This is clearly seen, as shown above, in their affirmation of the *divine* decrees. The elect are elected because of their calling *from God*, believed Augustine, and it is because of this divine decree by which they were called that they will, therefore, persevere unto eternal life.[87] Monergists find biblical support for God being the sole efficient cause of election through such verses as Acts 13:48, Romans 8:28–30, Romans 9:11–13, Romans 11:7, Ephesians 1:12, 1 Thessalonians 1:4–5, 2 Thessalonians 2:13, and 1 Peter 2:9.[88]

Synergists' View on Instrumental Means

Again, quoting Olson, "Arminians . . . hold a form of evangelical synergism that sees grace as the efficient cause of salvation and calls faith the sole instrumental cause of salvation, to the exclusion of human merits."[89] For synergists, faith is the condition for election, and therefore, in their view, the means (or cause?) by which election is received. This has been shown above. As such, the instrumental means of election is synergistic.

Monergists' View of Instrumental Means

The instrumental means (not cause) of election, for monergists, is not faith but merely the will of God. In other words, election is passive (not

---

86. Again, this is speaking with regards to the efficient cause of election. Monergists, as said above, do not deny that faith is in accordance with the foreknowledge of God. They do not deny that faith is involved with election. However, what they would deny is that faith has an involvement in the *cause* of election. Geisler appears to be placing faith in the cause of election, not as the means through which it is received like most Arminians/synergists do.

87. Augustine, "Treatise on Rebuke and Grace" in *Augustin*, 2.14–15, 477.

88. Grudem, *Systematic Theology*, 671–72.

89. Olson, *Arminian Theology*, 95.

active through faith) upon the individual. This is made clear by monergists' claim that God executes his will in an *unconditional* way. That is to say, in accordance with all the divine decrees as set forth, God accomplishes his efficacious plans in an unconditional way. They are not dependent upon foreseen faith or good works.[90] Should such choice be conditioned upon foreseen merit or response, a case could be made for active instrumental means. However, this is precisely what monergists reject.

This is not to say that monergists do not believe faith has no part to play in salvation; it is to say that faith is not the instrumental means by which one receives election. This is part of what is meant by *called* or *chosen*, the monergist would claim, citing John 15:16 as support: "You did not choose me but I chose you. And I appointed you to go and bear fruit," as well as Romans 9:15–16: "For he says to Moses, 'I will have mercy on whom I have mercy, and I will have compassion on whom I have compassion.' So it depends not on human will or exertion, but on God who shows mercy."[91] God purposed to elect (Rom 9:11, 2 Tim 1:9), and this election is a status that is granted. When asking the question, "How are the elect elected?," the monergists claim that God elected them from eternity past apart from foreseen merit or faith.[92]

As a matter of exegetical importance, it is worthwhile to note the subject of the verb ἐκλέγομαι. Mark 13:20 says that it was the Lord who *chose* the elect. John 15:16 states that it was Jesus who *chose* the disciples. Ephesians 1:4 states that it was God who *chose* disciples to be in Christ (a verse used often by monergists to show instrumental means as has already been noted). Second Thessalonians states that brothers and sisters (in Christ) are beloved in the Lord because they were chosen (by God) as the first-fruits of salvation. Regarding the noun form ἐκλεκτός, all but three references in the New Testament refer to being chosen *passively* by God.[93] As such, monergists conclude that, in accordance with all divine decrees, election is founded not only *in* God but is received *through* God.

---

90. Berkhof, *Systematic Theology*, 114–15.
91. Erickson, *Christian Theology*, 929–30.
92. Augustine, "Treatise on Rebuke and Grace" in *Augustin*, 2.14–15, 477.
93. See BDAG, s.v. ἐκλεκτός. The exceptions are in 1 Tim 5:21 referring to angels and Rom 16:13 and 1 Pet 2:4, 6 which refer to being "choice" or "excellent."

THE ASPECT OF ELECTION

A CRITIQUE OF THE SYNERGISTS' VIEW OF ELECTION

Both parties may affirm God as the efficient cause and therefore consider this to be a non-issue regarding monergism and synergism; however, is this *truly* the case? While Arminians and Calvinists may *claim* God as the efficient cause, it will ultimately depend not upon their mere claims but their theological construction.

While synergists do not typically deny that it is God who elects (therefore assuming God as the efficient cause), an examination of their theology may yield a different answer thereby showing the underlying synergism (and the underlying tension between Arminians and Calvinists). While synergists such as Roger Olson say that faith is the agency (specifically *instrumental cause*) of receiving election (thereby referring to instrumentation), classical Arminian theology as has been described here actually shows synergism (a cooperation) in the efficient cause.

This can be seen from two angles. First, election is not, for Arminians/synergists, a decree from eternity past carrying a certainty to the individual (as monergists would claim and has been shown above). This is an interesting move on behalf of the synergists given that they construe no other divine decrees in this way. Rather, in their view election is merely foreknowledge of who will freely respond to God's offer of salvation. Therefore, one becomes elect in a moment in time whenever faith is placed in Christ.

This is an interesting claim given such verses as Ephesians 1:4: "[H]e chose us in Christ before the foundation of the world." Naturally, monergists see this statement as God's eternal, immutable choice before time began thereby emphasizing that nothing can shake his determination to save his people.[94] But how would synergists address this verse? Interestingly, New Testament Arminian scholar William Klein states that this passage is referring to (corporate) election in a "pretemporal" way, "before the world was created."[95] He goes on to say, "God's pretemporal choice becomes evident when people accept the Gospel."[96] While the issue of whether election being corporate or individualistic, at this point, is not the issue, it is interesting at this point how Klein believes election is something that did, in fact, happen in eternity past and not in a moment in time like many other Arminians. Consider also C. Gordon Olson (also a synergist) on the matter of Ephesians 1 who states that Ephesians 1 refers to "foreordination" and

---

94. Vaughan, *Ephesians*, 14 and Polhill, *Paul and His Letters*, 362.
95. Klein, *The New Chosen People*, 179.
96. Ibid., 211.

"preappointment" to an inheritance to be received in a moment in time.[97] This is an interesting claim given that Olson also states that election is "conditioned upon the sinner's response to the gospel message in repentance in faith."[98] It is hard to understand how something could be "preappointed" and "foreordained" in eternity past whereby things should be a certain way but in time be conditional and uncertain. Norman Geisler also states that it is a "fact that only believers were chosen in Christ before time began" upon his commentary of Ephesians 1:4.[99] At the same time, Geisler also says (in commentary of Ephesians 1:4) that these people are not actually saved but only potentially saved, for God does not choose against the individual's will.[100] Others go on to say that election does not mean inevitable salvation.[101] The synergist, when facing such passages as Ephesians 1 (consider also Romans 9:11), exegetically admits that certain things are certain, but when the matter is applied to salvation, it becomes conditional. Again, the matter is whether election is something that did happen in eternity past or whether it takes place in active time. The synergists, while affirming foreordination, preappointment, and divine pretemporal choice, make a break in application when it comes to election.

Regarding conditional election, the synergists are adamant that foreseen faith is not the same as foreseen merit.[102] Should salvation and election be dependent upon merit or works, then one may have a right to boast; however, since it is all of grace, there is no room for boasting.[103] However, Welty (a monergist) raises the following consideration regarding those who believe that God elects because of foreseen faith and not merit: if faith originates from within the individual and is not a gift given only to some/the elect (as synergists believe), why would it not be meritorious?[104] Welty observes that exercising faith is something that pleases God (Heb 11:6) and choosing to disbelieve God and his commands will bring punishment and is a form of disobedience. If an independently exercised faith (albeit by prevenient grace) is shown, Welty claims that one could take credit (merit)

---

97. Olson, *Getting the Gospel Right*, 284–85.

98. Ibid., 290.

99. Geisler, *Chosen But Free*, 79. See also 83. He says this in the context of it being a fact that believers are chosen in Christ before time began but that Christ also died for all human beings knowing who would and would not believe. Still, the point holds that Geisler is not consistent in his claims.

100. Ibid., 83, 96.

101. Walls and Dongell, *Why I Am Not A Calvinist*, 81.

102. Geisler, *Chosen But Free*, 198–99; Olson, *Against Calvinism*, 128–29.

103. Walls and Dongell, *Why I Am Not A Calvinist*, 75–76.

104. Welty, "Election and Calling," 226.

THE ASPECT OF ELECTION

for showing it.[105] D. A. Carson, addressing this issue, applies the analogy of a judge who is just in condemning ten criminals but offers each of them pardon. Five accept the pardon but the other five reject it. While those who accept the pardon do not earn it, and certainly are the recipients of grace, they are distinguishable from those who rejected the offer because of their own decision to accept the pardon. It was their wisdom that separated them from those who rejected the grace which, Carson claims, becomes a legitimate boast, but not so when God becomes the one who elects solely by his choice and grace as in the monergistic model.[106]

The point being made here is that though synergists claim that God is the efficient cause, one sees that there is synergism in the efficient cause (in their view). God chooses people, but people must choose God.[107] Moreover, as election does not become active or realized until a specific moment in time (as shown above) when an individual places faith in God, it stands to reason that there is truly *cooperation* in the efficient cause. God chooses individuals, and individuals choose God thereby becoming and being grafted into the corporate body of Christ. Election does not become certain until it is received in faith.[108]

In so doing, synergists face monumental problems (even in their own admission) with how election can truly be in eternity past by the foreordained plan of God. Moreover, synergists also make a redefinition of terms. While monergists readily admit that salvation (particularly the aspects of conversion, regeneration, and justification to name a few) happen in a moment in time, election happens in eternity past. This is readily *admitted to* by the Arminian synergists mentioned above that hold to the position of divine decrees (such as: Arminius, Wesley, Olson, Geisler, and Forlines), but it is not readily *applied*. All of these theologians hold to foreordained certainties, even placing election in them; however, they later say that election is not certain or realized until a moment in time when faith is expressed. This is not consistent.

Moreover, the conditional system of election does give credit to the individual who was wise enough (as Carson stated) to exercise this free faith while others did not. Faith, then, is a contributing work (again, remember that synergists claim that one "*works* together" with God) which would allow one to boast. This is difficult to reconcile with Ephesians 2:8–9: "For by

---

105. Ibid., 226.

106. Carson, *Exegetical Fallacies*, 121–22. Welty also references this analogy in his aforementioned work.

107. Geisler, *Chosen But Free*, 40.

108. Walls and Dongell, *Why I Am Not A Calvinist*, 81.

grace you have been saved through faith, and this is not your own doing; it is the gift of God– not the result of works, so that no one may boast," for faith contrasts works (as shown in chapter 1) and that in showing faith one (according to the monergists' interpretation of these verses) has no room to boast. By claiming that an individual works together with God in election through faith, they are making the claim that faith is a work (though they will inevitably deny this). This is not merely an accidental misuse of the term "work." It is, in fact, embedded in this theology. Without humanity doing their synergistic work, God will not do his work.[109] Without an individual exercising one's ability of faith, God will not grant election. This is the standard definition and notion of faith as shown in chapter 1. As C. Samuel Storms observes concerning Arminian theology: "Thus the basis or ground for being chosen *by* God is one's own freewill choice *of* God, God's election of us is, in effect, no more than a divine echo of our election of him."[110] Storms, like most monergists, finds this difficult to reconcile with Romans 9:16, because it makes election synergistic, a joint or mutual effort on both God and the human which effects a given outcome.[111]

A second way in which one may see how synergists view the efficient cause of salvation to be synergistic (though this goes against their claims) regards the issue of apostasy. As was shown above, Arminius held to certain decrees of God, one of which stated:

> The second precise and absolute decree of God, is that in which he decreed to receive into favor those who repent and believe, and, in Christ, for his sake and through him, to effect the salvation of such penitents and believers *as persevered to the end*; but to leave in sin, and under wrath, all impenitent persons and unbelievers, and to damn them as aliens from Christ.[112]

---

109. A criticism has been levelled at the monergistic party along these lines. One author states, "The order of the Gospel is inverted (by monergists). 'Whosoever believeth' is made to imply that God loved not all men but only the elect whom he caused irresistibly to believe. On this basis no man is a real co-laborer with God (I Cor. 3:9)" (Slaatte, *The Arminian Arm of Theology*, 53; emphasis original). This accusation is unwarranted. Few monergists claim that God does not love all in some way, but more importantly they deny that there is no involvement of the human will in salvation. Strictly speaking, Arminians would agree that God caused them to believe because faith is a gift of God (according to Arminius). That monergists deny that one is a "real co-laborer with God" is undeniable when it comes to election is unquestionable, for one's election is by grace and not by co-laboring. Moreover, nothing in 1 Cor 3:9 remotely suggests that one is a co-laborer with God in the effecting of election.

110. Storms, *Chosen for Life*, 29.

111. Ibid., 29, 30.

112. Arminius, *Works of Jacob Arminius*, 185; emphasis added. Arminius held that

Certain modern day synergists likewise believe one may lose one's salvation should apostasy occur.[113] Whether or not this is possible (and the monergist would deny that it is possible) will not now be explored. What can be concluded is that this does relate to synergism in the efficient cause. Election is secure as long as faith is exercised in the synergists' view. When faith is not shown, election is lost (which is consistent with the synergistic belief that election is in a moment in time rather than a decree from eternity past—a fact that has already been shown to be contradictory). Faith, as is already admitted to by the synergists, is what is necessary in order to activate election, and should that be lost, so is the election.

Two considerations must be made to this which were also applied above. First, by synergists even making election conditional upon faith, they go against their own views on the divine decrees.[114] They must make a radical departure from the pattern of the divine decrees that they have already admitted to by claiming that election is conditional and activated in time. No other decrees work in that way.

Second, once again faith is made a work. Faith, however, contrasts works as synergists already admit.[115] Nevertheless, they insist that faith is the *work* which individuals do in order to become elect.[116] Regarding apostasy, as long as the work of faith is being performed, one will be elect (showing efficient cause); however, when this work of faith stops, so does the election. Admittedly, not all synergists hold to the belief that one can lose one's salvation.[117] However, it is almost necessary for their system.[118] If elec-

---

one could have assurance of *present* salvation but not *future* salvation, and Wesley, whose doctrine of assurance would change and develop significantly in time towards an uncertainty of assurance, believed one may have a relatively fair degree of assurance of salvation in this life, though some can and do fall away. See Noll, "John Wesley and the Doctrine of Assurance," 161–77. See also Harper, *The Way to Heaven*, 49.

113. See Forlines, *Classical Arminianism*, 303.

114. Again, it is acknowledged that some synergists (like Olson) do not hold to the divine decrees. This, however, is addressed to those who do.

115. Olson, *Arminian Theology*, 161 and Geisler, *Chosen But Free*, 198–99.

116. Wesley, *Calvinism Calmly Considered*, 22–23; Forlines, *Classical Arminianism*, 46; Moody, *The Word of Truth*, 341–42; Geisler, *Chosen But Free*, 242; Olson, *Against Calvinism*, 129.

117. Olson, *Against Calvinism*, 52–53.

118. According to Sell in *The Great Debate*, 20–21, the Remonstrants often substituted the word *predestination* with *foreknowledge* claiming that it preserves the ethical character of God. Later Calvinists (such as William Cunningham) claimed that the fore-knower knows what will occur, so the foreknowledge is tantamount to predestination. Still, to claim that God foresees faith that one will have denies that God is the only author of salvation, according to Sell. Because grace is resistible and requires cooperation, Sell thus concludes that one can have no true assurance of eternal security.

tion is conditional, it must also be conditioned upon continual faith. Should that faith not be exercised, it will be forfeited. That is because election, in their view, has as its synergistic efficient cause, both God and the individual showing faith. As shown through biblical survey above, the exegesis does not support this view.

Third, one may question the relation between unconditional love and conditional election in this view. Here, one may observe the claims of Grant Osborne. Osborne states: "Towards man he (the apostle Paul) is pessimistic (per. Rom 3), but when he considers the Father and the Son his rapture knows no bounds. Man may fail, but God will never fail, and the love of Christ is not dependent on the vicissitudes of man."[119] He then goes on to reference Arminius and Wesley in agreement. Osborne claims that Paul affirms God's love that cannot be separated by outward pressures.[120] However, is this really the case? If election is conditional, why is not the love that motivated that election conditional? Osborne goes on to state immediately following that one may apostatize. Salvation would be forfeited. One would no longer be a child of God but an enemy of God leading God to exercise wrath against the individual. Such apostasy would be the work of the human, so why would Christ's love not be "dependent on the vicissitudes of man"? Seemingly, conditional election that may be forfeited through apostasy also undermines the synergists' claim of unconditional love.[121]

A final critique will be offered regarding the synergists' view of instrumental means. Again, the monergists affirm (as shown above) that the instrumental means of election is in God's choice and not in humankind; that is, election is passive in their view. Synergists, however, maintain that election is active through the instrumental means of faith. It must be *received*.

It is difficult to understand, grammatically and logically, how one can receive the choice of another. Again, as shown above, synergists define election as God's choice. How the choice of another is to be received actively by faith is unclear in their writings. It would seem that the means from which election is sourced flows through the will of the chooser. As such, one is *chosen* because the *chooser chose*.

119. Osborne, "Exegetical Notes on Calvinist Texts," 179.

120. Ibid.

121. Perhaps the Arminian would say that God could still love the individual in an unconditional way and still exercise wrath against him or her for apostasy. Even monergists would affirm that God does love all, even those who do not come to salvation. However, such a statement as the Arminian party is making here is moving one from particular love back to universal love. If particular love was shown to an elect individual, and the elect individual apostatizes, he or she then must be removed from the particular love (as a child of God) back to the universal love of God only thereby showing conditional love in conditional election. See Packer, "The Love of God," 2:413–27.

THE ASPECT OF ELECTION

Nevertheless, an exegetical survey is in order. In the major passages of Scripture that deal with divine election the subject of the verb is never humankind, and the object of the verb is always humankind. Ephesians 1:4 states ἐξελέξατοἡμᾶς (He/God chose us), Romans 8:30 states οὓς δὲ προώρισεν, τούτους καὶ ἐκάλεσσεν (those whom predestined he also called), Romans 9:11 states ἐκλογὴν πρόθεσις τοῦ θεοῦ (God's purpose of election—on Jacob and Esau), Romans 11:5 states ἐκλογὴν χάριτος γέγονεν (*become chosen* by grace—notice passive language), 1 Corinthians 1:27–28 states ἐξελέξατο ὁ θεός (God chose, used three times in these two verses), 2 Timothy 1:9 σώσαντος ἡμᾶς καὶ καλέσαντος (God saved us and called us), and 2 Peter 1:10 ὑμῶν τὴκλῆσιν καὶ ἐκλογὴν (your calling and election— not the ones calling or electing but passively the ones who have received the calling and election).[122] God is both the source and the means through which his will flows.

One might also recall that synergists also hold to election to people, service, and means as mentioned above. In examination of each of these, one does not find faith as active instrumentation, specifically as an instrumental *cause*. Regarding the election of people, God's people in the Old Testament were often called "faithless" (see also Isa 30:9). Nevertheless, they were still God's *chosen* people. Regarding election to service, one finds that individuals such as Pharaoh were chosen by God (Romans 9) for service apart from faith in God. Finally, as the election of means is impersonal (that is not concerning an individual, per se but is rather an inanimate idea or activity), there is no ability to exercise faith. The monergists, on the other hand, who find the instrumental means as founded in God through the exercising of his will can remain consistent with the way election works throughout the Bible.

CONCLUSION

While there have been scores of material published by both Calvinists and Arminians regarding election, this study has attempted to show that there is an often neglected area which plays a significant part in the issue, namely monergism or synergism. The issue is oftentimes underlying, assumed, or ignored, but exploration into this matter may help clarify the issue.

As has been shown above, Calvinists (monergists) and Arminians (synergists) can find common ground on a definition but not a systematic application of election. It was shown that the Arminian synergistic party has

---

122. See Berkhof, *Systematic Theology*, 114–15 and Grudem, *Systematic Theology*, 670–72.

many proponents who hold to divine decrees, even making election a divine decree. However, in order to hold to election being a divine decree, the synergist must make radical departures from the typical pattern of other divine decrees. Admittedly, not all Arminians or synergists hold to divine decrees; however, those that do must stay consistent with the pattern or else give satisfactory explanation as to why election demands an exception (which as has been shown is not done).

Second, it was shown how synergists relate and oftentimes equate foreknowledge of future events with election. This leads them to say, therefore, that election is conditioned upon faith and activated in a moment in time. This has been shown to have numerous difficulties within the Arminian/synergistic tradition in itself. There is no shortage of proponents within this camp who claim that election happens before time began. However, at the same time they propose that election is activated in time. There is an obvious conflict within this system, for election cannot be founded (not just foreknown but *founded*) in time as well as activated in time. Moreover, it also makes the individual a part of the efficient cause of election though exegesis has shown God to be the subject of the verb election and humankind to be the object of the verb.

Third, faith is, in this system, a work. Because the efficient cause of election is both in God and in the believer, faith becomes a work. However, faith cannot be a work, for the two constantly and consistently differ from one another as admitted to by synergists and has been shown throughout this study.

Fourth, faith as the instrumental cause of election does not make logical sense or have exegetical support as has been shown. How the choice of another is to be received actively by faith is unclear. An exegetical survey was done to show how God chooses, and humankind is the object of that choice thereby showing divine instrumentality.

The monergists party, however, claims that God is the efficient cause of salvation. Moreover, their claims do maintain consistency with the established pattern of divine decrees. The monergists have significant exegetical and logical support on their side. Moreover, monergists are able to prove that conditional election does not, as the synergists claim, resolve the issue of the omni-benevolence of God. Instead, monergists rest in the sovereign will of God over his creation maintaining that he is indeed a God of love who chooses as he sees fit. It is in light of the aforementioned considerations that one may conclude that the aspect of election is monergistic.

Chapter 3

The Aspect of Regeneration

AN UNDEREMPHASIZED ISSUE

IN THE FAMOUS DISCOURSE between Jesus and Nicodemus recorded in John 3, Jesus said, "Truly, truly, I say to you, unless one is born again (γεννηθῇ ἄνωθεν) he cannot see the kingdom of God" (v. 3, ESV). In response to Nicodemus's inquiry on how one is able to enter again into the womb of one's own mother, Jesus said, "Do not marvel that I said to you, 'You must be born again,'" (v. 7, ESV).

Despite Jesus' command, many since the time of Nicodemus have marveled at the meaning of being "born again," a term referring to the soteriological aspect of *regeneration*. What is regeneration? How is one born again? Is regeneration active or passive? And, very importantly, what is the relationship between regeneration, the effects of sin, and faith? These issues have sparked lasting divisions within the church.[1]

While the heart of the Protestant Reformation is often considered to be the issue of justification, one could easily consider regeneration to be of at least equal importance. Some even claim that Martin Luther's work *The Bondage of the Will* drives at the heart of the Gospel and Reformation.[2] In this work, Luther writes against Desiderius Erasmus of Rotterdam concerning the depraving effects that sin leaves upon all persons and the inability of the human will to seek God apart from God's transforming and

---

1. The primary focus here will be between the Wesleyan-Arminian and Reformed perspectives. The Roman Catholic position on regeneration will be excluded at this point because the Catholic position on baptismal regeneration is thoroughly monergistic (though monergistic regeneration need not assume baptismal regeneration by default).

2. Packer and Johnston, "Historical and Theological Introduction," 40–41.

regenerating grace. It relates strongly, though not exactly, to the struggles between Augustinianism and Semi-Pelagianism concerning the ability of the will with specific attention to monergism and synergism.[3] Luther made the claim that the human will is bound to sin, incapable of willing and doing that which is pleasing to God, and the term *free will* is ultimately an empty term devoid of meaning given that the will is not ultimately "free."[4]

If that is the case, why are individuals called to exercise faith? Erasmus, on the other hand, strongly defended the notion of *prevenient* (or preceding) grace that overcomes the depraving effects of sin on the human will thereby liberating one to believe in or reject the Gospel.[5] As such, no direct accusations of Pelagianism or Semi-Pelagianism are warranted given that the bondage of the will to sin is not denied; rather, the will is liberated by the Holy Spirit enabling one to receive new life in Christ.[6]

Still, one must question whether this prevenient grace is full regeneration. If God overcomes the depraving effects of sin on the soul, is this not regeneration thereby implying that regeneration precedes faith? This was not the claim of Erasmus or the Wesleyan-Arminian tradition that follows similar beliefs. Dale Moody considered it to be one of the great errors of Calvinism that regeneration is considered to be before faith.[7] But if true *regeneration* is not both logically and temporally prior to faith, how can one truly believe in Christ without resorting to Pelagianism or Semi-Pelagianism?

As mentioned in chapter 1, much of the debate regarding salvation (regeneration in particular) revolves around the notion of ability. The common thread throughout Martin Luther's *The Bondage of the Will*, John

---

3. Sproul, *Willing to Believe*, 88. While Erasmus was a proponent of prevenient grace, at times his *On the Freedom of the Will* had traces of Semi-Pelagianism. Erasmus once said, "It is this flexible will which is called free choice and, although on account of the propensity to sin which remains in us, our will is perhaps more prone to evil than to good, yet no one is actually forced to do evil except with his own consent" (Erasmus, *On the Freedom of the Will*, 77).

4. Luther, *Bondage of the Will*, 148.

5. Erasmus, *On the Freedom of the Will*, 79–85. See also Olson, *The Mosaic of Christian Belief*, 280.

6. Interestingly, however, Slaatte, in *The Arminian Arm of Theology*, 56 states (concerning the Arminius's doctrine of faith and transforming grace in "Apology or Defense" in *Works of Jacob Arminius*, vol. 1., art. XXVII), "Arminius, again, is overtly 'semi-Pelagian' seeing this position (relation between grace and human free will that leads to synergism) as a means between extremes. Yet he can be said to be 'semi-Calvinists,' too. Neither freedom nor absolute election is adequate to define or describe the New Testament grace relation." As will be shown, others accuse this position as semi-Pelagian; however, this study will not necessarily challenge Arminianism on these grounds.

7. Moody, *The Word of Truth*, 322.

Calvin's *The Bondage and Liberation of the Will*, and Jonathan Edwards's *The Freedom of the Will* (to name a few) is that they all concern the notion of the ability (or better termed *inability*) of the human will because of the depraving effects of sin.

Is it possible that there is an underlying and underemphasized issue at hand? Given Jesus' words in John 3:3 that one *must* be born again in order to enter into the Kingdom of Heaven, it is important that these issues be explored, but is not a new methodology in order? This chapter will attempt to show the role of monergism and synergism in the theologies of these two opposing positions. By exploring these underlying and oftentimes underemphasized issues, further development may be made in understanding the precise nature of regeneration.

DEFINING REGENERATION

For regeneration to be understood, it must first be defined. However, in order to define *regeneration*, one must first define the need for regeneration and then the term *regeneration*. Simple lexical definitions will not be sufficient. It will only be in understanding the need for regeneration that the meaning of regeneration can be properly understood.

Grammatical and Lexical Examination of Regeneration

By dividing the prefix from the suffix, one may assume that regeneration simply means "to be born (generated/γεννάω) again."[8] As will be shown, regeneration does mean this; however, it is not limited to it. The aspect of regeneration is itself aspectual encompassing a variety of elements that must be overcome. As such, one may see that regeneration encompasses more than merely the issue of rebirth. In other words, one must look to the meaning behind regeneration recognizing it as a term that encompasses a variety of aspects given that the term itself (παλιγγενεσία) only occurs twice in the Scriptures (Matt 19:28 and Titus 3:5).[9]

---

8. The following definitions are supplied from Bauer, *A Greek-English Lexicon of the New Testament* [BDAG].

9. This approach is utilized by the non-Reformed tradition as they also observe the rare occurrence of παλιγγενεσία. See Stagg, *New Testament Theology*, 117–18. Notice therein where he states that all work of regeneration is to be attributed to God alone and not to the credit of human works. It is likewise used by the Reformed tradition. B. B. Warfield observes that it would be a grave mistake to disassociate the concept of regeneration from the rest of the biblical teaching on the subject just because the term (particularly in the Gospels) is rarely used. He, therefore, gives a helpful biblical survey on the doctrine of justification in *Biblical and Theological Studies*, 351–74.

The slightly more common synonym of regeneration in the Scriptures is 'born again.' The Greek New Testament uses both γεννάω ἄνωθεν (found only in John 3:3, 7) and ἀναγεννάω (found only in 1 Pet 1:3, 23) to refer to being "born again." Also occurring only twice is the verb συνεζωοποίεω which means "to make alive together with someone" (Eph 2:5 and Col 2:13). This is in reference to those who are dead in sins but brought to life through Christ. Still more, the verb γεννάω is used repeatedly in context to refer not to the initial birth into the world but a new birth in Christ (see also John 3:8, 1 John 2:29, 3:9, 4:7 et al.). James 1:18 refers to God "bringing forth" (ἀποκυέω) the believer as a first fruit of God that contrasts sin "bringing forth" (ἀποκύησεν) death in 1:15.[10] Regarding John 1:13 where it states: "who were born, not of blood or of the will of the flesh or of the will of man, but of God," non-Reformed scholar Frank Stagg states: "To say that salvation is not of 'flesh' is to say that it is not possible to human striving. 'Flesh' in this sense would describe all religious striving, including that of Nicodemus."[11]

It is important to note that the Reformed and non-Reformed parties are in agreement on these issues. Norman Geisler defines regeneration as "rebirth," "impartation of spiritual life," and "made alive by God."[12] Methodist scholar Thomas Oden also defines regeneration as "'[To] be generated again,' a *re*-creation by which the sinner becomes (a) child of God," and "new beginning."[13] This rests well with those of a stronger Reformed perspective who likewise translate *regeneration* as "new life," "begetting of the new life," and "born again."[14]

Given that there are numerous words that refer to the same aspect (namely regeneration), it will be important to define regeneration and the need for regeneration in light of the contexts of this line of thought. In other words, one must capture not only the term but also the concept of regeneration with its surrounding Scriptural contexts that highlight both the need for and the full meaning of regeneration. In so doing, one finds that the biblical authors refer to regeneration at times without necessarily using the terms.[15]

---

10. For a good treatment on the Old and New Testaments usages of this regeneration concept, see Garrett, *Systematic Theology*, 302–5.

11. Stagg, *New Testament Theology*, 116.

12. Geisler, *Systematic Theology*, 225.

13. Oden, *Systematic Theology*, 3:156.

14. Grudem, *Systematic Theology*, 699 and Berkhof, *Systematic Theology*, 465.

15. See for example Rom 8:5–13 where Paul refers to being dead in sin but alive in the Spirit. While no terms for regeneration are used there, the concept is present. See also Ezek 11:19, 36:26, and Acts 16:14 for more examples.

THE ASPECT OF REGENERATION

Theological Definition of Regeneration

Bruce Demarest helpfully gives four effects that sin leaves upon all humanity thereby necessitating regeneration. They are: (1) humankind is in a state of moral evil from which they need to be purified, (2) all humanity is spiritually sick and in need of spiritual health, (3) all persons are in spiritual darkness without Christ (desiring it to be this way) whereby they naturally resist God who is in the Light, and (4) non-Christians are in need of eternal life given that they face physical, spiritual, and eternal death.[16]

These effects will serve as an outline below allowing one to see how regeneration relates to each of these conditions. However, it is important to note that Calvinists and Arminians, monergists and synergists, all affirm, without reservation, the notion of *total depravity* which is what this ultimately concerns.[17] Sin has affected all persons in the totality of their being, in their view, and humankind is in need of a transformation from these effects. It is important for one to note the various levels of agreement between the two parties on the need for regeneration.

The Need for Regeneration

Though accusations are often hurled against Arminians that the binding effects of sin are denied (thus often being equated with Semi-Pelagianism), one may observe what Jacob Arminius himself said regarding sin and the Law of God:

---

16. Demarest, *The Cross and Salvation*, 292. Demarest also gives a fifth effect of sin that he says requires regeneration, namely that the unsaved are slaves to sin and must be liberated from their bondage of sin by Christ. While this is certainly true, this author views this matter not as regeneration but as redemption, a different aspect of salvation. It is important not to confuse the two as being the same even if they are related. Demarest also goes on to speak of the alienation that humankind has with God due to his sin and how regeneration restores this relationshi Again, while regeneration cannot be separated from a restored relationship with God, the mending of the broken relationship between humankind and God is best understood as reconciliation and not regeneration.

17. As has and will continue to be shown, most Arminians do uphold total depravity in a way compatible with the monergistic tradition. Some Arminians (alluding to Arminius himself for support) claim that because prevenient grace universally covers all persons thereby undoing the effects of the Fall (see below) that the sin of Adam on his posterity leads more to privation rather than depravation. In other words, some Arminians claim that Arminius holds to the absence of original righteousness after the Fall as that which produces sins rather than a corruption of the human will to the extent of depravity. See Clarke, *The Ground of Election*, 74–75.

This perverse depravity consists in sin working death by the law which is good, and in being made exceedingly sinful by the commandment which is just and holy, and that it might only become as it were a sinner above measure by its own wickedness, but also might be declared to be such by the indication of the law, which it has so shamefully abused to produce these effects.[18]

For Arminius, one could not, by natural ability, uphold the law and demands of God (contrary to Pelagius) because of depraving effects of sin which: work death, produce wickedness, and make one unable to produce the righteousness that God desires.[19] John Wesley, showing his agreement, said, "No man that ever lived, not John Calvin himself, ever asserted either original sin, or justification by faith, in more strong, more clear and express terms, than Arminius has done."[20] He also went on to say, "But still, as none of them ("heathens") were apprised of the fall of man, so none of them knew of his total corruption. They did not know that all were empty of all good and filled with all manner of evil. They were wholly ignorant of the entire depravity of the whole human nature..."[21] Roger Olson states that Arminians have a "commitment to (the doctrine of) total depravity."[22]

This is not far removed from what John Calvin himself said regarding the nature of original sin in all persons. He writes:

---

18. Arminius, "A Dissertation on the True and Genuine Sense of the Seventh Chapter of the Epistle to the Romans" in *The Works of James Arminius*, 170. See also Olson, *Arminian Theology*, 56.

19. Arminius, *The Works of James Arminius*, I. "A Declaration of The Sentiments of Arminius on Predestination"—3.XIII.1, 1:628–29. As will be seen in a latter chapter, Arminius would claim that regeneration does not overcome the depravation of humankind but rather prevenient grace does. This has serious flaws as will be shown. However, Arminius was not Pelagian or Semi-Pelagian. See Olson, *Arminian Theology*, 161–63.

20. Wesley, *Calvinism Calmly Considered*, 7.

21. Wesley, "On Original Sin," in *The Essential Works of John Wesley*, 133.

22. Olson, *Arminian Theology*, 56. Notable exceptions to this exist. One Arminian who denies total depravity is Cottrell, "Conditional Election" in *Grace Unlimited*, 68 where he states: "The fact is, however, that the Bible does not picture man as totally depraved. Man as a sinner is truly depraved and corrupted (Jer 17:9), even to the point of being dead in his trespasses and sins (Eph 2:1, 5; Col 2:13). This does not mean, however, that he is unable to respond to the gospel call." Dave Hunt, likewise, states, "The Bible does not, however, teach the inability of Total Depravity as defined in Calvinism: that all men are by nature unable to believe the gospel" (Hunt, *What Love Is This?*, 102). The reason for this is, as will be shown, because of the Wesleyan-Arminian view that prevenient grace universally covers all thereby undoing the effects of the Fall. Why, then, have a doctrine of total depravity? For some, such as Olson, the doctrine must be upheld (and rightly so), for it shows the need of great salvation and dismisses any (direct) charge of Semi-Pelagianism. Others, like Cottrell and Hunt, are on dangerous autosoteric/Pelagian grounds.

THE ASPECT OF REGENERATION

> First, we are so vitiated and perverted in every part of our nature that by this great corruption we stand justly condemned and convicted before God, to whom nothing is acceptable but righteousness, innocence, and purity... Then comes the second consideration: that this perversity never ceases in us, but continually bears new fruits—the works of the flesh... For our nature is not only destitute and empty of good, but so fertile and fruitful of every evil that it cannot be idle.[23]

As such, there is joint agreement between both parties that the will of humankind is in bondage to depravity and in need of transformation. As one will see, it is the effects of sinful depravity that regeneration addresses.

Inability to Please God

Genesis 8:21 states that the Lord said, "[T]he inclination of the human heart is evil from youth." Jesus called his hearers "evil" in Matthew 7:11 who can produce no good "fruit" (namely righteous works that are ultimately pleasing before God, v. 17). The biblical authors quote Solomon as having said there is no one who does not sin (1 Kgs 8:46, see also Prov 20:9, Rom 3:23). The psalmist said that there are none who do good or seek after God (Ps 14:1–3).[24]

---

23. Calvin, *Institutes of the Christian Religion*, II.I.VIII. While this depiction of the spiritual condition of every person may seem bleak and leave no room for any moral decency in the human race, Calvin readily admitted that certain members of humanity are capable of moral conduct, honorable living, and charitable acts. See Calvin, *Institutes*, II.III.III. However, Calvin saw these commendable acts as the grace of God still working in their lives, though it may not be to the full extent as providing full regeneration. Some have moved away from the common dictum *total depravity* to stress the point that sin does not destroy entirely a human being of bearing (even to some extent) the *imago Dei*. Rather, the term *radical depravity* has been adopted to emphasize that sinners are spiritually dead, incapable of producing works that make one worthy before God, and both corrupt and evil in nature. See George, *Amazing Grace*, 72–73 and Keathley, *Salvation and Sovereignty*, 63. One may agree with George and Keathley that one should distinguish total depravity from total corruption in the fullest extent; however, the whole notion of Molinism will not be treated here for the sake of focus. The point is, for Calvin, total depravity did not mean no capacity for any good in humanity but that no human activity can merit salvation. See Bouwsma, *John Calvin*, 139. Still, a claim of the Reformed tradition is that anything "good" is still tainted by sin. As the sixteenth-century Reformed theologian Franciscus Junius put it, "For the unregenerate necessarily sins, not even being able to will or to do anything (else) (until by the grace of regeneration he does something that is not polluted by some fault)" (Van Asselt et al., *Reformed Thought on Freedom*, 105).

24. See Sproul, *What Is Reformed Theology?*, 117–24.

These verses affirm to both parties that humankind is not able to be righteous or please God apart from divine grace. Those from a non-Reformed perspective uphold this. Consider Paige Patterson who said, "Prior to the exercise of regeneration and justification... there is not a single person, however religious or ethically moral he may be, who is righteous before God."[25] The Reformed party affirms this as well. While one may be able to do acts of goodwill towards one's neighbor, one cannot do so before God, monergists contend.[26] This affirmation has been widely upheld since the time of Augustine, though it was affirmed before him.[27] As such, humankind's need for regeneration revolves around the concern of moral inability to do spiritual good.[28] As said in Romans 8:8, "[T]hose who are in the flesh cannot please God." Jesus affirmed humankind's inability to please God alone when he said, "[A]part from me you can do nothing" (John 15:5), something agreed to by traditional Calvinists and Arminians without reservation.[29]

---

25. Patterson, "Total Depravity," 32. See also Wynkoop, *Foundations of Wesleyan-Arminian Theology*, 68–69.

26. Grudem, *Systematic Theology*, 497.

27. It was in the early fourth century AD when the nature of the soul became of prime importance in Christian theology. One can find Athanasius, Bishop of Alexandria, to be representative of this era of thought given that he wrote much concerning the topic. In his writings (both in *The Paradise or Garden of the Holy Fathers* and in *On the Incarnation of the Word*) Athanasius affirmed that humankind as a whole suffered a corruption (though not total loss) of their divine image whereby people lapsed into ignorance, wretchedness, and idolatry. See Kelly, *Early Christian Doctrines*, 346–47.

28. This was the essence of Augustine's writings against the Pelagians as already covered. Humankind, he believed, was not in a position to do actions that were acceptable before God to acquire salvation, forgiveness, or divine favor. After Augustine, this position was affirmed by the Council of Carthage in AD 417 and the Council of Orange in AD 529 It was also held by all of the major Reformers and many of the Puritans of the seventeenth–eighteenth centuries (such as Edwards, Owen, and Baxter). See Ahlstrom, *A Religious History of the American People*, 151–53.

29. For clarification, this aspect of *Inability to Please God* differs from the following aspect of *Hostility before God* in that the former highlights one's inability to perform acts that are acceptable to God for salvation while the second shows one's resistance towards God himself. In relation, the aspect for *Inability to Seek After God* certainly relates to the following aspect of *Spiritual Deadness*, though the first stresses one's spiritual aloofness towards God while the second stresses one's spiritual deadness. Said another way, the first highlights his insensitivity and the second highlights the reason for this insensitivity (namely death), though to a greater degree. For an Arminian perspective on these issues, see Forlines, *Classical Arminianism*, 16–17.

THE ASPECT OF REGENERATION

Inability to Seek After God

Moreover, both Reformed and non-Reformed scholars affirm that humankind is in need of divine regeneration in order to seek after God. Both parties affirm humankind's natural incomprehension of the things of God and, similarly, a resistance towards them apart from divine interaction. Non-Reformed scholar Norman Geisler affirms that both Calvinists and Arminians agree that it is not within one's ability to come to faith in Christ without divine assistance.[30] Arminius believed that one cannot conceive, will, or do any good at all apart from God's grace (even after one is regenerate, much less non-regenerate).[31] Supporters of this view find support in the first letter to the Corinthians: "But a natural man does not accept the things of the Spirit of God, for they are foolishness to him; and he cannot understand them, because they are spiritually appraised" (1 Cor 2:14, NASB). Such inability to comprehend (in a spiritually applied sense as opposed to intellectual assent) the things of God (such as the nature of the one, true God, salvation in Jesus Christ, the gravity of sin, etc.), is also seen by Reformed and non-Reformed alike in Romans 1:21–22 and Ephesians 4:18 where Paul speaks of those who are darkened in their understanding to the things of God, living in spiritual ignorance to the truths of God because of a hardened heart.[32]

---

30. Geisler, *Chosen But Free*, 61.

31. Arminius, "My Own Sentiments on Predestination" sect. IV in *The Works of James Arminius*, 190. It should be noted, though, that Arminius was referring to prevenient grace and synergistic cooperation which will be explored and evaluated below. That is to say, monergists, though they agree that God's intervention is necessary in order to seek God, would sharply disagree with Arminius's (and others) positions that cooperation is possible apart from full regeneration.

32. In both of these references to inability (the inability to please God and the inability to spiritually comprehend, realize, and strive for the truths of God), one would do well to remember the work of Jonathan Edwards on this matter. There, he states that moral inability consists of the impairment or obstruction of the individual's inclination to will or choose a certain thing. This is what is meant by inability. Sin has corrupted the good inclination of the heart to will or choose a certain thing (namely the things of God). As such, one pursues one's prevalent contrary motives which are hostile to the things of God (which the following paragraph deals with). See Edwards, *The Freedom of the Will*, 28–29. Millard Erickson uses a different term, *insensitivity*, to refer to the same thing whereby he states that, as an effect of sin, humankind rejects God's warnings and promptings of the heart to turn towards the Truth in *Christian Theology*, 634–35. For a non-Reformed perspective, see Olson, *Arminian Theology*, 144–46 that agrees in one's natural inability to seek after God.

Monergism or Synergism

Hostility Before God

Moreover, monergists and synergists similarly contend that due to the effects of sin, humankind is in a state of hostility towards God and the truths which he makes. Consider Jesus' statement, "And this is the judgment, that the light has come into the world, and people loved darkness rather than light because their deeds were evil. For all who do evil hate the light and do not come to the light, so that their deeds may not be exposed" (John 3:19–20). Moreover, Romans 8:7 states: "For this reason the mind that is set on the flesh is hostile to God; it does not submit to God's law– indeed it cannot." These verses are used to support the common view between Reformed and non-Reformed alike that there is hostility of the human will towards God. William G. T. Shedd does well in highlighting the fact that this is an active pursuit of the will, as though it actually pursues enmity with God, rather than it merely being a recoil of the will towards something unpleasing.[33] Paige Patterson likewise says, from a non-Reformed view, "*The direction of depraved man is away from God.*"[34] Said in a compatible way from the other tradition, R. C. Sproul says, "By nature, our attitude toward God is not one of mere indifference. It is a posture of malice."[35] As such, both monergists and synergists may agree that left unregenerate, an individual is both running away from God and in direct defiance against God.

Spiritual Deadness

This is not to leave out the obvious effect of sin and need for regeneration, namely that humankind is, by nature, spiritually dead. Monergists and synergists both contend that people are in need of actual, new birth in the spiritual sense. This is seen well in the following Ephesian discourse: "You were dead through the trespasses and sins in which you once lived, following the course of this world" (Eph 2:1–2a). As such, monergists and synergists both contend that people are in a state of spiritual deadness because of trespasses and sin.[36] Consider Norman Geisler who says, "Regeneration

---

33. Shedd, *Dogmatic Theology*, 2:124.
34. Patterson, *Whosoever Will*, 33; italics original.
35. Sproul, *The Holiness of God*, 229.
36. Vaughan, *The Letter to The Ephesians*, 40 and Wesley, "On Original Sin," in *The Essential Works of John Wesley*, 125–27. For a Wesleyan-Arminian perspective that is in full agreement with this, see Marshall, *New Testament Theology*, 520 where he states: "The metaphor of birth from God (John 1:13) or being born again (John 3:3, 5) conveys the fact that people are without life until they receive the divine gift. Such life is defined as knowing God and Jesus Christ (John 17:3), language that suggests something akin to a personal relationship."

is the impartation of spiritual life, by God, to the souls of those who were "dead in trespasses and sins" (Eph 2:1 KJV) and who were "saved" made alive (*sic*) by God."[37] This echoes a classical Reformed perspective of which Peter Van Mastricht can serve as example: "Before regeneration is effected, man is spiritually dead . . . in regeneration there is bestowed a new heart and a new spirit, on which is written the law of God."[38]

It should be pointed out here that, though there is an element of agreement between both parties that people are (as a result of sin) in spiritual deadness and natural passivity towards God, there is significant disagreement between the two camps as to what is necessary in order to overcome these depraved effects. While those of a strong Reformed perspective would claim that this spiritual deadness proves the need for regeneration by the Holy Spirit in a moment in time upon the individual, classical Arminianism claims that the cross of Christ (elsewhere attributed to prevenient grace by the Holy Spirit) removes on all persons (oftentimes said to have been accomplished at the time of the crucifixion of Christ in the first century) the spiritual deadness and does not render people utterly incapable of desiring God.[39] While this issue will be developed further below, one should still note that though there be disagreement in the emphasis of spiritual deadness as a result of sin in people, there is agreement to an extent in both parties that sin has a lethal effect upon the soul requiring the overcoming grace of God.

In sum, the condition of humankind's heart is seen by both Reformed and non-Reformed alike to be in drastic need of a regeneration that encompasses multiple facets. These facets are all related but distinct. Humankind is in a state of evil, rebellion, incomprehension, and death according to both views. Humanity is in need of a radical transformation that will overcome these effects. These matters are all which are agreed upon by most Calvinists/monergists and Arminians/synergists alike.

The Nature of Regeneration

With the need for regeneration clearly defined, and having shown how there is agreement between both parties on what the depraving effects of sin are

---

37. Geisler, *Systematic Theology*, 225.

38. Van Mastricht, *A Treatise on Regeneration*, 35. It must be stressed as strongly as possible that though there is agreement that there is spiritual death from which to be regenerated from, the way this is articulated and understood systematically differs significantly between Reformed and non-Reformed parties.

39. Olson, *Against Calvinism*, 43, 66.

Regeneration unto a Pleasing Life

As mentioned above, monergists and synergists agree that humankind has an inability to please God. Because their hearts are evil and set on the flesh (in both of their views, though neither party would deny that persons are as bad as they could possibly be or that people are incapable of doing some actual good), they are in need of a new life (oftentimes called *heart*) that is able to please God in righteousness. It is in this line of thought that Ephesians 2:3–5 addresses:

> All of us once lived among them in the passions of our flesh, following the desires of flesh and senses, and we were by nature children of wrath, like everyone else. But God, who is rich in mercy, out of the great love with which he loved us even when we were dead through our trespasses, made us alive together with Christ– by grace you have been saved.

Several things are noteworthy from this passage. First, the need for regeneration (as has been outlined above) is present whereby one is in a position of enmity with God (being children of wrath), living in lusts and desires of the flesh (which parallels being dead in transgressions and contrasts being made alive with Christ), and in need (as one who was formerly not a recipient) of God's rich mercy, love, and enlivening.[40] Second, God is the one who saw the individual in this condition, felt mercy and love, and as a result "made us alive together (συνεζωοποιέω) with Christ."[41] Regeneration supplied the need that sin incurred. This "making alive," or "new life," that is in the individual (as the following context would make clear) enables the individual to live a life that is pleasing to God, something agreed to by both Reformed and non-Reformed alike.[42]

By claiming that regeneration enables a person to live a pleasing life before God, it is meant that one is now in a position to live by faith. As

---

40. Vaughan, *The Letter to the Ephesians*, 42–47.

41. With the prefix removed, ζωοποιέω means "to make alive" in the soteriological sense with God, Christ, or the Spirit being the subject in the whole New Testament (Kittel, *Theological Dictionary of the New Testament* [TDNT], vol. 2 Δ–H, s.v. ζωοποιέω.) In Pauline thought, the Law is said to kill and cannot make one alive (Rom 8:2, 1 Cor 15:56, and Gal 3:21) but by the Spirit one is made alive.

42. Vaughan, *Ephesians*, 47 and Oden, *Life in the Spirit*, 80.

Hebrews 11:6 states: "And without faith it is impossible to please God, for whoever would approach him must believe that he exists and that he rewards those who seek him." While the individual once lived a life that was not pleasing to God because of a lack of faith, one now, by faith, lives a life that is pleasing to him. The shift from a life displeasing before God to a life that is pleasing to God being termed as *regeneration* is something that Arminian/synergistic theologians would agree in conjunction with the Reformed tradition (though they would claim that conversion precedes regeneration).[43]

Regeneration of the Senses

Humankind's further need in regeneration, as shown above, is sensitivity to the things of God. It has already been shown by the survey above how there is agreement between Reformed and non-Reformed alike that humankind is in a state of spiritual blindness and incomprehension to such things as holiness, salvation, the work of Christ, etc. due to the effects of sin. However, this is the very thing that both parties claim regeneration addresses.

While there is disagreement between the camps as to whether regeneration is instantaneous or progressive in time, there is an agreement that regeneration (when it actually happens) brings transformation of comprehension. James Arminius (who did not believe regeneration was an instantaneous act), said, "[A]s soon as ever it (regeneration) is perfected according to its essence, that is, through the renovation of the mind and affections, it renders the man spiritual, and capable of resisting sin through the assisting grace of God."[44] Martin Luther, likewise, affirmed that through regeneration the will of an individual is changed by the Holy Spirit and allows the will to act in inclination of its own freed (not free but *freed*) will and godly accord and no longer under the compulsions of sin.[45]

43. See Grenz, *Theology for the Community of God*, 434 and Olson, *The Mosaic of Christian Belief*, 280–81.

44. Arminius, "Certain Articles" in *The Works of James Arminius*, 2:344. Again, there is significant disagreement between the camps as to what causes regeneration and the level of involvement of the human will in this regard, factors which will be explored below. However, here one may affirm that there is agreement that regeneration does bring a renewal of the spiritual senses by both parties.

45. Luther, *The Bondage of the Will*, 102–3. This was said in staunch disagreement with the synergist Erasmus, but one should at least note that aside from the whens and hows of regeneration, when it does occur, there is a change brought in the spiritual awareness of an individual according to both parties. Luther likewise saw regeneration (again which can only be done by the work of the Spirit and not through human faculties) as bringing a "new discernment" beyond the capacities of natural reason which expresses itself through love for the things of God. See Gerrish, *Grace and Reason*, 72.

With this said, there is major disagreement at this point between both parties as to whether faith precedes regeneration or *vice-versa*. Both will agree that regeneration is necessary for salvation, and both agree that regeneration overcomes the depraving effects of insensitivity towards God. However, it remains to be seen whether regeneration precedes faith or faith precedes regeneration.

Regeneration of the Disposition

The aspect of being regenerated in disposition closely parallels the regeneration of the senses, though it is distinct from it. John 3 records Jesus speaking of a relationship between being in a state of darkness and being hostile towards the things of God: "And this is the judgment, that the light has come into the world, and people loved darkness rather than light because their deeds were evil. For all who do evil hate the light and do not come to the light, so that their deeds may not be exposed" (19–20). It is to this issue that one considers the need for regeneration of the disposition.

In an exposition of Romans 7, James Arminius highlighted the effects of sin upon the human disposition. He said:

> [S]in is so powerful in men who are still under the law, that it abuses the law to produce those effects in a man who is under subjection to it; by which abuse of the law, sin, on the other hand, takes away the reward from the law, that its own perverse and noxious disposition and tendency may be manifested by the indication of the law.[46]

For Arminius, the law of God which reveals His good will and calls for obedience is that which provokes the sin in humankind thereby leading to abuse and rebellion towards the law. This abuse and rebellion, Arminius claims, is a result of the "perverse and noxious disposition" of the human will as a result of sin. However, in the same discourse, Arminius states that those who are carnal (again, a reference to the disposition) can become regenerate by the Spirit and thereby be led by grace and not by one's carnal nature.[47]

Arminius shares some commonality (though by no means complete agreement) with Calvin in the area of a renewal of humankind's nature.

---

46. Arminius, "A Dissertation on the True and Genuine Sense of the Seventh Chapter of The Epistle to the Romans" in *The Works of James Arminius*, 2:171.

47. Arminius, "Seventh Chapter of the Epistle to the Romans," in *The Works of James Arminius*, 2:175.

THE ASPECT OF REGENERATION

Calvin spoke of the will being "evil" and "depraved," but the will could be changed and "created in Christ" to will and to do what God pleases.[48] Martin Luther, likewise, spoke of a "renewal and transformation of the old man, who is a son of the devil, into the new man, who is a son of God."[49] While Reformed and non-Reformed views differ in significant respects (which will be discussed below), there is agreement on the effects of regeneration to overcome the depraved disposition.

Regeneration Unto New Life

Like the other areas mentioned above, there is agreement between Reformed and non-Reformed alike that regeneration leads to new life. In fact, there is little disagreement between the parties that regeneration is, in fact, the beginning of the new life.

Consider John Wesley who spoke of believers being "born again of the Spirit to a new life" and a "newborn babe" who grows into maturity.[50] Luther, likewise, considered *rebirth* to be synonymous with *regeneration*.[51] Louis Berkhof also spoke of regeneration being the implanting of new life into an individual.[52] Again, it is not so much the issue of whether regeneration leads to a new life for individuals (as this is a standard lexical definition as shown above). The major area of contention between the opposing groups is *how* this new life is imparted.

PERSPECTIVES OF SYNERGISM IN REGENERATION

It has been shown thus far how Reformed and Wesleyan-Arminian scholars define regeneration. As shown above, there is a consensus amongst major proponents of each party in the depraving effects of sin and how regeneration addresses each of those. However, there is a significant amount of disagreement between the parties, and it will be shown how monergism and synergism lies at the heart of it.

---

48. Calvin, *Institutes*, II.III.VI.
49. Luther, *Bondage of the Will*, 187.
50. Wesley, "Salvation by Faith" in *The Essential Works of John Wesley*, 209.
51. Luther, *The Bondage of the Will*, 180 (Packer, Johnston edition). One should note that this was in direct rebuttal of the synergist Erasmus helping one to appreciate that there is still a large amount of disagreement on this issue between the parties, though an element of agreement can be found.
52. Berkhof, *Systematic Theology*, 469.

Faith Precedes Regeneration

Perhaps the greatest area of disagreement between the Reformed and non-Reformed parties is the ordering of faith and regeneration. As mentioned above, Dale Moody once stated that one of the great errors of Calvinism is holding to regeneration preceding faith and repentance.[53] E. Y. Mullins, likewise, said that the first and immediate result of expressing faith is regeneration and redemption.[54] Steve Lemke states that faith precedes new life in Christ and results in regeneration.[55] As one scholar put it (commenting upon the *Five Articles of the Remonstrants*), "Yet man's zeal to work out his own salvation and his desire to hear God's Word and to repent of his sins are useful and, indeed, necessary steps in the attainment of Faith and Regeneration. Efficacious Grace is not irresistible."[56]

However, given the survey above, one may very well question *how* one is in a position to exercise faith in God given the depraving effects of sin. The response provided by the Wesleyan-Arminian tradition is *prevenient grace*.[57] Prevenient grace is defined by synergists as: "the convicting, calling, enlightening and enabling grace of God that goes before conversion and makes repentance and faith possible."[58] It is the grace given by God that overcomes the depravity and inability of humankind with regards to salvation. Prevenient (oftentimes called *preceding* or *preventing*) grace can be found in the works of monergists such as Augustine, Luther, and Calvin as well as in synergists such as Erasmus of Rotterdam, Arminius, and John Wesley. As to what such prevenient grace accomplishes, however, the two camps will disagree.

---

53. Moody, *The Word of Truth*, 322.

54. Mullins, *The Axioms of Religion*, 10. See also Godwin, *What It Means to Be Born Again*, 30 who states that our choice to rebel against God is sin which gives us the need for regeneration. Then, he states that "The way to eternal life—a new quality of life that is unending—is to openly admit that you have gone against God's will and to openly commit yourself to God's will. Then he can make you a new creation—give you new life and make you born again" (30). The implication is that human will has led to spiritual death but human will can (with the work of God) lead to a new life (being *born again*) in Christ. Spiritual death and the ability to exercise the human will does not seem to be in conflict with this particular author.

55. Lemke, "A Biblical and Theological Critique," 137–38.

56. Harrison, *Arminianism*, 88.

57. Lemke, "A Biblical and Theological Critique," 137–38; Olson, *Arminian Theology*, 159–60.

58. Olson, *Arminian Theology*, 35. This definition accurately represents the views of most synergists who hold to prevenient grace.

THE ASPECT OF REGENERATION

Here one must observe the biblical rationale provided by the synergists for their doctrine of prevenient grace. While many within this party expound the doctrine of prevenient grace, few give their biblical rationale for it like John Wesley. For Wesley, one of the primary texts from Scripture pointing to prevenient grace was Philippians 2:12: "work out your own salvation with fear and trembling" of which he gave a famous sermon bearing the name "On Working Out Our Own Salvation." There, Wesley states that individuals are "dead in sin by *nature*"; however, there is not any who are left in their nature (unless the individual has "quenched the Spirit").[59] God has been at work in all people through prevenient grace which precedes the "call of man" for salvation. God is at work in this; therefore, individuals must work with God (synergistically) with the grace already given by placing their faith in Christ.[60]

Wesley's sermon "On Conscience" also gives some biblical rationale for prevenient grace.[61] His text here was 2 Corinthians 1:12: "Indeed, this is our boast, the testimony of our conscience." Based upon this text, Wesley states that one's conscience is the faculty of conscious regarding one's thoughts, words, and actions. He states that this is found in every soul born of humanity.[62] Wesley then uses two Scriptural proofs, John 1:9 ("The true light, which enlighteneth every man that cometh into the world") and Micah 6:8 ("He hath showed thee, O man, what is good.").[63] For Wesley, these verses teach the universal work of the Spirit, particularly in the area of conscience. He then alludes to 1 John 2:20 stating that the offices of conscience (temperament, rule to be directed, and ability to agree or disagree) need the "unction of the Holy One."[64] By this, the Holy Spirit works amongst people, causing them to feel convicted (or as Wesley put it "[T]o feel uneasy, when thou walkest in any instance contrary to the light which he hath given thee."[65] This is prevenient grace, for it shines light to the sinner in darkness, convicting them of their error, and stirring their soul towards the things

---

59. Wesley, "On Working Out Our Own Salvation" III.IV, in *The Complete Sermons*, 431.

60. Ibid., III.IV, in *The Complete Sermons*, 431.

61. That this sermon is reflective of Wesley's doctrine of prevenient grace, see Rogers, *The Concept of Prevenient Grace*, 26 and Burtner and Chiles, *John Wesley's Theology*, 150–51. As such, one should not assume that this author is selecting a sermon that is not in reference to prevenient grace in Wesley.

62. Wesley, "On Conscience," I.III–IV in *The Complete Sermons*, 517.

63. Ibid., I.V in *The Complete Sermons*, 517. Wesley does not quote the full verse.

64. Ibid., I.XI in *The Complete Sermons*, 518.

65. Ibid., I.V in *The Complete Sermons* of John Wesley, 517. See also Harper, *The Way to Heaven*, 37.

of God. In another sermon entitled "*The Great Privilege of Those that are Born of God*," Wesley alludes to Luke 15:20 (the Prodigal Son) who was far off but the Father called to him and 1 John 4:19 where God loved people before people loved God.[66] However, if an individual does not respond to this preventing work of God, God will withdraw from the individual and leave them in their sin, claims Wesley.

William Burt Pope, moreover, gave a clear exposition for his doctrine of prevenient grace. He points to Jeremiah 31:18: "[T]urn thou me, and I shall be turned" (KJV). Here, Pope states, "He who works in us to will is never represented as working so absolutely upon us that nothing is left to personal responsibility . . . There is no saying in the Word of God which, fairly expounded, represents the Divine Spirit as overruling the energy of the human object of His grace."[67] Pope also pointed to Matthew 13.23 in the parable of the Sewer. He attributes to preliminary grace the ability of an individual (symbolized by the good soil) to receive the Word of God (the seed) to God (but nonetheless stresses that an individual must receive this Word (seed) as well).[68] Pope, finally, references 1 Thessalonians 1:6 and 2:13, Colossians 1:6, and 2 Corinthians 6:1 as texts which declare that believers voluntarily receive the Word of God, Christ, or grace allowing for cooperation.[69]

In more recent times, one of the more thorough biblical rationales for prevenient grace from the Arminian tradition comes from Vernon C. Grounds. Though he does not use the term prevenient grace, he speaks of God's universal grace which he says means, "[M]erely that God is at work in Jesus Christ and by his Holy Spirit sovereignly and sincerely . . . providing the potential of salvation for every human being. But that potential depends

---

66. Wesley, "The Great Privilege of those that are Born of God," III.III in *The Complete Sermons*, 100. Again, these are allusions, not quotes, from Wesley. See also Cobb, *Grace and Responsibility*, 40–41.

67. Pope, *A Compendium of Christian Theology*, 2:365.

68. Ibid., 365–66.

69. Ibid., 366. It is not clear from Pope why he sees these texts as proofs for prevenient grace. It would seem that it is based upon his theology that such would not be possible unless prevenient grace first occurred. These are the only verses in Scripture that Pope expressly cites. He then gives a more theological treatise, saying "That the Spirit has the pre-eminence is equally the doctrine of all the Scripture, as indeed it is of common sense" (366). Though not citing any more texts, he references the Fall and the necessity of prevenient grace to redeem humanity. He then speaks how prevenient grace works through the preaching of the Word. Finally, he states that prevenient grace must clearly be evident because individuals are able to yield to it and thereby cooperate with God. He states, "The man determines himself, through Divine grace, to salvation: never so free as when swayed by grace" (367).

for its actualization on a believing response."[70] He also states that this universal salvific grace is that which allows individuals to be and do what they otherwise could not because of their sin.[71] As such, he is dealing with the issue of prevenient grace.

It is his biblical rationale that is reflective of most proponents of prevenient grace in synergism. There, he points to John 1:29, 3:16, Romans 5:17–21, Romans 11:32, 1 Timothy 2:6, Hebrews 2:9, 2 Peter 3:9, and 1 John 2:2. This list is likely not exhaustive but serves the purpose for Grounds nonetheless. These verses speak of God's universal love for humankind, the free gift of Christ coming to all persons unto justification, God having mercy on all, God giving Christ as a ransom for all, Christ tasting death for all, God not wanting any to perish but all to come to repentance, and the propitiation of sins for the whole world. Grounds thus states that God provides a universality of saving grace providing the opportunity for all people to be saved and make a favorable response to Christ in faith.

An examination (and critique) of the Arminian notion of prevenient grace will be provided below and will be dealt with more exhaustively on the chapter on *Conversion*. For now, however, the focus will be how synergism is found in the Wesleyan-Arminian theology of regeneration.

The Efficient Cause

If faith is a necessary condition in order to be regenerated (or perhaps better understood as that which leads to or activates regeneration), and if faith, which is an action of the individual, is that which brings forth new life, then perhaps one would assume that the efficient cause of regeneration in the Wesleyan-Arminian perspective is the individual believer. Interestingly, however, this is denied by many within the Wesleyan-Arminian tradition with claims that it is God, not the individual believer, who is the cause of regeneration. It remains to be seen, however, if this claim can be substantiated.

Consider Norman Geisler, a prominent synergist, who says, "The *Source* of regeneration is God."[72] Methodist scholar Thomas Oden shows his agreement with what he calls "scholastic exegetes" like Thomas Aquinas by stating, "[T]he resurrection (of Christ) is the effecting cause of our regeneration."[73] However, no one in this tradition was more adamant that

---

70. Grounds, "God's Universal Salvific Grace," 28.

71. Ibid., 24. It should be noted that Grounds expressly denies universalism in his exposition of the universality of saving grace (28).

72. Geisler, *Systematic Theology*, 225; emphasis original.

73. Oden, *Word of Life*, 433–34.

Monergism or Synergism

the efficient cause of regeneration is God than James Arminius. He says, "The efficient cause of this evocation, or calling out (for salvation), is God the Father, in his Son Jesus Christ, and Christ himself, through the Spirit . . . sanctifying and regenerating her (the church) to a new life."[74] As seen here, God the Father in the work of Jesus through the applying work of the Spirit is the efficient cause who not only sanctifies but also regenerates people into new life. He goes on to say, "The principal cause (of righteous actions of believers) is the Holy Spirit, who infuses into man, by the act of regeneration, the affections of love, fear, trust, and honour."[75] It is a consistent claim throughout Arminius's writings that regeneration found its origins in the will and work of God.

Upon preaching on "new birth" (a synonym for regeneration), John Wesley said that one is "born of God," that "the Spirit of God works in his heart," and that "God having quickened him by His Spirit" becomes alive to God.[76] For Wesley, God takes the initial and primary role (though synergism has its place in regeneration he would claim).[77]

As one considers these claims that God is the efficient cause of regeneration in the Wesleyan-Arminian view, one must also consider the constant emphasis that regeneration does not occur without the consent of the individual. Oden states: "God does not force godliness or regenerating grace upon human beings, for if forced it could be neither truly godly nor truly just. God draws persons towards salvation by calling, illuminating, convicting, and enabling faith . . . " by which one may resist.[78] Oden believes that the efficient cause of regeneration is still God, not the person, because the prevenient grace of God works operatively (not cooperatively) initially (thereby allowing the will to give free consent to the divine will which leads to regeneration).[79]

James Arminius, who (as said above) believed the efficient cause of regeneration to be God, nevertheless believed that regeneration (if not consented to synergistically by faith) can be resisted and rejected.[80] In other words, God leads one by prevenient grace to the point of decision making, and faith must be exercised by the individual in order to become regenerate;

---

74. Arminius, "Disputation L", in *The Works of James Arminius*, 2:87.
75. Ibid., "Disputation LXXIII," 122.
76. Wesley, "The New Birth," in *The Essential Works of John Wesley*, 219.
77. Olson, *Arminian Theology*, 169–70.
78. Oden, *Life in the Spirit*, 165.
79. Oden, *The Transforming Power of Grace*, 51–53.
80. Arminius, "Sentiments on Predestination, IV," in *The Works of James Arminius*, 1:190.

however, God (in his view) was still the efficient cause of regeneration. Interestingly, Arminius went on to say, "[W]e say that a regenerate man is one who is so called, not from the commenced act or operation of the Holy Spirit, though this is regeneration, but from the same act or operation when it is perfected with respect to its essential parts."[81] Rather, Arminius says the regenerate ones are those who repent and place faith in God.[82] Said another way, Arminius believed that God is the efficient cause of regeneration but not the sole cause of regeneration. One must work together (synergistically) with God by faith in order to be regenerate.

John Wesley, as mentioned above, likewise believed that regeneration was "of God." Nevertheless, he believed that through prevenient grace God allows the dead in spiritual nature to reach a point where one may cooperate with God (by faith) to become alive to God.[83] Roger Olson comments upon Wesley's theology: "Clearly, for him (Wesley) prevenient grace is regenerative even though actual salvation necessarily involves the person's free and willing cooperation with it by not resisting its saving work."[84] This goes slightly beyond what Arminius would claim (that prevenient grace brings one to a state of neutrality in choice). For Wesley, faith was a mark of believers.[85] Still, one was not fully saved and brought into new life until faith is shown, but God (in his view), was still the source of regeneration.

In sum, one may claim that there is a wide consensus in the Wesleyan-Arminian tradition that believes regeneration is founded in God and caused by God, though there is an element of cooperation that is necessary in order for regeneration to be effected in actuality. The way in which one thus cooperates with God is by faith in this view.

Instrumentality

Some within this tradition have no qualms in affirming that the aspect of regeneration is entirely passive upon the individual. While faith and synergism may be the necessary means of other aspects, Norman Geisler affirms, "the *means* of regeneration is the Holy Spirit."[86] Arminian scholar F. Leroy

81. Arminius, "A Dissertation on the True and Genuine Sense of the Seventh Chapter of the Epistle to the Romans," in ibid., 2:160.

82. Ibid., 2:160–62.

83. Wesley, "On Working Out Our Own Salvation," in *The Essential Works of John Wesley*, 328–29.

84. Olson, *Arminian Theology*, 170.

85. Wesley, "The Marks of the New Birth," in *The Essential Works of John Wesley*, 227.

86. Geisler, *Systematic Theology*, 225; emphasis original.

Forlines states: "Justification and regeneration are monergistic. They are solely the work of God."[87] While faith is not excluded from regeneration, it is neither the cause nor the means by which regeneration occurs in their view with respect to this particular aspect.

Such a view from this party, however, appears to be the exception rather than the rule. In fact, it is almost essential to the Wesleyan-Arminian system that the individual is not passive (but active) in regeneration because of their view (as a whole) that faith (in synergy with the prevenient work of God) precedes regeneration.

For Mildred Wynkoop, God overcomes the depraving effects of sin (mentioned above) by prevenient grace, and through cooperation with this grace by faith, one can become regenerate and saved.[88] Said another way, by faith one receives regeneration from God. Likewise, Steve Lemke (though he claims like almost all within this tradition that the human acts of cooperation do not merit one's salvation or allow one to boast in personal ability) speaks of the essential cooperation by faith necessary in order to be regenerate.[89] While he claims that salvation is provided for humans by God in a monergistic sense, it must be received synergistically through the means of faith for one to be regenerate and saved.[90]

The instrumental cause of regeneration being synergistic is also found in the classical writings of this tradition as well. While Arminius affirmed that the efficient cause (which he called "principal cause") of regeneration is the Holy Spirit, he went on to say that the "immediate cause" is the individual who has received prevenient grace.[91] For Arminius, regeneration did not occur until after faith is shown. Thus, until one exercises faith, one has not received regeneration, and should one reject the offer of new life, one will never receive this regeneration.[92] Erasmus, along similar lines, emphasized that God does not do violence against the will but allows (by prevenient grace) the ability to consent and cooperate with saving grace so that the individual can be made new.[93]

However, one of the more puzzling views in this tradition regarding the instrumentality of regeneration comes from contemporary Methodist

---

87. Forlines, *Classical Arminianism*, 88.

88. Wynkoop, *Foundations of Wesleyan-Arminian Theology*, 98–105.

89. Lemke, *Whosoever Will*, 136–37, 159.

90. Ibid., 159. This is a way of saying that the efficient cause of regeneration/salvation is God but that the instrumental means is synergistic.

91. Arminius, "Disputation LXXII," in *The Works of James Arminius*, 2:122.

92. Arminius, "Sentiments on Predestination," in ibid., 1:190.

93. Erasmus, *On the Freedom of the Will*, 80–81.

THE ASPECT OF REGENERATION

scholar Thomas Oden. As said above, Oden believes God is the efficient cause of salvation, but his view on the instrumental causation is unclear and conflicting. In speaking of the *"Agency in Spiritual Birth,"* Oden says, "Quickening is throughout scripture a work of God's Spirit ... The acting power or agent in regeneration is God the Spirit ... Through this work of the Spirit, the renewed individual is translated (*sic*) from one sphere of existence (realm, aeon, dominion, orientation) to another."[94] He also says, "New birth is the decisive work of God in the economy of salvation whereby spiritual life in Christ is *imparted by the Holy Spirit*,"[95] and "The agent of justification is the Son; of regeneration, the Spirit."[96] Still more, he speaks of: "[T]he single pivotal act of God's renewing (*sic*) of the human spirit in Christ."[97] In such talk of agency, the acting power *in* regeneration, and the impartation of spiritual life by the Spirit, it would appear that Oden believes God is also the instrumental cause. However, further commentary by him seems to conflict these statements.

Oden says that God's grace is offered but not intruded upon people. While claiming that humans are "self-determining," he says that the Spirit awakens cooperation of individuals to receive that which is imputed and imparted (namely new spiritual life).[98] New birth, according to Oden, by the Spirit does not occur without the will of the human; rather, the Spirit works in the individual's heart to transform the will and affections. This does not imply a force of godliness or even full regenerating grace upon humans, Oden would say, but rather the enabling of faith to be exercised.[99] As such, faith is an instrumental cause in both senses of the word. It is instrumental in significance and instrumental in agency.

PERSPECTIVES OF MONERGISM IN REGENERATION

Again, while there may be several areas of agreement between the Reformed and non-Reformed parties, there are many more areas of disagreement. The differences particularly relate to the efficient cause, instrumentality, the effects of regeneration, and how regeneration precedes faith.

---

94. Oden, *Life in the Spirit*, 164; italics original.
95. Ibid., 156; emphasis added.
96. Ibid., 158.
97. Ibid., 157.
98. Oden, *Transforming Power of Grace*, 37.
99. Oden, *Life in the Spirit*, 165.

Regeneration Precedes Faith

While the Wesleyan-Arminian tradition upholds faith prior to regeneration, the Reformed tradition upholds regeneration prior to faith. Consider chapter 10 of the *Westminster Confession of Faith*—"This effectual call is of God's free and special grace alone, not from anything at all foreseen in man, who is altogether passive therein, until, being quickened and renewed by the Holy Spirit, he is thereby enabled to answer this call, and to embrace the grace offered and conveyed in it."[100] Likewise, Article twelve of "The Third Main Part of Doctrine" in the *Canons of Dort* states:

> As a result (of regeneration), all those in whose hearts God works in this marvelous way are certainly, unfailingly, and effectively reborn and do actually believe. And then the will, now renewed, is not only activated and motivated by God, but in being activated by God is also itself active. For this reason, people themselves, by that grace which they have received, are also rightly said to believe and to repent.

Luther, against Erasmus, likewise stressed the passivity of the human will in regeneration and the effecting of faith through the Spirit's transforming work.[101] Such affirmation that regeneration precedes faith has been

---

100. Bordwine, *A Guide to the Westminster Confession of Faith and Larger Catechism*, 63. While this does not *expressly* state that regeneration precedes faith, it states that the quickening and renewal of the Spirit enables a person to embrace the grace offered (which while initiated in baptism) appears to occur by faith. Chapter XIV states, "The grace of faith, whereby the elect are enabled to believe to the saving of their souls, is the work of the Spirit of Christ in their hearts..." Here, people are enabled to believe by the work of the Spirit. While this does not mention *regeneration* specifically, the textual support given (2 Cor 4:13, Eph 1:17–19) appears to support this idea especially when considering the aforementioned statement of what the Spirit does in regeneration. The following agree that the WCF teaches regeneration prior to faith: Robertson, "The Holy Spirit," 1:83–84. In the *Larger Catechism*, see Vos, *The Westminster Larger Catechism*, 76. In the *Shorter Catechism*, see Whyte, *An Exposition on the Shorter Catechism*, 102–9.

101. Luther, *The Bondage of the Will*, 187. Luther, like Augustine, held to baptismal regeneration; however, as his *Small Catechism*, IV.III states, the power for regeneration is not in the water but the Word of God which is present in the water matched with faith which trusts the Word of God in the water. He likewise saw in baptism the forgiveness of sins and the giving of everlasting life to all who believe in IV.II. See Luther, "Luther's Small Catechism," 3:85–86. As such, it is difficult to define any specific *ordo salutis* in Luther. One may thus question (particularly in light of Luther's Preface to his commentary on Romans) if Luther's view held to faith preceding regeneration. See Klotsche, *The History of Christian Doctrine*, 177. Still, for Luther, faith is not the work of man which effects anything, but faith is the work of God binding an individual to Christ. See Ebeling, *Luther*, 257. Moreover, Luther believed baptism was a liturgical enactment of justification by faith alone. Baptism (a divine act) must be done in faith (which was a gift of God), and those who receive baptism in faith (faith preceding the act of baptism)

typical in the Reformed perspective.[102] John Calvin, however, is a notable exception to this.[103]

The Efficient Cause

The Reformed tradition unequivocally affirms that the efficient cause of regeneration is in God alone. Stressing the depraving effects of sin and moral inability of humankind in a classical Anti-Pelagian way, the Reformed tradition has, since the time of Augustine, denied that regeneration can be brought about by human achievement. This is not to say that the Wesleyan-Arminian tradition would oppose this position; in fact, as shown above, they agree with it in principle.

At the turn of the twentieth century, Herman Bavinck wrote a series of articles concerning the doctrine of immediate regeneration by the Holy Spirit. Comprised in book form, they have served for over a century as an influential work amongst Reformed theology. Therein, Bavinck states that the Holy Spirit penetrates the human heart apart from the intellect or will of the human. He stresses that the work of the Spirit is immediate and thus (unlike the Wesleyan-Arminian tradition) does not require the consent of the individual.[104]

Anthony Hoekema, in typical Reformed fashion, affirms human depravity and then affirms (after biblical survey) that God must actually *impart* new life and not merely lead people to a state where cooperation is possible but not certain.[105] Puritan scholar Peter Van Mastricht likewise states: "In regeneration there is bestowed a new heart and a new spirit, on which is written the law of God, which certainly is to be ascribed to God

---

are bathed and cleansed from sin. See George, *Theology of the Reformers*, 94. There, George also speaks of Luther's rationale for infant baptism. Luther believed children are brought to baptism by the faith of someone else, and thereupon Christ blesses the infant and grants the child faith leading to new life and the kingdom of heaven (again regeneration preceding faith).

102. Sproul, *What Is Reformed Theology?*, 185–87; Van Mastricht, *A Treatise on Regeneration*, 35; Cole, *He Who Gives Life*, 215.

103. See III.III of Calvin's *Institutes* where he speaks of regeneration by faith. He also states that "people are aroused by the word (preached) to seek regeneration" (Calvin, *The Bondage and Liberation of the Will*, 165). See also George, *Theology of the Reformers*, 225–26. Also observing that, for Calvin, faith precedes regeneration Crampton rightly observes that, for Calvin, regeneration is the result of God's effectual calling which prepares the heart for the individual to place faith in Christ in *What Calvin Says*, 74. As such, Calvin consistently avoids any guilt of being autosoteric.

104. Bavinck, *Saved by Grace*, 131–32.

105. Hoekema, *Saved By Grace*, 101.

alone."[106] Louis Berkhof says that it is essential to stress that regeneration is from God's work alone in order to claim truly that salvation is from God's work alone.[107] In all of these claims that God is the sole worker, it is meant that regeneration is sourced in the actions and will of God alone.

Instrumentality

While the Reformed position affirms that regeneration is sourced in God, one must also inquire as to how this Source operates in the lives of believers. Therein, this tradition affirms that the instrumental cause is also found in God.

Charles Spurgeon affirmed that faith is the evidence of (not the cause or means of) regeneration.[108] Paul Helm speaks on behalf of all within the Reformed tradition when he states that it is not the intent of the Holy Spirit to bypass or neglect the will of the individual. Rather through regeneration (in the full sense of the word, not merely prevenient grace), the will is enabled to be active in faith and repentance.[109] This is in accordance to what Luther stressed to Erasmus, namely that the individual is passive and does nothing by free will. Because of the depraving effects of sin (and the only solution being recreation, not mere neutrality as in prevenient grace), one must be regenerated by and through God's work.[110]

Faith, then, is not the instrumental cause of regeneration but a by-product of the instrumental cause (the Holy Spirit). As said before, monergists can be synergists in certain aspects, and for those monergists who embrace synergism in some respects, it is only after regeneration. J. Gresham Machen helps make that observation. He states:

> At the beginning of the Christian life there is an act of God and of God alone. It is called in the New Testament the new birth or (as Paul calls it) the new creation. In that act no part whatever is contributed by the man who is born again. And no wonder! A man who is dead . . . can do nothing whatever, at least in the sphere in which he is dead . . . But birth is followed by life; and though a man is not active in his birth he is active in the life that follows . . . Thus the Christian life is begun by an act of God alone; but it is continued by co-operation between God and

---

106. Van Mastricht, *A Treatise on Regeneration*, 35.
107. Berkhof, *Systematic Theology*, 465.
108. Spurgeon, *All of Grace*, 88–89.
109. Helm, *The Beginnings*, 16–17.
110. Luther, *The Bondage of the Will*, 187.

man. The possibility of such co-operation is due indeed only to God; it has not been achieved in slightest measure by us; it is the supreme wonder of God's grace.[111]

As one can see, in this tradition regeneration in the completed sense is required in order for faith to be exercised. While regeneration is a prevenient and preceding grace (that is, it is God that makes the first moves), prevenient grace (in the Wesleyan-Arminian tradition) is not sufficient enough for one to be brought to new life. Regeneration, in this view, is sourced and executed by God alone leading to a full (not partial) transformation.

AN ANALYSIS AND CRITIQUE ON THE VIEWS

In this chapter, the need for regeneration has been presented and both the term and effects of regeneration have been defined by both parties. There is considerable agreement between the two parties that sin leaves all persons in a state of evil, rebellion, incomprehension, and spiritual death. It has also been shown how there is agreement that regeneration is that which remedies these defects. Moreover, claims are made by both parties that God is the one from whom regeneration is sourced, and there is lesser (though significant) agreement that God (according to both parties) is the agent through whom regeneration occurs. So why are there still tensions and schisms related to this issue? The claim made here is that monergism and synergism are the underlying sources of tension.

An Analysis and Critique of the Wesleyan-Arminian Perspective on Efficient Causation

While the non-Reformed tradition *claims* that the efficient cause of regeneration is God, one must question whether this is truly the case. Indeed, it can be shown that the efficient cause of regeneration is synergistic (meaning that both God and the individual are at *work*) in their view, that it is inherent in their position that God is not the sole source, and that the claims for divine causation alone cannot be substantiated.

---

111. Machen, *What is Faith?*, 207–8. This would be the affirmation of most monergists who uphold some degree of synergism. Affirming that salvation has a beginning point but continues into the present and future, monergists uphold monergism up to the point of regeneration, conversion, and justification, but subsequently affirm synergism after the event of salvation has occurred.

Consider the notion of prevenient grace as it relates to the efficient cause. Again, prevenient grace is defined by synergists as: "the convicting, calling, enlightening and enabling grace of God that goes before conversion and makes repentance and faith possible."[112] It is that which overcomes the depraving effects of sin to bring one to a place where one may exercise faith and then receive new life.[113] In other words, though one was formerly lost in sin, through prevenient grace the individual is brought to a crossroads whereby one may exercise faith and be transformed (regenerated) or refuse and still be in sin.[114]

While this is obviously not an issue of Pelagianism or Semi-Pelagianism given that God is that which overcomes the depraving effects of sin and that original sin is not denied, this is an issue of synergism in the efficient cause. In order for regeneration to occur, God must give his consent, and the individual must give consent as well. This does not even address the issue of agency or instrumentality at this point, simply the source or ultimate cause of regeneration. While the non-Reformed party does not suggest that the individual is the *regenerator*, they do claim that regeneration will not occur apart from the free act of the will through faith. Faith from the person is a contributing cause of regeneration.[115]

---

112. Olson, *Arminian Theology*, 35. This definition accurately represents the views of most synergists who hold to prevenient grace. It is also something that many monergists could agree with as well, though the "enabling" factor of prevenient grace would entail full regeneration in their view rather than the crossroads view in Arminian theology.

113. Erasmus, *On the Freedom of the Will*, 79–85.

114. Arminius, "Sentiments" in *The Works of James Arminius*, 1:190.

115. Cox says, "Thus the salvation of man is dependent upon man's response by prevenient grace to the saving grace of God . . . Here is a form of synergism understood in the midst of a monergism. Initially God works and after His work begins, then it is possible for man to cooperate with Him" (Cox, "Prevenient Grace—A Wesleyan View," 147–48. Granted, after this, he states that this does not count as merit to the individual for all is of grace. Yet one may legitimately question this claim. Prior to these quotes, Cox stated that God universally prevenes over all people thereby undoing the effects of the Fall. Through this prevenient grace, God gives the individual the ability to work together with God. God begins the work, but this work will not be completed until one contributes faith. As he said, "the salvation of man is dependent upon man's response" and the response one gives in synergism (meaning working together) to "cooperate with Him" is faith. Faith is becoming a contributing work which an individual does in conjunction with the work of God to effect the outcome of salvation. As will be shown above, one of the criticisms levelled against this tradition is that due to universal prevenience and the effects of the Fall being undone, one is now able to exercise faith from within their own initiative. Though God overcomes the depraving effects, one then becomes the necessary dependent source that effects in cooperation with God salvation.

THE ASPECT OF REGENERATION

Consider the words of Thomas Oden who (as quoted earlier) said that regeneration is founded in God: "The doctrine of regeneration is that part of teaching of salvation that focuses upon the new birth of life *that follows from faith*."[116] New birth (a term synonymous with regeneration) *follows from* the faith of the individual in his view.

John Miley states:

> Regeneration is a true sphere of the divine monergism. There is also a sphere of synergism. Regeneration is not an absolute work of the Spirit . . . There must be an earnest turning of the soul to God, deep repentance for sin, and a true faith in Christ. Such are the requirements of our own agency. There is no regeneration for us without them.[117]

Two thoughts are necessary regarding Miley's quote. First, faith is an implied work because it is a necessary cause that (in cooperation with God) leads to the effect of regeneration. Second, faith is made to be an implied work because regeneration is not a "work of the Spirit" alone but of "synergism" (a working together).

It was shown above how an essential part of the Wesleyan-Arminian tradition is that faith precedes regeneration. This is not the same thing as saying, "Faith comes through regeneration." Faith is that conditional cause that (in *cooperation* with God) activates or effects regeneration according to this tradition. Oden is clear on this point when he says that new birth by the Holy Spirit does not occur without the human will.[118] Arminius said (as quoted above), "[T]hat a regenerate man is one who is so called, not from the commenced act or operation of the Holy Spirit," but by those who repent and place their faith in Christ.[119] He goes on to say, "A regenerate man is he who has a mind freed from the darkness and vanity of the world (by the Holy Spirit) . . . and with faith . . . " carries out good deeds.[120] As one can see in Arminius's definition of what a "regenerate man" is, it is those who have a passive work of God in being freed from darkness (i.e., prevenient grace) *and* exercise faith. Those are the ones that Arminius calls the "regenerate." This is in contradiction to their previous claims that God is the sole efficient cause.

---

116. Oden, *Life in the Spirit*, 156; emphasis added.

117. Miley, *Systematic Theology*, 2:336.

118. Oden, *Life in the Spirit*, 165.

119. Arminius, "A Dissertation on the True and Genuine Sense of the seventh Chapter of the Epistle to the Romans," in *The Works of James Arminius*, 2:160, 161–62.

120. Ibid., 162.

Reformed scholar Louis Berkhof incorrectly associates Arminians with Semi-Pelagians because of their view that the efficient cause of regeneration is the human will while also claiming that both of these parties (Arminians included) deny total depravity.[121] While both of these claims have been proven false, it is perhaps better to say that the effects of sin, the death of the old life, and the darkness which one is in are satisfied and overcome not through the work of Christ by application of the Spirit alone but through the cooperation of the individual. While this is never affirmed by proponents of this tradition (in fact it is vehemently denied[122]), it is the ultimate conclusion of their claims. Unless faith is shown and the human will is active, regeneration unto a life pleasing to God, regeneration of the senses, regeneration of the disposition, and regeneration unto a new life will not occur. While many of Luther's criticisms of Erasmus are overly harsh and in some cases unwarranted, it is here where Luther's claims that God's glory is robbed (though perhaps more appropriately termed *lessened* since God, in the Arminian view still has the primary role to play) and there is room for boasting in one's ability can be substantiated.[123]

Faith as a Work in the Instrumental Cause

As has been shown, this tradition vehemently denies (and rightly so) salvation by works. Monergists must respect this view and dismiss accusations of autosoterism. However, monergists (and synergists) should also seek to understand how faith is used in this system, namely whether it is an effecting mechanism or a receptive mechanism.

Consider Oden who says, "Grace prepares the will and coworks (*sic*) with the prepared will . . . Insofar as grace accompanies and enables human willing to work with divine willing, it is called cooperating grace."[124] For Oden, one is enabled to work with the divine will through "willing." That is, to will is to work. In a sermon entitled *On Working Out Our Own Salvation*, John Wesley spoke how God's work *begins* with prevenient grace, and by faith one may *work together* (synergistically) with God to complete salvation.[125] On commenting on this sermon of Wesley's, Olson says, "For him

---

121. Berkhof, *Systematic Theology*, 473.

122. Olson, *Arminian Theology*, 36–37, 165–66 and Olson, *Against Calvinism*, 155–58.

123. Luther, *On the Bondage of the Will*, 251–53.

124. Oden, *Transforming Power of Grace*, 47.

125. Wesley, "On Working Out Our Own Salvation," in *The Essential Works of John Wesley*, 326–27.

THE ASPECT OF REGENERATION

(Wesley), as for all true Arminians, 'God works; therefore you *can* work... God works therefore you *must* work.'"[126] Arminius, likewise, said:

> Let the word "unregenerate" be taken for a man who is now in the act of the new birth, though he be not yet actually born again; let "the pleasure" which God feels be taken for an initial act, let the impulsive cause be understood to refer to the final reception of the sinner into favor, and let secondary, subsequent, cooperating and entering grace be substituted for "saving grace."[127]

For Arminius, one is unregenerate who has not actually been born again (i.e., regenerated), but when God works upon the individual (through prevenient grace), one may cooperate (which again means *work together*) with the initial and prevenient works of God in order to receive saving and regenerating grace. One should notice that cooperation (working together) is necessary, and (as has already been shown) in Arminius's view the work which one does is faith.[128] Olson says, "That Arminius believed humans must cooperate with God's grace for salvation is beyond dispute."[129] Speaking on behalf of classical Arminianism, Forlines states: "Active participation in faith on the part of the believer means that it cannot be otherwise than *synergistic*."[130]

Faith, in this view, is a cooperative activity between God and the human which leads to a given outcome. Thus, it appears to be an effecting mechanism and not the receptive mechanism as in the monergistic tradition. Granted, this goes against their claims (and the Scriptures as they would admit). Olson, commenting upon Wesley's sermon *On Working Out Our Own Salvation*, said that for Wesley and all classical Arminians, the "work" which one does is by God's grace and does not mean that salvation depends upon human works.[131] But if a work is an action which causes an effect (as shown in chapter 1), and salvation is dependent upon the person's faith, then salvation *does* depend upon human works. Arminian scholars Walls and Dongell stress that the Bible does not portray faith as a work

---

126. Olson, *Arminian Theology*, 170, emphasis and ellipsis original.

127. Arminius, "Article XVI," in *The Works of James Arminius*, 1:247.

128. See Arminius, "A Dissertation on the True and Genuine Sense of the Seventh Chapter to the Epistle to the Romans" in ibid., 2:160–163. Therein (as shown above), Arminius believes that the regenerate are those who cooperate with God through faith and prevenient grace.

129. Olson, *Arminian Theology*, 143.

130. Forlines, *Classical Arminianism*, 261; emphasis original.

131. Olson, *Arminian Theology*, 170.

that merits salvation or forces God to act.[132] Nevertheless, there is constant reference to synergism, to working together, and to cooperation in their writings. Moreover, their theology demands that in order for something (i.e., regeneration) to be accomplished, one must *work* and contribute in order for it to be accomplished.

This is far removed from the monergist perspective, mentioned above, which sees God as not only the source of regeneration but the cause through which it occurs. For the monergist, regeneration is entirely passive, and though faith is related to regeneration, it is not conditioned on it nor a contributing synergistic activity. This, no doubt, is an underlying tension between the parties, and the support best favors the monergists' position.

An Evaluation of the Arminian View of Prevenient Grace

Further examination must now be given on how the Wesleyan-Arminian tradition construes its doctrine of prevenient grace besides the shortcomings of how it is applied to the efficient cause as shown above.[133] First, one must be reminded of what this tradition affirms about the depraving effects of sin. As shown above, this tradition affirms that sin leaves one in a state of moral evil, rebellion against God, incomprehension to divine and holy things, and spiritual death. It has also been shown how the Wesleyan-Arminian tradition believes that regeneration overcomes these effects.

However, is this truly the case? Is it not prevenient grace that overcomes the depraving effects of sin and not regeneration in their theology? It has been shown repeatedly throughout this study that this party believes that full regeneration does not occur until faith is expressed. Faith can only be expressed, in this view, when God exercises prevenient grace upon the human will. In that state of grace, this party claims that one has the effects of sin overcome whereby one may exercise faith and then regeneration may occur.[134] This is not to say that regeneration is not a form of prevenient grace. On the contrary, the monergist party recognizes throughout that regeneration precedes any act or volition of the human. It truly *prevenes* and goes before. But what the Wesleyan-Arminian tradition wishes to claim is that prevenient grace has all of the positive features of overcoming sin but not in bringing new life. Certainly Arminians hold to the necessity of regeneration

---

132. Walls and Dongell, *Why I Am Not A Calvinist*, 78.

133. Again, see the chapter on *Conversion* for a more complete critique of the Wesleyan-Arminian tradition of prevenient grace.

134. Picirilli, *Grace, Faith, Free Will*, 154; Lemke, "A Biblical and Theological Critique," 159–60; Olson, *Arminian Theology*, 160–61.

THE ASPECT OF REGENERATION

for salvation and should be reckoned to be Christian; however, the concern has to do with what activity overcomes one's depravity—full regeneration or the Arminian notion of prevenient grace. As shown through the biblical survey above, it is full regeneration which overcomes the effects of sin *and* imparts new life. Moreover, the Wesleyan-Arminian tradition affirms that it is *regeneration* that ultimately overcomes these effects, though at the same time they say it is prevenient grace that overcomes them. If prevenient grace overcomes these effects of sin, then why would these persons still be accountable for (and in a very real sense *affected by*) them?

Moreover, one must question as to what would actually be chosen by a person in a state of mere neutrality where obedience or rejection were the two options. Biblical scholar E. Earle Ellis comments on this aspect:

> Some suppose that if our will is "free" to accept or reject Christ, many will accept him. But is that true? If our first parents (Gen 1—3), whose wills were truly free, chose against God, do we suppose that any of their children, sullied by sin from earliest experiences, would make a more godly choice than they? Would we, who were at enmity with God, controlled by ego, surrounded by a thousand temptations (Adam and Eve faced one), make a better choice than they? Hardly . . . "Free will" is precisely what God permits to the terminally unrepentant, and it is a one-way ticket to destruction in Hell. If salvation came through our free choice, we would all be lost. No one would be saved except Jesus Christ.[135]

Here one may address the common objection that if prevenient grace is denied then violence is done against the human will. Consider Oden's claim: "God does not force godliness or regenerating grace upon human beings, for if forced it could be neither truly godly nor truly just. God draws persons toward salvation by calling, illuminating, convicting, and enabling faith wherever there is an opening amid human resistances."[136]

However, two things must be noted here. First, the monergist would affirm that there is nothing gracious about leaving one in sin, rebellion, darkness, death, and ignorance that the Wesleyan-Arminian tradition affirms (as shown above) as the depraving effects of sin. Instead, God liberates the human will to will that which is good and holy. This is a common teaching as exposed by Luther, Edwards, and Calvin. Regeneration brings new *life* as opposed to death which is, in their opinion, the most gracious thing. Second, while this concept will be explored further in the chapter of

---

135. Ellis, *The Sovereignty of God in Salvation*, 5.
136. Oden, *Life in the Spirit*, 165.

Monergism or Synergism

Conversion, it must be noted that the Wesleyan-Arminian tradition already affirms that there is, to some extent, a sovereign usurping of the human will apart from the will of the individual. Through their own doctrine of prevenient grace, the sinful nature is overcome apart from their own desire. This was not caused or consented to by the individual. Rather, the individual (in the Wesleyan-Arminian tradition) is totally passive. While one is still in one's sin and rebellion, God overcomes the depraving effects of sin apart from any assent or cooperation of the individual. Their doctrine does affirm a divine interference and overcoming of the sinful nature of humankind.

Moreover, in the doctrine of prevenient grace as composed by the Wesleyan-Arminian tradition, the person does not have new life until faith is exercised. Does this imply that one is still dead in his or her transgressions? Surely not, for such should be undone by prevenient grace. However, those in prevenient grace are still unregenerate. What state does this leave an individual in? While still dead (or at least not *alive* in the Spirit), the person is allowed to choose to become alive (though he or she is not alive). This confusing issue poses a difficult problem for the Arminian tradition leading one to find, on balance, more coherent support from the monergists.

Finally, as one considers biblical support, an analysis of the biblical texts used by Arminians is warranted. Ben Witherington makes the following observation about Wesley: "Wesley's concept of prevenient grace is frankly weakly grounded if we are talking about proof texts from the Bible."[137] Indeed, biblical references for their doctrine of prevenient grace are difficult to find and follow exegetically making Witherington's quote applicable to others besides Wesley. Through exegetical survey contrary to the claims of Wesley, Witherington provides a convincing critique of Wesley's view. While God does exercise a universal love, such does not negate the overwhelming textual passages that speak of universal sin (Pss 5:9, 7:9 and 12, 14:3, Rom 8:19–20) according to Witherington. He also states that those who articulate such a doctrine of prevenient grace are "filling in gaps that the Bible does not speak to, and before long you distort what it does say about correlative matters."[138] As such, monergists such as Witherington do not dispute that there is a prevenient grace which goes before the acts of a sinner thereby undoing the effects of the Fall; rather, what is in dispute is the universality of prevenient grace that overcomes universal sin in all people in order to preserve one's pre-existing theology.

The proof texts cited above by the Arminian camp to support their doctrine of prevenient grace are not convincing. Again, Wesley cited

---

137. Witherington, *The Problem with Evangelical Theology*, 207.
138. Ibid., 209.

THE ASPECT OF REGENERATION

Philippians 2:12 on working out one's own salvation. He states that one may do so because God was first at work to allow one to work out such salvation. However, he makes two fundamental mistakes. First, as has already been stated, Philippians 2:12 is speaking to people already converted (not yet to be converted). They are to work out the implications of a salvation they already have entered into. Second, nothing in this text (or surrounding context) reflects the preliminary work of God in a way construed by prevenient grace in Arminian theology. Nothing in Philippians 2 suggests that the preliminary work of God is a "convicting, calling, enlightening and enabling grace of God that goes before conversion and makes repentance and faith possible."[139]

Wesley's support for prevenient grace in his sermon "On Conscience" likewise lacks convincing biblical support. This topical sermon on the human conscience is based upon an abbreviated quote from 2 Corinthians 1:12 which, in full, states: "Indeed, this is our boast, the testimony of our conscience: we have behaved in the world with frankness and godly sincerity, not by earthly wisdom but by the grace of God– and all the more toward you." Wesley makes no reference to the surrounding context of Paul's suffering for the sake of the Gospel of which he is informing the church of Corinth in this text. Wesley, instead, gives a treatise on the human conscience claiming that John 1:9, Micah 6:8, and 1 John 2:20 support a universal work of the Holy Spirit to convict individuals of their sin and stir the heart towards God. John 1:9, however, speaks of the incarnation of Christ, not the universal prevenient grace of the Holy Spirit. Wesley only quotes part of Micah 6:8 of which nothing teaches their doctrine of prevenient grace. The complete reference of 1 John 2:20 (which Wesley only alluded to a portion of it) states: "But you have been anointed by the Holy One, and all of you have knowledge." This contrasts those who professed Christ and a relationship to the true church but were, in fact, actually not of them. Nothing here supports the "convicting, calling, enlightening and enabling grace of God that goes before conversion and makes repentance and faith possible."[140] The Prodigal Son reference in Luke 15 has its own difficulties in supporting prevenient grace, for there the agent is the Father (not the Spirit). Finally, the numerous passages used by Wesley of God's universal love for humankind do not support his doctrine of prevenient grace. Rather, it seems to be the basis for this party's construal of their doctrine of prevenient grace.[141]

---

139. Olson, *Arminian Theology*, 35.

140. Ibid.

141. See Rogers, *The Concept of Prevenient Grace*, 26, Rogers states that the texts used by Wesley to support prevenient grace are: Rom 1:19, 2:12–14, 8:32, John 1:9, and Micah 6:8, many of which were examined here. One can see the minimal biblical

Regarding William Pope's analysis of prevenient grace, one observes that (like Wesley) Pope only uses portions of single texts without references to the surrounding context. Jeremiah 31:18: "[T]urn thou me, and I shall be turned" (KJV) would benefit from the surrounding context whereby Ephraim (a synonym for Israel) is the one speaking (not God). As such, Ephraim is pleading that God would accept them back into fellowship. This does not teach God sending the Holy Spirit universally to undo the effects of the Fall to allow people the opportunity to be saved in Christ. The same could be said with the Matthew 13 reference where too much is being based upon a parable (of whose context is entirely left out by Pope). Finally, as was noted above, Pope (whose actual biblical references to prevenient grace were rare) claims that prevenient grace is assumed by all the references to one receiving the Word, Christ, etc. Again, biblical support is not given but assumed. The monergists, however, are able to provide convincing arguments that the way individuals are able to receive the Word, Christ, grace, and more is through regeneration, not the Arminian notion of prevenient grace.

Arminius himself rarely gave Scriptural support for his doctrine of prevenient grace. His most thorough exposition of prevenient grace found in Scripture is found in *Disputation XI* "On the Free Will of Man and Its Powers" n.XIV. His textual support is Philippians 1:6, 1 Peter 1:5, and James 1:17. While all of these texts are wonderful references to God's grace, they do not teach prevenient (non-regenerating) grace as Arminius and his followers suggest. Rather, it seems to be a necessary element constructed to uphold a preconceived theological system. As Keith D. Stanglin observes regarding Arminius on prevenient grace; "Without such contingent human

---

support used by Wesley for this doctrine, and he references Scripture for this belief more than most others. An interesting observation is made by Rogers (who is sympathetic to Wesley's doctrine). He states: "[T]he term "preventing grace" and the more explicit theological content of the notion seems, for Wesley, to come from the theological tradition of the church" (ibid., 27). McGonigle, in *Sufficient Saving Grace*, 320–23 states that the two biggest influences that led to the development of Wesley's doctrine of prevenient grace was Philippians 2:12–13 (observed above and elsewhere) and the sermons of William Tilly. Tilly helped Wesley reconcile original sin and human inability with the free offer of salvation. One may here notice that it was a theological/philosophical system that was serving as the primary rationale for prevenient grace in Wesley, not Scripture. One may also note that Wesley expounded his doctrine of prevenient grace most in his sermons *The Scripture Way of Salvation* and *On Working Out Our Own Salvation*, but no support (other than Phil 2:12–13) is used to support his doctrine of prevenient grace. The point to observe, here, is that there is minimal Scriptural support for this belief (much if not all which can be easily deconstructed). It, rather, seems to be the natural by-product of a predetermined system.

THE ASPECT OF REGENERATION

freedom, Arminius (and virtually every other "anti-Calvinist") cannot see how God can justly reprobate or damn sinners."[142]

John Fletcher occasionally spoke of prevenient grace in his sermons, but the biblical references are not reflective of the biblical basis for prevenient grace as much as how prevenient grace works. Fletcher states:

> Up, then, thou sincere expectant of God's kingdom! Let thy humble, ardent free-will meet prevenient, sanctifying free-grace in its weakest and darkest appearance, as the father of the faithful met the Lord when "he appeared to him in the plain of Mamre" as mere mortal: "Abraham lifted up his eyes, and looked, and lo, three men stood by him!" So does free grace, if I may venture upon the allusion, invite itself to thy tent: nay, it is now with thee, in its creating, redeeming, and sanctifying influences.[143]

Howard Slaatte, commenting upon Fletcher, states that Fletcher's synergistic theology *implies* prevenient grace (of which theological/philosophical rationale is given, but not biblical support).[144] This appears to be the norm on this issue from this tradition.

However, what should one make of the biblical references supplied by Vernon Grounds (mentioned above) on God's universal love and grace for humanity? Does not this teach prevenient grace? Here, one should observe what has already been stated: none of these verses expressly teach that the Holy Spirit universally prevenes upon all people in a way that undoes the effects of the Fall and makes all people able to respond in faith to Christ. In fact, Grounds never makes that claim. He provides no single verse that supports his claim that "God is at work in Jesus Christ and by His Holy Spirit sovereignly and sincerely . . . providing the potential of salvation for every human being."[145] Rather, it seems that Grounds assumes God must work in a universally prevening way to undo the acts of the Fall; otherwise, God could not genuinely love all and extend grace to all. Again, his philosophical judgments of prevenient grace appears to have greater influence than do the Scriptures.[146]

---

142. Stanglin, *Arminius on the Assurance of Salvation*, 87; parenthetical remark original.

143. Fletcher, *On Perfection* in *Christian Perfection*, 53.

144. Slaatte, *The Arminian Arm of Theology*, 108.

145. Grounds, "God's Universal Salvific Grace," 28.

146. Page, *Trouble with the Tulip*, 40–43 outlines what appears to be the pre-set system (or set doctrinal beliefs) which necessitate prevenient grace. They are the nature of God (being a God of love) and human free-will/integrity/responsibility. This appears to be the case across the board where monergism would be a violation of God's love or goodness (many such as Page assume that monergism implies TULIP Calvinism) and/or a violation of human free will (accusing the other party of fatalism).

Even still, how would monergists respond to Ground's use of Scripture? Thomas Schreiner gives a helpful examination of these verses to see if they teach prevenient grace. Regarding John 1:9, Schreiner states that in Wesleyan theology the illumination refers to the overcoming grace that undoes the effects of Adam's sin. However, Schreiner observes that the word *enlighten* (*phōtizō*):

> [R]efers not to inward illumination but to the exposure that comes when light is shed upon something. Some are shown to be evil because they did not know or receive Jesus (John 1:10–11), while others are revealed to be righteous because they have received Jesus and have been born of God (John 1:12–13).[147]

Schreiner's use of the surrounding context contrary to Grounds is in his favor as well as his references to John 3:19–21. He observes the Johannine teaching of the light exposing human wickedness and their need for redemption while also noting that John 1:9 does not teach in any way (whether explicitly or by suggestion) that the incarnation gives all people the ability to choose salvation.[148]

Schreiner makes similar observations regarding Titus 2:11. There, Schreiner shows an engagement with what the text actually says (rather than drawing inferences) when he claims that God's grace is shown through the crucifixion but does not supply the ability for all people to believe based upon this verse.[149] The same is true for John 12:32. However, Schreiner also observes John 6:37 and 44. He states: "The Johannine conception of drawing is not that it makes salvation possible, but that it makes salvation effectual. Those who are drawn will come to Jesus and believe in Him."[150]

Regarding such passages as Romans 2:4, Matthew 5:48, 11:28–30, and more, Schreiner observes that Wesleyanism is guided by the logic and rationality of their theology, not the Scriptures. There, synergists claim that God would not give certain commands or calls to people unless they were able to do them (which must logically be supplied by prevenient grace). Schreiner responds that the commands of God are good (such as the Law being good,

---

147. Schreiner, "Does Scripture Teach?," 2:376. See also Carson, *The Gospel According to John*, 124.

148. Schreiner, "Does Scripture Teach?," 2:376.

149. Ibid., 377.

150. Ibid., 378. Here, Schreiner also observes the surrounding context of John 12:32. Schreiner observes that the cross will break the power of Satan allowing the Gentiles to come to Jesus. He states, "The Wesleyan theory that prevenient grace is provided in the atonement so that people are given ability to choose salvation cannot be supported from the context of John 12" (378). See also Carson, *John*, 293.

THE ASPECT OF REGENERATION

Rom 7:12) though none can keep it perfectly (Rom 8:7–8). God, claims Schreiner, can still expect his good commands to be carried out (because of the goodness in them) despite the lack of goodness in an individual.[151] However, here one might go beyond what Schreiner states and observe that God *does* give individuals the ability to do what they cannot do naturally, and that comes through regeneration which is expressly taught in Scripture. One can therefore affirm that God *saved* (Titus 3:5) and did not just make one *savable*.

Recently, W. Brian Shelton has written a response to Schreiner's interpretation. He questions how much Schreiner's interpretation is based upon a predetermined commitment to limited atonement.[152] Such is understandable, for just as Arminians may have predetermined systems in place for their doctrine of prevenient grace, Calvinists like Schreiner may be too heavily influenced by Limited Atonement.

Shelton, then, gives the following arguments on why John 1:9 (which he states is the "most impressive verse that posits prevenient grace"[153]) teaches enabling, prevenient grace: it teaches that there must be some work of Christ where human condition or self-understanding is altered (which he claims is enabling or convicting grace), and it is incongruent to interpret (as Schreiner is accused of doing) "enlightens all humankind" as applying to the elect only.[154]

What Shelton does not show clearly is how the incarnation of Christ is an enabling activity of the Spirit that overcomes human depravity allowing one to believe in Christ for salvation. He claims in his first reasoning that John 1:9 teaches enabling *or* convicting grace. Schreiner would hold to the latter but not the former. Yet *how* the incarnation enables (by the Holy Spirit) individuals as taught by this verse is not made clear by Shelton. Regarding his second argument on how John 1:9 supports prevenient grace, one may observe that this is not a statement of support for his view but a criticism of the opposing view. He goes on to write against limited atonement (which many monergists would oppose alongside Shelton).[155] He speaks of the necessity for people to receive and believe in Christ (John 1:12–13). Yet how the incarnation provides "universal potential for salvation described in this verse (John 1:9)" is not made clear.[156] If this is the most impressive verse

---

151. Schreiner, "Does Scripture Teach?," 2:378–81.

152. Shelton, *Prevenient Grace*, 24.

153. Ibid.

154. Ibid., 27–28.

155. In chapter 7, it will be shown that a commitment to monergism does not suppose a commitment to limited atonement.

156. Shelton, *Prevenient Grace*, 28.

that teaches prevenient grace (according to Shelton), then one may question how impressive the other verses will be. In fact, Shelton goes on to say (in his John 1:9 discourse):

> Some may object that the idea of prevenient grace is only implicit in these verses, and the Arminian would agree. We would be presumptuous to expect John to spell out an entire incarnational-forensic-pneumatological-salvific formula solely through his use of "light" metaphors.[157]

This is to show what has been stated above that the Arminian doctrine of prevenient grace appears to be a formulation built upon philosophical grounds to maintain their belief that faith precedes regeneration. As Shelton opens up his discourse on the "Scriptural Depiction of Prevenient Grace," he says he will consider three essential sets of biblical texts. First, he will show how human beings are incapable of doing meritorious good before God, including repentance and belief (so as to avoid Pelagianism). Next (and important to the point here), he says he will explore, "Passages that depict how enabling grace is available to all people, a category that will specifically establish the biblical justification for the doctrine of prevenient grace."[158] Finally, he will explore passages that seem to go against universal prevenient grace.

It is this second claim that merits attention. His intention is to explore (primarily through "light" passages) how enabling grace is available to all, and based upon that one may see the "biblical justification for the doctrine of prevenient grace." He does not actually provide biblical justification for prevenient grace but tries to make the point that rationally it must be there. His scriptural support (and his rationale as will be shown below) is not convincing.[159]

---

157. Ibid., 30.

158. Ibid., 13.

159. Shelton's other use of Scripture come from other "Light Verses" such as Prov 29:13, Ps 19:8, Eph 1:18 and 3:9, and Rom 1:18–32. Monergists would not contend with Shelton that God shines light in the darkness and opens up the eyes of the spiritually blind (see the first section of this chapter). What they would say is that this is what regeneration refers to, not prevenient grace as defined by the Arminians. He also speaks of John 3:14–15, 6:44, 12:32 and other passages which speak of God drawing individuals to himself. Again, monergists do not argue with Shelton that God does draw, woo, and convince. The question at hand is in what order does God do this? Can someone who is spiritually dead respond to wooing? Monergists would say no. Would someone who is spiritually blind follow the drawings of someone asking to be followed? However, upon regeneration, when an individual is enabled (which is what Shelton is ultimately after with his desire for enabling grace) to respond to the wooing and drawing of God, then he or she may respond favorably. There is engagement of the will for

In light of such analysis, monergists would do well to find the strengths found in the Arminian notion of prevenient grace. First, as has been shown, their construal of prevenient grace takes seriously the depraving effects of sin. Second, direct accusations of Pelagianism or Semi-Pelagianism are thus unwarranted. Third, it stresses divine initiative before human response in a way similar to the monergists' portrayal. However, on balance, the Arminian doctrine of prevenient grace lacks sufficient biblical support and appears to be based upon philosophical assumptions. So far, the monergists have the stronger claim of biblical support with full regeneration as being the measure of prevenient grace shown by God.

Other Considerations

Benjamin B. Warfield addressed the issue of regeneration and the will of an individual against what he called the "anti-Calvinistic party." He speaks against the "Congruists," namely those who believe in prevenient grace that leads one to synergism. He states that in that system, "[I]t is not the sovereign choice of God, but a native difference in men, which determines salvation, and we are on expressly autosoteric ground."[160] While this may be slightly overstated or exaggerated, it stands that it is the will of the individual who works for new life in the Wesleyan-Arminian system. It is ultimately up to the consent and work of faith that brings one into a new life that is pleasing to God in this system.

Naturally, this claim would be denied by those in this non-Reformed tradition. While most commentary on this subject by this tradition affirms that there is some *activity* or *active working* that is to be done (i.e., the exercising of faith), in an interesting turn, the opposite is, in fact, affirmed. Some within this tradition affirm that the cooperation or work done by the individual is merely consent or allowing for God to do his work.

Two illustrations are provided by two respective synergists. One is by Steve Lemke who gives the illustration of one who is stranded and drowning in a vast ocean. The individual could not swim to shore and thus not save himself or herself (hence, no Pelagianism or Semi-Pelagianism). The rescue ship throws a life buoy to the individual, but the person is too weak even to accept it (which itself is an acceptable position to many within this party and thus in conflict). Thus, the rescuer jumps from the ship, swims to the individual, and picks up the person to be delivered into the safety of the rescue ship. Lemke then states: "The only thing humans would have to do is

---

monergists, but it does not effect a given aspect like regeneration.

160. Warfield, *The Plan of Salvation*, 94.

assent to be rescued, or at least not resist being rescued."[161] Lemke compares this to his view of salvation, namely that one does not save oneself, but that God is the Savior. However, in that model, the individual *must* (he says, "The only thing humans would *have to do*") is give assent (actively) *or* at least not resist being saved (passively).

A similar illustration is provided by Roger Olson. In his example, one falls into a deep pit that has slippery sides. One is not able to climb out on his or her own (no Pelagianism/Semi-Pelagianism), but he rejects the thought of one throwing down a rope, climbing down, wrapping the rope around the individual, and bringing him or her to safety apart from any cooperation (which he attributes to the monergists). Instead, he says that one (i.e., God) throws down a rope, calls for the individual to grab on to it, and he will pull (note also that this position would be acceptable to many in his party and thus in contradiction with others). Olson goes on to say, though, that this is not enough because the individual is helpless. As such, the rescuer will pour water into the pit and calls them to, "Relax" and "Float." Olson then says that the response of the person being rescued is simply to "[L]et the water lift him or her out of the pit. It takes a decision, but not an effort. The water, of course, is prevenient grace."[162]

Several things are noteworthy about these illustrations which are part of the Wesleyan-Arminian soteriology. First, as shown, there is conflict within the models. It is ultimately bound up within this model that one *must* grab hold of the life buoy or grab onto the rope in order to be saved. There must be an active reaching out in order to be saved and receive new life. However, and secondly, this party wishes to affirm a form of passivity. Simply "not resisting" or "allowing" certainly cannot be considered an active work (of faith). It is, in fact, the monergists who wish to affirm passivity in regeneration, not the Wesleyan-Arminians. This has the appearance of still taking a form of credit (or at least affirming one's active cooperation and work) when one, in this case, is still entirely passive.

Finally, one may see a measure of inconsistency in these illustrations. As mentioned above, faith must be exercised and consent must be given in order to become regenerated. In these cases, there was ultimately no consent. The individual did not consent for a rescue ship to be sent nor that the rescuer grabs him or her to be taken to the ship. The individual did not consent to have the water be poured down into the well. Naturally, the monergist would have no problem affirming these things, but the synergists, however, would.

---

161. Lemke, "A Biblical and Theological Critique," 160.
162. Olson, *Against Calvinism*, 172–73.

This ultimately relates to the critique that prevenient grace still has a strong measure of overcoming apart from any consent of the individual.

CONCLUSION

This study has attempted to show that the tensions concerning the aspect of regeneration between the Reformed and Wesleyan-Arminian tradition have an underlying and underemphasized issue of monergism and synergism. Through biblical survey, as well as an examination of the proponents of both parties, the need for regeneration and the effects of regeneration were provided.

It was shown that both parties affirm the effects of sin and how regeneration resolves those effects. However, the Wesleyan-Arminian tradition later changes commitments to say that it is prevenient grace that overcomes these depraving effects. Through prevenient grace, they claim, one can believe in Christ, have the ability to see the goodness of God, and turn away from sin. However, did this party not earlier claim that regeneration (in the full sense) is that which accomplishes these results? Does not Scripture (as shown above) claim that regeneration undoes the depraving effects of sin (not a limited version of prevenient grace as defined by the Wesleyan-Arminian tradition)? The monergists, by affirming full regeneration that overcomes the depraving effects of sin, have the more coherent view.

It was also shown that though there is agreement between both parties that the efficient cause of regeneration should be God, only the monergists stay true to that claim. Both through admission and omission of their doctrinal system, the Wesleyan-Arminian tradition, it has been shown, holds to synergism in the efficient cause. This leads to numerous problems. It is difficult to see how one could be an efficient cause of bringing new life into oneself whenever one has not been fully regenerate (for their notion of prevenient grace falls short of regeneration—the impartation of spiritual life). Naturally they would not claim that an individual could be an efficient cause of regeneration. However, their claim is that God gives an unregenerating prevenient grace that enables individuals to do an action that causes an outcome (faith causing regeneration). This activity (while met with prevenient grace) is an essential activity that produces (not receives) an outcome which may rightly be understood as an efficient cause. This activity, moreover, is done by one who is still unregenerate. This is difficult to balance.

Moreover, it has been shown that the instrumentality in this non-Reformed party holds faith to be a work (instrumental *cause*) in contrast to their own admissions and biblical portrayal. If an individual shows the work of faith, it leads to the outcome of regeneration. Faith, one may thus see, is made into a work which produces the effect of regeneration. This is contradictory, counter-biblical, and contrary to their own admission.

Monergists, on the other hand, remain consistent in their view of the depraving effects of sin and regeneration as the sole remedy. They give consistent and logical grounds matched with biblical support on how regeneration is the sole work of God (as the efficient cause) as executed through the instrumental cause of divine initiative. This does not mean that faith has no part to play in salvation, nor does it mean that there is no relationship between regeneration and faith. Rather, it affirms in a consistent way that God overcomes the sinfulness of humans, imparts new life to them, and enables them to believe in Christ unto salvation. The monergists have the more coherent view when it comes to the aspect of regeneration.

Chapter 4

The Aspect of Conversion

SOURCES OF TENSIONS

IN THE PRECEDING CHAPTERS, the passive aspects of election and regeneration were explored. It is now time to explore a further passive aspect of salvation, though as will be shown there is division as to whether this aspect is active or passive between the Arminian and Reformed traditions. This chapter will explore the aspect of conversion which closely relates to the aspect of regeneration covered in the preceding chapter.

As one could imagine, tensions abound concerning the aspect of conversion. Indeed, it was of such importance that it consumed much of the church's attention in the fifth and sixth centuries (as evidenced by the councils of Carthage and Orange). Because Pelagianism was dealt a fatal blow at Carthage for attributing abilities to humankind in the work of conversion apart from divine grace, the opposing position of Augustinianism was the only remaining alternative. Some, however, found the teachings of Augustine to be an unfounded and unacceptable alternative. Consider John Cassian, the fifth-century monastic pioneer, who tried to find middle ground between what he saw as the harsh criticisms of human inability in Augustine's theology and the natural ability of humankind apart from divine intervention in Pelagius's theology.

Cassian sates:

> [I]t is in our own power to follow up the encouragement and assistance of God with more or less zeal, and that accordingly we are rightly visited either with reward or with punishment, because we have been either careless or careful to correspond to

His design and providential arrangement made for us with such kindly regard.[1]

Cassian, widely viewed as a Semi-Pelagian, believed that Adam's sin did transmit to the entire human race and that divine grace was necessary in order to attain salvation (contrary to Pelagius). However, at times, the first inclinations of a good will originate from within one's own volition, and God merely confirms and strengthens those desires.[2] In other words, humankind was still able at times to place their faith in God for salvation on their own, though due to the effects of inherited sin, they were in need of the cooperating grace of God to attain salvation fully. As one can see from Cassian's quote above, he, along with other Semi-Pelagians, recognized the necessity of God's activity in the role of sinful humankind, but the role of God is that of "encouragement" and "assistance" thereby leaving much of the rest of the activity up to the human. Humankind is still naturally able to attain salvation, in his view, though they need divine encouragement to attain salvation. This is also evidenced in the following claim: "How then is it true that our salvation does not depend upon ourselves, if God Himself has given us the power either to hearken or not to hearken?"[3]

The synergism of Semi-Pelagianism is also shown in the writings of Faustus of Rhegium. Though joining the list of those against Pelagius, Faustus strongly opposed the Augustinian doctrines of predestination and conversion. While not denying that the Fall of Adam left humanity as a whole in a state of corruption and that sin reigns over all, Faustus believed that the will of humans is merely impaired. As church historian Adolf Harnack writes of Faustus's view, "Our being saved is God's gift; it does not rest, however, on an absolute predestination, but God's predetermination depends on the use man makes of the liberty still left him, and in virtue of which he can amend himself (prescience)."[4] Harnack writes that the underlying assumption of Faustus's view of the ability of the impaired will (as well as

---

1. Cassian, *The Works of John Cassian*, Book 1 Conf. III, ch. XIX, 328.

2. Kelly, *Early Christian Doctrines*, 371. Cunliffe-Jones, *A History of Christian Doctrine*, 168. See also Hägglund, *History of Theology*, 144 who states about Cassian: "When man is converted it is sometimes God who takes the initiative, but on other occasions He waits for us to decide, so that our will anticipates God's will."

3. Cassian, *The Works of John Cassian*, Book 1 Conf. III, ch. XXI, 329. See also Kelly, *Early Christian Doctrines*, 371 who states that, for Cassian, this view was based upon his belief that Adam retained knowledge of good despite the Fall, the human will is not dead but merely sick, and predestination is conditioned upon foreseen behavior.

4. Harnack, *History of Dogma*, ch. 5.1, 5:253.

THE ASPECT OF CONVERSION

many Semi-Pelagians) lies in the understanding of faith being a work and achievement,[5] a concept that will be discussed in more detail below.

Semi-Pelagianism was condemned as heresy at the Council of Orange in AD 529. The main fault according to the Council of Orange with Semi-Pelagianism was that cooperation with God unto salvation is not possible without God taking the first steps in the process. In other words, Semi-Pelagianism, while still affirming inherited sin from Adam's Fall, denied total depravation and inability of the human will to attain salvation independently from the divine intervention of grace.[6] Individuals were able to cooperate with God leading to salvation in their natural state in the Semi-Pelagian concept, a view the Council of Orange and the prevalent Augustinian tradition heartily rejected.

While Pelagianism and Semi-Pelagianism were no longer considered orthodox options for the church, the strong notions of predestination and divine interference over the human will were also not acceptable to some. There has been a consistent movement since the Council of Orange to affirm inherited sin, corruption, and inability to attain salvation on one's own while also affirming that it is the individual who must exercise free will in order to be converted. But how could one affirm the depraving effects of sin while also not fully affirming Augustinianism? An appendix to the canons of the Council of Orange opened a door. It states: "The sin of the first man has so impaired and weakened free will that no one thereafter can either love God as he ought or believe in God or do good for God's sake, unless the grace of divine mercy has preceded (*praeveniret*) him."[7]

Said another way, God must first work in the hearts of sinners to overcome the effects of sin, a notion that Augustine's followers and critics could both affirm. However, the Council of Orange did not state as to what extent God must work in the human heart in order to be fully converted or if there was some room for an individual to cooperate with God through the exercise of one's will in order to be saved.

It has been in this area where much of the debate lies. While both parties may affirm depravity and the necessity of God to overcome such sinful bondage, to what extent must God work before the individual may respond in such a way as to be converted? Must God lead one to total regeneration before one can be converted (the Augustinian view), or must God merely "prevene" in such a way to bring one to a point of responsibility and choice

---

5. Ibid., 253–54.
6. See Olson, *Arminian Theology*, 80–81, 142–43.
7. "The Council of Orange" in Leith, *Creeds of the Church*, 43.

whereby one may respond in repentance and faith and thus be converted and regenerated (an Arminian view)?

James Arminius, as one would expect, held to the latter view. Divine grace is championed and praised by Arminius because it precedes (or it is "primary" to) the work of the individual in conversion.[8] This is not to say that the individual does not exercise one's will before conversion in Arminius's mind. Rather, God's work is primary to the work of the individual. When God inclines one's heart and mind by grace to be sensitive to one's own sin and need for Christ, the individual is thereby able to assent to that grace.[9] Said another way, God overcomes the effects of sin to a point where one is able to make a decision for or against Christ. Should faith be expressed, it leads to conversion (and thus regeneration), and should faith continually not be expressed, it leads to condemnation.

Arminius's view has been upheld by others within his tradition. Arminian scholar F. Leroy Forlines is critical of the opposition (namely the Reformed/Augustinian tradition) because it claims that the Holy Spirit, by prevenient grace, is the *cause* of conversion (the expressing of faith) rather than the One who *assists* and *influences* the expression of faith (the Arminian view).[10] John Wesley, who strongly affirms the corruption of sin and the necessity of divine intervention, describes God's activity as that which "draws," "woos," and "inspires."[11]

This has come under harsh criticism by the opposing party. One author, on commenting on the Arminian view, writes:

> One can readily see how a shift from a God-centered message of human sinfulness and divine grace to a human-centered message of human potential and relative divine impotence could create a more secularized outlook. If human beings are not so badly off, perhaps they do not need such a radical plan of salvation. Perhaps all they need is a pep talk, some inspiration at halftime, so they can get back into the game. Or perhaps they need an injection of grace, as a spiritual antibiotic, to counteract the sinful affections. But in Reformation theology, human beings do not need help. They need redemption.[12]

---

8. Arminius, "Article XVII," in *The Works of James Arminius*, 1:247–48.

9. Arminius, "On the Vocation of Sinners to Communion With Christ, and to a Participation of His Benefits," 2:342.

10. Forlines, *Classical Arminianism*, 131–32.

11. Wesley, *Calvinism Calmly Considered*, 49–50 and "Awake Thou that Sleepest" in *The Essential Works of John Wesley*, 166–67.

12. Horton, "Evangelical Arminians," 293–94 likewise says, "What lies at the heart of his (Calvinists—note, not Calvin) soteriology is the absolute exclusion of the

THE ASPECT OF CONVERSION

The accusations are quite clear. The Arminians, it is claimed, have a human-centered view of salvation whereas the Reformed view is God-centered. As such, the Arminian not only places a high view on one's own ability (merely needing a "pep talk" or "inspiration" from the Holy Spirit to be saved thus equating it to Semi-Pelagianism), but one also makes God an "impotent" partner in the process. Though some divine assistance may be needed, all that is truly necessary is an "injection" to cure the maladies of sin and not full redemption.[13]

While the Reformed and non-Reformed traditions continue to debate in this area, one may question whether there are certain underlying issues in this aspect of conversion that are the sources of the conflict. Might much of the disagreement in conversion have to do with the one(s) that work and wrought this aspect (the issue of monergism and synergism)? Might too much be assumed (in both parties) on the notion of prevenient grace? And, is the terminology used by both parties consistent? This chapter will suggest that monergism and synergism lie at the heart of these tensions, and when these areas are defined (and the terminology associated with them is clarified) progress may be made in the debate.

TOWARDS A DEFINITION OF CONVERSION

There is not considerable disagreement in the simple definition of *conversion* between the Reformed and non-Reformed traditions. Non-Reformed scholar Thomas Oden even references John Calvin in his definition: "Conversion is a reversal of disposition and personal direction. Conversion involves a turning away from sin (repentance) and a turning to Christ (faith), two phases of a single act of turning (Calvin, *Inst.* 3.3)."[14] Kenneth Keathley agrees with Reformed scholar Wayne Grudem on a definition of conversion as "our willing response to the gospel call, in which we sincerely repent of

---

creaturely element in the initiation of the saving process, that so the pure grace of God may be magnified. Only so could he express his sense of man's complete dependence as sinner on the free mercy of a saving God; or extrude the evil leaven of Synergism by which, as he clearly sees, God is robbed of His glory and man is encouraged to think that he owes to some power, some act of choice, some initiative of his own, his participation in that salvation which is really all of grace." Warfield goes on to call synergism a "degree of autosoterism" (in ibid., 294). These accusations are severe and not reflective of Arminian theology.

13. A synergist would, typically speaking, not make such a claim. Even Arminius, as well as modern day synergists, would claim that even faith is a gift of God's prevenient grace as will be shown below. See Olson, *Arminian Theology*, 159.

14. Oden, *Life in the Spirit*, 101.

sin and place our trust in Christ for salvation."[15] This is very similar to the definitions of the Reformed party. Consider Millard Erickson's definition: "Conversion is the human's turning to God. It consists of a negative and a positive element: repentance, that is, abandonment of sin; and faith, that is, acceptance of the promises and the work of Christ."[16]

Appearing 1,056 times, the Hebrew verb שוב (often translated as "to turn" or "to convert") is an important theme in the Old Testament.[17] Out of those 1,056 usages, 118 of them are used in a religious sense of turning away from sin and turning to the Lord with the result being the restoration of relationship and blessing.[18] Again, one can see that conversion (in the Old Testament) is a twofold act: the turning away from sin and the turning towards God.[19]

In the New Testament, the word that refers to religious conversion is ἐπιστροφή, being translated as "conversion" (along with its verb form ἐπιστρέφω which is translated as "to turn, to turn around" including in areas of conduct).[20] When referring to salvation, it refers to turning away from sin and turning towards God.[21]

Non-Reformed author E. Stanley Jones, in his book entitled *Conversion*, utilizes John 1:12–13 that was also observed in the preceding chapter for the Arminian doctrine of regeneration. Again, it states there: "But to all who received him, who believed in his name, he gave power to become children of God, who were born, not of blood or of the will of the flesh or of the will of man, but of God." Jones states that conversion is not hereditary (as coming from one's biological parents), not through self-driven effort, and not through the will of others but solely from God.[22]

Building upon the narrative of Acts 16:23–40 of Paul and Silas's imprisonment (as well as all relevant passages from Luke and Acts), Joel B. Green speaks of conversion entailing a response to the Gospel which entails baptism—(not so much the ritual act as a desire to embrace God, his plans,

15. Keathley, "The Doctrine of Salvation," 728; Grudem, *Systematic Theology*, 709.

16. Erickson, *Christian Theology*, 888.

17. Koehler and Baumgartner, *The Hebrew and Aramaic Lexicon of the Old Testament*, s.v. שוב.

18. Peters, "The Meaning of Conversion," 235.

19. See Waltke, *An Old Testament Theology*, 282–83.

20. Bauer, *A Greek-English Lexicon of the New Testament*, s.v. ἐπιστροφή, and ἐπιστρέφω.

21. Kittel, *Theological Dictionary of the New Testament*, vol. 7, Σ, s.v. ἐπιστρέφω. See also Peters, "The Meaning of Conversion," 235–38. For a thorough biblical survey of the Old and New Testament uses of conversion, see Wells, *Turning to God*, 31–52.

22. Jones, *Conversion*, 37–38.

and his community), repentance—(behavior that demonstrates that one has committed oneself to God's purposes), and faith.[23] Through exegetical analysis of most usages of ἐπιστρέφω and ἐπιστροφη, Steven W. Waterhouse (also non-Reformed) speaks of conversion as "turning to Christ in saving faith" and follows up this definition with, "It (conversion) does not mean a person must total change his lifestyle before salvation is granted. Conversion is turning to Christ in faith for salvation."[24]

This is not unlike the Reformed definition of *conversion*; indeed, as was shown above, the non-Reformed quote the Reformed on this matter. Still, William G. T. Shedd said, "The converting activity of the regenerate soul moves in two principal directions: (a) faith, which is the converting or turning of the soul to Christ as the Redeemer from sin, and (b) repentance, which is the converting or turning of the soul to God as the supreme good."[25] Michael Horton, likewise, states that conversion means to repent and believe, and though these are human responses, they are gifts of grace.[26] As such, there is not considerable disagreement between the two parties on the definition of conversion.

CONVERSION AS AN ACTIVE OR PASSIVE ASPECT

When one understands conversion as the act of repenting from sin and turning in faith towards Jesus Christ, one assumes that this aspect is active (not passive). Indeed, repentance (whether the initial act in conversion or the continual act of obedience by the believer after conversion) is always thought of as an action to be carried out by an individual. Consider the Greek word μετάνοια. Μετάνοια, the New Testament word for repentance, is primarily translated in the noun form as "a change of mind, turning about, conversion."[27] Some lexicon authors believe μετανοέω carries a connotation of remorse for what one has done in an effort that the individual will cease to commit the sin.[28] Some argue such an assertion because of the middle/passive verb μεταμέλομαι, which definitely carries the connotation of regret in their view.[29]

23. Green, *Salvation*, 113–15.
24. Waterhouse, *What Must I Do To Be Saved*, 31.
25. Shedd, *Dogmatic Theology*, 772.
26. Horton, *The Christian Faith*, 576.
27. BDAG, s.v. μετάνοια.
28. Ibid., s.v. μετανοέω.
29. Brown, *The New International Dictionary of New Testament*, s.v. "Conversion—μεταμέλομαι," 1:356.

Monergism or Synergism

It would be unthinkable that God is the one repenting or even forcing repentance upon an individual. Likewise, the thought of God having remorse or forcing remorse poses ontological fallacies.

However, this study has sought to discern who the efficient cause is and how that cause works instrumentally. Hardly a monergist anywhere would claim repentance and faith is not an activity done by an individual. Faith and repentance are rightly understood as active endeavors performed by an individual. This, however, does not address the issue of causality.

As was observed above (though it will be explored more thoroughly below), Arminians believe conversion is an active aspect. God's work of prevenient grace matched with the faith of an individual provides the synergism necessary to lead one to conversion. Because faith is (in this view) an instrumental (or efficient?) cause of conversion, they consider conversion to be an active aspect.[30]

Monergists, on the other hand, view conversion passively. Art. II.IX of the Formula of Concord states:

> Also, whereas Dr. Luther has written that the will of man in conversion is *purely passive*, that is to be received rightly and fitly, to wit: in respect of divine grace in kindling new motions, that is, it ought to be understood of the moment when the Spirit of God, through the hearing of the Word or through the use of the sacraments, lays hold of the will of man, and works conversion and regeneration in man.[31]

God is the efficient cause of conversion, and he works through the instrumental cause of regeneration. Regeneration, then, may be thought of as the instrumental cause of conversion. Because regeneration (a passive aspect in their view) is the work of God alone, such instrumental causation makes conversion (its effect) passive. The individual was not an instrumental factor in the conversion process albeit one, once converted, becomes enabled to be an instrumental factor in other respects (such as justification).

PREVENIENT GRACE

As mentioned in the previous chapter, prevenient grace is defined by synergists as: "[T]he convicting, calling, enlightening and enabling grace of God

---

30. Charles Finney, interestingly, believed regeneration was passive, being effected by the Holy Spirit, though he remains consistent with this tradition that conversion is the activity of the individual and not of God. He even spoke of a sinner who "turns or converts himself." See Finney, *Lectures on Systematic Theology*, 282.

31. Schaff and Schaff, "The Formula of Concord," 3:113; italics original.

that goes before conversion and makes repentance and faith possible."[32] It is the grace given by God that overcomes the depravity and inability of humankind with regards to salvation. Prevenient (oftentimes called preceding or preventing), grace can be found in the works of Reformed theologians such as Augustine and Calvin as well as synergists such as Erasmus of Rotterdam, Arminius, and John Wesley. As to what such prevenient grace accomplishes, however, the two camps will disagree.

Prevenient grace is a major aspect of Wesleyan-Arminian theology. Though accusations were (and are) often hurled against Arminius (who reacted against the monergistic claims of his teacher Theodore Beza and others of the Reformed movement) that his views deemphasize the grace of God in favor of the ability of humankind, Arminius held to natural inability and the necessity of God to intervene on the sinner's behalf (as has already been affirmed). He wrote:

> In this manner, I ascribe to grace the commencement, the continuance and the consummation of all good—and to such an extent do I carry its influence, that a man, though already regenerate, can neither conceive, will, nor do any good at all, nor resist any evil temptation, without this preventing and exciting, this following and co-operating grace.[33]

As one can see, for Arminius, such prevenient grace (or "preventing" grace) was what enabled the sinner to cooperate with God for the acquiring of salvation.

What is more, prevenient grace was also a universal gift that has been given to all people thereby enabling everyone with the opportunity to embrace or resist God's offer of salvation. Such grace, though overcoming the sinner's corrupt disposition, merely brought the ability to cooperate with God to salvation, but such cooperation was volitional and could be resisted. On his section *The Grace of God*, Arminius wrote: "I believe, according to the scriptures, that many persons resist the Holy Spirit and reject the grace that is *offered*."[34]

---

32. Olson, *Arminian Theology*, 35. This definition accurately represents the views of most synergists who hold to prevenient grace. While this matter was explored in the preceding chapter, a thorough examination and critique was reserved for this chapter.

33. Arminius, "My Own Sentiments on Predestination," in *The Works of James Arminius*, 1:190.

34. Ibid.; emphasis added. It is important to note that such "grace" as Arminius referred to here did not mean *prevenient* grace but *saving* grace. This, as I will point out below, is an inconsistency on how grace is defined. While Arminius, and other synergists, sees prevenient grace as an imposed, universal "gift" that cannot be resisted (see the section below), saving grace is resistible and merely "offered," and such saving grace

Monergism or Synergism

Viewing saving grace as an *offer* that can be either accepted or resisted can also be seen in the five point confession of the Remonstrants, often called the *Remonstrance* or *The Arminian Articles*. Article IV, referring to saving grace, states: "But as respects the mode of the operation of this grace, it is not irresistible, inasmuch as it is written concerning many, that they have resisted the Holy Ghost."

Arguably, after Arminius, John Wesley was the next greatest theologian to promote soteriological synergism in conjunction with prevenient grace. Like Arminius, Wesley recognized one's natural inability and the need of supernatural prevenient grace for salvation. He wrote:

> "[P]reventing grace" (is) all the drawings of the Father; the desires after God, which, *if we yield to them*, increase more and more;—all that light wherewith the Son of God "enlighteneth every one that cometh into the world"; showing every man "to do justly, to love mercy, and to walk humbly with his God";—all the convictions which His Spirit, from time to time, works in every child of man—although it is true, the generality of men stifle them as soon as possible, and after a while forget, or at least deny, that they ever had them at all.[35]

It is important to note that, to Wesley (and most other synergists), prevenient grace is universal to all of humankind; hence, the effects of the Fall, though *applicable* are not *affective* because intervention is provided "in every child of man."[36] Indeed, one source exploring the prevenient grace in

---

is what Arminius is referring to here. That prevenient grace is also irresistible grace, see Barrett, *Salvation by Grace*, 273–75. See also Bavinck, *Saved by Grace*, 20–25 and Bavinck, *Reformed Dogmatics*, 4:84–86. Commenting on Wesley's view of prevenient grace, Harper, in *The Way to Heaven*, 34 states, "Literally, *prevenient grace* means "the grace that comes before." Before what? Before any *conscious* personal experience of divine grace. Through his doctrine of prevenient grace, Wesley was saying that the first move is God's, not man's" (italics original). Again, grace here is bestowed, and it undoes the depraving effects of sin (which is exactly what regeneration does). Arminians find this as a fault in monergistic theology that God's grace overrides the sinful will; however, they admit as much with their doctrine of prevenient grace.

35. Wesley, "The Scripture Way of Salvation," in *The Essential Works of John Wesley*, 148; italics added.

36. This is not to say that, in Wesley's view, sin would not affect the individual. Indeed, he often spoke of it hardening the heart and depraving the senses. This is to say that though sin universally affects all people, God extends a universal grace (for an unspecified amount of time) that overcomes the effects of sin allowing individuals to place faith in Christ for salvation. Does this mean that those who do not hear the Gospel of Christ are able to respond to the Gospel without hearing it? Naturally, strong evangelists like the Wesleys would want to share the Gospel throughout the world, and in no way did he diminish the importance of evangelization. In his sermon, "The General

Wesley states, "Hence Wesley's black description of man in his fallen state above, while true in theory, is not true in fact because of the grace of God which immediately moved upon man after the fall. No man, who is alive, is without prevenient grace ... The purely natural man does not exist."[37] That is to say that though sin universally affects all persons, prevenient grace also universally affects all persons whereby the effects of the universal sin are overcome.[38] What is more is that prevenient grace places before the individual desires after God, but such desires do not belong to the individual until he or she so chooses to yield to them. As Wesley goes on to say, many persons stifle this prevenient work with the implication being that they have chosen not to be converted.

The similarities between Arminius, the Remonstrants, and Wesley are clear. Though the effects of original sin exist in all of humanity, God has universally covered all people with a prevenient grace that enables them either to accept or reject the saving grace that is offered.[39] Indeed, this is

Spread of the Gospel" he referenced in n. 24 those "heathen nations in the world" that have no access to the Gospel. He asks how they can believe without having access to the Gospel, and commenting upon Romans 10:14 Wesley states that God is able to use a variety of means to supply them with a preacher of the Gospel. Nevertheless, in his sermon "On Charity," Wesley (also commenting on Romans 10:14) poses the question about what happens to the eternal state of those who do not hear the Gospel. Therein, he states that one cannot know what will truly happen to those who die without hearing the Gospel and that God will merely judge them based upon what "light they have." He also seems to imply that if they responded to this "light" in a way that "feareth God and worketh righteousness" they will be saved and be "accepted of him." See Wesley, "On Charity" in *The Complete Sermons*, 457–58. This is telling of the Wesleyan-Arminian perspective. Though the Fall of Adam binds all people, universally, in sin, God, in an indiscriminate and wide-reaching way, extends grace whereby all persons are able to respond to the Gospel. Should they not have access to the Gospel, God may choose to raise other means of getting that person access to the Gospel or merely not hold that person responsible for failing to respond to the Gospel. This further proves the point that though sin is applicable but not affective. See also Oden, *The Transforming Power of Grace*, 48–49.

37. Reist, "John Wesley's View of Man," 29–30.

38. Taylor, "Historical and Modern Significance," 64. Taylor sees no conflict in prevenient grace being universally bestowed and effective while also not being irresistible. Note that he is not speaking of saving grace but prevenient grace not being irresistible.

39. This universal coverage of prevenient grace by God does not necessarily mean that the Arminian/Non-Reformed view claims that a person will always stay neutral or at the "crossroads" of faith or disbelief. Indeed, Wesley, as mentioned above, held to the view of hardening one's heart making it more difficult for the individual to believe. It is likely, though this is not universally affirmed by the non-Reformed party, that the more resistance that is shown to the prevenient grace and Gospel presentation, the more difficult it will be for them to repent and place their faith in Christ. Again, what is meant by the universal coverage is not that it leaves people in a permanent state of neutrality but that it universally covers people whereby they may make a decision for or against Christ.

representative of the majority of synergists post the Council of Orange. Roger Olson affirms that God (in a universal and non-selective way) draws all people (in a prevenient way) to come to Christ through an enabling by the Spirit that restores the human will with the freedom either to believe or reject Christ for salvation.[40] Mildred Bangs Wynkoop states: "Saving grace begins with prevenient grace extended to all men. No man is found in the "state of nature" . . . All men come in under the cover of God's free grace."[41]

The Reformed tradition, as said above, also holds to prevenient grace, but in a dramatically different way. While the term *prevenient grace* is used more often by the non-Reformed tradition, it does not need to assume the non-Reformed view. Again, prevenient grace is the grace that goes before any action of the individual, but as to what that grace does and to what extent it is involved, the parties differ.

Augustine, an adherent of prevenient grace, would deny the notions of prevenient grace mentioned above. In Augustine's *Anti-Pelagian Writings*, the bishop affirmed that God "prevenes" (or "anticipates") the will of an individual to desire the things of God without which the individual would stay in sin.[42] However, he is critical against those who would say that this anticipatory grace does not infringe upon a "reluctant heart."[43] If God did not infringe upon reluctant hearts, Augustine said that it was the individual, by good merit, who brought about the salvation.[44] While this statement is directed at the Pelagians (not Arminians), it is also indicative of Augustine's perspective. God does not work in a universally prevening way, and in order to save the elect, his grace would precede their sinful desires and move them to the point of conversion.[45] This is different from the previous perspective

---

40. Olson, *Against Calvinism*, 129–31.

41. Wynkoop, *Foundations of Wesleyan-Arminian Theology*, 99.

42. Augustine, "A Treatise Against Two Letters of the Pelagians," in *Augustin: Anti-Pelagian Writings*, 2.21, 401–2.

43. Ibid., 2.22, 401.

44. Ibid. Augustine spoke more on this issue in ibid., 4.15, 423 whereby he called it human pride to say that it was the individual who made the final choice to salvation. All, believed Augustine, must be attributed to divine grace.

45. To be clear, Augustine did believe God universally prevenes upon all people in some way because any good thing which comes from a person (saved or not) comes from God's grace preceding their sinfulness. See ibid., 2.21, 400. However, as prevenient grace relates to salvation, it was conferred (for infants) through baptism. See Augustine, "A Treatise on the Merits and Forgiveness of Sins and on the Baptism of Infants," in *Augustin*, 1.23, 23–24. Adults, likewise, could receive such prevenient grace (apart from which salvation would not occur); however, such is not conferred upon all of the human race. See Augustine, "A Treatise on Nature and Grace" in ibid., ch. 4, 122. Some, to be clear, "convert" (repent and believe) but later fall away. They were not amongst the elect. This can be seen well in his treatise "On the Gift of Perseverance," specifically chs.

of the non-Reformed tradition that states that God, in a universal way for all humankind, brings one to a crossroads and allows them to decide without infringing upon or forcing the will.

John Calvin, likewise, attributed all matters pertaining to conversion to the grace of God even more so than just a preparatory way. While not doubting that God intercedes and goes before any will of an individual, Calvin said that further grace must be shown to bring about conversion. His view is that humanity simply cannot fulfil what is required by God by human merit. Grace must begin and complete the work leading Calvin to affirm that conversion is not a cooperative work between God and an individual whereby God is the instigator and the human is the fulfiller.[46] Martin Luther, likewise, did not have an issue with the fact that God (through the Holy Spirit) precedes any action of the sinner and must overcome the effects of sin. For him, the issue is that God's prevenient grace must not fall short of full regeneration lest the individual not truly be saved.[47]

SYNERGISM AND PREVENIENT GRACE IN CONVERSION

As one can see, the meaning of prevenient grace, and the extent which God must prevene, differs between the two parties. However, it is in making

---

9, 12, 14, 19, 33. Augustine illustrated this point well in his teaching on marriage and divorce which he compares to salvation in Christ. Like in divorce, an apostate does not lose one's sacrament which he or she received at baptism (like in marriage); however, upon apostasy (similar to divorce) he or she is cut off from one's relationship to Christ. The sacrament remains after apostasy, but that will be used against the individual. See "On Marriage and Concupiscence," in *Augustin*, 1.11, 268. To the point, though, it is important to note that God does overcome reluctant hearts in Augustine's theology of prevenient grace and that one is elect because God chose the person, not because the person chose God. Augustine says, "But it was because they had been chosen, that they chose Him; not because they chose Him that they were chosen. There could be no merit in men's choice of Christ, if it were not that God's grace was prevenient in His choosing them," in "On Grace and Free Will," ch. 38 in *Augustin*, 460. This does not mean that, for Augustine, the operative prevenient grace destroys free will; rather, it is a wooing of the will to respond freely. As one author put it, "God is the infallible seducer—he wins the soul, but in such a way that the soul responds gladly and freely" (Lane, *A Concise History of Christian Thought*, 51). For more on Augustine's view of predestination matched with prevenient grace, see González, *A History of Christian Thought*, 2:46–47. Still, one should observe that in Augustine, one who is predestined for good is said to receive the preparation of grace. See Augustine, *On the Predestination of the Saints*, ch. 19. For a critical examination of this view, see Wetzel, "Snares of Truth," 124–38, specifically 124–25.

46. Calvin, *Institutes of the Christian Religion*, II.V.VIII–IX, 325–36.
47. Luther, *On the Bondage of the Will*, 289.

this distinction that one is able to see where synergism plays a role in the non-Reformed tradition. While the Reformed party affirms that God must intercede and prevene by grace in the will of the individual, they believe that God, in a monergistic fashion, must bring a person to full regeneration in order for repentance and faith to be expressed. The non-Reformed party, however, believes that God prevenes upon the will in order to bring about a measure of freedom from the bonds of sin whereby one may believe or disbelieve in the Gospel. It is there that synergism is advocated for by the non-Reformed tradition.

There appears to be a twofold perspective amongst Arminians in how synergism plays a part in conversion due to prevenient grace. The first of these is that the individual at hand cooperates with God simply by not resisting the Spirit's work. Stanley Grenz presents the fourfold prevenient work of God in the aspect of conversion that is widely accepted by the Reformed and non-Reformed tradition alike: conviction, call, illumination, and enablement.[48] Interestingly, Roger Olson, an Arminian, builds upon Grenz's work and says, "No person can repent, believe and be saved without the Holy Spirit's supernatural support from beginning to end. All the person does is cooperate by not resisting."[49] Olson then goes on to reference Arminius. Olson claims that Arminius's soteriology was synergistic because the human's role was simply not to resist the grace of God.[50] As such, the first way that humankind cooperates with God (in this view) is by not resisting the Spirit's work.

The second way synergism is portrayed concerning conversion is through the individual responding to the prevenient grace by repentance and faith. While the other mode of synergism advocated by the non-Reformed discussed above was passive in nature (the act of not resisting), this mode is active. The way in which an individual cooperates is by response. Consider Thomas Oden's words: "Grace prepares the will and coworks with the prepared will. Insofar as grace precedes and prepares free will it is called prevenient. Insofar as grace accompanies and enables human willing to work with divine willing, it is called cooperative grace."[51] Oden goes on by saying that God's work is to change one's disposition towards reception of grace, to give holy thoughts, pious plans, and motion of good will towards

---

48. Grenz, *Theology for the Community of God*, 412–15.

49. Olson, *Arminian Theology*, 160. Notice that this statement from Olson follows his reference of Grenz, but upon exploring Grenz's own statements, Grenz (whose theology is characterized as Arminian) says nothing of such cooperation or synergism in conversion.

50. Ibid., 165. See also 166.

51. Oden, *Transforming Power of Grace*, 47.

THE ASPECT OF CONVERSION

the human, and to complete the work of conversion in the human soul.[52] The cooperating work of the human, then, is free consent to God and the response of faith.[53]

Arminian scholars Joseph Dongell and Jerry Walls describe the synergism in Arminianism through the analogy of one who has been imprisoned in a terrorist camp. Being bound, gagged, blindfolded, and drugged, the individual is in no position to save himself or herself (hence no Pelagianism or Semi-Pelagianism). God, in their view, breaks into the camp, injects a "serum" that will clear the mind of the person, he takes off the gag from the mouth, shines light in the darkness, and enables him or her (through wooing and speaking the truth) to leave their current state and to follow him for a better situation if they will trust him to save them and follow him.[54] In this analogy, God prevenes upon the helpless individual and makes the way towards freedom. He presents an offer for salvation, and the individual is thus free to accept this salvation or reject it, but he does not force the individual to action. It is merely an offer and invitation. The response of faith (which they claim is not a meritorious work) is how cooperation occurs, and it is a necessary part in order to receive this redemption. In a typical Arminian fashion, F. Leroy Forlines states that the Arminian view of faith is synergistic because any exercise of human faith (to the consenting of God for salvation) is synergistic.[55] Norman Geisler, in a similar way, writes, "[A]lthough no one can believe unto salvation without the aid of God's saving grace, the gracious action by which we are saved is not monergistic (an act of God alone) but synergistic (an act of God *and* our free choice)."[56]

This view is built upon the teachings of Arminius himself. Arminius believed that cooperation with the Holy Spirit was vital to the conversion of sinners. It began in the preparatory work of God without which no one could be saved, but it is accompanied by faith from the individual and can thus be understood as cooperative.[57] Viewed from the opposite perspective, Arminius elsewhere said that when one resists and fails to yield assent to God, the individual does not cooperate with God.[58] Consider these words by Arminius:

---

52. Ibid., 51–52.
53. Ibid., 47–54.
54. Walls and Dongell, *Why I Am Not A Calvinist*, 68–69.
55. Forlines, *Classical Arminianism*, 24.
56. Geisler, *Systematic Theology*, 3:136.
57. Arminius, "Examination of the Treatise," in *The Works of James Arminius*, 3:249–50.
58. Arminius, "On Predestination," in ibid., 1:169.

> This [repentance and faith, i.e., conversion] is effected by the word of God. But persuasion is effected, externally by the preaching of the word, internally by the operation, or rather the co-operation, of the Holy Spirit, tending to this result, that the word may be understood and apprehended by true faith. These two are almost always joined. For God has determined to save them, who believe by the preaching of the word, and the preaching of the word, without the co-operation of the Holy Spirit, is useless, and can effect nothing.[59]

John Wesley, in similar fashion, believed that God works first thereby enabling individuals to work. That is to say, God (in what he called "preventing grace") takes the initial work in salvation apart from which no one could be saved. He liberates the will whereby one is able to work out one's own salvation by the expression of faith through the freed will.[60]

This is not to leave out the other area of synergism whereby an individual cooperates with God *after* conversion to sanctification. However, this is not the issue at hand, for there are examples of Reformed and non-Reformed who affirm synergism after conversion.[61] The question is whether synergism takes place *before* conversion. The non-Reformed tradition says "yes" while the Reformed tradition says "no."[62]

ORDER OF REGENERATION AND CONVERSION

With this distinction in mind, one can see the differences in the two parties' *ordo salutis*. Does one repent and believe in order to become regenerate, or does one repent and believe because one is regenerate? The non-Reformed party holds to the former while the Reformed party holds to the latter.

There are reasons why Arminius chose to believe faith and repentance precede regeneration. First, he believed that it was the biblical perspective. In his commentary on Romans 7, Arminius sought to prove that "true and

---

59. Arminius, "Examination of the Treatise," in ibid., 3:249.

60. Wesley, "On Working Out Our Own Salvation," in *The Essential Works of John Wesley*, 328–29. See also Knight, "Love and Freedom," 62–63.

61. For example, see Sproul, *Willing to Believe*, 73.

62. Again, this is generally speaking the main views concerning each party. Notably, exceptions exist. Anthony Hoekema, a Reformed scholar, believed conversion was synergistic because of God's work of changing the disposition and humankind's work of expressing faith. See *Saved by Grace*, 114–15. Likewise, Stanley Grenz in the non-Reformed tradition, affirms that faith and repentance are responses to the divine work but never calls them work or synergistic effort. See *Theology for the Community of God*, 409–11.

living faith in Christ precedes regeneration strictly taken," and "Christ becomes ours by faith, and we are engrafted into Christ ... that we may draw from him the vivifying power of the Holy Spirit, by which power the old man is mortified and we rise again into a new life."[63] For Arminius, he believed it to be the plain teaching of Scripture that one must believe and repent before one can be made alive again; hence, he cited numerous Pauline passages to support his position that faith precedes regeneration.[64]

A second reason why Arminius believed faith precedes regeneration concerns the integrity of the human will. As said above, Arminius held to prevenient grace. God gives individuals a will and calls upon them to exercise that will. While they were once condemned and bound by the enslaving effects of sin, God has "prevened" upon humanity thereby enabling them to respond to or reject Christ.[65]

In a similar fashion, Wesley was critical of regeneration preceding faith particularly on theological grounds. Wesley denied the notion of irresistible grace which, he claimed, was essential if regeneration was to precede faith. If God were to work in fully transforming the will and spiritual life of the individual before he or she has had the opportunity to exercise faith, then such a thing is logically irresistible (according to Wesley). Naturally, this relates to the doctrine of predestination, and for Wesley predestination could only be conditional (upon faith) rather than absolute (by divine decree).[66]

The non-Reformed tradition has continued this belief that faith and repentance must precede regeneration. Steve Lemke provides numerous Scriptural references that he says supports his view that repentance and faith precedes conversion.[67] Then, he claims that it is difficult to see how the view that regeneration precedes faith plays out in real life. He claims that it is theoretically possible (in Reformed theology) for one to be regenerated on one day but not be converted for some considerable time later. Moreover, if regeneration and conversion occur simultaneously (which he admits is

---

63. Arminius, "A Dissertation on the True and Genuine Sense of the Seventh Chapter of the Epistle to the Romans," in *The Works of James Arminius*, 2:163.

64. Ibid., 162. His support comes from such places as Eph 1:18, 4:22–24, 2 Cor 3:18, Rom 6:2, 6, 7, 11, Gal 2:20, and others.

65. Arminius, "An Examination of the Treatise of William Perkins Concerning the Order and Mode of Predestination—Part 2 Concerning Predestination," in *The Works of James Arminius*, 3:379–80.

66. Wesley, "The Question, 'What Is An Arminian?' Answered," in *The Essential Works of John Wesley*, 1172–73.

67. Lemke, "A Biblical and Theological Critique," 138–39. He references Mark 16:15–16, John 1:12, 20:31, Acts 13:39, 16:31, 18:8, Rom 1:16, 10:9–10, 1 Cor 1:21, and Heb 11:6.

the Reformed view), then why do some people attend church services for a season before they are regenerated?[68]

Roger Olson, like Arminius and Wesley, believes that God enables all people to respond synergistically in repentance and faith leading to new life and that such a gift is not given only to the elect but to all persons.[69] Thomas Oden, however, says that there is truth on both sides of the argument (on whether faith precedes regeneration or regeneration precedes faith). He says, however, that "the prevailing logical-consensual order in interpreting the sense of scripture is that faith's first work is repentance, and penitent faith is the condition of regeneration."[70]

The Reformed tradition, however, holds to the opposing view. According to this party, regeneration must precede faith. The previous chapter has already shown the Reformed (monergist) tradition's view on regeneration, particularly concerning the effects of sin and how regeneration (in the full sense) is necessary to overcome humankind's depravation. An exhaustive treatment of this issue again is not necessary given its thorough treatment in the preceding chapter; however, the major conclusions found there can be reiterated. First, both Reformed and non-Reformed parties affirm that sin has left all persons in a spiritually destitute state whereby they have no ability to please God without divine grace, no ability to seek after God for salvation without divine grace, and are in a state of spiritual deadness and incapacity. Second, these areas of depravation are the very things that regeneration addresses. Third, it is widely claimed by the Reformed tradition that regeneration (in the full sense) is the only possible explanation for how faith can be expressed by an individual.[71]

THE EFFICIENT CAUSE OF CONVERSION

With the presentation of views made thus far, one is now in a position to see how the efficient cause and instrumental means of conversion are in conflict in these two traditions. Little attention is given to this matter, but it is of utmost importance that this area be explored to understand underlying sources of disagreement.

---

68. Ibid., 139–40.
69. Olson, *The Mosaic of Christian Belief*, 281.
70. Oden, *Systematic Theology*, 3:103.
71. Luther, *The Bondage of the Will*, 187. Sproul, *What Is Reformed Theology?*, 185–87, Van Mastricht, *A Treatise on Regeneration*, 35, Cole, *He Who Gives Life*, 215. Calvin is a notable exception to this as has already been noted.

THE ASPECT OF CONVERSION

The non-Reformed tradition, as said above, believes there is synergy between God and humankind in the role of conversion. According to Thomas Oden, God's work is the work of prevenient grace whereby he enables the human will to respond, and the human's work is the response (repentance and faith) itself.[72] That is to say, conversion occurs when God works upon an individual's heart to overcome the effects of original sin and when the individual thus responds in repentance and faith. As such, the efficient cause (namely that which brings about and serves as the source cause) of conversion is the synergistic activity of the prevenient grace of God and the willing response of the individual at hand.

In this non-Reformed view, synergist Norman Geisler views God as the primary efficient cause that gives the power of free choice to the individual, but there is still a secondary efficient cause found in the free choice of the believer who has been divinely enabled to express remorse and faith.[73] Geisler is not alone. Using the view of "Middle Knowledge" from the works of the Catholic Counter-Reformer Luis Molina, William Lane Craig proposes that God, by his prevenient grace, gives to all people a will that can cooperate with God unto salvation through faith or reject the offer of salvation in unbelief. This *freed* will has the effect of procuring justification "for those who assent to its operation."[74] Likewise, in his defense of the Arminian view, Roger Olson says that synergism is the belief that salvation is all due to the grace of God but requires cooperation (through faith) in order for such conversion to be activated. Such grace to conversion, however, is conditioned upon the willing response of the individual, and should the individual respond in faith the outcome will be new life.[75] The efficient cause, therefore, is clear. God must work in the individual's heart, and the individual must work in light of the divine enablement by faith. The result is conversion, and this was brought about through the synergistic activity of God and humankind.

The Reformed view, however, views the efficient cause to be God (and his work) alone. Denying synergism and upholding monergism, the Reformed tradition views regeneration as the cause of conversion, and because regeneration is monergistic so too is conversion.[76] As said in the preceding chapter, in order for faith to be exercised (which it cannot due to the effects of sin), the individual must be regenerated (in the complete sense) from

---

72. Oden, *The Transforming Power of Grace*, 51–54.
73. Geisler, "God Knows All Things," in *Predestination and Free Will*, 78–80.
74. Craig, "Middle Knowledge," 157.
75. Olson, *Against Calvinism*, 156, 170–74.
76. Helm, *The Beginnings*, 15–16.

the state of spiritual deadness in order to make any response of faith and repentance, claims this view. Michael Horton states:

> Only because of God's one-sided act of regeneration does anyone repent and believe. So even though Arminianism should not be equated with Semi-Pelagianism, it does in fact deny that the new birth is a unilateral act of God's grace. Every person is graciously enabled to believe (in the Arminian view), and the new birth is the consequence rather than the source of that decision.[77]

While not denying that repentance and faith are an essential part of regeneration, Bruce Demarest states that they are the by-products of the divine work of regeneration not the cause of it.[78] That is to say, conversion finds its efficient cause in the monergistic work of regeneration. When God transforms the heart of the sinner (in the full sense, not in the Arminian sense), then one is thereby enabled to respond with repentance and faith. Thus, while repentance and faith are the actions of the individual, they were caused and sourced in the divine, monergistic work of God in regeneration. Without the cause of regeneration, the effect of conversion would not occur.

As such, there is no notion of synergism in the Reformed view of conversion. While Calvin never denied (in fact he affirmed) that faith is the conscious activity of the individual, he attributed the ability to exercise faith to the supernatural work of the Holy Spirit.[79] In Calvin's view, faith is something that is exhibited by the human spirit; however, if this human spirit is dead (which he affirms it is), God must divinely enable one to believe.[80] Faith is thus not the efficient cause of conversion. Charles Spurgeon, in similar fashion, wrote: "Grace is the first and last moving cause of salvation, and faith, essential as it is, is only an important part of the machinery which grace employs. We are saved 'through faith,' but salvation is 'by grace.'"[81] As such, in the Reformed tradition, the efficient cause of conversion is God, for it is by God that one is enabled to repent and believe.

---

77. Horton, *For Calvinism*, 104–5.

78. Demarest, *The Cross and Salvation*, 246–47.

79. Calvin, *Institutes*, III.II.XXXIII. It is true that Calvin viewed the origins of conversion in the will. See ibid., II.III.VI; however, one must ask what the efficient cause of the will willing was. There also, in ibid., II.III.VI, Calvin affirms that this comes from God. When the will's inclination is changed by grace, then one can desire to repent and believe. See Hoitenga, *John Calvin and the Will*, 52.

80. Calvin, *Institutes*, III.I.IV. As said in the preceding chapter, Calvin held to faith preceding regeneration; however, this did not mean that he saw anything but monergism in efficient causation in conversion.

81. Spurgeon, *All of Grace*, 43.

THE ASPECT OF CONVERSION

THE INSTRUMENTAL MEANS OF CONVERSION

The instrumental means, in the Reformed tradition, is therefore clear in light of its monergistic position on regeneration. God, as the efficient cause, works through the Holy Spirit's transforming, regenerating work to bring about the conversion (faith and repentance) of the individual. Regeneration, thus, is not only the efficient cause but the instrumental cause through which individuals are able to respond in faith and repentance. This is to say that the aspect of conversion is completed when one exercises repentance and faith; however, such repentance and faith must (in this view) be brought about from God and through God through the divine work of regeneration. When God does the regenerating work (discussed in the previous chapter) of reviving the human spirit, transforming the senses, and changing the disposition of the individual at hand, it is only then that repentance and faith are possible.[82] It should be clearly noted that in the Reformed tradition, repentance and faith (i.e., the aspect of conversion) are the by-products of monergistic regeneration, and though they are activities of an individual, it was not necessarily through an active instrumental means by which this aspect came about. Said another way, it would be illogical to say that conversion occurred through the means of faith, for conversion entails faith as a part of its definition.

The non-Reformed tradition, however, has a differing notion of the instrumentality through which one becomes converted. Again, in the non-Reformed view, God intervenes through prevenient grace to bring one to a point of decision making. If one acts in faith, then one will be converted and thus regenerated (for faith precedes regeneration in their view as shown in the previous chapter). Oden says that God exhibits prevenient grace upon the human will and works together with the human will to bring about the conversion and redemption of the individual at hand.[83] Olson, likewise, says that salvation (including the aspect of conversion) occurs when the individual (as a result of prevenient grace) accepts, does not resist, and actively exercises the will.[84] As such, it appears that in the non-Reformed tradition, the instrumental cause of conversion is the human will, freed from the ef-

---

82. Bavinck, *Saved by Grace*, 157–58. Bavinck speaks of the instrumentality of the Word as an important means through which people become converted; however, he also says that the agent which accomplishes such conversion is God through the Holy Spirit. As such, one should not (in his view) deny the divine monergistic power that is at work and not attribute it to anything else. As a side note, one need not assume that Bavinck's pedobaptism views are representative of all the Reformed tradition.

83. Oden, *The Transforming Power of Grace*, 52–54.

84. Olson, *Arminian Theology*, 164–65.

fects of sin through the prevenient work of God and enabled to exercise faith and repentance.

AN EVALUATION OF THE VIEWS

With the opposing views clearly defined, it is now time for a thorough evaluation of both parties to see which tradition (if either) provides the better arguments. This evaluation will begin with the matter of prevenient grace.

Prevenience

As said above, both traditions hold to prevenient grace. The difference between the two parties is to what extent God must prevene for an individual to repent and believe. As such, one can see that though the same terminology is used, there is a difference in definitions.

The first point of observation in the Wesleyan-Arminian tradition's view of prevenient grace concerns the prevenient state of an individual. As said above, in this view God prevenes upon an individual's natural sinful condition to bring him or her to a point of liberated decision making. The individual is thus free to respond affirmatively or negatively to the Gospel. Should faith and repentance be exercised, the individual will be saved, and should continuous disbelief remain, the result will be condemnation.

While few would question (even between both of these traditions) that the Scriptures portray humanity in states of either sin and rebellion or in grace and redemption, one may very well question whether there is evidence of a third state of being for individuals, namely that of neutrality and decision making.[85]

James Dunn comments upon the Pauline view of Romans 8. There, Dunn states (with particular attention to v. 7) that all individuals are either living according to the flesh (a reference to sin which does not please God) or according to the Spirit (a reference to faith and obedience which does please God). Claiming that there is no other alternative, Dunn states that one is either in sin and rebellion or in faith and favor.[86] In a similar fashion, David Wells describes the personal conversion of Paul. He states that Paul described himself in one of two conditions—either dead in trespasses and

---

85. Arminians (like Roman Catholics) would see the state of prevenient grace as being in a state of grace and not sin; however, one must observe that this is not saving grace (as Arminians would fully affirm) for faith has not been yet expressed. One must then question whether this intermediate state is Scriptural.

86. Dunn, *Romans 1–8*, 442–43.

THE ASPECT OF CONVERSION

sin or alive in the Spirit. There was the state of being "in Christ" and "in the Spirit" and a state of being under the law and in sin.[87] A third (and somewhat intermediate) state, however, is the logical consequence of the Wesleyan-Arminian claim, for there the life of flesh that is hostile towards God is overcome with the prevenient grace of God, but they are not in a position of living in faith and obedience to God yet.[88]

The Reformed tradition, however, does not have this trouble, for their view is that one is either in a state of sin or a state of salvation. There is, in their view, the children of God or the children of the devil (to reference John 8), not both.[89] As such, one truly converts from one state to another in the Reformed view which appears to coincide with the meaning of conversion as described above. For the Reformed tradition (in light of their interpretation of Eph 4:18–19), unbelief is a result of one's ignorance, darkness of understanding, and hardness of their heart, but that state ends whenever the Holy Spirit regenerates the individual allowing faith and repentance to be expressed.[90] There is no third state, only one or the other.

A second observation concerning the Wesleyan-Arminian tradition's view of prevenient grace is to what extent God must intervene before repentance and faith are possible. As shown above, the Reformed tradition believes full regeneration is necessary while the non-Reformed tradition believes that God must simply enable a person to make a free choice.

Here one must carefully observe the language of the definition of prevenient grace. It is defined as: "[T]he convicting, calling, enlightening and

---

87. Wells, *Turning To God*, 54–64.

88. See MacDonald, "The Spirit of Grace," 86–87. He states that God cannot and will not regenerate someone unless they "admit him" (86). How can one admit him given one's fallen, depraved condition? MacDonald states: "One without God sleeps in the death of his sins, but when God's call awakens him, he can respond in faith, or he can resist the Spirit and go back to sleep in death" (87). His textual support for this is Eph 5:14 which certainly relates to regeneration from death (or spiritual sleep). One wonders, however, if MacDonald is making too much of the notion of sleep John 11:10–12 speaks of Lazarus who fell asleep (who, Jesus told his disciples plainly, was dead). Jesus woke Lazarus up through resurrection of the dead. It is in this sense that Eph 5:14 speaks of one who is asleep. They are spiritually lifeless unless Christ wakes them up through regeneration. MacDonald sees something different. He sees one not so much in spiritual death but spiritual sleep that can wake up and go back to sleep. During the wake time, the individual is still unregenerate in his view. This means that one is somewhere between life and death which Scripture does not teach. Eph 5:14 should be understood in light of Eph 2:1, 5–6 which speaks of an individual who is dead but made alive (συνεζωοποίησεν—see the chapter above that shows this is a term for regeneration) in Christ. This refers to an actual movement from former existence (darkness) to a new existence (light). See Thielman, *Ephesians*, 350–51.

89. Beasley-Murray, *John*, 134–35.

90. Vaughan, *The Letter to the Ephesians*, 98–101.

enabling grace of God that goes before conversion and *makes repentance and faith possible*."⁹¹ To clarify, it is the work of God that goes before any act of an individual so that repentance and faith (i.e., conversion) are possible. In this process, God convicts, calls, enlightens, and enables the human heart to turn away from sin and believe in Christ. The question then becomes—*is this not precisely the definition of regeneration?*

The Arminian says that this prevenient grace entails "convicting." It was shown in the preceding chapter how an aspect of regeneration is making the human heart sensitive to sin whereby the individual feels convicted over sin. Apart from regeneration, the individual at hand would never be sensitive to such conviction. As such, the previous chapter concluded that conviction is the result of regeneration. Also, the Arminian says that prevenient grace involves "calling." Calling the dead to life, calling the individual in a way which one can hear though the effects of sin have left one spiritually deaf and insensitive, are effects of regeneration, as was shown in the previous chapter. In claiming that prevenient grace entails "enlightening," even the Reformed tradition says, "Yes," but this enlightening of the senses to be sensitive to the things of God is the result of regeneration in their view. Furthermore, claiming that this grace is "enabling grace" is to say that one is enabled (as the definition goes on to say) to repent and believe in Christ. Said another way, it is what overcomes one's sinful depravation and enables repentance and faith. This is the standard definition of regeneration.

However, the Wesleyan-Arminian party does not wish to affirm this prevenience as full regeneration. Olson says that this is merely "partial" regeneration by prevenient grace, and that it is only when repentance and faith are shown that one receives "full" regeneration.⁹² Arminius, likewise, believed in some kind of partial regeneration, for he claimed that the Holy Spirit, through regeneration and renewing, infuses faith to the individual.⁹³ It would not be complete, however, until "God may then will and work together with man, that man may perform whatever he wills."⁹⁴

This effort to define regeneration as prevenient grace, to admit that it is, in fact, regeneration, and to assign all the effects of regeneration to prevenient grace without calling it as such, appears to be merely an attempt to preserve a preconceived theology of the human will. Said another way, the Arminian doctrine of prevenient grace appears to be an attempt to

91. Olson, *Arminian Theology*, 35.

92. Ibid., 36.

93. Arminius, "My Own Sentiments on Predestination," in *The Works of James Arminius*, 1:189–90.

94. Ibid., 190.

ensure that free will and personal choice are preserved and never usurped. Whether this tradition succeeds in preserving their view of free will or not will be explored below. However, one may reasonably conclude that while this tradition wishes to affirm that free will and faith precede regeneration, they in effect are admitting that regeneration is prior to free will and are merely trying to redefine terms to uphold preconceived notions that are central to their theology.

The Reformed tradition, however, remains consistent in terminology. While this tradition does not use the term *prevenient grace* as often as the non-Reformed party, the idea of God going before and preceding any actions on the human will to overcome the effects of sin is overwhelmingly present. For this tradition, however, they affirm that prevenient grace is regeneration and therefore appear to have the most consistent framework.

Grace

In the Wesleyan-Arminian tradition of prevenient grace, the concept is twofold. First, it is *prevenient* in terms of it going before the actions of the individual (as was just covered), and secondly that it is *grace*. The notion of grace in prevenience in this tradition, however, must fully be explored to determine if it can be substantiated.

As shown above, the non-Reformed tradition has two unique perspectives concerning prevenient grace. First, God's prevenient grace brings not a result but a choice, an offer, a possibility to accept the gift or deny it. Second, this choice must be made by the free (or perhaps better termed *freed*) will of the person. Grace, as one synergist claims, creates free will and enables the cooperation to accept or reject God's offer of salvation.[95]

Concerning the first aspect of prevenient grace bringing an offer which may be accepted or denied, it is interesting to note that only once in the Scriptures is the term "offer" used in conjunction with salvation (1 Cor 9:18).[96] Therein, Paul states: "What then is my reward? That, when I preach the gospel, I may offer the gospel without charge, so as not to make full use of my right in the gospel" (NASB).

There is hardly a synergist anywhere who would affirm that this verse teaches that salvation is something that is offered for the choosing. The most common interpretation is that Paul shares the Gospel without placing financial obligation upon the recipients, preaching out of volition and not obligation or charge whereby neither he nor the recipients of his message

---

95. Olson, *Arminian Theology*, 66.
96. See Nettles, *By His Grace and for His Glory*, 387–88.

are found in debt.⁹⁷ Still, the synergist may say that the idea or concept is there throughout Scripture. As shown above, the synergist claims that one must not resist the prevenient grace of God and one must actively receive it and respond to it in faith.

Several things are noteworthy concerning the notion of salvation as an offer to be chosen. First, one could easily argue that *grace*, *gift*, and *salvation* (all used interchangeably) are not gifts to be offered but gifts that are bestowed. 2 Timothy 1:8–10 states:

> Do not be ashamed, then, of the testimony about our Lord or of me his prisoner, but join with me in suffering for the gospel, relying on the power of God, who saved us and called us with a holy calling, not according to our works but according to his own purpose and grace. This grace was given to us in Christ Jesus before the ages began, but it has now been revealed through the appearing of our Savior Christ Jesus, who abolished death and brought life and immortality to light through the gospel.

The participles *saved* (σώσαντος) and *called* (καλέσαντος) modify Lord (κυρίου), matching in gender, number, and case whereby it was the Lord Jesus who has saved and called. Such was done not according to any human works, according to this verse, but rather his purposes and grace. Monergists contend that Paul is conveying over to Timothy that salvation was not something that was done by the human but by God.⁹⁸ His position of Lordship enables him to do as he pleases. Claiming that Christ is the agent for imparting grace, Donald Guthrie affirms that grace is not only unearned by human works but also determined before the world began. By being "determined," the gift will certainly have its effect of bringing about salvation which is reflective of the bestowal view mentioned here.⁹⁹

Monergists also turn to such passages as Philippians 1:29: "For he has graciously granted you the privilege not only of believing in Christ, but of suffering for him as well." There, monergists contend that believing in

---

97. Polhill, *Paul and His Letters*, 190.
98. Mounce, *The Pastoral Epistles*, 482–83.
99. Guthrie, *The Pastoral Epistles*, 129. Here, one may question whether monergists believe in a free offer of the Gospel. Indeed they do. Hoekema, in *Saved by Grace*, 68–79 speaks of the general call of the Gospel to all people. He even expounds upon the Canons of Dort (ch. II, a. 5 and III–IV, a. 8) that deal with the "well-meant offer" of the Gospel (77–78). This well-meant offer, however, does not abolish the doctrines of election and atonement to monergists as Hoekema contends (78). This general call of the Gospel should be distinguished from the effectual call which is something bestowed upon individuals in salvation and is the work of God alone as described by Hoekema in ibid., 80–92.

THE ASPECT OF CONVERSION

Christ is much like suffering; though one did not ask on one's own to believe in Christ, one likewise did not ask to suffer for Christ; however, this is "graciously granted" to those and should be considered a "privilege" that is bestowed on all who truly believe.[100]

More references could be made to support the view that grace is bestowed as opposed to offered;[101] however, such exegetical debate and proof texting has only led to more arguments and has not resolved this issue. Interestingly, though, one need not address the issue from exegetical grounds alone. One needs simply to look at the Wesleyan-Arminian's tradition alone to see how they also view grace not as an offer but as something that is bestowed.

By the admission of the Wesleyan-Arminian tradition, God works by prevenient grace upon the rebellious hearts of sinners so that the effects of their own depravity are overcome and they are enabled to make a response for or against Christ. This, it is said, is necessary to preserve the dignity of the human will, for God does not save (i.e., regenerate) the unwilling but considers their free will.

The interesting thing to consider is that nothing in this notion preserves the dignity of the human will or shows the Reformed view to be either inferior to or different from the non-Reformed view. In this Wesleyan-Arminian view, God must overcome by his grace the depraving effects of sin. While the individual is still in a state of hostility against God, while one is still opposed to the things of God, while the human will is set against godliness, God overcomes and supersedes the human will. There is a radical change in the heart of the individual whereby one is no longer bound to the depraving effects of sin like one once was. One is now able, because of

---

100. This verb is also used in conjunction with a superior giving pardon to an inferior (see 2 Cor 12:13 for example). Friedrich, *Theological Dictionary of the New Testament*, 9:396, s.v. χαρίς. See also Hawthorn, *Philippians*, 60–61.

101. Sproul does an exegetical survey of Acts 9 in the conversion of Saul. There he states that the transformation of Saul the persecutor to Paul the apostle was sheer sovereign grace that was bestowed upon Saul but withheld from Pilate and Caiaphas. Sproul states, "There was no merit to which Saul could point as the reason for this visitation of grace. Paul, by his own testimony, was the chief of sinners. Christ did not wait for Saul to repent or otherwise incline his soul toward Christ before He manifested himself to him. Let others argue about the doctrine of irresistible grace. Paul did not debate it. He was redeemed by it. He knew that the grace he received in that hour was completely unmerited and was, to him, irresistible" (Sproul, *The Glory of Christ*, 216–17). This is a significant observation for many reasons. Regeneration, in this tradition, must precede conversion/faith, for it is the only thing that will allow one to see Christ for who he really is (as Pilate and Caiaphas could not). Second, grace is bestowed and not merely offered for the optional taking. Third, there may be grounds of considering the human response as "merit" if one is the instrumental cause in effecting regeneration.

God's interfering and prevenient grace, to believe in Christ apart from any permission or forethought given by the individual. This prevenient grace was simply bestowed upon the individual and not presented as an option to be received or rejected. An individual did not ask to have this prevenient grace come upon his or her will. The individual did not give consent for God to overcome his or her natural hostilities towards God. God simply acted on his own initiative in overcoming the obstinacy of the individual by bestowing prevenient grace.[102] This is the Wesleyan-Arminian view.[103]

This is not unlike the Reformed doctrine of prevenient-regenerating grace. God simply works in the heart of the individual, superseding the hostile will, and working before any human response to bring this person to faith. Even members of the Wesleyan-Arminian tradition have come to admit that prevenient grace is itself irresistible, though they will quickly emphasize that this irresistible grace provides the ability to resist grace.[104] Still, the Wesleyan-Arminian tradition's own teachings show grace as something that is bestowed, not merely offered. It does what the Reformed tradition clearly affirms, namely that God must work in the life of an individual before one can repent and believe.

Consider further the Arminian's view of passivity that is vital to their view of synergism. As shown above, synergism (in their view) has two

---

102. This observation is also made by Barrett, *Salvation by Grace*, 273–75 and Bavinck, *Reformed Dogmatics*, 4:84–86. Most importantly, it has been admitted to by some Arminians. See Collins, *The Theology of John Wesley*, 80–81. See also Reasoner, "John Wesley's Doctrines," 186. Granted, as Reasoner goes on to state, though everyone is under common grace, one may resist the preliminary grace given (bestowed?) on an individual. In other words, one may reject the promptings of the Spirit towards faith, and one may harden his or heart towards the things of God leaving them in a permanently lost state; however, one should still observe that this initial prevenient grace overcame their sinful disposition apart from consent.

103. See Rogers, *The Concept of Prevenient Grace*, 128–29. There, Rogers observes how this prevenient grace comes before any freedom or will in humanity in Wesley's theology. He also states that in Wesley's theology prevenient grace "is bestowed" (129). See also Shelton, "Initial Salvation," 1:485. There, Shelton states, "Wesleyan-Arminian theology has historically emphasized that the grace of God is universally offered but may be resisted by the perverse will of sinful humanity." Directly following this, he states, "Grace, however, enables fallen humanity to respond in faith." On the one hand, Shelton (and the Wesleyan-Arminian tradition as he also said) states that grace is never imposed on anyone. It is merely offered for the taking but can be refused or resisted. Immediately following, he states that all fallen humanity has been enabled with grace to respond in faith. This, however, was imposed. Shelton (like most within the Arminian tradition) does not clearly state *how* the Holy Spirit prevenes upon all humanity. He simply states that he does. However, even in this, the grace was issued, imposed, and became effective. It effected the ability to respond in faith. This is a conflict of terms.

104. Knight, "Love and Freedom," 60.

forms. There is an active part whereby one must repent and believe and a passive part where one simply does not resist.[105] Passivity is another way of saying that God acts upon a person (by his grace) apart from any act done on behalf of the individual. This clearly is not an offer or invitation. It is a bestowal of grace.

As such, the Reformed tradition which sees God working beforehand through regeneration by his grace to lead a person to repentance and faith appears to be the more consistent of the two parties. God does show prevenient grace in the Reformed view, but the prevenience is regeneration and the grace is bestowed and efficacious. He does not, in this view, bring one merely to a point of decision making leaving it up to him or her to exercise free will. The quote from E. Earle Ellis is worthy of mentioning again:

> Some suppose that if our will is "Free" to accept or reject Christ, many will accept him. But is that true? If our first parents (Gen 1–3), whose wills were truly free, chose against God, do we suppose that any of their children, sullied by sin from earliest experiences, would make a more godly choice than they? . . . "Free will" is precisely what God permits to the terminally unrepentant, and it is a one-way ticket to destruction in Hell. If salvation came through our free choice, we would all be lost.[106]

Another consideration should be made whether grace is a gift that is offered or bestowed. It deals with the efficacy of the atonement. Gordon H. Clark makes the observation that in Arminianism, Christ died not in order to save some but to make salvation possible. He did not, according to Clark, procure reconciliation for anyone or receive a chosen people. Instead, he merely removed the obstacle to make people salvable. This leads Clark to say that (according to the Arminian view) the atonement has no efficacy insofar as application goes, it makes salvation a work of the human's free will (because one chooses to be more spiritual, clever, determined, or sensitive than others), it is up to an individual (not Christ) to apply redemption, and it conflicts certain Scriptural passages (such as Isa 53:11).[107] However, it is not only the accusations of the monergists that the atonement offers potentiality and not actuality; it is the admittance of the Arminian party. Thos Summers, in addressing the question of whether the atonement reconciled

---

105. Olson, *Arminian Theology*, 160.

106. Ellis, *The Sovereignty of God in Salvation*, 5.

107. Clark, *The Atonement*, 139–40. George Smeaton makes a similar observation in *Christ's Doctrine of the Atonement*, 372–73. He says the Arminian view where reconciliation is merely possible strips the atonement of all its efficacy. He does so elsewhere in *The Doctrine of the Atonement According to the Apostles*, 537–40.

God to humanity, states that Christ satisfied reconciliation of God to humanity thereby *offering* pardon to the world through the atonement (though not actually securing anyone into that atonement in particular).[108] While one should note that not all monergists affirm this perspective (as it comes very close to affirming Limited Atonement—found amongst many but not all monergists), it is still worth noting that the Arminian tradition believes Christ's work on the cross had no direct efficacy in securing humanity into a right relationship with God. Such would violate the human will. However, texts such as Ephesians 1:7–10, Colossians 1:20–22, and Hebrews 9:12 seem to indicate something different.

Faith

Another area worthy of consideration is the notion of faith, particularly in the non-Reformed tradition. As said above, synergism is advocated for in this tradition through a passive act (not resisting) as well as by an active act (faith). Again, Thomas Oden said, "Grace prepares the will and coworks with the prepared will. Insofar as grace precedes and prepares free will it is called prevenient. Insofar as grace accompanies and enables human willing to work with divine willing, it is called cooperative grace."[109] Oden went on to say that the cooperating work of the human is free consent to God and the response of faith.[110]

Again, to reiterate, Dongell and Walls used the illustration of one who was bound, gagged, blindfolded, and drugged inside a prison where one received a serum that overcame these effects and allowed them to escape should they trust and follow their rescuer. The synergism, here, is the act of leaving the current state and following the rescuer to salvation from this misery. Faith is made to be a non-meritorious work which is shown by the individual leading to redemption.

Wesley, likewise, believed that God liberates the will to work out one's own salvation by the expression of faith.[111] The Holy Spirit takes the first initiative in salvation through prevenient grace (something Wesley sometimes referred to as "revelation"); however, as one commentator on Wesley's views

---

108. Summers, *Systematic Theology*, 238–39.

109. Oden, *Transforming Power of Grace*, 47.

110. Ibid., 47–54.

111. Wesley, "On Working Out Our Own Salvation," in *The Essential Works of John Wesley*, 328–29. See also Knight, "Love and Freedom," 62–63.

THE ASPECT OF CONVERSION

states: "God alone makes the encounter possible. But God cannot effect this encounter unless His human partner responds to the divine overture."[112]

Faith, they claim, is the activity of humankind which cooperates with God's prevenient grace. God is the superior worker in this view because of his work in prevenient grace; however, the individual is none-the-less important in this cooperative process, even called at times a "crucial partner."[113]

As has been shown throughout this study, one of the central flaws in the Wesleyan-Arminian tradition is faith is reckoned to be an activity which effects an outcome. As shown in chapter 1, each tradition surveyed here understands "work" to be that which acquires, achieves, and effects. This is far different from a response or result. Faith can still be the act of an individual, but it need not be a work that contributes to a specific end. As shown from chapter 1, if an individual is a cause that leads to an effect, this is a work. While this tradition claims that faith is a non-meritorious work, it is a work in their view nonetheless. However, as shown in chapter 1 and throughout this study, faith contrasts works.[114] This is not merely a matter of being careless with terminology. It is embedded in their theology. Unless faith is shown by and from the individual, regeneration will not occur. The faith and repentance, they claim, is the contributing factor (not the result of divine work) in bringing about new life. Through their actions, the effect is brought about. This relates to the next matter of efficient cause and instrumental means.

---

112. Staples, "John Wesley's Doctrine of the Holy Spirit," 94. One Wesleyan scholar states that, for Wesley, "When he turns to God, it is grace (prevenient) co-operating with grace (redemptive). And this redemptive grace is conceived of as infused rather than imputed. It effects not simply a changed relationship but a changed nature" (Peters, *Christian Perfection and American Methodism*, 43; parenthetical remarks original). This is an interesting observation. God works through prevenient grace allowing one to turn to God. He or she then cooperates (synergistically) with God in redemptive grace in the act of turning away from sin and placing faith in Christ (conversion). Faith and repentance, again, are shown to be works. Notice, moreover, that they are causes that lead to an effect. They lead to an infusion (not imputation) of redemptive grace. Synergism leads to (or effects) redemptive grace. This is showing human activity as a work.

113. Olson, *The Mosaic of Christian Belief*, 277. Note also that here Olson contrasts synergism and the "cooperative project" with monergism which believes salvation is "entirely the work of God." As Olson goes on to say here, salvation cannot be "entirely the work of God" because an individual must exercise faith, which means he or she is synergistically/cooperatively involved. The meanings of synergism and cooperation (as "work together") should not be minimized, though, to be clear, Olson and other Arminians fully affirm (perhaps inconsistently) that their view does not make faith a work.

114. See also Grudem, *Systematic Theology*, 730–32; Erickson, *Christian Theology*, 954; and Demarest, *The Cross and Salvation*, 262–63.

Efficient Cause

The Reformed tradition, as said above, believes that the efficient cause of conversion (and regeneration) is monergistic. God works in the lives of the individual so that they may express godly sorrow and faith. Repentance and faith are evidences of God's monergistic work through the prevenient act of regeneration.

The non-Reformed tradition, as shown above, does not hold to this view. For them, the cause for conversion is the synergistic activity between God's prevenient grace and the human who gives assent to the operation of God.[115] Through this combined effort, the result will be conversion.

Paul Helm rightly clarifies the issue. He states that repentance is a necessary aspect of true conversion; however, it is not a condition to be fulfilled so that one may be converted or find favor with God.[116] Faith, he goes on to say, accompanies true repentance. The faith, however, is not some self-effort or moral reform invoked upon personal choice and volition. Rather, God grants this awareness and enables the person to respond to Christ the way one should.[117] John R. W. Stott says well that humankind is not justified "by" faith (or because of it as if it were a work that God rewards) as much as "by" God's grace and the blood of Christ; therefore, one is saved by God's grace and the sacrifice of Christ with humankind's faith being what unites him or her to Christ.[118]

In one of the foundational texts that show the contrast between faith and works, Ephesians 2:8–9 states: "For by grace you have been saved through faith; and that not of yourselves, it is the gift of God; not as a result of works, so that no one may boast." Again, the Wesleyan-Arminian tradition says that the work which individuals do is faith; however, faith in this text contrasts works.[119] Moreover, faith (if it is a work) is grounds to boast because these individuals heeded the prevenient grace of God leading to everlasting blessing and joy while others did not. Since the faith is

---

115. Craig, "Middle Knowledge," 157.
116. Helm, *The Beginnings*, 65.
117. Ibid., 81.
118. Stott, *The Cross of Christ*, 190.
119. NIDNT, s.v. "Grace," 119 states, "The apostle (Paul in light of Rom 3:24–26) unfolds the reality and power of *charis* in a stubborn conflict with Rab. ideas of justification by works and synergism ... This leads him to set up in contrast two antithetical, mutually exclusive series of ideas: grace, gift, the righteousness of God, superabundance, faith, gospel, calling, in grace and hope on the one side; and law, reward, sin, works, accomplishment owed, one's own righteousness, honour, worldly wisdom, futility on the other side."

the contributing work of an individual, and certain individuals exercised it while others did not, there is certainly grounds for boasting.[120]

The Reformed tradition, however, does not make faith a work. God is the efficient cause of conversion. He brings it about because of regeneration, and faith and repentance are the by-products of regeneration. Genuine repentance and faith are still shown in this view; however, they are not works that acquire a certain end.[121]

Instrumental Means

While the Reformed tradition's view of the instrumental means mentioned above is fairly straightforward (namely that God is also the instrumental means through which conversion occurs), the non-Reformed tradition's view is quite complex. Here one must keep in mind their notion of prevenient grace whereby God overcomes the effects of sin so that a person may freely illicit a response via a free will.

As said above, the Wesleyan-Arminian tradition's view of the instrumental cause is the human will. Through prevenient grace, one is able to make a choice to be converted or not to be converted. If the individual wills conversion, one will be converted. Such willing could not occur without the work of God; hence, it is called cooperative.[122] Olson says that it is a free response towards the Gospel, to desire to repent and believe.[123] The instrumental cause of conversion, in their view, is not faith but the willing to have faith and a desire to believe in the things of God.[124] When one desires to believe in God, then one will believe in God leading to conversion.

While the Reformed tradition would not deny that an individual does, in fact, desire to believe in Christ and turn away from sin (the essence of conversion), it would question if *self-driven* desire through the liberating

120. Carson, *Exegetical Fallacies*, 121–22.

121. Warfield, *Biblical and Theological Studies*, 363 makes a helpful observation reflective of monergists. There, he states that there is synergism taught in the New Testament (particularly Eph 2:10 and elsewhere). One does engage in synergistic activity in relation to regeneration; however, it is only after regeneration has occurred. To carry out good works in faith and faithfulness and to repent from sin is something that one does in cooperation with God, but this is not in order to become regenerate but because one is regenerate, according to Warfield. One sees here how such actions are not efficient or instrumental causes that lead to an effect but are the effect themselves.

122. Oden, *Transforming Power of Grace*, 51–55.

123. Olson, *Arminian Theology*, 159–61.

124. This has to be the only logical alternative. It would be irrational to believe that the instrumental means of conversion is faith because conversion itself is faith (and repentance).

work of God was the means to conversion.¹²⁵ In the non-Reformed view, God prevenes upon all people whereby they are at a crossroads. If one chooses to go in the direction of faith, then one will be converted, and if one goes in the direction of disbelief, one will not be converted.

Once again, it appears that it is the human will that must perform its work so that conversion may be accomplished. The human desire (albeit freed by God from its depraving effects) must perform its duty so that conversion may occur. This has been unsettling to many within the Reformed party, most notably Martin Luther, who claims that one can do nothing simply from within themselves but is entirely dependent upon grace to be made new and become a new creation. The Spirit of God must recreate (in the regenerative sense) the hearts of people whereby they can begin to will as they should. Such desires do not, he would claim, come from within but only from without.¹²⁶

CONCLUSION

This study has surveyed the traditions of the Reformed and non-Reformed parties and their perspectives on the aspect of conversion. Some underlying and underemphasized issues were raised as potential sources for disagreement. An evaluation of these perspectives was done whereby one may make the following conclusions.

First, the non-Reformed tradition affirms prevenient grace whereby God overcomes the effects of sin and allows individuals the opportunity to believe. However, their definition of prevenient grace is virtually identical with and corresponding to the definition of regeneration (which is the Reformed view). Though different language is used, the functionality is the same leading one to support the monergists' notion of regeneration.

Second, the non-Reformed party wishes to present grace as an offer to be accepted or rejected in an effort to preserve the goodness of God who would not force his will upon the unwilling. However, this study has shown how the Wesleyan-Arminian tradition's notion of prevenient grace does exactly that, namely imposing divine will upon the unwilling. The Reformed tradition, however, views this as a sign of God's (regenerating) grace while the non-Reformed tradition views this as contrary to the goodness of God.

125. While Joachim Jeremias certainly sees repentance as an activity of an individual, he rightly states, "Repentance is not an act of human humility or human self-mastery; it is being overwhelmed by the grace of God . . . Repentance takes place in the light of the gospel; only the opening of his eyes to God's goodness makes a man recognize his guilt and the distance that separates him from God" (*New Testament Theology*, 157).

126. Luther, *The Bondage of the Will*, 289.

THE ASPECT OF CONVERSION

Given their notions of prevenient grace whereby God interposes his divine transforming will upon the unwilling, this tradition fails to be consistent, and the argument best supports the monergistic view.

Third, the non-Reformed tradition continually makes faith as a work, often unknowingly. It is a contributing, efficacious effort on behalf of humankind. Through biblical survey provided throughout this study, one may affirm along with the monergistic party that faith is not a work and may furthermore conclude that it is the by-product of regeneration.

Finally, because faith is made a work, the Wesleyan-Arminian party views the efficient cause of conversion to be synergistic. However, when one views faith not as a work but as a response to the divine work of regeneration (i.e., the monergistic view), then one is not presented with the difficulties of this matter. God, then, can rightly be called the Savior, and the human can rightly be called the blessed recipient. As such, this study concludes on balance that conversion is monergistic and that the monergistic tradition presents the most conclusive and consistent argumentation between the two parties.

Chapter 5

The Aspect of Justification in the Monergistic Protestant Tradition

THE APPROACH OF EXAMINATION

ARGUABLY, THE ASPECT OF salvation that is debated more than any other is the aspect of justification. It is the aspect that has caused a lasting schism between Catholics and Protestants since the Reformation Period. This is not to mention the divides amongst the Protestant tradition especially in light of new proposals brought forth by E. P. Sanders, James D. G. Dunn, and N. T. Wright (to name a few) which have come to be known as *The New Perspective on Paul*.

Interestingly, while the previous aspects of salvation covered thus far particularly concern divisions in the Reformed and non-Reformed traditions of Protestant theology, there is not significant disagreement between these two camps on the notion of justification, particularly whether it is monergistic or synergistic.[1] That is to say that Arminian synergists and Re-

---

1. Hence, while some may consider themselves synergists, there are aspects in soteriology where they could be considered monergists (and *vice-versa* as shown in chapter 1). See, for example, Roger Olson who claims that the Arminian doctrine of justification (stemming from Jacob Arminius's own doctrine of justification) sees the Holy Spirit as the efficient cause of justification, Christ as the meritorious cause of justification, and faith as the instrumental cause of justification in *Arminian Theology*, 206. This is not to say that there are not significant differences and even some fractions towards synergistic justification. For example, Thomas Nettles explores what was covered in the previous chapter on conversion on how some are able to place their faith (an essential element to justification in the Protestant tradition) in Christ while others

JUSTIFICATION IN THE MONERGISTIC PROTESTANT TRADITION

formed monergists find common ground (as a whole) in the monergistic aspect of justification.[2] Such cannot be said for those parties and the Roman Catholic Church.

Given the various interpretations of justification between these two traditions (monergistic Protestantism and Roman Catholicism), this chapter will examine both of these perspectives individually looking for possible underlying and underemphasized issues particularly focusing on whether or not synergism or monergism have a role. To carry out this task, comparative analysis will be used beginning with, in this chapter, the monergistic Protestant tradition (hereafter simply monergistic tradition) followed by an examination of the Roman Catholic position.

Before such an examination of the monergistic view can be done, however, one must be mindful how this tradition arrived at its conclusions. As such, a historical survey is in order followed by the monergistic tradition's understanding of righteousness in their biblical interpretation.

TRACING THE DEFINITION AND DEBATE

While it is simple enough to say as many do that the Scriptures use the Hebrew term *tsedek* (צדק) and the Greek term *dikaios* (δίκαιος) in connoting forensic imagery in the doctrine of salvation, what is not as simple is how one should translate and define these terms and their cognates into modern English as well as how one is to understand these terms (or aspects) doctrinally. The various uses of the צדק and δίκ- roots are translated into modern English as: "right," "righteous," and "righteousness," as well as "just," "justice," "justify," and "justification."[3] With such a variety of meanings, it is no wonder that these terms have sparked centuries' worth of debate, a

---

do not. He claims that (as it relates to justification) faith is a gift given to the elect by effectual grace and not the human will. See *By His Grace and For His Glory*, 287–88. See also the James Hervey and John Wesley controversies in Nettles, "John Wesley's Contention with Calvinism: Interactions Then and Now," in Nettles, *The Grace of God, The Bondage of the Will*, 2:306–9. The point being made is that there are not significant contentions within the Reformed and non-Reformed parties that justification is based in Christ's righteousness through union with him by faith, though there are some exceptions to this.

2. Slaatte, in *The Arminian Arm of Theology*, 55 states: "The Arminian view of justification by faith is basically that held by the Reformers."

3. Koehler and Baumgartner, *The Hebrew and Aramaic Lexicon of the Old Testament*, s.v. צדק and Bauer, *A Greek-English Lexicon of the New Testament*, s.v. δίκαιος. References will be made here and throughout to the δίκ- root. While not a word in itself, it is the root for various derivatives such as δίκη, δικαιοσυνη, δικαίος, δικαιωσις, and others.

lasting schism in the Christian church, and, more recently, debate of the meaning of the terms from the *New Perspective on Paul*.[4] A historical survey will show the various understandings of these aspects.

The Patristic Era

While the Protestant Reformation of the sixteenth century certainly brought to a head the definitions and redefinitions of the צדק and δίκ- word groups (requiring the attention of various councils such as Trent and, later, Vatican II), the original debate over the meaning and significance of these terms came much earlier (during the fourth and fifth centuries), through the influential works of Augustine of Hippo.[5] Indeed, Augustine's own definitions of righteousness would develop throughout his lifetime making one appreciate the difficulty in defining the terms.

While earlier in his Christian life, Augustine thought that the beginnings of faith and a right relationship with God were a result of human free will to call upon God to save, upon questions regarding predestination by Simplicianus, Augustine was forced to redevelop and redefine his understanding. The result was that one's free will was held captive by sin but liberated by the justifying work of God. Such justification, according to Augustine, progressively *made* one righteous (by the operating grace/monergistic work of God) as opposed to *declaring* one righteous, and through cooperation with God (synergistically), the individual pursues a lifelong process of bringing that justification to perfection and completion.[6]

---

4. This study will break up the aspect of δίκ- into two parts. Given the uniqueness of the two different Greek words δικαιοσύνη and δικαίωσις, this study will first examine righteousness and then justification. One may well ask why there should be separate sections for "righteousness" and "justification" when the Hebrew and Greek terms can mean either. As will be shown below, there is a distinction between justification (the legal pronouncement) and righteousness (that which covers the believer through union with Christ).

5. This is not to say that matters of justification and righteousness were not of importance during the first three centuries of the church. Rather, the mentioning of these aspects was minimal as the focus of theological attention was given largely to Christological and Trinitarian issues. Likewise, much of the discussion regarding justification was related to the concept of *liberum arbitrium* (free will) and *meritum* (merit) making the timely response of Augustine's doctrine of justification and righteousness all the more significant to the debate. See McGrath, *Iustitia Dei*, 33–38.

6. Ibid., 38–44. See also Garrett, *Systematic Theology*, 2:290–92. Augustine himself once affirmed, "[T]he assistance of the divine grace towards our justification, by which God co-operates in all things for good with those who love Him, and whom He first loved—giving to them (a renewed nature) that He might receive from them" (Augustine, "A Treaties on the Grace of Christ, And On Original Sin" in *Augustin*, 1.55,

JUSTIFICATION IN THE MONERGISTIC PROTESTANT TRADITION

Having greatly influenced Western Christianity with his views on justification, Augustinian debate over the nature of righteousness (and the full meanings and implications of the צדק and δικ- word groups particularly with regards to whether it is imputed or infused, operative or cooperative, stative or progressive) carried over into the Middle Ages.

The Middle Ages

Just how closely related the terms *righteousness* and *justification* should be and how these aspects ought to be appropriated gave medieval theologians much to debate. Indeed, the church of the Middle Ages explored in great detail exactly how the God who justifies cooperates with the sinner to make the individual righteous, largely due to the influence of Augustine. Since such synergism begs the question of the ability and freedom of the will, much attention was given to the effects of sin, the types of grace, and the modes of infusion/reception. However, what concerns this study is that the prevalent teachings of the day juxtaposed the human works of the sacraments against the divine work of justification.

The relationship between the sacraments and righteousness is seen clearly in the writings of perhaps the greatest Medieval Catholic theologian, Thomas Aquinas. While it should be stressed that for Aquinas, like Augustine before him, salvation is not a human merit but, rather, a divine gift of grace through Christ, he also believed that grace was dispensed by the priests through the sacraments from the source of all righteousness, which is Christ.[7] The sacraments, then, were the consent of the believer to the co-operation of God who desires the individual to exercise free will.

Aquinas's views can be seen well in the following statement which highlights God being the justifier, humankind the consenting cooperator, sacraments as the vessel of grace, grace (namely righteousness) being infused, and provision being made for those like infants (and others that are impaired to exercise their free-will):

5:236. Augustine's synergistic view that justification involves the making (rather than declaring) of individuals as righteous is not indicative of the views of the majority of modern monergists who agree with him in many other respects. As stated in chapter 1, one can be monergistic in certain areas and synergistic in others. Augustine is an example of this.

7. Hill, *The History of Christian Thought*, 160. It should be noted that for Aquinas and other Medieval theologians, the sacraments, while performed by humans, were themselves seen as a divine grace in and of themselves. See also Pfurtner, *Luther and Aquinas on Salvation*, 82–89.

> Hence in him who has the use of reason, God's motion to justice does not take place without a movement of the free-will; but He so infuses the gift of justifying grace that at the same time He moves the free-will to accept the gift of grace, in such as are capable of being moved thus. Infants are not capable of the movement of their free-will; hence it is by the mere infusion of their souls that God moves them to justice ... he does not obtain justifying grace by the exterior rite of Baptism, or of any other sacrament, unless he intended to make use of this sacrament, and this can only be by the use of his free-will.[8]

As to what constituted a sacrament and how the sacrament should be administered, there was much disagreement; however, Peter Lombard in his *Libri Quattuor Sententiarum* systematized seven sacraments which were widely accepted throughout the church and later developed by Aquinas. The seven sacraments were: baptism, confirmation, communion, matrimony, penance, extreme unction, and ordination.[9] These sacramental acts, it was viewed, *infused* or *injected* righteousness (oftentimes called "grace"), to the believer almost as though righteousness were a substance or force that is imparted to the believer and must be acquired to a sufficient level before one has a fully restored and right-standing relationship with God.[10]

With such an overwhelming amount of authority (and money) given to the church (particularly to the priests who performed the sacraments), it is of no wonder that abuses developed over the issue of righteousness. If righteousness was attainable by human actions, albeit with divine assistance, the question then becomes, "What of those believers who have not attained complete righteousness?" Naturally, this led into the doctrine of purgatory, the selling of indulgences, and formalized works of penance. It is against these abuses (amongst others) that Martin Luther would protest bringing the precise nature of righteousness and justification to its most public and divisive point.

The Reformation

It is ironic that the tradition that founded its sacramental theology upon and prided itself in the Augustinian tradition would later be accused of succumbing to Pelagianism by Martin Luther. While Luther and Augustine

---

8. Aquinas, *Summa Theologica*, I/II, q. 113, a. 3.
9. Berkouwer, *Studies in Dogmatics*, 28–36. See also McGrath, *Iustitia Dei*, 117–28.
10. Berkouwer, *Dogmatics*, 16, 32–34. Baillie, *The Theology of the Sacraments*, 52.

would differ on the doctrine of justification, the two would find agreement on the doctrine of grace.[11]

In his challenge against the abuses of the sacraments in the church, Luther, in "The Babylonian Captivity of the Church," spoke against those who would, "[M]easure righteousness and holiness by the greatness, number, or other quality of the works! But God measures them by faith alone, and with him there is no difference among works, except insofar as there is a difference in faith."[12]

By late AD 1515, Luther departed from the soteriology of the *via moderna* emphasizing more of a *fides Christi* in contrast to the seemingly Pelagian notions of the Catholic Church at the time.[13] In contrast to the late medieval church, Luther contrasted the righteousness which belongs to God bound in his essence with the righteousness which is freely given by God through faith in Christ.[14] For Luther, one becomes justified by turning away from sin and seizing Christ in faith whereby God imputes (or reckons through legal pronouncement, not *infuses* various amounts through sacraments) Christ's righteousness to the believer giving the believer a new, right status before God, namely one that is justified.[15]

As the abuses of the medieval church had worldwide effects, many within Europe welcomed John Calvin's contributions on justification by faith. He writes, "On the contrary, justified by faith is he who, excluded from the righteousness of works, grasps the righteousness of Christ through faith,

---

11. McGrath, *Iustitia Dei*, 209, 224. To be clear, while the Reformers thought that Augustine was forerunner for their doctrine of grace (and indeed they were agreed in terms of divine priority to human action), Augustine did believe (contrary to the Reformers) that grace operates in individuals for the increase of merit that will lead to final salvation. See González, *A History of Christian Thought*, 2:47. Still, B. B. Warfield is correct in saying that the Reformation was a revival of Augustine (not in terms of justification but) in terms of grace, particularly prevenient grace, in Warfield, *Calvin and Augustine*, 322–23. As Forde in *On Being A Theologian of the Cross*, 29 observes, there was agreement in the Catholic Church that it is impossible to be saved without grace. The issue at hand was whether someone was able to do works which would prepare him or her for grace, something which Luther would (as evidenced by thesis 13 of the *Heidelberg Disputation*) reject. See also Lane, *Justification by Faith in Catholic-Protestant Dialogue*, 68.

12. Luther, "The Babylonian Captivity of the Church," 199.

13. McGrath, *Luther's Theology of the Cross*, 126–29.

14. Ibid., 114.

15. McGrath, *Iustitia*, 227, 229. See also Garret, *Systematic Theology*, 294–95. These two authors show that there is a strong tradition that distinguishes (though does not separate) righteousness from justification. Righteousness is that which is imputed (or to some *infused*) to the believer in faith while justification is the legal pronouncement that one has a right standing in the eyes of the Judge, namely God. See also Köstlin, *The Theology of Luther*, 2:411 and Lane, *A Concise History of Christian Thought*, 159–60.

and clothed in it, appears in God's sight not as a sinner but as a righteous man."[16] Calvin, like Luther, believed that righteousness is imputed to the believer who lays hold of Christ in faith bringing together (though he still distinguished) imputation and union with Christ.[17] By one's unity with Christ by faith, one is imputed with Christ's righteousness, clothing the believer with a grace that makes him or her acceptable to God.[18]

The Modern Period

Being sixteen centuries departed from the biblical authors, however, has made some recent scholars question whether Martin Luther, John Calvin, and the Protestant church as a whole have understood the New Testament

---

16. Calvin, *Institutes*, III.XI.II.

17. Mackinnon, *Calvin and the Reformation*, 237–38.

18. Wendel, *Calvin*, 258. Here it is worthwhile to note that Calvin did speak of faith being an instrumental *cause*. This is found in III.XIV.XVII of his *Institutes*. Does this mean that Calvin held to faith being the human instrument that causes salvation? Calvin's response would be a vehement, "No." In fact, that is the very thing that he addresses in this section, which is entitled "*In no respect can works serve as the cause of our holiness*" of which he contrasts faith and works. Indeed, he speaks of faith as that by which one is received into grace out of mercy. See also III.XI.VII and III.XVIII.VIII. For further discussion that Calvin saw faith as an instrument and not as that which merits righteousness as though it were a work, see Lane, *Justification by Faith in Catholic-Protestant Dialogue*, 22 and Garcia, *Life In Christ*, 117–19. So why would Calvin speak of an instrumental cause if he did not see faith as a cause which leads to the effect of salvation? In this same section where he speaks of faith as instrumental cause (III.XIV.XVII), Calvin says, "The philosophers postulate four kinds of causes to be observed in the outworking of things. If we look at these, however, we will find that, as far as the establishment of our salvation is concerned, none of them has anything to do with works." The editor (John T. McNeill) provides a helpful footnote to Calvin's referent, which is Aristotle, *Physics* ii.3,7 in *Basic Works* and Aquinas, *Summa Theologica*, I.xix.VIII; II/II.xv.I–II. Calvin appears to be merely working within their framework (which is the attempt of this study) with attempts to qualify elsewhere that faith itself does not cause the effect of salvation. This is different from how the Roman Catholics (and others) view instrumentality because, for them, they are not merely working within a philosophical framework but are articulating faith as a cause that effects a given outcome. For Calvin, entry into the covenant was entirely of grace, and faith and obedience were responses to that covenant not actions (or works?) which effect the covenant. See Hoekema, "The Covenant of Grace in Calvin's Teaching," 55–56. Moreover, see the excellent analysis of Calvin's use of the four causes by Jonathan H. Rainbow. He observes how Calvin utilized the Aristotelian model of causation because of its usefulness in expressing the unity and complexity of salvation. Regarding the *causa instrumentala*, Rainbow observes that, for Calvin, faith did not cause salvation. He states that the death of Christ is the cause of salvation, and God acts through faith in such a way to carry out efficacy for his saving act. Such was the theology of Calvin. See Rainbow, *The Will of God and the Cross*, 94 and 89–109.

JUSTIFICATION IN THE MONERGISTIC PROTESTANT TRADITION

doctrine of justification properly. It is unquestionable that the apostle Paul (who wrote on the doctrine of justification and righteousness more than any other biblical author) was not faced with abuses of sacraments and the financial abuses of indulgences as were the sixteenth-century reformers. Could Luther, Calvin, and Zwingli been influenced by the religious discord of their day to such an extent where they eisegete sixteenth-century problems onto a first-century text? Some scholars in modern Pauline scholarship would affirm so. This has led these individuals to study how a first-century audience would have understood the doctrines of justification and righteousness in light of covenant expectations and the makeup of the community of God.[19] Vatican II, moreover, reaffirmed traditional Roman Catholic understanding of justification by means of the sacraments, though it softened the Church's stance on salvation outside of the Catholic Church.[20]

Much more could be said about the history and development of justification and righteousness throughout Christian history; however, this survey has gone far enough to make the necessary following conclusions: 1. There is ambiguity on how one should translate צדק and δικ- word groups. 2. There is disagreement on whether righteousness is imputed or infused, operative or cooperative, stative or progressive. 3. Union with Christ takes a considerable role of importance in the monergists' understanding of righteousness. 4. Monergism and synergism may play a significant role in the division between church traditions.

---

19. This area of study, often called the "New Perspective on Paul," is considerable and cannot be dealt with thoroughly here. For an overview of this tradition, see Waters, *Justification and the New Perspectives on Paul*.

20. See *Vatican Council II*, "Lumen Gentium" 5.40, 157 where it states, "The followers of Christ, called by God not for their achievements but in accordance with his plan and his grace, and justified in the lord Jesus, by their baptism in faith have been truly made children of God and sharers in the divine nature, and are therefore really made holy." Notice that the Church affirms that this is all by grace and not by works, but notice also that it comes by baptism and that an individual is "made holy" rather than "reckoned holy." The next sentence after this one, though, says, "This holiness, therefore, which they have received by the gifts of God, they must maintain and perfect by their way of life" (156–57). Entry is by grace, though one must maintain (by certain acts as expressed through the sacraments) this status. See the next chapter for how the Roman Catholics softened their stance on salvation outside of the church.

THE ASPECT OF RIGHTEOUSNESS IN THE MONERGISTIC TRADITION

Monergistic Protestants' View of Righteousness in Scripture

The term *righteousness* has multiple references in the monergist tradition. Sometimes monergists emphasize the judicial aspect of righteousness, others the relational aspect of righteousness, and some the aspect of appropriate moral behavior. However, what is readily affirmed by the monergistic community is that righteousness must be understood in accordance with the character of God.[21] That is to say that such emphasis on the relational and judicial aspects of righteousness must be understood as it relates to the divine nature.[22]

It is particularly important to understand monergists' interpretation of the righteousness of God in the Old Testament. Thomas Schreiner gives a helpful insight at this point that is reflective of the monergistic community. For him (and other likeminded monergists), righteousness in the Old Testament has to do with fulfilling the requirements of a covenant relationship; however, it is not limited to it. He cites Genesis 38 as an example where Tamar (though she acted as a prostitute and thus being morally unrighteous) is reckoned to be more righteous than Judah because she carried out obligations of the covenant *and also* (and very importantly states Schreiner) conformed to a norm.[23] He further supports his claim that righteousness (in the Old Testament) refers not just to fulfilling expectations but also conforming to a norm by referencing Leviticus 19:36: "You shall have just balances, just weights, a just ephah, and a just hin: I am the Lord your God." When applied to God's people, their actions must also (says Schreiner) conform to a norm, and the norm (which Schreiner says is codified in the Old Testament law) that they should conform to is God himself.[24] Bruce Waltke, in a similar fashion, states: "[T]he righteousness that pleases God is rooted in faith in the truthfulness of his promises and in the goodness of his character."[25] This is to say that the righteous activity of God's people is a reflection of the righteous character of God which is based in himself.

---

21. Waltke, *An Old Testament Theology*, 289. Dyrness, *Themes in Old Testament Theology*, 53–55. Though dated, Ropes gives a helpful Old Testament survey in light of these matters in "'Righteousness' and 'The Righteousness of God,'" 211–20.

22. Buchanan, *The Doctrine of Justification*, 269.

23. Schreiner, *40 Questions About Christians and Biblical Law*, 109.

24. Ibid., 109–10.

25. Waltke, *An Old Testament Theology*, 289.

JUSTIFICATION IN THE MONERGISTIC PROTESTANT TRADITION

With this framework in mind, monergists go on to explain the other ways in which righteousness may be understood. As one author observes, righteousness is a relationship word.[26] While the basis for righteousness is in the character of God, it allows one to have proper relationship or standing before God or others (hence there is a judicial aspect whereby one may be reckoned as righteous—namely fulfilling expectations and conforming to the norm or unrighteous—a failure to meet expectations). Bringing all these concepts together, George Ladd states: "Basically, 'righteousness' is a concept of *relationship* . . . The righteous person is the one who in God's judgment meets the divine standard and thus stands in a right relationship with God. The norm of righteousness depends entirely on the nature of God."[27]

It is this judicial aspect (as it relates to justification) that concerns the attention of most monergists. What has been widely (though never universally) accepted by the monergistic community is that the δίκ- word group relates to one's right standing (or ability to be accepted and considered *just*) before God.[28] Monergists contend that first-century Jews believed that through meticulous observance of the law (Mosaic Law in particular) one could store up merit that would be used at the time of judgment to sway the verdict in favor of the offending individual.[29] While faith was always a condition of the covenant, monergistic Pauline interpreters view Paul's Jewish audience as having made faith a kind of work itself which brings forth merits for the Day of Judgment. Through Romans 3:20, Galatians 2:16, Ephesians 2:8–9, and others Paul (according to this tradition) reacts against any notions that an individual is able to bring about a right standing before God on one's own.[30] Simply observing the covenant expectations again will not satisfy the matter given that the transgressions go beyond the breaking of a moral code but are considered *sinful* before a God whose nature is the opposite of sin.

Since observance of the law after one becomes a transgressor is not the means for justification, the monergist position (as will be shown) views Paul explaining a new means by which individuals may be considered righteous.[31] Paul provides an illustration paralleling how one becomes unrighteous-

---

26. Graesser, "Righteousness, Human And Divine," 134.
27. Ladd, *A Theology of the New Testament*, 481; emphasis original.
28. See Buchanan, *The Doctrine of Justification*, 226.
29. Ibid., 54–57. This assumes the traditional perspective on Paul.
30. See Guthrie, *New Testament Theology*, 501.
31. This view is not exclusive to the monergist position; however, it is an important part of the monergistic position so as to show that the means of righteousness is not found in the abilities of humankind but in union with Christ.

ness with how one becomes righteous in Romans 5:12–21. Stating that in one man, Adam, all sinned and death spread to all humankind (v. 12), so judgment results to all humankind because all were in Adam (v. 19, see also 1 Cor 15:45–49). That is to say, by nature, one has a union with Adam that results in unrighteousness.[32]

Such union with Adam is contrasted with union with Christ according to the monergist tradition. Christ, who is called the second (or last) Adam (1 Cor 15:45, see also Rom 5:14), is believed to have succeeded in obedience where the first Adam failed in disobedience.[33] Romans 5:19 states: "For as through the one man's (Adam's) disobedience the many were made sinners, even so *through the obedience* of the One (Jesus, the second Adam) the many will be made righteous" (emphasis added). Monergists claim obedience is a reference to Christ's perfect obedience to the will and nature of God in his sinlessness as well as by his obedience to the point of death on the cross.[34] Just as those who are in Adam through sin are unrighteous, those who are in Christ through faith are considered righteous (Rom 3:22, 5:19, 8:30, Gal 2:16, 3:24).[35] There is therefore no fear of condemnation for those who are in Christ by faith because of what Christ has accomplished (Rom 8:33–34).[36]

To conclude, exegetically speaking monergists define righteousness as that which is right based upon the character of God. It is what allows for right standing or relationship before God and others. In that, there is a judicial aspect whereby the righteous are the ones who are declared to be in the right while the unrighteous would be declared to be in the wrong (thus guilty), for they failed to meet expectations. However, because righteousness also involves conformity to a norm, and the norm is bound up in the

---

32. Eldon Ladd, *A Theology of the New Testament*, 443.

33. Calvin, *Institutes*, II.XII.III and II.XVI.V–VII. For a non-Pauline view, see McCartney, "Atonement," 181–82.

34. Guthrie, *New Testament Theology*, 364; Ziesler, *Pauline Christianity*, 54–55; Polhill, *Paul and His Letters*, 173. Some claim that the obedience of Christ is his obedience to the Law which humankind failed to do whereby he is able to impute this obedience to the Law to believers who are united by faith to him. Others simply view this obedience to the obedience of death on a cross. It is perhaps best not to see these as two separate or conflicting ideas but rather accept both as true and valid. This is oftentimes called Christ's passive and active obedience where the former relates to his substitutionary death on the cross while the latter refers to his obedience to the entire Law of God. Without his active obedience, he could not have performed the passive obedience, and without the passive obedience, the active obedience could not be applied to believers. See White, *The God Who Justifies*, 94–96. One should observe, however, that many monergists make no mention of the active or passive obedience to Christ or do not emphasize it as a major issue. See, for example, Moo, *The Epistle to the Romans*, 225.

35. Tuckett, *Christology and the New Testament*, 52–53.

36. Berkhof, *Systematic Theology*, 448–51.

perfection of God, to be unjust is not just to be considered "in the wrong" but wicked and evil.[37]

Righteousness Defined Theologically

Having defined what monergists mean by righteousness, one must now consider how they use the term theologically. What is the relationship between righteousness and union with Christ? While a person is considered righteous through faith, is this righteousness merely reckoned to the believer or actualized in the believer? Is this righteousness complete within the individual or does a person need to do works that will acquire more righteousness to one's account? These are all questions monergists attempt to address.

The Aspects of the Aspect

What is of critical importance is to understand how righteousness relates to union with Christ in this tradition. As shown above, the righteousness of believers is external (or foreign) to themselves in this view. This righteousness comes about as a result of Christ's death, resurrection, and perfect life. This is to say that righteousness is an aspect (or part of) union with Christ and not its totality.

In Pauline writings, the phrases *in Christ, in the Lord, in Jesus Christ, in Him*, etc. appear two hundred and sixteen times and twenty-six times in the Johannine literature.[38] As such, these prepositional phrases combined with a noun referencing Jesus refer to what is being called here *union with Christ*. While the phrase is common, one may examine the different usages of the phrase to find numerous meanings.

Pauline epistles speak of being buried and raised *with Him* through faith (Gal 2:20, 5:24, Col 2:12, Rom 6:4, 11, 2 Tim 1:1 et.al.), being saved *in Christ* (2 Tim 2:10), being reconciled *through Christ* (Rom 5:11), and being members in Christ's body (Rom 12:5, 1 Cor 12:27). The Gospel of John speaks of abiding *in Christ* as the only means to bear spiritual fruit (signs that there is spiritual life and membership to the source of spiritual life, i.e., the vine) in John 15:5. Being in Christ carried the promises of fellowship with each member of the Trinity (John 17:21, see also 1 John 2:24). The idea is that one's union with Christ leads to death of the old self, salvation

37. Graesser, "Righteousness, Human And Divine," 135.
38. Demarest, *The Cross and Salvation*, 313.

of the new self, reconciliation, ability to do works that are pleasing to God, and more.[39]

The point to make is that union with Christ carries with it multiple facets and effects. That is to say, union with Christ, while being an aspect of salvation, is itself aspectual.[40] This is brought out best, perhaps, by John Calvin who wrote:

> Both things (mortification of sinful flesh and vivification of the human spirit) happen to us by participation (Lat. *participatione*, often translated *union*) in Christ. For if we truly partake in his death, "our old man is crucified by his power, and the body of sin perishes" (Rom 6:6 p.), that the corruption of original nature may no longer thrive. If we share in his resurrection, through it we are raised up into newness of life to correspond with the righteousness of God.[41]

For Calvin, the faith that binds the individual to Christ allows for the believer to experience a variety of benefits as a result of that union, namely the death of the old life which was in unrighteousness and the corresponding new life which is righteous before God.[42]

While lengthy discourses for each aspect of union with Christ are warranted, what concerns this study is how monergists define and use the term *righteousness*. As has been already shown, this party believes that to be in Christ is to be righteous; however, is this a righteousness that is actualized within the believer (meaning that one actually has the righteousness of Christ) or is the believer merely considered to have the righteousness of Christ?

---

39. Clowney, "The Biblical Doctrine of Justification by Faith," 46–50. See also Carson, "The Vindication of Imputation," 73.

40. Some theologians would state that union with Christ is not an aspect of salvation but simply a term for the whole of salvation. Millard Erickson would be one such example where he states, "[U]nion with Christ is an inclusive term for the whole of salvation; the various other doctrines are simply subparts" (*Christian Theology*, 961). While one can appreciate the significance of union with Christ in its entirety, this view is inadequate given that it fails to take into account the multi-aspectual nature of union with Christ and the way those aspects (and the aspect as a whole) relates to the other aspects of salvation. In other words, it is not that the whole of salvation is union with Christ, for union with Christ (while being strongly related to the other aspects) is not the other aspects itself. This will be made clearer below when one sees that union with Christ is the *basis for* (not the *same thing as*) justification.

41. Calvin, *Institutes*, III.III.IX.

42. See Wendel, *Calvin*, 256–58.

JUSTIFICATION IN THE MONERGISTIC PROTESTANT TRADITION

The Actuality of Righteousness

Theologians, particularly in the monergistic camp, are divided as to whether a believer actually *receives* the righteousness of Christ or is merely *reckoned* to have it. Calvin believed that, through one's union with Christ, the power of Christ's righteousness is actually transfused (Lat. *transfundit*) to the believer, though this is not the same thing as saying Christ's righteousness is transfused to the believer.[43] However, this language is used in reference to the sin of Adam being *communicated* to all persons by which Christ therefore communicates his righteousness to believers. As will be shown below, Calvin vehemently rejected any notion of the infusion of the essential righteousness of Christ whereby Christ imparts his own righteousness which is an eternal aspect of his divine character.[44]

However, the more dominant description that Calvin gave concerning righteousness is that it is *imputed* to believers through faith.[45] Despite interchangeable terms (though arguably not interchangeable ideas), the believer, according to Calvin, is fully engrafted into the body of Christ because of the union that the believer has whereby one is also a participator in the actual righteousness and fellowship of Christ's righteousness.[46] Luther, likewise, believed that believers actually have the righteousness of Jesus Christ. Like a bridegroom who fully takes in his bride and bestows what is his, so Christ takes in the believer and bestows every good blessing, including his righteousness, upon the individual.[47] He also said, "Through faith in Christ, therefore, Christ's righteousness becomes our righteousness and all that he has becomes ours; rather, he himself becomes ours."[48] Having the righteousness of Christ is also advocated for by modern monergists as well, though

---

43. Calvin, *Institutes*, II.I.VI. Here Calvin states "[I]t is well known that this (the hope of life) occurs in no other way than that wonderful communication whereby Christ transfuses into us the power of his righteousness" (248).

44. Ibid., III.XI.V. See also Lane, *Justification by Faith in Catholic-Protestant Dialogue*, 25.

45. See almost all of Calvin, *Institutes*, III.XI. The most common language is that of imputation (reckoning) paralleling the sin that is imputed to all persons by Adam.

46. Calvin, *Institutes*, III.XI.X. See also Wendel, *Calvin*, 256–57. Here it must be stressed that Calvin rejected any notion of the essential righteousness of Christ indwelling the believer (though he did affirm the mystical union one experiences as an engrafted member of the body of Christ, in accordance with 2 Peter 1:4, in *Institutes* III.XI.X). As such, one receives righteousness through imputation because of union with Christ rather than receiving the essential righteousness (or indwelling) of Christ as Calvin criticized Andreas Osiander of believing. See Wendel, *Calvin*, 236. See also Calvin, *Institutes*, III.XI.V.

47. Luther, *On Christian Liberty*, 32.

48. Luther, *Two Kinds of Righteousness*, 135.

never in terms of Christ's essential righteousness which is unique only to the triune Godhead.[49]

Some monergists (and others) claim that Christ's righteousness is merely reckoned to the believer but not actualized. Wayne Grudem would be one such example. Though Grudem would claim that the righteousness of Christ is actual to a believer (even claiming that it is "given" to the believer[50]), he would claim that it is actual in God's reckoning and proclaiming only. In other words, since God (in his act of justifying) considers a believer to have the righteousness of Christ, one has it (but only in the eyes of God, not in actuality). Grudem claims that if one actually had righteousness, this would be righteousness *in oneself* and therefore not *in Christ*. He also claims that if one were actually righteous, one would be changed to be internally righteous, and if changed internally righteous, then how could one stay without sin for the remainder of one's lifetime?[51] Michael Horton likewise states: "It is crucial to point out that the Reformation position has never been that *God's righteousness* is imputed . . . [T]his assumes that righteousness is a substance or a commodity that is transferred from one person to another."[52]

While it appears that these views are in conflict, remembering how monergists understand righteousness will clarify the issue. Before God, this tradition affirms that individuals stand guilty and in the wrong because of sin. This is an actual status held by them but does not mean that the status of unrighteousness is a substance infused within them. Righteousness in this tradition, as said above, connotes forensic imagery of legal status. Because one is *in Christ*, the individual shares the right standing before God that Christ does. Nowhere in the definition of righteousness given above do monergists state that an individual shares Christ's deity, absolute inherit perfection, or other incommunicable attributes. As such, this is a matter of perception. In this tradition, there is a sense where the individual does not share Christ's actual righteous, for Christ alone has perfectly fulfilled God's expectations and displays the perfected "norm." As such, the righteousness which one has by faith in Christ is not one's own inherent righteousness. Nevertheless, the judicial verdict that God pronounces is (in this tradition) according to what he actually sees. One is not unrighteous anymore due to union with Christ because of a status one actually has.[53]

49. For example, see White, *The God Who Justifies*, 94–95.
50. Grudem, *Systematic Theology*, 726.
51. Ibid., 727.
52. Horton, "Traditional Reformed View," 93.
53. To clarify the distinction and to resolve this tension, see White, *The God Who*

For Scriptural support, monergists supply the following: Romans 5:17 speaks of receiving the gift of righteousness (through faith in Christ), and verse 21 of the same chapter speaks of grace reigning through righteousness unto eternal life in the believer (contrasting the sin that once reigned in the believer).[54] In the letter addressed to the Corinthians who were said to be immoral, greedy, and idolatrous, Jesus is said to have washed, sanctified, and justified them (1 Cor 6:9–11), actually becoming sin so that they would become the righteousness of God in Christ (2 Cor 5:21, see 1 Cor 1:30).[55] Monergists furthermore affirm that Christ's righteousness is *imputed* (or reckoned) and not *infused*. Guy Prentiss Waters states that if Christ's righteousness were infused in the believer then the believer's sin would also be infused into Christ, which he claims goes against 2 Corinthians 5:21, "Him who knew no sin."[56]

A final point to make regarding the actuality of righteousness is that those who are united to Christ are not merely neutral in the eyes of God. While unrighteousness made the individual have a negative position, forgiveness would place the individual in a neutral position, as if nothing wrong had been done. However, this is not the position that monergists (and they would say the New Testament) would take given that a right standing before God is the essence of righteousness. In other words, a positive stance, not just neutrality, is received based upon one's union with Christ which is what is required (as will be shown) in justification.[57]

The Extent of Righteousness

The question then becomes, if a believer is righteous before God, to what extent is one righteous? In other words, does this righteousness increase over time as an individual pursues righteous acts, or is one completely righteous and in need of no further increase? It is at this point that all monergists would agree that righteousness is completed in the believer with no room (whether speaking metaphorically about completeness or inability to accept) for increasing righteousness.

Justifies, 88–91. Luther called this being *simul Justus et peccator*. For Calvin's affirmation of this, see Wendel, *Calvin*, 258.

54. Forrester, *A Righteousness of God For Unrighteous Men*, 119–23.

55. See Seifrid, *Christ, Our Righteousness*, 88.

56. Waters, *Justification and the New Perspectives on Paul*, 172.

57. Grudem makes this point in *Systematic Theology*, 725–26. See also Horton, "Traditional Reformed View," 95.

Naturally, this was at the heart of Martin Luther's theology of the Reformation. While in reference to the Roman Catholic Church's sacramental theology (which will be dealt with more thoroughly in chapter 6) that claimed that righteousness must be increased in an individual's life through participation in the sacraments, Luther claimed that something external to the individual's ability must produce Christian righteousness given that acts of the sacraments could be "done by any wicked person."[58] The language often adopted by Luther was that of "works." "Works" (defined as anything an individual must do in order to acquire, merit, or perform for salvation) of an individual bring condemnation in unrighteousness which contrast the "work" (referring to the *completed* work) of Jesus Christ in his death, burial, and resurrection which effects salvation for those who believe.[59]

Whether humankind has full or partial righteousness proved to be at the heart of Calvin's tensions with the German theologian Andreas Osiander. Calvin claimed that Osiander made a fundamental mistake when he defined righteousness as "essential" righteousness whereby Christ imparts his actual essence (i.e., moral perfection) to the believer through continual use of the sacraments.[60] Calvin responded to Osiander's objection that God does not justify those who are indeed wicked (by "wicked" he meant sinners whose nature is opposite of the divine nature, and because of that wicked nature they required a divine nature) by affirming that God does not justify apart from regenerating and beginning the lifelong process of sanctification (which is not the same thing as deification as Calvin claimed Osiander seemed to confuse).[61] That is to say that sanctification (becoming holy) is progressive while righteousness (having a right standing in the eyes of God) is not, and though they are related, they are distinct. God, Calvin said, does not justify and declare righteous in part (as would be the case in Osiander's theology), nor would any mere portion of righteousness make one actually pleasing to God, but rather the believer has been imputed with

---

58. Luther, *On Christian Liberty*, 5.

59. Ibid., 8–11. Alister McGrath notes that by late 1514, Luther came to the realization that the righteousness which God requires comes through the humiliation of humankind (an admittance that the individual is in all ways helpless, hopeless, and incapable of bring about justification), and that the means through which one might receive this righteousness is only through faith (an admittance of one's own helplessness and the sufficiency of Christ's work on the cross). See McGrath, *Luther's Theology of the Cross*, 153–55.

60. Calvin, *Institutes*, III.XI.V–XII. See also Horton, "Traditional Reformed View," 94.

61. Calvin, *Institutes*, III.XI.XI. See also Gossett, *The Doctrine of Justification*, 70–76.

the righteousness of Christ through union with Christ making the believer righteous (not divine) in whole in the eyes of God.[62]

THE EFFICIENT CAUSE OF RIGHTEOUSNESS

Having hopefully clarified the meaning of the ambiguous δικ- root (showing how it has been defined historically, biblically, and theologically) in this tradition, one is now in a position to examine how the monergist camp views the efficient cause of righteousness.

A helpful place to begin in examining the efficient cause is to be reminded of where righteousness cannot be sourced according to this tradition. As has already been shown, monergists affirm that sin results in unrighteousness. To break God's law (i.e., sin) is to result in an unfavorable status in the eyes of the Judge. The monergist position has shown throughout this study that humankind has sinned and is in a state of unrighteousness. Since righteousness and unrighteousness are antonyms, the efficient cause of righteousness cannot be in the individual person. As has been shown, any denial of sin (and thus unrighteousness) and its depraving effects upon humanity amounts to Pelagianism and not a viable option to this party. Moreover, it has also been shown that, since the individual is unrighteous, he or she is incapable of progressively attaining righteousness through works of faith and obedience. According to monergists throughout church history, humankind is in need of a foreign, eternal righteousness, but where does this righteousness come from if not from within?

In the opening of Book Three of the *Institutes*, John Calvin stated that by faith one communes with Christ by which all believers partake in his benefits. However, it is not just Christ's benefits but Christ *himself* that the believer receives.[63] It is here that one sees Calvin's understanding of causation. The Father (specifically his mercy and love) is the efficient cause, Christ's obedience (to be discussed below) is the material cause, and faith is the instrumental cause.[64] Through union with Christ by faith, believers receive righteousness imputed to them by God the Father.[65]

---

62. Calvin, *Institutes*, III.XI.XI. This relates to what Calvin (and Luther) referred to as double justification where first God justifies the sinner and places him or her in a right standing in the eyes of the metaphorical court, and the second is the justification of the justified whereby one (by the grace of God) carries out acts of righteousness. See Wendel, 259–62.

63. Calvin, *Institutes*, III.I.I. See also Horton, "Traditional Reformed View," 88.

64. Calvin, *Institutes*, III.XIV.XVII and III.XIV.XXI. See also the footnote reference above in this chapter about Calvin and whether faith is the *cause* of salvation.

65. Turretin, *Justification*, 27–35.

However, if the believer's righteousness is found in Christ, then what is the efficient cause of Christ's righteousness that is imparted to the believer? Here one must recall what was only briefly mentioned before, that the efficient cause of Christ's righteousness is in his *active* and *passive* obedience.[66]

The *active* obedience of Christ refers to his perfection in keeping the law of God.[67] While in life, Christ yielded perfect obedience to the law of God making him the only worthy One to credit others with this obedience (through his passive obedience which will be discussed below). As said above, it is important to understand Christ as the second Adam.[68] As Louis Berkhof observes, Christ as the last Adam took the place of the first Adam (whose descendants were destined to death for disobedience to the law) and acquired perfect obedience and eternal life by keeping the law of God for all of his descendants (namely those who exhibited faith).[69]

The position of Berkhof is a typical representation of the monergist position. Berkhof states that God demands obedience to the law lest one be subjected to penalty. If one is obedient, then no penalty will result. However, if the law is transgressed, a penalty will result. If Christ obeyed the law but did not pay the penalty, then he would have nothing to give to the sinners who have transgressed the law. If he had paid the penalty but not fulfilled the law, it would still be left for humankind to find a way to fulfil the Law

---

66. A criticism could be hurled against this view claiming that Christ had to be righteous before the incarnation; therefore, the active and passive obedience is no efficient cause for Christ's righteousness (as if righteousness is the same thing as divinity). One should make the following observations. God (that is the Triune God in all three persons) is and forever will be righteous. This is because he does that which is consistent with his own will and perfect actions. God the Son was and is righteous, having always had a right standing before the Father and having done what is right in his sight. However, humanity was the transgressor of the divine law. It was necessary for someone to be righteous with regards to the law to be a substitute for death and imparter of righteousness. The transfer of righteousness could not have taken place apart from the cross, for God would not be just in punishing unrighteousness apart from the cross. It is important, moreover, to distinguish between righteousness and divinity. While Christ has both, they are not the same thing. God declares believers to be righteous but not divine. This settles some matters with regards to deification given that Christ in no way confers his deity to an individual (something proponents of *theosis* would also readily admit), only righteousness. Moreover, it also addresses the issue that Christ has and always will have his divinity but that righteousness was acquired or earned (as the perfect Man on behalf of the unrighteous) through active and passive obedience. On a different note, it is important, as with most things, to distinguish but not separate Christ's active and passive obedience. The distinctions will be made clear, but his active obedience could not have occurred without his passive obedience, and *vice-versa*.

67. White, *The God Who Justifies*, 95.

68. Best, *Studies in the Person and Work of Jesus Christ*, 109–15.

69. Berkhof, *Systematic Theology*, 380–81.

on their own. The passive obedience, then, is Christ's obedience to God in paying the penalty of sin for humankind on the cross. Therefore, through active obedience (matched with the passive obedience) Christ fulfilled the law and paid the penalty.[70] Anthony Hoekema holds a similar view stating that Christ had to do a twofold work, namely to suffer the penalty for humankind's sin (and all future sins) as well as to render to God perfect obedience to his law which would therefore allow for the payment for transgressions and obedience to the Law.[71]

Through active and passive obedience, the monergist tradition claims Christ fulfilled all that was necessary with regards to the demands of God. If, as has been said, to be righteous is to have a right standing before God, to be just and right before him with no penalty or unfavorable sentence made, then such righteousness is found in Jesus Christ alone (in this view). He alone could perform the active and passive obedience necessary to satisfy God.[72] But how does this tradition claim that righteousness is reckoned to another?

THE INSTRUMENTALITY OF RIGHTEOUSNESS

The monergist position claims that the means by which one becomes righteous is (and has always been) through faith. Bruce Demarest gives a helpful presentation of the monergists' view through his analysis of Romans 4. He claims that the Pauline view is that God credits righteousness to the account of individuals not by works but by faith, and to prove the point, Paul (according to Demarest), refers back to Genesis 15:6 where Abraham believed God and it was reckoned or credited to him as righteousness.[73]

Leon Morris likewise comments on Romans 9:30–32 where he believes Paul contrasts righteousness attained through faith against a "law" (later defined as "works" in v. 32) that does not lead to righteousness. Morris claims that the Jews sought a righteous standing before God through meritorious works, yet the argument Paul is making (according to Morris) is that the Gentiles (who did not seek God before) now have a righteous standing through their faith in Christ.[74]

---

70. Ibid., 381.

71. Hoekema, *Saved by Grace*, 182. See also Buchanan, *Doctrine of Justification*, 307, and White, *The God Who Justifies*, 94–95.

72. Shedd, *Dogmatic Theology*, 542–43.

73. Demarest, *The Cross and Salvation*, 371.

74. Morris, *The Apostolic Preaching of the Cross*, 275–76.

Monergism or Synergism

Looking outside of Pauline epistles, monergists find additional support for their view that one becomes righteous through the means of faith. Demarest sees the thief on the cross' plea to Christ to remember him when Christ enters into his kingdom (matched with Christ's response that the thief will be with him in paradise) as support that trusting in Christ is the means to stand before God. Additionally, Demarest sees contrast in human works versus faith in John 6:28–29 where the disciples (according to Demarest) believed that if they do many works of the law they can please God. Christ's response of "to believe in him whom he has sent" shows to Demarest and others that Christ too affirmed faith as the means by which divine favor may be granted.[75] Moreover, through a study of James, Peter, and Jude, Dan McCartney states: "Christ's suffering, the righteous for the unrighteous, enacted a unique covenantal union between him and his people, enabling him to bring them to God and delivering them from bondage."[76]

Through the historical survey mentioned above, it has already been shown that righteousness through faith was at the heart of the Protestant Reformation and of utmost importance in the theology of Luther and Calvin (not to mention Zwingli). Still, others such as Charles Spurgeon noted that the basis for salvation is God in his grace, but the means through which one is saved (and thereby becomes righteous) is through faith in Jesus Christ.[77] Millard Erickson affirms what is often implied by most monergists that faith includes personal trust as well as the assenting of facts.[78]

In an effort to be clear, monergists are quick to affirm that the ground of such righteousness is not faith, only the means of receiving it. By faith, it is meant that one accepts Christ's work on the cross as the grounds of justification, that one relies upon it completely, and that one rejects one's own works or efforts to gain a right standing before God.[79] Faith, then, is an instrumental means, not an instrumental cause, of justification because (in this view) faith does not cause justification (albeit the means through which one receives justification).

---

75. Demarest, *The Cross and Salvation*, 372.

76. McCartney, "Atonement in James, Peter, and Jude," 189. McCartney is clear that such union is for those who believe.

77. Spurgeon, *All of Grace*, 43.

78. Erickson, *Christian Theology*, 953. The assenting facts being such things as the deity of Christ, the historicity of the cross and resurrection, etc.

79. Ladd, *A Theology of the New Testament*, 490.

CONCLUSION ON RIGHTEOUSNESS IN THE MONERGISTIC TRADITION

For the purpose of comparing and contrasting positions, this section has sought to present the monergistic position of righteousness. In so doing, the following conclusions have been made: first, righteousness is an aspect within a wider aspect, namely union with Christ in this tradition. As one becomes united to Christ, one becomes righteous (meaning in the forensic sense that one has a right standing before God). This does not mean that one actually possesses Christ's essential righteousness. However, one does possess (in actuality) the standing that Christ himself has before God. Christ, therefore, is the efficient cause of righteousness in this tradition. Moreover, the monergist tradition also affirms that the instrumental means of receiving righteousness is by faith. Contrary to the *New Perspectives on Paul*, such instrumental means in the monergistic tradition is faith (in terms of belief and trust as mentioned above) and not faithfulness to set expectations.[80]

It has also been shown that this tradition believes that the righteousness that one receives through faith in Christ is actualized in the life of the believer. It is not that God merely pretends that those united to his Son are righteous; rather, he has declared them righteous in actuality not because of inherent righteousness but because of a vital union that believers share in Christ. Moreover, one receives the righteousness of Christ in full, not in part in this view, for this is a status (not a substance) that one has. This does not mean that one becomes divine (in terms of sharing certain incommunicable attributes of God or that a person becomes inherently righteous). Rather, the same status that Christ has before his Father with regards to right relationship, blamelessness, and favor are all the same for those who have been united to him by faith.

JUSTIFICATION

Having explored the monergists' understanding of righteousness, one then is able to turn to the Greek word δικαίωσις and the subject of *justification*.[81]

---

80. Stuhlmacher, *Revisiting Paul's Doctrine of Justification*, 63–66.

81. The Greek term δικαίωσις is itself rare in the New Testament, appearing in Rom 4:25 and 5:18. Translated, it means "*justification, vindication, acquittal*" in BDAG, s.v. δικαίωσις; italics original. On a separate note, as one turns to this section on justification, it must be reiterated here (as it was at the beginning of this chapter) that monergists, in this sense, included the Reformed and non-Reformed (Wesleyan-Arminian) traditions in contrast to the Roman Catholic tradition. While there are certain areas of disagreement between these traditions in certain aspects, there is not major disagreement as it relates to the aspect of justification.

As was said above, righteousness and justification (though they share the same root word) are distinct according to this tradition. Michael Horton states: "[T]he Reformers taught and evangelicals teach that . . . justification is a verdict that declares sinners to be righteous even while they are inherently unrighteous, simply on the basis of Christ's righteousness imputed to them."[82] Righteousness, then, is the basis for the verdict of justification, according to this perspective.

The various ways justification has been understood throughout church history have already been shown above needing, at this time, no further development. What is necessary is to explore these historical understandings in light of the monergist position, particularly on what justification actually means, the efficient cause of justification, whether justification is imputed or infused righteousness, and the means of becoming justified.

DEFINING JUSTIFICATION BIBLICALLY

Wayne Grudem defines justification in the typical monergistic fashion as, "[A]n instantaneous legal act of God in which he (1) thinks of our sins as forgiven and Christ's righteousness as belonging to us, and (2) declares us to be righteous in his sight."[83] Certain points of emphasis need to be pointed out in this definition. First, justification (like righteousness) is instantaneous and not progressive or increasing. Second, it is a legal act of God, drawing upon forensic parallels. Third, justification leads to a right standing on the basis of Christ's righteousness. Finally, this is a declaratory and reckoning verdict of righteousness, not an infusing of righteousness.

Francis Turretin, the seventeenth-century Swiss-Italian Reformed theologian, gives five reasons to support the forensic definition of justification. First, he states that when Scripture deals with the matter of justification, it abounds with legal language such as "law," "accused persons," "guilty," "justice," "punishment," and others (citing Job 9:3, Ps 143:2, Rom 3:28 and 4:1–3, Col 2:14, 1 John 2:1 et al.). Second, Turretin observes what justification is opposed to in his analysis of Scripture which he claims is the forensic term *condemnation* (citing Rom 8:33–34). Third, Turretin states that biblical authors use the following phrases as equivalent terms for justification which can be understood in no other way but legal terminology: "not to come into judgment," "not to be condemned," "to remit sins," and "to impute righteousness" (citing John 5:24, John 3:18, Rom 4 and 5:10, 2 Cor 5:19). Fourth, Turretin sees that a major concern amongst first-century Jews

---

82. Horton, "Traditional Reformed View," 85.
83. Grudem, *Systematic Theology*, 723.

was how they could withstand divine judgment and God's wrath. Turretin claims that there was confusion whether through works of the law or some other means that the Jews could stand blameless before the judgment seat of God and that Paul sought to alleviate those concerns by pointing them to faith in Christ. As such, Turretin claims one must admit to a forensic sense. Finally, unless justification is understood in a forensic sense then it becomes equivocal with sanctification (in his view) which he claims Scripture clearly proves that they are distinct.[84]

While not all monergists would agree with every detail of Turretin's views, they are reflective in a significant way of the traditional Protestant view.[85] Gerhard Kittel notes that the New Testament use of δικαιόω is legal/forensic, and when used by Paul (though it is not limited to him) it refers to God's judgment that the ungodly who believe are regarded, on the basis of Christ's death and resurrection, just or righteous (that is, again, in God's reckoning and not as if moral qualities have been infused into them).[86] Donald Hagner comments on Matthew 12:36–37 which states: "For by your words you will be justified (Greek root δικαιόω), and by your words you will be condemned." Hagner observes that the preceding verse (v. 36) informs the reader that such a judicial verdict will be rendered on the day of judgment emphasizing the point that the words one uses during one's lifetime will reflect the words one hears on judgment day. As the justified are juxtaposed against the condemned, this should be understood in a forensic sense, he claims.[87] J. A. Ziesler, in a similar fashion, said the debate on whether δικαιόω can mean "declare righteous" must be regarded as closed given its parallels in biblical Greek and that in secular Greek there is only one instance of it being used as "to make righteous."[88]

Regarding Pauline literature, the monergist tradition states that justification according to Paul (as he used the δικ- words) is generally referring to a forensic sense. Donald Guthrie observes that (as mentioned above) righteousness is a relationship word, and what is at stake is humankind's

---

84. Turretin, *Justification*, 4–5.

85. For a thorough exegetical treatment of justification in the legal sense according to the monergist tradition (including matters of imputation and what it contrasts) see Morris, *The Apostolic Preaching of the Cross*, 251–98. See also Horton, "Traditional Reformed View," 91–92.

86. TDNT, s.v. δικαιόω.

87. See Hagner, *Matthew 1–13*, 351 who rightly states that words (like deeds, per James) are a reflector of one's discipleship to Jesus and one's true inner identity. This is building upon the imagery of the tree and its fruit in Matt 7:16–20. The point being emphasized here is that justification is a declaration (a reference to speaking and hearing words).

88. Ziesler, *The Meaning of Righteousness in Paul*, 48.

relationship to God. As such, Guthrie states that justification cannot be understood as anything but forensic.[89] John Polhill likewise states that for Paul, justification (a legal term) is how one gets right with God, and the means by which one becomes right with God is through righteousness (acquired by grace through faith).[90] Exploring the epistle to the Romans, James Denney makes an exegetical point to prove a theological point. He claims that beyond such debated issues as the imputation or infusion of righteousness, legal fiction or actual attainment of righteous status, and the judiciary verdicts from the judgment seat (and the like), one need only to look at Paul's dealings with Christ on the cross as proof of the judicial framework of justification. Denney claims in Christ God satisfied the penalty of the law. Sin (a failure to measure up to the law) was judged by God on Christ, making Christ be declared as the guilty one. By satisfying the demands of the law through the death of Christ, God may then justify sinners in light of the righteousness of God founded in Christ through their union with him by faith.[91]

A final exegetical point is made by Millard Erickson. He concludes through his examination of Old and New Testament scriptures the notion of righteousness refers to one's standing before the law or covenant as determined by a judge, that justification contrasts condemnation, and that justification refers to declaring one righteous as opposed to making one righteous (just as there are examples in Scripture of individuals declaring God to be righteous as opposed to making him righteous). However, he goes beyond by providing one further evidence that is helpful in understanding the declarative and forensic nature of justification. Linguistically, when a Greek verb ends in -όω, it does not mean "to make something a particular way." Rather, the verbal ending -άζω (as in ἁγιάζω- "to make holy") would be used. As δικαιόω ends in -όω, it does not mean "to make one justified" but to "declare one justified."[92]

DEFINING JUSTIFICATION THEOLOGICALLY

Through an examination of the biblical text, monergists would thus affirm that justification is a forensic term that refers to God's reckoning of believers

89. Guthrie, *New Testament Theology*, 500–501.
90. Polhill, *Paul and His Letters*, 174.
91. Denney, *The Death of Christ*, 163–94.
92. Erickson, *Christian Theology*, 969–70, quoting Moulton and Howard, *New Testament Greek*, 397; Sunday and Headlam, *A Critical and Exegetical Commentary on the Epistle to the Romans*, 30–31.

as righteous through instantaneous declaration. However, what do these conclusions that the monergists make mean theologically? Particularly, what is the relationship between union with Christ, righteousness, and justification? Who is the efficient cause of justification? What is the means of receiving justification? And what is the relationship between justification and good works?

Justification, Union with Christ, and Righteousness

It has already been shown above how union with Christ is the basis for the believer's righteousness in this view. The righteousness that one has through faith is certainly affirmed to be foreign to oneself; however, it is still personal in this view. As such, to be in Christ is to be justified. To be righteous is to be just. The δικ- root carries both meanings (in this tradition), and though they can be distinguished, they are intricately related. But what is the nature of this relationship?

The Westminster Confession of Faith (WCF) may be used as an example of the monergists' response to this issue. Chapter 12 of this famous document reads in part:

> Those whom God effectually calleth, He also freely justifieth: not by infusing righteousness into them, but by pardoning their sins, and by accounting and accepting their persons as righteous; not for any thing wrought in them, or done by them, but for Christ's sake alone; nor by imputing faith itself, the act of believing, or any other evangelical obedience to them, as their righteousness; but by imputing the obedience and satisfaction of Christ unto them, they receiving and resting on Him and His righteousness by faith; which faith they have not of themselves, it is the gift of God.[93]

In this clause, the WCF has two seemingly conflicting statements. On the one hand, God does not infuse righteousness into believers; he merely calls them to be righteous. However, God also gives righteousness by faith ("they receiving and resting on Him and His (Christ's) righteousness by faith . . . it is the gift of God").

Here one can see not a conflict but the connection. Through faith in Jesus Christ the believer receives by the gift of God the righteousness of Jesus Christ by which one may be effectually called, pronounced, and reckoned through a legal verdict by God to be just. Justification, still, is not the

---

93. Williamson, *The Westminster Confession of Faith for Study Classes*, 103.

making of one righteous. Union with Christ makes one righteous (positionally speaking). Justification, then, is the formal declaration that God judges according to what he sees.[94]

Here one becomes reminded of some disagreement amongst monergists (such as Wayne Grudem) who claim that believers do not have the righteousness of Christ which was covered above. However, there may be no real disagreement but rather a necessity to be clear. Any monergist may readily agree with Michael Horton in his "Traditional Reformed View" where he says, "(I)t is crucial to point out that the Reformation (also monergistic) position has never been that *God's righteousness* (meaning his essential righteousness that he possesses as a divine quality) is imputed . . . [T]his assumes that righteousness is a substance or a commodity that is transferred from one person to another, rather than a legal status."[95]

God's righteousness is, indeed, the righteousness belonging to God bound up in his character. This is not given to the believer thereby implying God no longer has it himself or that it mutates into a substance which is shared. Rather, as Horton goes on to say, Christ has credited his active and passive obedience rather than his divine attribute of righteousness to the believer whereby Christ becomes the believer's righteousness as the second Adam.[96] To have something to one's credit is certainly to have it. That is, the righteousness truly belongs to the believer; however, this is in terms of credit, not substance. All that is true of Christ in terms of obedience to the law now belongs to the believer.[97]

James Buchanan states that this was the view of the Reformers. What was required by the Law of God was obedience which was fulfilled by Jesus' active and passive obedience through which, by the grace of God in the working of the Holy Spirit, one becomes enabled to receive the righteousness of Christ through faith.[98] This righteousness should not be thought of as a substance that is passed on, nor should it be confused with sanctification; rather, righteousness is that ground of acceptance which is received by faith and allows one to rest entirely upon Christ for salvation.[99]

It should be made clear, however, that not all monergists affirm the active and passive obedience motif as the grounds by which Christ's

94. Stott, *The Cross of Christ*, 189–92.

95. Horton, *Justification*, 93.

96. Ibid., 94; Fesko, *Justification*, 154–57.

97. For an excellent exposition of the Trinitarian role of justification in light of God's essential righteousness, the active and passive obedience of Christ, and the role of the Spirit, see John Webster, "*Rector et iudex*," 50–55.

98. Buchanan, *The Doctrine of Justification*, 117–18.

99. Ibid., 116, 120.

righteousness may be imputed. Michael Bird would be one such example. Critiquing the notion that Christ's active and passive obedience merits status, Bird states that the problem humanity has is not a lack of moral merits but a broken relationship. What is necessary is for reconciliation to fix the break of relationship of which righteousness refers. Christ came to bridge the gap between humankind and God, which (claims Bird) is contrary to any notion of storing up merit through obedience to the law.[100]

Nevertheless, the fact that the believer receives the same reckoning as does Jesus is of utmost importance in how God may be both just and the justifier (Rom 3:26) according to this tradition. It would be legal fiction (and contrary to the just nature of God) if he judges one to be righteous when in fact one is not. This accusation is hurled against those who hold to imputation, for they contend that God does not make one righteous but declares one to be righteous.[101] Since individuals are not made righteous, nor do they share the essential righteousness of Christ but are merely reckoned to have it, the monergists (one could argue) believe in legal fiction if this is the grounds for God's verdict. However, as James White aptly puts it, "God does not say something is so when it in fact is not. When God says that the penalty of the law has been fulfilled and that the believer stands positively righteous before the Eternal Judge, then this is the case. It cannot be otherwise."[102] Again, justification is the declaration that one is righteous, not the making of one righteous. However, God may justly declare that one is righteous because he has also made the individual righteous through one's union by faith in Jesus Christ.[103]

A final word may be given about how God imputes righteousness to an individual based upon union with Christ. While many have made this observation, Constantine Campbell, perhaps, has treated it with the most

---

100. Bird, "Progressive Reformed Response," 115–16. Bird, however, may be simply describing another aspect of salvation rather than clearly articulating justification. Bridging relationship is an effect of justification, but the actual act of restoration is *reconciliation*, another aspect of salvation. Nevertheless, whether one considers Christ's active and passive obedience as the grounds by which he may impute righteousness or not, one may think of the matter on different terms. By Christ fulfilling (not necessarily meriting) perfect obedience to the law of God, he has (with regards to the Law which humankind has violated) a status of being in the right. Thereby having such status, he is in a position to impute (or better termed *share*) his status with all who will be united to him by faith. This is not the acquiring of merit (as is found in the Roman Catholic tradition) but merely the fulfilment of expectations and the sharing or imputing of such a status to all who are united to him in faith.

101. Buchannan, *The Doctrine of Justification*, 334–38.

102. White, *The God Who Justifies*, 94.

103. Clowney, "The Biblical Doctrine of Justification by Faith," 48–49.

detail in recent times. There, Campbell states that in one's union with Christ by faith, the individual actually participates in the death, burial, and resurrection of Christ in the spiritual sense. It is because of this union (by faith) that an individual is (before God) dead to sin and alive in righteousness.[104]

The Actuality of Justification

Monergists fully affirm that justification is stative and not progressive. That is to say that justification happens in a moment and not over time. This is because justification is a verdict whereby one (upon expression of faith and union with Christ) receives pardon, assurance, and peace with and from God. Since justification is a judicial act of declaring (and not a process of renewal) one's standing (not necessarily condition) is actualized in a moment in time.[105]

This was at the heart of the Reformation. For Luther, the sacraments were abused by priests as works which (if enough were acquired) could be used as a basis for one's justification. It was this progressive justification through works of the sacraments that Luther, in his "The Babylonian Captivity of the Church," wrote so harshly against. Luther thus said, "It cannot be true, therefore, that there is contained in the sacraments a power efficacious for justification, or that they are 'effective signs' of grace. All such things are said to the detriment of faith, and out of ignorance of the divine promise."[106] The verdict of "just" (in this tradition) is received the moment faith in Christ is expressed. Since this is a legal pronouncement (and not an infusion of moral uprightness), justification is actualized in a moment in time and is not progressive.[107]

THE EFFICIENT CAUSE OF JUSTIFICATION

Just as the efficient cause of righteousness is founded in God, monergists (as one would suppose given their name) also affirm God as the efficient cause of justification. This is largely due to their belief that justification is a forensic term and that righteousness is not a substance that is acquired progressively.[108]

104. Campbell, *Paul and Union With Christ*, 349–52, 405, 412–14.

105. Berkhof alludes to this in *Systematic Theology*, 513.

106. Luther, "The Babylonian Captivity of the Church," 189.

107. Berkhof, *The History of Christian Doctrines*, 220. See also Demarest, *The Cross and Salvation*, 367.

108. To see a treatment on the grounds of justification using the methodology

JUSTIFICATION IN THE MONERGISTIC PROTESTANT TRADITION

All monergists believe the basis and grounds for justification is the righteousness of Christ which he imputes to believers who are united to him by faith. The only dispute is on what is the efficient cause of Christ's righteousness (which was covered above). Most monergists, however, believe that the grounds for justification is the virtuous life of Christ in his active obedience to the will of God followed by his passive obedience to death on the cross.[109]

The forensic imagery that has been fully affirmed by this tradition should not be overshadowed. God is the judge and humankind is the transgressor. God is the one who alone may justify or condemn. One should clearly distinguish who does the justifying. Even if an individual is righteous or just, he or she is not the justifier. That is to say, though one is in the right, one is not the one who declares that they are in the right. That right alone belongs to the judge. God, in the case of justification, is the judge according to the monergists' interpretation of the Scriptures.[110]

Moreover, monergists are quick to affirm that even the basis for this verdict is not in themselves.[111] Through union with Christ who atoned for sin through the cross, monergists contend that sin was transferred to Christ (by imputation, not infusion) so that his death pays the penalty for human sin. Because Christ fulfilled all righteousness through active and thus also passive obedience, he too may (through one's union with him by faith) impute his righteousness.[112] Hence, monergists affirm that good works, attempts to fulfil perfectly the law of God, or even (should this have been the original intent of Paul) should one observe Jewish ceremonial customs before becoming a Christian are not the grounds by which one may be justified.[113]

To further prove the point, monergists affirm (in conjunction with the Protestant Reformers) that justification is not on the basis of worth or personal merit. Claiming that the New Testament's consistent message is

---

incorporated here with Aristotle's Efficient Cause and Instrumental Cause (Means) see Sproul, *Faith Alone*, 73–75.

109. Sproul, *What Is Reformed Theology?*, 67; Demarest, *The Cross and Salvation*, 369; Fesko, *Justification*, 146–57.

110. Ladd, *A Theology of the New Testament*, 481.

111. Jüngel, *Justification*, 54–55, 64–65.

112. Sproul, *What Is Reformed Theology?*, 68.

113. Seifrid, *Christ, Our Righteousness*, 99–103. For this latter view of whether works refer to becoming Jewish first, see Bird, "Progressive Reformed View," 117, 135. There, Bird states that Paul's discourse in Galatians and Romans focus primarily not on salvation by good deeds by whether or not one must become a Jew in order to become a Christian.

that pedigree or personal piety are not the means to favor with God, all of humanity is in need of an alien righteousness given their failure to observe the law perfectly.[114]

By saying that the basis of justification is not in themselves, monergists thus also affirm that faith is also not the efficient cause of justification.[115] If this were the case, it would prove problematic for many reasons. First, faith would be considered a work that effects justification. Second, it would leave one reason to boast. But very importantly, faith itself does not solve the predicament that one finds oneself in. Having faith in a judge who condemns transgressors does not seem like any rational way to be pardoned. However, if one is united to one who is righteous, the Judge (i.e., God) may make a verdict in accordance with what he actually sees.

THE INSTRUMENTALITY OF JUSTIFICATION

The grounds of justification are in one's union with Christ, or said another way in the righteousness of Christ that is imputed. However, one must then question how one becomes justified or receives this verdict. This is where one finds once again the active instrumental means of faith.[116]

Monergists use the following Scriptures to support their view: Romans 3:28: "For we maintain that a man is justified by faith . . . " Romans 5:1: "Therefore, having been justified by faith, we have peace with God through our Lord Jesus Christ." Galatians 2:16: "[Y]et who know that a man is not justified by works of the law but through faith in Jesus Christ, even we have believed in Christ Jesus, in order to be justified by faith in Christ, and not by works of the law, because by works of the law shall no one be justified . . . " Galatians 3:24: "[W]e may be justified by faith."[117]

G. C. Berkouwer makes the historical and theological point that for the Reformers and monergists (though he did not use that term) faith is

---

114. Demarest, *The Cross and Salvation*, 368. Stott, *The Cross of Christ*, 189.

115. Horton, "Traditional Reformed View," 89. Buchannan, *The Doctrine of Justification*, 366–73.

116. It should be noted that Luther understood the human to be passive towards justification as he adopted (not unlike Augustine) a concept of operative grace where the human is passive towards first grace. This does not mean that Luther excluded all human activity in justification. Faith was certainly something the human did (which can therefore rightly be understood as active); however, the action taken in faith by an individual is that of reception, not acquisition. See McGrath, *Luther's Theology of the Cross*, 130. See also Bayer, "Justification," 83–84.

117. Turretin, *Justification*, 85–98 gives thorough scriptural support for the monergistic view.

indeed a human act, though it honors the gracious justifying act as it affirms one's own emptiness and vacuity (serving, as he would say, like a telephone between God and the believer).[118] Faith, in this tradition, has immense value, though it does not earn or cause justification.[119]

One must be clear, however, in discussing instrumentality in order to stay consistent with the meaning of justification. If justification is the legal pronouncement of God that an individual is righteous on the basis of the work of Christ, then how is humankind truly justified through faith? It would seem that means of justification is the pronouncement rather than by faith as this tradition affirms. Louis Berkhof provides a possible solution. He claims that the Bible says God justifies by faith, making faith an instrument of God (see also Romans 3:30). This does not mean that this is through God's faith. Rather, God who brings the individual to faith takes hold of this faith and brings justification to him or her. Second, Berkhof affirms that faith is also the instrument of humankind. One exhibits faith concurrently with God who brings justification about.[120]

JUSTIFICATION, FAITH, AND GOOD WORKS

If the verdict of justification is founded in righteousness through one's union with Christ, and the means for receiving this justification is through faith, then where do works of charity and ethical living fit in? While the monergists would be quick to affirm that charity and responsible living

118. Berkouwer, *Faith and Justification*, 178–79.

119. See Crampton, *What Calvin Says*, 76 who says about Calvin (and the rest of the Reformers), "Faith is in no way to be considered as meritorious (*Institutes*, III. XI.XXIII). Faith, of course, means trusting in Christ who alone justifies. Salvation is by God's grace (*sola gratia*) through faith (*sola fide*). Faith is the instrument by which one is saved, not the cause of one's salvation." Here, one may question this claim from monergists, as Arminians or (specifically here in the doctrine of justification) Catholics claim the same. One will observe the difference, however, in that monergists claim faith is simply an instrumental means and not an instrumental cause of justification. Justification comes by means of faith as one is united to Christ which is an entirely different concept than meriting by means of grace-filled faith the merits of Christ through the sacraments which cause the infusion of righteousness.

120. Berkhof, *Systematic Theology*, 522. Here, one may question the role of the sacraments in the Reformed tradition. Because the Reformed tradition is comprised of multiple Protestant traditions, their understanding of the sacraments varies. Some, following the likeness of John Calvin, believe that the sacraments can confer grace (see *Institutes*, IV.XIV.I, VII); however, Calvin was also clear that the sacraments, themselves, do not confer righteousness in themselves, apart from faith in III.XIV.I. See also IV.XIV.XIV where he said, "[A]ssurance of salvation does not depend on participation in the sacraments, as if justification consisted in it."

(simply called here *good works*) are not the grounds or means by which one is justified, they are also quick to affirm that good works are essential if there has been justification.[121]

James White descriptively addresses this concern by saying, "*Sola fide* (referring to justification through faith alone) has never, ever meant '[J]ustified by a barren, dead faith that is not Spirit-borne nor accompanied by all the rest of the work of God in His redeemed people.'"[122] The monergist fully affirms with James 2:24: "You see that a man is justified by works and not by faith alone," when properly understood. Just as was said above in regards to good works and righteousness, so one must understand the proper order and place of works with regards to justification. Works do not lead to justification or are the means of acquisition; rather, they are evidence of a true, saving faith that has received justification.[123]

CONCLUSION

What has been laid forth thus far is the monergistic position on justification. Herein, it has been shown how this tradition views justification as a legal pronouncement whereby one is declared on the basis of righteousness founded in Christ through union with him by faith to be righteous. As the name would suppose, this tradition believes justification is entirely monergistic given that God is the justifier, and the means through which justification is applied is through the vessel of faith and not through human merit.

What has also been stressed is that this tradition believes justification happens in its completeness (meaning it is stative and not progressive) once faith has been shown in Christ resulting in union with Him. It is not something to be continuously acquired as though it were a substance. Because this status has been conferred, one has peace with God through faith in Christ and no longer faces the condemnation that was once deserved. In light of such contrast between condemnation, righteous, peace, and guilt, this tradition affirms that justification is primarily a judicial term relating to one's transgressions of sin requiring pardon through the work of Christ.

While Protestantism has continually been contrasted with Roman Catholicism, this chapter has sought to present a view of justification that is monergistic. As it turns out, it is the traditional Protestant position; however,

---

121. Shedd, "Justification and Personal Christian Living," 170–75. For this teaching in the theology of John Calvin, see Barth, *The Theology of John Calvin*, 166–67.

122. White, *The God Who Justifies*, 108. See also Berkouwer, *Faith and Justification*, 195–96.

123. Sproul, *Faith Alone*, 160.

what is often left out in the Protestant view is how this aspect of justification is in actuality monergistic. With the understanding that this view is monergistic, it can be contrasted with Catholicism to see if synergism plays a part in the tensions between these parties.

Chapter 6

The Aspect of Justification in Roman Catholicism

A HISTORIC AND MODERN ISSUE

As mentioned in chapter 1, Thomas Aquinas (the great medieval scholastic whose works have influenced Roman Catholic doctrine for over 700 years) built upon the Aristotelian philosophy of causation. The efficient cause (which Aquinas called the *principal cause*) is the cause of action. This, Aquinas affirmed, is to be distinguished from the *instrumental cause*, which is the means through which the principal cause works. Aquinas analyzed this issue as it relates to the doctrine of salvation. He posed the following objection:

> Further, an instrument acquires no merit or demerit in the sight of him that uses it; because the entire action of the instrument belongs to the user. Now when man acts he is the instrument of the Divine power which is the principal cause of his action . . . Therefore man merits or demerits nothing in God's sight, by good or evil deeds.[1]

Aquinas's response to this objection is that: "Man is so moved, as an instrument, by God, that, at the same time, he moves himself by his free-will . . . Consequently, by his action, he acquires merit or demerit in God's sight."[2] God, believed Aquinas, was the principal cause of salvation; however, there is an element whereby an individual must acquire merit instru-

---

1. Aquinas, *Summa Theologica*, I/II, q. 21, a. 4.
2. Ibid.

mentally from the efficient cause. This notion of acquiring merit before God through the exercise (or instrumentality) of one's free-will proved to be the central issue of the Protestant Reformation. That is to say, the Thomist doctrine of causation was, indeed, a central issue of the Reformation, though this factor does not always receive the attention it deserves.

Martin Luther, though he was familiar with the concept of principal causation,[3] never developed a thorough philosophy of causation or attacked his opponents on these grounds. This is not to say that he did not react against his opponents on the grounds of who does what in justification; rather, he appealed more to the Augustinian tradition of the freedom (or lack thereof) of the human will. That is to say, Luther explored the notion of ability, the nature of merit, the depravity of the soul, and the integrity of the sacraments as they relate to one's standing before God rather than the notion of causality.

The notions of monergism and synergism are by no means foreign to the Protestant Reformation debate. Indeed, Luther and Erasmus had a heated exchange over the subject as will be discussed below, and they are the subject of debate even currently over justification issues. However, what has not been satisfactorily examined is the role of monergism and synergism in Protestant/Catholic dialogue with particular examination to the Thomist notion of causation which has been the approach throughout this study and will be the methodology incorporated here. It is to this matter that this study now turns.

THE MEANING AND BASIS OF JUSTIFICATION IN ROMAN CATHOLIC THEOLOGY

The history of justification as it pertains to the Roman Catholic Church and the Protestant Reformation was covered in chapters 1 and 5, and as such there will be no intent to reiterate it here. However, what one may do is explore how the Roman Catholic Church defines justification and how this has been understood historically.

While the doctrine of justification has a rich history in the Catholic Church which dates back to the time of Augustine, the clearest exposition of the doctrine is found in the proceedings of the Council of Trent which were approved on January 13, 1547.[4] It is worth noting that though this chapter does not take a diachronic approach to exploring the Roman Catholic doc-

---

3. Luther, *On the Bondage of the Will*, 241.

4. O'Collins and Rafferty, "Roman Catholic View," 265, 269–71. Much of the historical doctrines on justification that precede the Council of Trent will be explored below.

trine of justification, the Catholic Church affirms uniformity throughout the ages in its doctrine making a synchronic approach to analysis merit-worthy.[5]

To begin, one must first understand the Roman Catholic Church's doctrine of sin whereby the need for justification may be understood. While the notion of sin and justification are by no means absent from the earliest councils and church fathers, it was not until the Council of Orange in AD 529 that the Catholic Church (in response to the Pelagian controversy) formulated a precise statement concerning sin. Canon 1 of the Council of Orange states:

> If anyone denies that it is the whole man, that is, both body and soul, that was "changed for the worse" through the offence of Adam's sin, but believes that the freedom of the soul remains unimpaired and that only the body is subject to corruption, he is deceived by the error of Pelagius and contradicts the scripture . . .[6]

The Council of Orange went on to state that this sin of Adam affected all his descendants (thus all humanity) and that free will along with works of the law cannot lead to one's righteousness before God (as shown through canons 2, 6–8, 10, 13–25). As for the consequences of sin, Orange stated that it led to such things as corruption, punishment, and godlessness. The Council of Trent, which convened over 1,000 years later, affirmed the same in their fifth session. In this session, they made five decrees that affirmed original sin, the universal scope of original sin, and the inability of individuals to remove this sin based upon human works. The consequences of sin according to Trent were the death of the soul, the wrath and indignation of God, and captivity to the devil.[7]

While rejecting the notions of Pelagianism and Semi-Pelagianism, the Roman Catholic Church affirmed (and continues to affirm) that there was not an utter corruption on the part of the person as a result of Adam's sin. The image of God, though occluded severely, was not destroyed.[8] Canon 5 of Trent anathematized anyone who would claim that the free-will of an in-

---

5. This was shown historically at the Council of Trent where it claims that the Catholic (i.e., Universal) faith purges errors so as to "remain complete and unsoiled in its integrity" (Council of Trent, "Decree Concerning Original Sin," Session V, ¶ 1, in Tanner, *Decrees of the Ecumenical Councils*, 665). A modern example can be seen from Vatican II as shown by Pope John Paul II's introduction in *Catechism of the Catholic Church*, 2–6.

6. "The Council of Orange," in Leith, *Creeds of the Church*, 38.

7. Council of Trent, "Decree Concerning Original Sin," Session V.1–3, in Tanner, *Decrees of the Ecumenical Councils*, 666.

8. O'Collins and Rafferty, "Roman Catholic View," 267–68.

dividual is lost or extinguished through Adam's sin. As such, human beings, as people who still retain the image of God, still retain a freedom of the will which may be moved (by God's grace) toward God.[9]

It is here that the Roman Catholic Church develops its doctrine of prevenient (or prepatory) grace. Chapters 5–6 of the sixth session of Trent speak of the necessity and manner of preparation for justification for "adults" (which are to be distinguished from infants whose means are different). The prevenient grace of God which leads to justification is said to happen through, "God's grace inciting and helping them, to turn toward their own justification by giving free assent to and co-operating with this same grace."[10] Notice that this inciting and helping grace must be assented to and cooperated with. However, the nature of this inciting and helping grace is described further: "God touches a person's heart through the light of the holy (sic) Spirit, neither does that person do absolutely nothing in receiving that moment of grace, for he can also reject it."[11] Again, the prevenient grace of God touches one's heart through the work of the Holy Spirit, yet the individual must also actively do something to receive that inspiration. One finds in the sixth chapter of this session of Trent that the work of God is in illuminating individuals by the Holy Spirit through revelation of the truths and promises of God (particularly with regards to their sin and divine justice and mercy). Moreover, the way an individual must cooperate with this prevening grace is through penance and baptism.[12]

The *Catechism of the Catholic Church* also spoke to something called the "preparation of man" which may be understood as prevenient grace. It states:

> The *preparation of man* for the reception of grace is already a work of grace. This latter is needed to arouse and sustain our collaboration in justification through faith, and in sanctification through charity. God brings to completion in us what he has begun, "since he who completes his work by cooperating with our will began by working so that we might will it:" Indeed we also work, but we are only collaborating with God who works, for his mercy has gone before us.[13]

---

9. Ibid., 268.

10. Council of Trent, "Decree on Justification," Session VI.5, in Tanner, *Decrees of the Ecunemical Councils*, 672.

11. Ibid.

12. Ibid.

13. *Catechism of the Catholic Church*, §2001, 484; italics original. The quotation comes from Augustine, *De gratia et libero arbitrio*.

Again, one can see that God is at work in preparing the soul of an individual for justification, yet this must be cooperated with through one's own works. While §537 in the *Catechism* states that through baptism one is assimilated into Jesus and adopted as a "beloved son in the Son," continual observance of the other sacraments is still required in order to receive justification (which will be explored below).

This thinking is in line with the medieval theologians as well. Aquinas referred to the preparation of the human soul as "first grace." It is the grace that precedes habitual (i.e., sanctifying) grace as expressed through the sacraments. For Aquinas, God prepares the human soul to respond in habitual grace through the first grace of inspiration (similar to what was mentioned above). However, the individual must prepare his or her soul in cooperation with the preparation of God by turning away from sin and engaging his or her will (and actions) in habitual grace (through the sacraments).[14] Anselm of Canterbury, similarly, said that just as no one receives uprightness before God without being willing for it, no one can have such righteousness without prevenient grace. The will, through prevenient grace however, must still freely choose uprightness before God making it clear that the prevenient grace being referred to does not entail full regeneration as was the case for the monergistic Protestants.[15]

As for a workable definition of *justification*, Trent supplies the following: "[Justification is] a transition from that state in which a person is born as a child of the first Adam to the state of grace and of adoption as children of God through the agency of the second Adam, Jesus Christ our savior."[16] It goes on to state: "(The justified are those who) become innocent, stainless, pure, blameless and beloved children of God, *heirs indeed of God and fellow heirs with Christ*, so that nothing at all impedes their entrance into heaven."[17]

These definitions raise questions (which the rest of the Canons of Trent seeks to answer) particularly with regards to the notions of "a transition from that state" and "*become* innocent, immaculate, pure ... (etc.)." Is the translation of one's state from being a child of Adam to a child of

---

14. Aquinas, *Summa Theologica*, I/II, q.109, a. 7–a. 8.

15. Anselm of Canterbury, *De Concordia*, 456. See also Maurer, *A History of Philosophy*, 57–58.

16. Council of Trent, "Decree on Justification," Session VI.4, in Tanner, *Decrees of the Ecunemical Councils*, 672.

17. Ibid., "Decree Concerning Original Sin," Session V.5, 667; italics original. It should be noted that there were some exceptions within the Catholic Church during this time period (notably Gasparo Contarini) who allowed for imputed righteousness in justification. See Lane, *Justification by Faith in Catholic-Protestant Dialogue*, 48–49.

God something that happens instantaneously or progressively?[18] How does someone "*become*" innocent, immaculate, pure, etc.? Why is one not merely reckoned to be these things, and what efforts on behalf of the human acquire such an outcome? These issues, which were central to the Reformation, must wait for analysis.

These definitions of justification are built upon Aquinas's own beliefs. Just as Trent said that justification is the translation of an individual from the state of the first Adam to the second Adam, so Aquinas says, "[T]he justification of the ungodly is a movement whereby the soul is moved by God from a state of sin to a state of justice."[19] The soul is moved by God, believed Aquinas, from state to state whereby the first state is ungodliness and the second is justice. The notion of the state of *justice* is of critical importance in understanding the Roman Catholic doctrine of justification as will be shown.

While the means by which an individual is transferred from state to state will be explored below, it is important at this point to recognize how differently the Roman Catholic Church defines justification distinctively from their Protestant counterparts. As mentioned in chapter 5, the Protestant tradition (as a whole) does not deny that justification has non-forensic associations to the term. However, what was shown there is a widely accepted consensus that justification is primarily a judicial term. What must be affirmed here, however, is that the Roman Catholic understanding of justification is not primarily forensically based (that is to say that justification has to do with acquittal of guilt).[20]

That justification is primarily non-forensic was made clear through Trent because one is able to observe, through the canons, what justification primarily accomplishes. As was stated above: "[The justified are those who] become innocent, stainless, pure, blameless and beloved children of God, *heirs indeed of God and fellow heirs with Christ*, so that nothing at all impedes their entrance into heaven."[21] Notice that being "become innocent"

18. As will be shown, justification in the Catholic view is a progressive movement or change from unrighteousness to righteousness whereby nature (i.e., original sin) is driven out and new is brought in. See Chemnitz, *Examination of the Council of Trent*, pt. 1, 470.

19. Aquinas, *Summa Theologica*, I/II, q. 113, a. 6.

20. Just as Protestants do not deny (as a whole) that justification can mean things in a non-judiciary way, so the Roman Catholics also affirm that justification can, at times be forensic. The difference is that the Roman Catholic Church denies that this is its primary meaning, unlike the traditional Protestant position. See, for example, Kenrick, *The Catholic Doctrine on Justification*, 82.

21. Council of Trent, "Decree Concerning Original Sin," Session V.5, in Tanner, *Decrees of the Ecumenical Councils*, 667.

connotes some forensic imagery. However, one must also notice that there is no language of acquittal nor does forensic imagery pervade the definition.

A classic work on the Roman Catholic doctrine of justification that makes this point abundantly clear came from Bishop Francis Patrick Kenrick in his book *The Catholic Doctrine on Justification Explained and Vindicated*. Therein, Kenrick writes, "It is an erroneous supposition that the sacred writers ordinarily use the imagery of judicial procedure to express the act of God justifying the sinner."[22] He says elsewhere, "There is no warrant in the comparison, or in the context (of Rom 5:14) for understanding justification to mean a mere judicial acquittal, unaccompanied by any moral change, or sanctification."[23]

The reason for such a non-judicial understanding of justification relates to the Council of Trent's definition of who the justified are. They are those who are "made innocent." They are not those whose sins are acquitted. They are not those whose transgressions against the Law are merely reckoned to another (i.e., Christ). This, they would claim, is legal fiction. Kenrick makes this point clear. He says that the judicial verdict of justification assumes that there is actual purity of conscious and a lack of guilt within the individual. The legal pronouncement of justification would have to be a statement of actuality, he claims. The way the individual is actually made innocent (in accordance with the Trent definition) is by: "[W]ashing from defilement, the raising from death to life, the communication of heavenly gifts, by which the soul is made the temple of God."[24]

This is to say that one must be actually made just. There must be an internal change within the individual and not just a reckoning in the eyes of the judge. This is made clear in the sixth session of the Council of Trent where it says, "[A]ctual justification, which consists not only in the forgiveness of sins but also in the sanctification and renewal of the inward being by a willing acceptance of the grace and gifts whereby someone from being unjust becomes just . . . "[25] Here, it becomes clear that justification is not merely the remission or acquittal of sins as the Protestants would suggest. Rather, justification and sanctification (belonging together and almost interchangeable) leads one to the transfer from the state of the first Adam to the second Adam (Jesus) mentioned above.[26]

22. Kenrick, *The Catholic Doctrine on Justification*, 75.
23. Ibid., 80.
24. Ibid., 83. See also 82.
25. Council of Trent, "Decree on Justification," Session VI.7, in Tanner, *Decrees of the Ecunemical Councils*, 673. See also Chemnitz, *Examination of the Council of Trent*, pt. 1, 538–43.
26. See Baker, *Fundamentals of Catholicism*, 3:62–64.

THE ASPECT OF JUSTIFICATION IN ROMAN CATHOLICISM

This concept is found in Thomas Aquinas as well. Aquinas does not object to justification as the remission of sins, outright. Rather, he qualifies what this means. He states:

> The infusion of grace and the remission of sin may be considered in two ways: first, with respect to the substance of the act, and thus they are the same; for by the same act God bestows grace and remits sin. Secondly, they may be considered on the part of the objects; and thus they differ by the difference between guilt, which is taken away, and grace, which is infused.[27]

This statement is revealing. Infused grace (a matter of some importance later) and the remission of sins can be thought of in a solitary act of God in justification. That is to say, negatively sins are remitted while positively grace is infused. Justification, however, is not a legal pronouncement but an act of increasing one's merit (the term Aquinas preferred) before God. Forensic imagery is not denied (Aquinas here mentions guilt), though a judiciary verdict as formulated by the Protestant position is not evident.

Before Aquinas, Anselm of Canterbury, claimed something similar. In his classic work, *Cur Deus Homo*, Anselm states that in Adam's sin, all people incurred loss. God still requires his original intents for creation which humanity (tainted by sin) cannot perform. However, God by his grace completes that which humanity is unable to do (thus continuing that which he begun, by making one right before him).[28] Again, how God makes one righteous (and the involvement of the individual in this regard) is of critical importance, though it must wait for further analysis. The point being made is that for Aquinas and Anselm, justification was not merely a forensic term. There must be an internal change wrought within the individual for one to be right before God.

This concept of justification has remained consistent even as recently as 1992 through the publication of the *Catechism of the Catholic Church* under the direction of Pope John Paul II. Therein, the *Catechism* expounds upon justification in this way: "The grace of the Holy Spirit has the power to justify us, that is, to cleanse us from our sins and to communicate to us "the righteousness of God through faith in Jesus Christ" and through Baptism."[29] Again one should notice that "to justify" is "to cleanse us from our sins" as righteousness is communicated (Lat. *communicandi* similar to the notion of transferal from state to state in Aquinas) to the individual. This is to show

---

27. Aquinas, *Summa Theologica*, I/II, q. 113, a. 6.

28. Anselm of Canterbury, *Why God Became Man*, 308–15 and 317–19.

29. *Catechism of the Catholic Church*, §1987. The quoted reference therein is from Rom 3:22; see also 6:3–4.

that justification in the Roman Catholic sense requires not merely a verdict but a cleansing, internal change so one may be moved into righteousness.

THE INCREASE OF MERIT AND THE PROGRESSIVE NATURE OF JUSTIFICATION

Protestants and Catholics concur that Scripture (and experience) teach that one does not become sinless and completely Christ-like in one's lifestyle at the moment of faith. The struggle with sin continues and that conformity to Jesus takes time (both would agree). The difference between the two parties, however, lies in their respective understandings of justification and sanctification.

As mentioned in chapter 5, the traditional, monergistic perspective distinguishes justification from sanctification. John Calvin brought this out clearly in Book 3 of his *Institutes*. Therein, Calvin states that justification can only be by faith alone and not by works, though works must be provided as a means to sanctification apart from which one does not truly belong to Christ.[30] In other words, sanctification is the by-product of justification, and good works are evidence of (not the means to) justification.[31] Karl Barth (who was starkly opposed to the Roman Catholic position at this point) affirmed similarly to Calvin that though justification and sanctification belong together, they are distinct and must be understood in the proper order. Barth claimed that the Catholic Church transferred justification into the sphere and control of the Church through means of the sacraments thereby controlling over others the means of grace which (wrongly he believed) combined justification and sanctification into one.[32]

The Catholic Church, however, sees the two not as essentially the same thing but as the accomplishment of the same end. One author claims that, substantially, justification and sanctification are aspects of the same thing and are parts of one gift.[33] Another author says, "Justification is the spiritual *process* by which a person, through faith in Jesus Christ, receives the sanctifying grace of God."[34]

---

30. Calvin, *Institutes*, III.XVI.I.

31. See McGrath, *Iustitia Dei*, 255.

32. Barth, *Church Dogmatics*, IV.I.§61.4, 625. Note Küng's response to Barth's criticisms below.

33. Kenrick, *The Catholic Doctrine on Justification*, 94–95.

34. Baker, *Fundamentals of Catholicism*, 62; italics original. There is also an understanding in Roman Catholic theology that conversion (not just justification) is progressive in nature, though here justification and conversion are almost interchangeable

THE ASPECT OF JUSTIFICATION IN ROMAN CATHOLICISM

Consider chapter 7 of session six of the Council of Trent: "[A]ctual justification, which consists not only in the forgiveness of sins but also in the sanctification and renewal of the inward being . . ."[35] While the Church recognizes their distinction, the two accomplish the same goal—sanctification and renewal of one's disposition. This is not unlike the concept proposed by Hans Urs von Balthasar who claimed that in Christ one is able to fulfil the original purpose of creation (to be engaged with God) through a divine-human synergy.[36] That is to say, being united (or what he calls "engaged") together with God entails cooperation of being rid of sin and submissive to the will of God. This is different from the traditional Protestant understanding that says cooperation with and conformity to Christ are a result (not means to) one's engagement with God. It also differs in the role of the sacraments and continual participation in the Church, which Balthasar claims, is the means by which one pursues this process.[37]

The product of such a progressive pursuit (or the progressive movement from state to state as was mentioned above) is oftentimes called "merit." The *Catechism of the Catholic Church* gives a precise definition of the term *merit*. It states: "The term 'merit' refers in general to the *recompense owed* by a community or a society for the action of one of its members, experienced either as beneficial or harmful, deserving reward or punishment."[38] In other words, merit is the recompense or reward based upon the action of a person (in the positive sense). When applied in a soteriological sense, the *Catechism* goes on to state:

> Since the initiative belongs to God in the order of grace, *no one can merit the initial grace* of forgiveness and justification, at the beginning of conversion. Moved by the Holy Spirit and by charity, *we can then merit* for ourselves and for others the graces

---

ideas. The idea is that one progressively, throughout one's lifetime, conforms into the personhood of Jesus which is to be thought of as a progressive conversion (turning away from the world and towards a new life in Jesus). See Curran, *Moral Theology*, 48, 72–73. This is very different from the Protestant understanding of conversion which (like justification) happens in a moment in time though the effects of it are long-lasting.

35. Council of Trent, "Decree on Justification," Session VI.VII, Tanner, *Decrees of the Ecunemical Councils*, 29.

36. Balthasar, *Engagement with God*, 71.

37. Ibid., 31, 37. Balthasar says God works through his community (i.e., the Church), and through participation in that community (via the sacraments) one becomes truly human because of one's involvement or engagement with God. As such, one can see how he bridges together into a unity engagement with God with acts of godliness.

38. *Catechism of the Catholic Church*, §2006; italics original.

needed for our sanctification, for the increase of grace and charity, and for the attainment of eternal life.³⁹

God, they fully affirm, takes the initial steps to begin justification and conversion. However, it is within one's grace-assisted ability to "*merit* for ourselves and others" the graces that increase and lead to the attainment of eternal life. Words such as "merit," "attainment," and "increase of grace" unto eternal life were (and are) significant issues not accepted by Protestants.

Alister McGrath observes that initially the notion of merit stems from Augustine who claimed that the merits of Christ were conferred upon believers by grace to justify the sinner without any notions of works-righteousness that require human acquisition (as would later be the understood case). McGrath goes on to state that by the twelfth century, the meaning and notion of merit had changed significantly from the time of Augustine. A distinction was made between *merit* and *congruity*. Humanity cannot merit justification through works; however, humans can make their justification congruous (meaning that one may dispose a meritorious character towards justification).⁴⁰ While many during the Medieval Ages understood justification sourced in the divine gift (rather than reward), there grew a trend in the thirteenth century to understand merit in terms of that which obligates God to justify the sinner and a progression to understanding justification as an ontological change in the individual who performs acts of merit.⁴¹

It is not difficult to understand why merit would be thought of in terms of a reward to be acquired. First, the Council of Trent spoke of justification

---

39. Ibid., §2010; italics original.

40. McGrath, *Iustitia Dei*, 138–41. McGrath, here, observed the difference that developed between *meritum de congruo* and *meritum de condigno* and how the two would, in time, blend. Condign merit refers to service and return. It requires a reward for service. *Meritum de congruo* is also a bestowal of merit but on the grounds of mercy and love (not justice or demand). There became a development of *de congruo* merit to human good works, and then a blending of this with *meritum de condigno* (which Catholic authors admit is "a sort of crypto-Pelagianism") per Osborne, *Reconciliation and Justification*, 108. See also González, *A History of Christian Thought*, 2:275 where he comments upon the view of Aquinas, "[D]ivine justice demands that man prepare himself through acts of merit to receive this unmerited gift." A. N. S. Lane observes that condign merit and congruous merit were both developed during the medieval ages, and the Tridentine decree specifically excluded condign merit but left open the possibility for justification by congruous merit in *Justification by Faith in Catholic-Protestant Dialogue*, 198. In the theology of Gabriel Biel (medieval Catholic scholastic), Heiko Augustinus Oberman observes that there was a threefold condition of acceptance of *meritum de condigno*, namely being a friend of God, righteous acts directed to God free from venial sins, and (concerning the rewarder) an acceptance or agreement required based upon the merit earned. See Oberman, *The Harvest of Medieval Theology*, 167–68.

41. McGrath, *Iustitia Dei*, 142–43.

being able to be increased through cooperation with good works.[42] As more synergistic works are accomplished, the more an individual is justified. Second, Trent spoke of merit as a "reward." Consider chapter 16 of session six: "Thus, to those who work well right to the end and keep their trust in God, eternal life should be held out, both as a grace promised in his mercy through Jesus Christ to the children of God, and as a reward to be faithfully bestowed, on the promise of God himself, for their good works and merits."[43] Notice that the results of this combined activity (grace and good works) are merits and reward which relate to the aforementioned "life eternal." It is easy to understand why merit would be thought of as a reward for good works (albeit they are sourced in the grace of God).

Thomas Aquinas spoke of merit and reward often as it relates to justification. He states:

> What falls under merit is the reward or wage ... For God gives men, both just and wicked, enough temporal goods to enable them to attain to everlasting life; and thus these temporal goods are simply good ... And thus as life everlasting is simply the reward of the works of justice in relation to the Divine motion, as stated above (AA[3],6), so have temporal goods, considered in themselves, the nature of reward, with respect to the Divine motion, whereby men's wills are moved to undertake these works, even though, sometimes, men have not a right intention in them.[44]

Thomism teaches that justification is measured in relation to merit, which is reward or wage. God gives an individual that which is necessary to attain life everlasting, even claiming that it is the reward of works of justice. One is able to work, and thus acquire the reward, because of the grace of God that moves one's will, yet it is up to an individual to undertake these works to receive eternal life.

Naturally, the notion of working to attain the reward of eternal life was troubling to the Reformers (and Protestant theology) albeit if grace assists these works. Erasmus of Rotterdam fully affirmed the notion of merit and reward that leads to elevated righteousness of an individual before God.[45] Luther saw this (whether rightly or wrongly) as *condignum meritum* and

---

42. Council of Trent, "Decree on Justification," Session VI.X, in Tanner, *Decrees of the Ecunemical Councils*, 675.

43. Ibid., Session VI.XVI, 676–78.

44. Aquinas, *Summa Theologica*, I/II, q. 114, a. 10.

45. Erasmus, *On the Freedom of the Will*, 87.

claimed that it is "plainly a denial of Christ" and "a more ungodly degree (*sic*) than the Pelagians themselves."[46]

One must be clear in observing what is not being advocated for when the Catholic Church speaks of "merit." Alister McGrath observes that merit in Thomism does not indebt God to humanity but is rather an act of grace flowing from his nature as a reward for faithfulness.[47] Humanity does not have a just claim before God where they can demand what is owed, and Thomism (in accordance with centuries' worth of tradition) affirms the prevenient grace of God in a denial of Pelagianism.

Moreover, Hans Küng wrote vehemently against Karl Barth's accusations of merit in Catholic theology. Küng affirms that a strict doctrine of merit whereby one boasts of works before God does not justify and is the essence of "Pharisaic morality."[48] Küng claims that humans are not equals with God who have contractual rights but are rather unworthy servants who hold on to a promise of a reward of grace.[49]

THE INFUSION OF RIGHTEOUSNESS AND THE NOTION OF PURGATORY

As has been shown, there is a progressive (not stative) aspect of justification in Roman Catholic theology. While the Protestant tradition affirms the actuality (that is a non-progressive view) of justification, the Roman Catholic position views justification as increasing and ever changing. Here the contrast between imputation and infusion becomes of issue.

As mentioned in chapter 5, the traditional, monergistic perspective holds primarily to a view of imputed righteousness. Built upon the doctrine of Luther (though proponents of this tradition will claim it arises from Scripture), the view of imputation means that the righteousness of Christ is external to a believer and refers to one's right standing in God's reckoning because of the union that one has by grace through faith in Jesus Christ.[50] Because their view of justification is primarily forensic, justification has to do with the declaration that one is in the right and thus not guilty of the penalty of sin leading to the status of "righteous."

This is different from the Roman Catholic view expressed by Canon XI of Trent which anathematized anyone who says that people are justified

---

46. Luther, *On the Bondage of the Will*, 321.
47. McGrath, *Iustitia Dei*, 144.
48. Küng, *Justification*, 270.
49. Ibid., 271. Whether this affirmation upholds or not will be observed below.
50. McGrath, *Iustitia Dei*, 229, 233.

THE ASPECT OF JUSTIFICATION IN ROMAN CATHOLICISM

"solely" by the imputation of Christ's justice.[51] This is not to say that the Council (and modern Catholics) rejected imputation definitively. Rather, their understanding is that the merits (or justice) of Christ is effectually communicated to individuals whereby one is not "solely imputed (or reckoned to be right with God) but is actually and effectually infused with the righteousness of Christ."[52] In other words, it is not by merely imputing (or reckoning) Christ's merits (or righteousness) over to an individual that makes one just before God. Instead, God makes an individual righteous (progressively) which leads to the reckoning of justification.

This making righteous, as said above, is infusion, and is received in a process. While Catholic theologians do speak of justification as a "state," what is meant is that one is in a state of being made progressively righteous through infusion. Consider the following quote: "In addition, sanctifying grace is a supernatural state of being, which is infused by God, and which permanently inheres in the soul."[53] As such, one is in a permanent state of progressively attaining sanctifying grace through acts of infusion. The result is that one's essence is changed substantially in the soul, it sanctifies (or makes holy) the once wicked disposition, and it leads one to becoming a new creation.

Consider Aquinas at this point: "Hence in him who has the use of reason, God's motion to justice does not take place without a movement of the free-will; but He so infuses the gift of justifying grace that at the same time He moves the free-will to accept the gift of grace, in such as are capable of being moved thus."[54] Infusion (while they claim it is all from God as will be shown through the efficient cause) takes place through the cooperative efforts of the human and God with the result of God infusing justifying grace into the individual. However, notice what Aquinas goes on to say: "By every meritorious act a man merits the increase of grace, equally with the consummation of grace which is eternal life. But just as eternal life is not given at once, but in its own time, so neither is grace increased at once, but in its own time, viz. when a man is sufficiently disposed for the increase of grace."[55] This is very revealing of the Catholic doctrine of justification. One must increase in this grace through "every meritorious act a man merits."

---

51. Council of Trent, "On Justification," Session 6, canon XI, in Tanner, *Decrees of the Ecunemical Councils*, 679.
52. Kenrick, *The Catholic Doctrine on Justification*, 98–99.
53. Baker, *Fundamentals of Catholicism*, 63.
54. Aquinas, *Summa Theologica*, I/II, q. 113, a. 3.
55. Ibid., I/II, q. 114, a. 8.

When merit reaches "the consummation of grace" an individual may receive "eternal life."

The notion of increasing in righteousness through infusion to a satisfactory level raises two concerns: what if an individual does not reach the consummation or fullness of merit in this lifetime, and can one have any assurance in this lifetime that one is actually justified? Beginning with the second of these questions first, the Council of Trent responded with a resounding "No." Canon XV made this clear: "If anyone says that a person reborn and justified is bound to believe as a matter of faith that he is certainly in the number of the predestined: let him be anathema."[56] It also states in Canon XXIII, "If anyone says that a person, once justified, cannot sin any more or lose grace . . . let him be anathema."[57] Chapter 15 of session six states that justification can be lost through infidelity and "mortal sins" which include not only unbelievers but "also the faithful if they are guilty of fornication, adultery, wantonness, sodomy, theft, avarice, drunkenness, slander, plundering, and all others who commit mortal sins . . ."[58] The *Catechism of the Catholic Church* (upon commenting upon the canons of Trent) softened the language on this matter, though it no doubt upheld it in Part Three §2005 where it claims that one cannot know for certain that one is justified, for feelings and works are unreliable.[59] Though little support is given for his claim, Bishop Francis Kenrick states: "[I]t is vain to assert the infallible certainty of our justification."[60] Moreover, Kenneth Baker makes the interesting observation that an individual may be justified yet not die in a state of grace (for eternal life).[61] This revealing statement shows how one may be in the process of justification yet not remain in it (thus forfeiting one's soul to hell).

Moving to the first question of what happens to an individual who does not achieve the proper level of merit in this lifetime, Aquinas was prepared for an answer with his doctrine of Purgatory. While Aquinas spoke of Purgatory throughout the *Summa*, perhaps the clearest explanation of what Purgatory does (of which he cites Augustine for support) is found in the

---

56. Council of Trent, "On Justification," Session VI, canon XV, in Tanner, *Decrees of the Ecunemical Councils*, 680.

57. Ibid., canon XXIII, 680.

58. Ibid., canon XV, 677.

59. *Catechism of the Catholic Church*, §2005.

60. Kenrick, *The Catholic Doctrine on Justification*, 113; see also 111–22.

61. Baker, *Fundamentals of Catholicism*, 29–30. This is an interesting claim because Baker states that an individual is indeed justified (though not fully) yet can lose this whenever the individual ceases to act in faithfulness. This shows, as will be shown below, the synergistic role an individual plays in justification.

THE ASPECT OF JUSTIFICATION IN ROMAN CATHOLICISM

following reference (which has the context of whether Christ's descent into hell automatically released people from Purgatory):

> From this passage of Augustine it cannot be concluded that all who were in Purgatory were delivered from it, but that such a benefit was bestowed upon some persons, that is to say, upon such as were already cleansed sufficiently, or who in life, by their faith and devotion towards Christ's death, so merited, that when He descended (into hell), they were delivered from the temporal punishment of Purgatory. Christ's power operates in the sacraments by way of healing and expiation. Consequently, the sacrament of the Eucharist delivers men from Purgatory inasmuch as it is a satisfactory sacrifice for sin.[62]

Notice that Aquinas believed that those released from purgatory are those who were "cleansed sufficiently" therein or who acquired enough merit to be delivered. Notice also that the Eucharist is a means by which the living can intercede on behalf of the dead to assist them in their deliverance from Purgatory.

Interestingly, Aquinas seems to assume much when he speaks on Purgatory, for though he spoke of what Purgatory does, he never clearly spoke on what Purgatory is. The *Catechism of the Catholic Church* gives a helpful definition: "All who die in God's grace and friendship, but still imperfectly purified, are indeed assured of their eternal salvation; but after death they undergo purification, so as to achieve the holiness necessary to enter the joy of heaven. The Church gives the name *Purgatory* to this final purification of the elect . . ."[63]

The Council of Florence (most notably Session 8 which was approved on 22 November 1439) acknowledges Purgatory but does not expound the doctrine. Trent, on the other hand, made a formal decree providing an official Roman Catholic affirmation of the doctrine. Therein, Canon XXX of Session VI anathematized anyone who would claim that justification blots out all sins whereby there is no debt left to be paid in the afterlife. Moreover, Session XXV claims that the suffrages of those in Purgatory are helped (i.e., years are taken off of the suffering) by the "acceptable sacrifice of the altar" (which it later explains are "Masses, prayers, alms and other works of piety" on behalf of faithful Christians).[64] The *Catechism* cites in support of this

---

62. Aquinas, *Summa Theologica*, III, q. 52, a. 8.
63. *Catechism of the Catholic Church*, §1030 and §1031; italics original.
64. Council of Trent, "On Justification," Session VI, canon XXX, in Tanner, *Decrees of the Ecunemical Councils*, 681 and "Decree Concerning Purgatory" Session XXV, ¶1, 774. See also Chemnitz, *Examination of the Council of Trent*, pt. 3, 229–30.

teaching 2 Maccabees 12:45: "Therefore he (Judas Maccabeus) made atonement for the dead, so that they might be delivered from their sin."[65] As one author puts it, Purgatory has two primary purposes: to punish those who have not fully satisfied the punishments due to mortal sins, and to punish those who have not obtained pardon of venial sins.[66] This is all in accord with the sentiments of Aquinas mentioned above.

THE EFFICIENT CAUSE

With the aforementioned background established, it is time to examine what the Roman Catholic Church believes to be the efficient cause in justification followed by an examination of the instrumental means. This will clarify how the Roman Catholic Church affirms synergism in their doctrine of infused righteousness.

The appropriate place to begin exploring the efficient cause of justification in Roman Catholic theology is with the person who first gave the clearest explanation of these terms—Thomas Aquinas. Again, the efficient cause explores who (or what) brings about a change. It explores the person who causes a particular effect, which in this case is justification.

It is unquestionable that Aquinas (as well as the rest of the Roman Catholic Church as will be shown) claimed God was the efficient (or principal) cause of justification.[67] Aquinas said, "The justification of the ungodly is brought about by God moving man to justice. For He it is 'that justifieth the ungodly' according to Rom 4:5."[68] This can rightly be understood as the affirmation that God is the efficient cause, though it needs to be understood in what Aquinas said immediately following:

> Hence He moves man to justice according to the condition of his human nature. But it is man's proper nature to have free-will.

---

65. Other supporting scriptures used in support of the doctrine of purgatory are: 1 Cor 3:15, 1 Pet 1:7, and Matt 12:31. See *The Companion to the Catechism of the Catholic Church*, §1031.5–7.

66. Kenrick, *The Catholic Doctrine of Justification Explained and Vindicated*, 203. There is a long list of what is defined as "mortal sins" (things such as sexual sins like rape, infidelity, and pornography as well as non-sexual sins such as blasphemy, murder, and abortion) which are deemed to be more severe than venial sins (which include things such as hate, lying, and filthy speech).

67. Whether Aquinas (and Roman Catholic theology for that matter) can support their claim that God is "the" efficient cause rather than "an" efficient cause awaits further analysis. Nevertheless, Aquinas claimed that God was *the* principal cause of justification.

68. Aquinas, *Summa Theologica*, I/II, q. 113, a. 3.

THE ASPECT OF JUSTIFICATION IN ROMAN CATHOLICISM

> Hence in him who has the use of reason, God's motion to justice does not take place without a movement of the (human) free-will; but He so infuses the gift of justifying grace that at the same time He moves the free-will to accept the gift of grace, in such as are capable of being moved thus.[69]

This statement is revealing of the Thomist doctrine of justification. God, Aquinas affirms, is the one who "moves man to justice." God, thus, is the cause of justifying an individual. Notice, however, that the way God operates as the efficient cause "does not take place without a movement of the (human) free-will." While Aquinas affirms that "He (God) so infuses the gift of justifying grace" (showing the efficient cause), it is done "at the same time He moves the free-will to accept the gift of grace." Thus, while God is the efficient cause, the cause does not have the effect (of infusing justifying grace into the individual) apart from the individual utilizing the free will to accept this grace. The cause does not effect, necessarily, but requires cooperation in order to effect infused righteousness.

Consider Aquinas further on the subject:

> As stated above (A[3]) a movement of free-will is required for the justification of the ungodly, inasmuch as man's mind is moved by God. Now God moves man's soul by turning it to Himself according to Ps 84:7 (Septuagint): "Thou wilt turn us, O God, and bring us to life." Hence for the justification of the ungodly a movement of the mind is required, by which it is turned to God. Now the first turning to God is by faith, according to Heb 11:6: "He that cometh to God must believe that He is." Hence a movement of faith is required for the justification of the ungodly.[70]

God is still the justifier in this case (Aquinas never affirmed that the human justifies oneself); however, understanding the precise nature of causation is important. For justification to occur, according to Aquinas, free will and faith must be exercised in order for justification to occur. As he said, "[A] movement of faith is required for the justification of the ungodly (to occur)." God moves the mind of an individual to exercise the free will (a rather obscure reference to prevenient grace thereby dismissing any notion of Pelagianism), and because God moves the will initially he thus gets all the credit and glory (according to Aquinas). However, the efficient cause does not cause the effect of justification without another cause that is "required for the justification of the ungodly." The other cause required is free-will and

69. Ibid.
70. Ibid., a. 4.

faith. Notice that free-will and faith are not the means by which the efficient cause works (as the Protestant tradition affirms). Rather (as Aquinas used the term "required" three times above) faith must be present in order for the effect of justification to occur.

A final reference from Aquinas will be observed before exploring the rest of the Catholic Church's stance on the subject. Aquinas states:

> There are four things which are accounted to be necessary for the justification of the ungodly, viz. the infusion of grace, the movement of the free-will towards God by faith, the movement of the free-will towards sin, and the remission of sins. The reason for this is that, as stated above (A[1]), the justification of the ungodly is a movement whereby the soul is moved by God from a state of sin to a state of justice. Now in the movement whereby one thing is moved by another, three things are required: first, the motion of the mover; secondly, the movement of the moved; thirdly, the consummation of the movement, or the attainment of the end. On the part of the Divine motion, there is the infusion of grace; on the part of the free-will which is moved, there are two movements– of departure from the term "whence," and of approach to the term "whereto"; but the consummation of the movement or the attainment of the end of the movement is implied in the remission of sins; for in this is the justification of the ungodly completed.[71]

Four things are *"necessary"* for justification to occur, according to Aquinas. First, God must infuse grace. He, as such, is reckoned to be the principal cause. Notice, however, that Aquinas does not see this as the completion of justification, for three other things are "necessary for the justification of the ungodly." The second and third necessary things (or could it have been said "the second and third necessary causes"?) required for justification to occur is a movement of an individual's free will towards God by repentance and faith. While the definitions of "repentance" and "faith" require proper understanding (and will be explored below), it is clear that repentance and faith are required for justification to occur. This may not sound troubling at first glance, for even Protestants would agree that repentance and faith are necessary in order for one to be justified. However, there is a significant difference. As was shown above (and will be shown below), justification is progressive. It must be acquired through acts of merit. Repentance (as will be shown below) is not merely a remorse and turning away from sin as the Protestants affirm. The Catholic Church developed

---

71. Ibid., a. 6.

THE ASPECT OF JUSTIFICATION IN ROMAN CATHOLICISM

certain *acts of penance* which must be done in order for repentance to occur. Moreover, though Aquinas affirmed that faith is a necessary condition for justification (something Protestants would agree), it will be made clear below (though it was mentioned above) that the faith being referred to is *acts of faith* as expressed through the sacraments. As such, one must merit justification (as mentioned above) through the sacraments. Though the efficient cause is reckoned to be God, further analysis must be done to see if there may be an underlying (synergistic) efficient cause. Finally, the fourth necessary thing for justification to be complete is the actual remission of sins, the consummation of justification.

Moving on, the Council of Trent could not be clearer in its affirmation of the efficient cause. They state: "The causes of this justification are: final cause, the glory of God and of Christ, and eternal life; efficient cause, the God of mercy who, of his own free will, washes and sanctifies, placing his seal and anointing... meritorious cause, his most beloved and only-begotten Son, our Lord Jesus Christ..."[72] They go on to say (in a way not unlike Aquinas did) that Jesus is the meriting cause of justification through his passion. Interestingly, this same chapter on the causes of justification immediately claims that justification only occurs when the merits of Christ's passions are communicated to an individual not through faith alone but through faith expressed through means of the sacraments.[73] Trent is clear that faith does not merit justification (again, the meritorious cause of justification is the Passion of Christ); however, Trent makes it clear that one will not receive "individually his own justness... (without) each one's dispositions and cooperation."[74] As such, human faith and the work of God cause justification to occur making one reconsider the claim that God is the sole efficient cause.

Hans Küng provides a puzzling view which amounts to the same notions as Aquinas and Trent. Küng (in response to the criticisms of Karl Barth) claims that though Trent advocates synergism in justification, it is not a notion of justification coming partly from God and partly from the human. Affirming that there is no co-justifier view in Trent, Küng states: "God Himself produces justification."[75] Yet how does God produce justification?

72. Council of Trent, "Decree on Justification," Session VI.7, in Tanner, *Decrees of the Ecunemical Councils*, 673.

73. Ibid.

74. Ibid. The "cooperation" required to receive the merits of the Passion are the sacraments. Notice that this "cooperation" implies "working together," or synergism with God in the sacraments.

75. Küng, *Justification*, 266; see also 264–65. Though Küng does not use the term "efficient cause," the notion is certainly there given that he claims "God Himself produces justification."

The answer, claimed Küng, is synergistic. God gives justice to an individual, yet he does so in accordance with the human will. Küng states: "The sinner himself is incapable of doing anything for his justification. But through God's grace man is highly active, precisely in his passive receptivity."[76] How someone can be actively passive is unclear, yet Küng tries to explain himself by saying that one must show faith (through the sacraments) which is active, yet it is also passive since this is only by grace, yet human activity is also an essential requirement, yet everything in this act of cooperation is from God and not of the human.[77] Küng is less than clear with his view and has been questioned as to his conclusions on the matter.[78] Nevertheless, there are enough parallels with his view and the Tridentine and Thomist views to conclude that, for Küng, the efficient cause of justification is in God though the human must exercise one's will in order to effect justification.

THE INSTRUMENTAL CAUSE

Now is the time to observe exactly how one is made righteous by observing instrumentality. Again, the instrumental cause (the term used by Aquinas) is a secondary cause that produces the effect which owes its efficacy to the efficient cause. In other words, one is now considering how one is justified, not who is the one who justifies.

As mentioned in the quote from Thomas Aquinas above, the Thomist view of instrumental causation comes through repentance and faith.[79] Through these acts, one acquires merits (also mentioned above). However, how is one to understand repentance and faith?

In the traditional Protestant position, repentance is defined as: "[A] heartfelt sorrow for sin, a renouncing of it, and a sincere commitment to forsake it and walk in obedience to Christ."[80] This is viewed as the negative side of conversion (as was explored in that respective chapter) whereby an individual turns away from sin. The positive side of conversion is faith which may be defined as: "[T]rust in Jesus Christ as a living person for forgiveness of sins and for eternal life with God."[81] Faith, in the Protestant understanding, is belief and trust in the promises of God. No doubt this tradition believes this faith must be evidenced by works, lest it not be true

76. Ibid., 264.
77. Ibid., 264–65.
78. McGrath, *Iustitia Dei*, 414.
79. Aquinas, *Summa Theologica*, I/II, q. 113, a. 6.
80. Grudem, *Systematic Theology*, 713.
81. Ibid., 710.

THE ASPECT OF JUSTIFICATION IN ROMAN CATHOLICISM

saving faith (as shown in chapter 5), yet faith understood as "faithful works" has no place in this tradition.

Roman Catholic theology, on the other hand, has a different understanding of repentance and faith. Examining repentance first, the Roman Catholic Church, because of their understanding of justification, defines repentance not only as remorse for sins but acts which show that one is truly sorrowful for sins. It is not enough to say, "I am sorry" to God for sins, believes the Catholic Church, for this is not genuine sorrow. Just as in earthly relations, forgiveness (they claim) acknowledges that wrong was done, asks for forgiveness, make efforts not to repeat the offence, and make amends for the offence.[82]

The *Catechism of the Catholic Church* makes this clear. It claims that the sinner (in order to recover from the effects of sin) must make satisfaction for one's own sins through penance, which are works which correspond to the gravity and nature of the sin, with the results being that one is configured to the likeness of Christ and may then be allowed to be co-heirs with him.[83] As for how penance should be carried out, the *Catechism of the Catholic Church* suggests prayer, offerings, acts of mercy, charity, and "patient acceptance of the cross we must bear,"[84] though this does not seem to be an exhaustive list.

While it was in the twelfth century that the Catholic Church formalized specific acts to be performed to make amends for the offence of sin, it was Tertullian, in the second century, who gave a historical basis for what would later be known as the sacrament of penance or the sacrament of reconciliation.[85] Consider Tertullian on the following:

> Well, since, God as Judge presides over the exacting and maintaining of justice, which to Him is most dear; and since it is with an eye to justice that He appoints all the sum of His discipline, is

---

82. Johnson, *Why Do Catholics Do That?*, 47.

83. *Catechism of the Catholic Church*, §1459–§1460. The *Catechism* goes on to cite a quote from Trent that says that Christ is the one whose sacrifice allows one to be accepted by God and not by human works or cooperation.

84. *Catechism of the Catholic Church*, §1460. Kevin Johnson observes the historical acts of penance required for sin as involving such things as wearing sackcloth and ashes in a public square for several weeks, wearing a sign in public arenas confessing one's sin, and walking to the Church of the Holy Sepulchre in Jerusalem (and back), in *Why Do Catholics Do That?*, 50.

85. While the Vatican has always referred to the penitential rite as "Sacrament of Penance," recently local parishes have changed the title to "Sacrament of Reconciliation" for pastoral reasons. See Cooke, *Sacraments and Sacramentality*, 208–9. It is important for the reader to know that *sacrament of penance* and *sacrament of reconciliation* will be used interchangeably.

there room for doubting that, just as in all our acts universally, so also in the case of repentance, justice must be rendered to God?—which duty can indeed only be fulfilled on the condition that repentance be brought to bear *only* on *sins*.[86]

For Tertullian, justice must also be rendered with repentance. In his treatise *On Reconciliation*, Tertullian made no mention of acts of penance which must be performed in order for sin to be absolved. Nevertheless, he did set a historical precedent for tying forgiveness of sin with the rites of the Church.[87]

Anselm of Canterbury, in his classic work *Why God Became Man*, likewise understood repentance as recompense. In the dialogue with Bono, Anselm states:

> [I]f it came about that you took that glance contrary to the will of God: what recompense could you make for this sin ... You do not therefore give recompense if you do not give something greater than the entity on account of which you ought not to have committed the sin ... And God cannot raise up to a state of blessedness anyone who is to any extent bound by indebtedness arising from sin.[88]

So where and how did acts of penance for the remission of sins come about? There are three primary texts from the New Testament that the Roman Catholic Church uses to support their doctrine of penance: Matthew 16:16, 18:18, and John 20:22–23. However, even prominent Catholic exegetes affirm that reading the sacrament of penance into these texts is eisegesis rather than exegesis, though they would also affirm that their sacrament of penance is in accordance with it. Rather, these exegetes affirm that the sacrament of penance was birthed through pastoral need and practical application under guidance from the Holy Spirit.[89]

The *Canons of Basil* (c. AD 370) list various acts of penance which must be performed when certain acts of sin occur. Each relates directly to the offence made meaning that public sins will be accompanied by public repentance, and the length of penance may be as small as a year and go on to 10 years depending upon the offence.[90] By the fifth century, Pope Leo the Great claimed:

---

86. Tertullian, "On Repentance," 3.2, 3:658; italics original.
87. Stasiak, *Sacramental Theology*, 57.
88. Anselm of Canterbury, *Why God Became Man*, 306–7.
89. Osborne, *Reconciliation and Justification*, 19–21.
90. Basil, "The First Canonical Epistle," Can. 2–4, 604.

THE ASPECT OF JUSTIFICATION IN ROMAN CATHOLICISM

> The manifold mercy of God so assists men when they fall, that not only by the grace of baptism but also by the remedy of penitence is the hope of eternal life revived, in order that they who have violated the gifts of the second birth (i.e., baptism), condemning themselves by their own judgment, may attain to remission of their crimes, the provisions of the Divine Goodness having so ordained that God's indulgence cannot be obtained without the supplications of priests.[91]

This telling statement reveals many things. Baptism is the grace of God by which an individual receives eternal life (something that will be explored further below), yet eternal life may be lost through sin. Penitence is that which restores an individual back to good graces (and God assists in this as well), yet penitence requires measurable acts (done in cooperation with the priests) in order to restore one's right relationship with God.

More could be said about how the church developed the sacrament of penance, yet one may say in summary that by the twelfth century, it was widely recognized that repentance entailed formalized acts of penance.[92] The Council of Trent gave thorough consideration to the sacrament of penance as this was the subject of Session XIV. The closing statement of Trent on this matter states:

> [W]e are able to make satisfaction before the Father not only by penances voluntarily undertaken by us to atone for sin, or those imposed by the judgment of the priest according to the extent of the fault, but also (and this is the greatest proof of love) by the temporal afflictions imposed by God and borne by us with patience.[93]

One should note from this text that the official Roman Catholic position (upheld by the *Catechism of the Catholic Church*) claims that an individual (through the assistance, or what could be understood as cooperation of Jesus Christ) can make satisfaction to God through voluntary punishment of the self, punishment as ascribed by the priest, or punishment ascribed by God. As one modern author puts it, one has to make up for (or pay for) one's sins, and this may be done in this life or the next. Should one

---

91. Leo I, "Letters of Leo the Great," CVIII.II, 80.

92. For a history and development of the sacrament of penance, see McGrath, *Iustitia Dei*, 117–28.

93. Council of Trent, "On the Most Holy Sacrament of Penance and Extreme Unction," Session XIV.IX, in Tanner, *Decrees of the Ecumenical Councils*, 709. For what acts constitute satisfaction, Trent says, "[F]asting, almsgiving, prayers and other devout exercises of the spiritual life," in "Decree on Justification," Session VI.XIV, 677.

want to atone (as he puts it) for one's sin, one may do "[T]oken acts like the familiar 'five Our Fathers and five Hail Marys.'"[94]

Again, Aquinas (and the Roman Catholic Church) believes that repentance is necessary in order to be justified; however, what is meant by repentance is acts of penance formalized by the Church and prescribed by the priests. An individual must do certain acts of penance which are measurable and fit the offence of sin if forgiveness is to occur. They do not do this, however, without grace assistance. As such, it is appropriate to consider penance as a synergistic activity of the instrumental cause by which an individual becomes righteous. However, this is only one half of the equation.

Not only must acts of penance be performed, but faith must be present as well. How Protestants define faith was mentioned above, yet is this how the Roman Catholic Church defines justifying faith? Asked another way, does belief and trust in the work of Christ on the cross alone (what Luther would call *sola fide*) lead one to justification?

Robert A. Sungenis, in his book *Not By Faith Alone*, answers in the negative. In this massive work, Sungenis claims that the Apostle Paul never once (in all his writings) ever stated that an individual is justified by "faith alone." Sungenis also points to James 2:24 where it states "You see that a person is justified by works and not by faith alone."[95] This is not to say that Sungenis believes justification is by works of the law. In fact, he denies such. Rather, what Sungenis suggests is that justification is not by faith *alone* or works of the law *alone* but a combination of faith *and* works together. Together, faith and works are the grounds and establishment for justification.[96] When Paul condemns salvation by works of the law, Sungenis argues that Paul condemned salvation by means of ceremonial law (customs, rituals, and rites of Judaism) and moral law (summed up in the Decalogue). Sungenis also claims that there is a universal law (citing Romans 2:14–15 as his textual support) which is a law written on people's hearts. It is a law that convicts one of sin. This too does not save; however, God still demands obedience to the law. Sungenis, thus, says, "This connection is so strong that it is quite biblical to state that without obedience to the law it is impossible to be justified and enter the kingdom of heaven."[97] One is thus justified by God assisting the individual to fulfil the heart of the law (not by faith alone and not by works done alone performed via unassisted merit), by grace

---

94. Johnson, *Why Do Catholics Do That?*, 49.
95. Sungenis, *Not By Faith Alone*, 1–3.
96. Ibid., 8–12, 16.
97. Ibid., 32.

assisted synergism.⁹⁸ Sungenis claims that Christ did not take away the guilt and punishment that humans deserved for their sin, for such is done in hell; rather, he became a propitiatory sacrifice which appeases the wrath of God and allows all people to attain salvation through participation in God's grace.⁹⁹ Yet how does this synergistic activity relate to Catholicism? What he spends much of the rest of his book doing is showing how baptism is the entry point into justification, that righteousness is something progressively attained synergistically, and that sanctification and justification belong together as one in the same end. The point of all of this is to say that faith alone (as defined as belief and trust in the saving work of Christ alone) is not the means by which an individual is justified. Synergistic works must be accompanied though they are not to be thought of things done in order to put God into humanity's debt (as if he were obliged to receive them).

This is in accordance with Trent. Consider Canon IX: "If anyone says that the sinner is justified by faith alone, meaning thereby that no other co-operation is required for him to obtain the grace of justification, and that in no sense is it necessary for him to make preparation and be disposed by a movement of his own will: let him be anathema."¹⁰⁰ Clearly, faith alone is not how one is justified in Roman Catholic theology, for cooperation is necessary in order to obtain justification. Notice how "to cooperate" (Lat. "*cooperetur*" which means "to work together") contrasts "faith alone" as it relates to "the obtaining the grace of justification." Belief must be accompanied with synergistic works in order for justification to be obtained.

Yet what works must accompany faith? The short answer is the sacraments, beginning with baptism. The first article on justification in the *Catechism of the Catholic Church* makes this affirmation through its claim that God justifies an individual by communicating Christ's righteousness into an individual by means of faith and baptism.¹⁰¹ Trent claimed that the merits of Christ leading one to justification come through the instrumental cause of the baptism sacrament, though it must be accompanied by faith.¹⁰² Trent goes on to say, though, that righteousness (or justice) must be increased

---

98. Ibid., 38–39, 46.

99. Ibid., 115.

100. Council of Trent, "On Justification" *Council of Trent*, Session VI, canon IX, in Tanner, *Decrees of the Ecumenical Councils*, 679.

101. *Catechism of the Catholic Church*, §1987. See also §1992, §1993, §1997, §1999, §2003.

102. Council of Trent, "Decree on Justification," Session VI.VII, in Tanner, *Decrees of the Ecumenical Councils*, 673. This same chapter goes on to state that the Holy Spirit ("Ghost") distributes justice within individuals through human cooperation (Lat. "*cooperationem*" i.e., synergism).

(clarifying that baptism alone is not sufficient to make one righteous). It claims that faith must cooperate with good works for the increase of justice. Trent clarifies what the instrumental cause is that leads to increase of justice through this claim: "[It is] the most holy sacraments of the church by means of which all true justness either begins, or once received gains strength, or if lost is restored . . . (the sacraments being) baptism, confirmation, Eucharist, penance, last anointing, order, matrimony."[103]

This historic dogma is in line with current Catholic theology. Pope Benedict XVI (formerly Joseph Ratzinger) affirms that justification is through faith and not by works, yet he also explains that the way faith must operate (for God does not impose his will upon a passive human) is initially through the sacrament of Baptism and then progressively through the Eucharist (which he claims embraces one to Christ and purifies an individual from sin).[104]

The use of the sacraments as instrumental cause to acquiring merit is in accordance with their definition of justification mentioned earlier. To be justified is to be *made* righteous. One is made righteous through the infusion of merit through the sacraments. The Church claims throughout that this is not to be thought of as works-based-righteousness. Rather, as said above, God desires to work with the human will, and the way the free-will cooperates (synergistically) with God is by sacraments done by faith.

The point to conclude is that the Roman Catholic Church (while attributing all things to grace) believes that justification occurs through the instrumental cause of penance and sacraments (acted out in faith). This is not to be understood in the way Protestants understand repentance and faith, for Protestants deny specific acts of penance to be done for repentance and specific sacraments to be done to acquire merit by faith. This also affirms that the instrumental cause, in the Roman Catholic Church, is both admittedly and logically synergistic in both forms: penance and sacraments.

SALVATION OUTSIDE THE CHURCH?

The sacraments (according to Trent) were to be administered only by the Church. Through the priests (as mentioned above) one may be ascribed acts of penance and receive the sacraments which lead to acquired justice (or merit) before God. This raises the question, since repentance and faith are

---

103. Council of Trent, "Decree on the Sacraments," Session VII. Proem and Canon I, in Tanner, *Decrees of the Ecumenical Councils*, 684. See also Session VI, ch. vii where it speaks of the causes of justification (the sacraments being the instrumental cause).

104. Benedict XVI, *Jesus of Nazareth*, 235, 237.

THE ASPECT OF JUSTIFICATION IN ROMAN CATHOLICISM

not defined in the same way the Protestant position defines them and because penance and the sacraments fall under the jurisdiction of the Church: is there salvation outside of the Roman Catholic Church?

The Latin phrase *extra ecclesiam nulla salus* has a long and rich history. Simply put, it means, "No salvation outside the church." While tracing the history of this statement would side-track this study from its present course, it may nonetheless be affirmed that this motto has been upheld by the Roman Catholic Church for centuries.[105] However, at Vatican II, the church (though it claims not to have changed their historic stance) clarified their position. While it affirms that there is no salvation outside of Christ, and Christ works through his Church by means of the sacraments for salvation, Vatican II softened exclusivist language and allowed the possibility that others, outside of the Roman Catholic Church, can be saved.[106]

EVALUATION OF THE EFFICIENT CAUSE OF SALVATION IN ROMAN CATHOLIC THEOLOGY

The areas of synergism in Roman Catholic theology should thus be clear. While God is the justifier in this tradition, justice (or merit) must be acquired through mutual cooperation between God and the human. The work of God is the infusion of merit, and the work (according to their own terminology) of the human is acquiring merit by means of acts of penance and utilization of the sacraments. As has been shown, the Catholic Church affirms throughout that this acquisition of merit is (in their understanding) not works-based or earned salvation whereby God is indebted to an individual; rather, it is God's generous utilization of the human's free will and response in holiness. This claim, however, must be analyzed.

It is beyond dispute that the Catholic Church has a firm stance that Jesus Christ has acquired all merit and is thus the only source by which people may be justified. Moreover, Trent affirmed the Council of Orange which

---

105. For a full history of salvation outside of the church, see Sullivan, *Salvation Outside the Church*.

106. See Sullivan, *Salvation Outside the Church*, 145–51. See also Rahner, "What is a Sacrament?," 280 who says that though Vatican II affirmed the Roman Catholic Church as the sacrament of grace to the world, individuals may still be saved without being baptized into this community. Vatican II states: "Relying on scripture and tradition, it ["This holy council"] teaches that this pilgrim church is required for salvation" (*Vatican Council II*, "Lumen Gentium" 2.14, 20). The implication is that there is no salvation outside the church. However, as said above, Vatican II, while affirming that God works through the Church for salvation, recognized that there are "separated brethren" outside of the church.

condemned Pelagianism (and Semi-Pelagianism) while also affirming prevenient grace thereby affirming an individual's inability to justify oneself. These points must be conceded upon. However, the issue of efficient cause (or principal cause according to Aquinas) does not concern *where* justification is *sourced*; it concerns *how* justification is *caused*.

As mentioned above, the Catholic Church affirms through Trent, Aquinas, Vatican II, and the *Catechism of the Catholic Church* (to name a few) that the efficient cause of justification is God. However, it was also shown that this Cause does not work *upon* individuals; He works *with* individuals in cooperation. While this perhaps would not be an issue to the monergistic position of the Protestants at first glance (for they affirm that justification is an active aspect of salvation requiring a human response of faith), it becomes a concern to this party when one observes that the way the Efficient Cause (i.e., God) works *with* humanity is by synergistic works that acquire merit as expressed through specified acts of penance and sacraments.

Consider again the following reference from Aquinas: "There are four things which are accounted to be necessary for the justification of the ungodly, viz. the infusion of grace, the movement of the free-will towards God by faith, the movement of the free-will towards sin, and the remission of sins..."[107]

This quote was analyzed in detail above, but one will recall what was observed. For Aquinas, there are four things that are *necessary*. God must infuse grace (a reference to prevenient grace, not full justifying grace, for God does not justify without the other "things" in this list). Once God prevenes upon the individual, one may move one's free will away from sin and towards God. While this sounds like something that the Protestant tradition would adhere to as well, it was also shown that for Aquinas (and later Catholicism), repentance involved formalized "acts of penance" not merely remorse and a turning away from sin, and faith was acts of faith as formalized in the sacraments. This leads to the fourth necessary criterion in Aquinas which is "the remission of sins" which leads to justification. Recall, however, that this justification does not occur at once (as is believed by the Protestant party). Rather, one gets infused with justifying grace (or merit) to a degree, though more is required. When one thus reads Aquinas with this understanding, Aquinas claims that four things are necessary (required, essential) for justification to occur: prevenient grace, acts of penance, and sacraments. These things will lead one to becoming progressively justified. Should enough merit not be acquired, one will undergo purgatory.

One will also recall this quote mentioned above from Aquinas:

---

107. Aquinas, *Summa Theologica*, I/II, q. 113, a. 6.

> Hence He moves man to justice according to the condition of his human nature. But it is man's proper nature to have free-will. Hence in him who has the use of reason, God's motion to justice does not take place without a movement of the (human) free-will; but He so infuses the gift of justifying grace that at the same time He moves the free-will to accept the gift of grace, in such as are capable of being moved thus.[108]

This quote (which is in accordance with the later Tridentine canons) claims that God will not justify an individual without a movement of one's free will. One may well question how "free" the will is in Thomism given that Aquinas states that God must move the will to accept the gift of grace (as this quote above mentions).[109] Nevertheless, the reader will observe that God does not justify without the free-will's engagement. While this may seem appropriate to the monergist, one must recall (as has been shown thoroughly above) that repentance and faith are defined differently than traditional Protestants understand.[110] Penance and sacraments are the means by which one exercises one's free will. God will not justify without sacraments and acts of penance. He will not effectually cause (as the sup-

---

108. Ibid., a. 3.

109. This, as mentioned above, could be an obscure reference to prevenient grace. Notice, however, that Aquinas differs from other proponents of prevenient grace in claiming that God moves an individual to accepting the grace. This is different from the Arminian claim that God overcomes one's depravity and presents the opportunity for one to respond freely to justification. This is not what Aquinas claims. Aquinas claims that God moves an individual to receiving justification. The clearest example of this is infant baptism. Aquinas claimed Infants are not capable of the movement of their free-will; hence it is by the mere infusion of their souls that God moves them to justice. Now this cannot be brought about without a sacrament, in Aquinas, *Summa Theologica*, I/II, q. 113, a. 3. Infants do not exercise their free will. Rather, God moves them to justice through the sacrament of infant baptism. In that sacramental act, God infuses merit into their souls and moves them to justice. While Roman Catholicism does see infant baptism as an act of prevenient grace, it is much different from the Wesleyan-Arminian notion of prevenient grace that allows an individual to exercise free will to receive salvation. In this view, God moves an individual to receiving merit through his movement, even upon unwilling infants. One may very well question how this notion maintains the integrity of free-will as Aquinas claims.

110. Here, the criticism against Aquinas is not that a motion of the will is required for justification. Monergists affirm as much when they claim that justification is by faith. The concern, rather, is the cause of justification. Aquinas affirms that God must move the will (something monergists gladly affirm) while also claiming that this is free will. How free is a will that is forcibly moved by God? Moreover, and more to the point, the movement of the will required in Thomism is engagement in the sacraments (matched with penance). When sacraments and penance are matched with the "prevenient" grace of God as defined by Aquinas, the result (or effect) is justification which goes far beyond what monergists would affirm.

posed Efficient Cause) justification, without a priest mediating penance and sacraments on an individual.

One may thus rightly question the Roman Catholic notion that God is *the* efficient cause of justification. He may be reckoned to be "an" efficient cause, but he cannot appropriately be reckoned to be "the" efficient cause despite the denial of this by Roman Catholicism. The reason for this, again, is because Aquinas himself observed that the principal (efficient) cause is the agent who brings about a cause so that a particular effect may occur. The effect of justification will not occur without God and the human working together (synergistically) through infusion on God's part and penance and sacraments on the human's part. Consider the Catholic position as set forth in the *Joint Declaration on the Doctrine of Justification*: "They (Catholics) do not thereby deny that God's gift of grace in justification remains independent of human cooperation."[111]

Catholicism does not hesitate to affirm that the sacraments themselves are both symbols of grace and causes of grace. As one author states: "They (the sacraments) confer grace and they symbolize the conferring of that grace. This is what the Scholastic formula meant when it said that the sacraments effect (cause) what they signify, and that they signify what they effect."[112] Yet how are those sacraments carried out? This same author says that the Latin phrase *ex opera operato* (by the work worked—a reference to doing rightly the sacraments in a non-passive way) is how the sacraments are to be carried out. Said another way, one must "approach the sacraments in faith" and when this is rightly done, justification is effected.[113] When one puts these two concepts together, the efficient cause becomes clear. Sacraments effect justification. Sacraments must be done in faith. Faithful activity in the sacraments effects, causes, merits justification. The sacraments should not be considered only as the means by which grace is conferred; they should be understood as the cause of grace. Hence, the efficient cause of justification is synergistic whereby God is the justifier who justifies through one's participative work in the sacraments. Both are required to effect justification.

---

111. *Joint Declaration on the Doctrine of Justification*, 19.

112. Stasiak, *Sacramental Theology*, 36–37.

113. Ibid., 38–39. This same discussion can also be found in Bokenkotter, *Dynamic Catholicism*, 175–79. There he claims that the sacraments are not mere symbols, but they actually cause the effect of justification. Bokenkotter also observes (historically speaking) that one must cooperate with this grace in the sacraments. When one puts all this together, one must synergistically work by faith in the sacraments with God which has the effect of justification.

THE ASPECT OF JUSTIFICATION IN ROMAN CATHOLICISM

Yet what should one do with all the affirmations made by the Catholic Church of justification being by grace? First, one must recall that the notion of merit is prevalent in this tradition, a matter which will be analyzed more below. Second, one should not suppose that because something is affirmed that it is also actualized, for a statement of fact may (in actuality) be contrary to fact.[114]

First, one must examine the language employed by Catholicism as it relates to justification. Recall the proceedings of Trent on this matter: "[T]hey grow and increase in that very justness they have received through the grace of Christ, by faith united (Lat. *cooperante*) to good works."[115] One must be cooperating with good works so that there may be an "increase in that very justness." Cooperation, as has been shown throughout this study, is synonymous with synergism. One must "work together" by means of good works (mentioned as observing the commandments of God and the Church) in order for justification to be infused. If the term "cooperation" were not clear enough, it is very clear that one must exercise an activity in order to acquire (for the belief is that one does not attain in a solitary act) justification. This matches well with Canon IX of Trent which states that one must cooperate with divine grace in order to be justified. Aquinas likewise said, "I answer that, As shown above (AA[1],3,4), our works are meritorious from two causes: first, by virtue of the Divine motion; and thus we merit condignly; secondly, according as they proceed from free-will in so far as we do them willingly, and thus they have congruous merit . . . "[116] He goes on to say, "And thus as life everlasting is simply the reward of the works of justice in relation to the Divine motion, as stated above (AA[3],6), so have temporal goods, considered in themselves, the nature of reward, with respect to the Divine motion, whereby men's wills are moved to undertake these works, even though, sometimes, men have not a right intention in them."[117] Apart from any analysis of these references, one will simply want

---

114. Again, this is not to accuse the Roman Catholic Church of Pelagianism, Semi-Pelagianism, or that Jesus Christ is not the source of all righteousness as was stated above.

115. Council of Trent, "Decree on Justification," Session VI.X, in Tanner, *Decrees of the Ecunemical Councils*, 675.

116. Aquinas, *Summa Theologica*, I/II, q. 114, a. 6. Aquinas's notion of moral causality through the principal cause of God through the sacraments has been questioned and refuted by Catholic theologians in this regard. Aquinas claimed that the sacraments were both symbol and cause of justification; however, can this really be the case? Liam G. Walsch observes that the Thomistic model here does not uphold, for signs (i.e., the sacraments) must be the effect of work not the cause of work. See Walsh, "Sacraments," 345.

117. Aquinas, *Summa Theologica*, I/II, q. 114, a. 10.

to observe that the Catholic tradition in no way shies away from using the term "work" when it comes to acquiring merit and receiving the reward (i.e., effect) of justification. It was also observed that Catholic scholars fully affirm "works" in conjunction with the grace of God as a means of acquiring merit before God.[118] Faith means faith-assisted works as observed through the sacraments in this tradition. The point to notice, here, is that the Catholic Church, by its own terminology, does support works as a cause to acquire merit for justification.

While the evaluation of the instrumental cause of sacramental works awaits further analysis below, the issue of efficient causation, being the focal point at this time, must be observed. While the Catholic Church affirms all is of grace, it also qualifies this statement that the grace requires a human cause to effect justification. This is contrary to the Protestant position which states that faith is the means through which justification is received, and it further differs from the Protestant view of works being evidence of justification (and not the means by which it is acquired). The terminology utilized by the Roman Catholic tradition is important. God works, but so must an individual. When the two work together (as the causes), the effect is justification. While this tradition claims this is all of God, it qualifies this statement repeatedly by saying that God (as efficient cause) works together with the human (which must also be understood as an efficient cause) because synergistic activity leads to an infusion of justice.

Consider Vatican I on this issue. It states, "And so faith in itself, even though it may not work through charity, is a gift of God, and its *operation is a work belonging to the order of salvation*."[119] Again, faith is a gift of God, and human cooperation is by God's grace; however, faith is also a voluntary act of obedience that cooperates with God's grace. The act itself is a "work belonging to the order of salvation" (Lat. *actus eius est opus ad salutem pertinens*). While faith could not be expressed without grace, it still is a work that appertains to salvation in cooperation (synergism) with God.

A second important factor to notice is that though the Catholic Church attributes all things to grace, the notion of merit is contrary to this statement. As stated above, justification is progressive in this view. It must be acquired. The substance that must be acquired is called "merit" which comes from Jesus Christ. Because Jesus is the one who acquired all merits

---

118. Sungenis, *Not By Faith Alone*, 32–46; Baker, *Fundamentals of Catholicism*, 14–15; O'Collins and Rafferty, "Roman Catholic View," 268, 275–76.

119. *First Vatican Council* in *Decrees of the Ecumenical Councils*, vol. II, session 3, ch. 3, 807; emphasis added.

because of his Passion on the cross, the Tridentine claim is that it is solely by grace that an individual is justified.[120] This claim, however, is questionable.

While the point of Jesus as the acquirer of all merit in Roman Catholic theology has been deemed incontestable, what is contestable is the definition of "grace." Grace, as understood by Protestants, means: *unmerited favor*.[121] The Catholic definition of this, however, appears to be the opposite. While grace may be favor from God, it would be merited favor. This comes from their own admission.[122]

Thomas Aquinas, as said above, did not shy away from using terms such as *merits* and *reward*.

> What falls under merit is the reward or wage ... For God gives men, both just and wicked, enough temporal goods to enable them to attain to everlasting life; and thus these temporal goods are simply good ... And thus as life everlasting is simply the reward of the works of justice in relation to the Divine motion, as stated above (AA[3],6), so have temporal goods, considered in themselves, the nature of reward, with respect to the Divine motion, whereby men's wills are moved to undertake these works, even though, sometimes, men have not a right intention in them.[123]

Merit, according to Aquinas, is closely related to reward or wage, and God gives such merit as the "reward of the works of justice." This, as was shown above, is not merely a medieval understanding of merit. The *Catechism of the Catholic Church* affirms the same: "The New Testament speaks of judgment primarily in its aspect of the final encounter with Christ in his second coming, but also repeatedly affirms that each will be rewarded immediately after death in accordance with his works and faith."[124] Notice that those who do "works and faith" are "rewarded" at the final judgment. Faithful works lead to a reward.[125] As such, one may conclude that initial

---

120. Council of Trent, "Decree on Justification," Session VI.III, in Tanner, *Decrees of the Ecumenical Councils*, 672.

121. Kearsley, "Grace," 280.

122. Aquinas said, "By every meritorious act a man merits the increase of grace, equally with the consummation of grace which is eternal life" (*Summa Theologica*, I/II, q. 114, a. 8). See also the rest of that section. He also said that one may merit the increase of grace for another in I/II, q. 114, a. 6. See also Supplement, q. 21, a. 2. The *Catechism* states in §2027, "Moved by the Holy Spirit, we can merit for ourselves and for others all the graces needed to attain eternal life."

123. Aquinas, *Summa Theologica*, I/II, q. 114, a. 10.

124. *Catechism of the Catholic Church*, §1021; see also §1821, 448 and §2006.

125. Monergists will gladly affirm the notion of reward for labor in accordance

grace is of God, yet as one is moved by the Spirit (to engage in penance and the sacraments) there is an increase of grace that is called "merit" which leads to the "attainment" of eternal life.[126]

Hans Küng weighs in on this matter which was briefly mentioned above. He claims that merits do not justify an individual in Roman Catholic theology as if they were some type of Pharisaic moralism. Rather, the work an individual must do is not remain passive (but rather active) in growing in holiness (for sanctification and justification are corollaries).[127] One of the reasons for this is because the human and God are not on equal footing whereby an individual can put God in debt. God merely blesses and rewards out of his lavish grace upon an unworthy servant.[128] This view of not indebting God to pay, reward, and merit an individual (while not succumbing to Pharisaic morality as Küng affirms) must be questioned, however.

An illustration will help prove this point. Say there is an individual in desperate need of money in order to survive, and an employer sees this individual in his need and calls him to work for the employer. The employer freely gives an individual all the tools necessary to do the job that was requested, and at the end of the day, after successful completion of the work assigned to the individual, the employer gives the individual his paycheck which the individual receives with joy and thanksgiving. In this illustration, the employer is the possessor of all the wealth, he freely gives the individual all the tools necessary to carry out a particular job, and the individual (who

---

with Luke 6:23, Rom 2:6, 1 Cor 3:8, et al. Calvin believed the faithful will receive "a compensation for their miseries, tribulations, slanders, etc." and called eternal life a "recompense" (*Institutes*, III.XVIII.IV). However, he, like most monergists, insists that this does not mean works are the cause of justification; see *Institutes*, III.XVIII.I–II. This has been a perpetual tension between Protestants and Catholics. See Lane, *Justification by Faith in Catholic-Protestant Dialogue*, 58–59 in his discussion of the Colloquy of Regensburg.

126. For Aquinas, he believed that if the will is to be free, it must by definition be free from all restraint. That is to say that if something binds the will, the individual cannot be blameworthy. It is based upon this principle that Aquinas develops his philosophy of merit. As one author puts it, "We could hardly merit or demerit by performing acts impossible not to have done. Any doctrine which ultimately removes the notion of merit removes also that of morality, and must be considered as a philosophical—*extranea philosophiae*. If there is nothing free in us, if we are necessarily determined in our willing, then deliberations and exhortations, precepts and punishments, praise and blame, in a word, everything which moral philosophy deals with, would quickly disappear and lose all its meaning" (Gilson, *The Christian Philosophy*, 245). This is the basis for Aquinas's philosophy of merit. The will is free to merit. It is by grace that the will is free to merit, but it is now the responsibility of the will to merit (or acquire) grace.

127. Küng, *Justification*, 270–72.

128. Ibid., 271. See Sungenis, *Not By Faith Alone*, 32–34 who gives a similar analogy and affirmation.

was in a dire, helpless situation) receives the orders and the wages with joy. This does not mean, however, that the individual did not acquire, work for, and deserve recompense or wages for the work being done. This does not mean that the *effect* of wages was not *caused* by the work done by the individual. The fact that the employee gladly received the offer to work does not mean that the individual did not merit a reward at the end of the day. Though the employer gave the individual all the tools necessary to do the job (which the employee could not provide), it was nonetheless the employee who did the work to acquire the wages in the end. The calling of an individual to work for the employer, the giving of the tools necessary to do the job, and the giving of the paycheck may appropriately be thought of as the work of the employer, but it was not a completed work because the task at hand was not accomplished. It required the work of an individual to do the task at hand. Hence, there is synergism in this area. However, the actual work needs to be performed by the employee if the wage is to be received.[129]

This is parallel to the Roman Catholic doctrine of justification. God sees individuals in their desperate need. He gives them the grace necessary to acquire merit, and he rewards (as was Aquinas's terminology) the work of individuals with merit. This notion of "grace" however is not unmerited. One must merit, acquire, and work for the end result. It must be progressively attained. One receives what is due to him or her. While Aquinas (and others) affirmed that there is no equal footing between God and the human, their claim that God is not indebted to individuals does not hold. An employer is above the employee, yet the employer is still indebted to the employee for work performed.

Consider further the claims of Küng: "[M]an confronts God not as a partner with equal contractual rights, but always as an unworthy servant..."[130] Also, "The God who justifies in Christ remains, even in justification, the God of the covenant who—by reason of His new gracious election—wants a true partner, not a robot or a puppet..."[131] For Küng, one is an inferior partner with God void of "contractual rights" but a part-

---

129. All analogies break down at some point, and in this case the Roman Catholic Church, likely, would not affirm that God would leave the employee to do the work all alone without assistance along the way. Still, the analogy upholds the point that though God gives individuals the things necessary to carry out the work, the individual must work in order to receive the wage.

130. Küng, *Justification*, 271. See also Karl Rahner who says, "The doctrine of merit, therefore, does not infringe on the freedom of God's decrees and of his grace. Man does not 'co-operate with' God as if the two were independent agents, but God enables man to work freely and thus really 'bring forth fruit'" (in Rahner and Vorgrimler, *Dictionary of Theology*, 306, s.v. "merit").

131. Küng, *Justification*, 265.

ner nonetheless. As it relates to justification, God accomplishes everything for justification while also including (by necessity) the participation of the individual (hence a true partnership). Interestingly, the New Testament only speaks of partnership in the Gospel with those who are already saved. Nevertheless, Küng states that God does not want a robot (for such would imply that the human would not exercise will but be merely an obedient servant doing things by orders), yet is that not what he would mean with an "unworthy servant"? To be clear, monergists do not believe in a justification that is void of any human activity. They reject complete passivity in justification, much like Küng's comments about God not wanting robots. But is the role between God and the human a partnership that leads to a given outcome? If so, the cause/effect synergistic activity would make the human an agent in the efficient cause. However, if an individual is truly an unworthy servant, he or she will receive whatever comes to him or her from the Master (which, in the case of justification would be the *reception* not *acquisition* of righteousness).

Moreover, Küng explains what is meant by the Tridentine notion of synergism claiming that the work of an individual should not be thought of as self-justification because, "The sinner himself is incapable of doing anything for his justification. But through God's grace man is highly active, precisely in his passive receptivity."[132] How one can be actively passive has already been questioned, though Küng states that active passivity means giving personal assent to the gracious verdict of God. Nevertheless, seven pages after affirming the passivity of an individual in justification, Küng states: "As in Scripture, the Council's (i.e., Trent's) only concern is that man should not remain in a state of indolent passivity, burying his talents, but put them to use."[133] On the one hand, Küng states that merit is acquired from active passivity (implying one acquires merit passively by merely receiving and assenting to it). This is later contradicted by a statement against passive reception, something Küng calls "indolent passivity." Was not active passivity just recently praised?[134] Did not Küng just state that active passivity (which is the human's role in cooperation) was merely assent, or what he calls, "[A] highly active 'Yes and Amen' of the repentant sinner awakened by God's gracious verdict"?[135]

132. Ibid., 264.

133. Ibid., 272.

134. Naturally, monergists (like Catholics) would not approve of indolent passivity. As has already been shown, the Reformers (and later monergists) reject antinomianism. Justification is by faith alone and not by works, but faith is never without subsequent works. The point here is that Küng is self-contradictory. Here, the author notes there is a difference between the adjectives *active* and *indolent*.

135. Ibid., 264.

THE ASPECT OF JUSTIFICATION IN ROMAN CATHOLICISM

Finally, Küng states in this same context that the cooperative works which an individual is responsible for performing (according to Trent) are works asked of the one who is already justified. Küng thus affirms what was also affirmed at Trent (to be discussed below) of the objective event and the subjective process of salvation. For Küng, as in Trent, there is initial justification followed by progressive justification. Küng states that there is no *cooperari* in the objective event of salvation, only in the subjective process through active passivity (as mentioned directly above). Is the subjective process of justification synonymous with Protestants' doctrine of sanctification? Küng sees a distinction, though he does not see them as opposed to one another. For Catholics, sanctification is "[P]rimarily the objective and ontological holiness (*heiligkeit*) achieved in man by God ... (not) the subjective and ethical sanctification (*heiligung*) brought about by man (as in the Protestant position)."[136] Again, for Küng (and the whole of Roman Catholicism), justification is the act (and process) of making someone just. This progressive justification does have a beginning point to it in an objective reality; however, it is not complete. Synergism is still a cause that leads to an effect in this given aspect. This differs from the Protestant understanding of sanctification for one who is fully just in the eyes of God.

Because justification is viewed as progressive, and merit must be acquired continually through the sacraments, it is logical to assume that the human (albeit by the grace of God) is a cooperator in the efficient cause of justification. When an individual carries out a sacrament, it effects infused righteousness with the assistance of God. God does not infuse righteousness apart from an individual's free consent as expressed through a sacrament. When the human's free assent to God through the sacrament is matched with the infused grace of Christ's righteousness, the individual is made more righteous. As such, the cause of justification is the cooperative works of God and the human. This goes contrary to their admission but is indicative of their theology. Even as late as late as the *Joint Declaration on the Doctrine of Justification*, Catholics affirm (see §2010) that no one can merit forgiveness and justification. However, notice how one Catholic author nuances this claim:

> The Roman Catholic position on merit is highly nuanced. Catholics teach cooperation between God's grace and human freedom. Justification has been merited for us by the Passion of Christ. No one can merit the *initial grace* of forgiveness and justification. However, after this initial grace, again through the grace of the Holy Spirit, Catholics hold that "we can then merit

---

136. Ibid., 268.

for ourselves and for others the graces needed for our sanctification, for the increase of grace and charity, and for the attainment of eternal life."[137]

This is an interesting observation. When Catholics speak of justification being unmerited, it is not because it is not progressively attained through synergism. Rather, it is because initial merit (or the source of merit) is found in Christ's work on the cross. It is then up to an individual to acquire this merit (which they claim is an act of grace, though such may be questioned).

Here, one may recall what was mentioned in the previous chapter about the foundation of one's righteousness through union with Christ. No doubt, the Roman Catholic Church has a strong doctrine of union with Christ, but it should be noted how this contrasts the formula as defined by the monergists in the previous chapter. As shown previously, monergists hold to an actuality of righteousness found in one's union with Christ in faith. The union is an established relationship through incorporation and indwelling.[138] The monergist party is not likely to deny any act of *participation* in Christ, but they would insist that such participation in Christ does not mean to imply that one's union with Christ occurs only when someone participates in Christ through certain acts (such as the sacraments). However, in the Catholic tradition, it appears that one is united to Christ through participation primarily (or possibly solely) through participation in the sacraments. The *Catechism* states, "Spiritual progress tends toward ever more intimate union with Christ. This union is called 'mystical' because it participates in the mystery of Christ through the sacraments—'the holy mysteries'—and, in him, in the mystery of the Holy Trinity."[139] Naturally their conception of *transubstantiation* lends itself to this concept of union with Christ.[140] Furthermore, as one is able to be severed from Christ and lose salvation in their view, it makes sense that one's union with Christ is intrinsically linked with

---

137. Wood, "Catholic Reception," 49, emphasis added. One will notice that this last quote comes from the Council of Trent as referenced above.

138. Campbell, *Paul and Union with Christ*, 412–13.

139. *Catechism of the Catholic Church*, §2014. See also §1391 where Holy Communion is said to augment union with Christ, and as one partakes of the Eucharist one receives the "principal fruit" of union with Christ. This is not to say that one sacrament, over another, is the only means through which one receives union with Christ. §1227 speaks of Baptism leading one into communion with Christ and §1309 speaks of Confirmation doing such as well. To be clear, the Holy Spirit is said to be the one bringing someone into communion with Christ in §1108, but this statement also said that the way the Holy Spirit works in this regard is through "liturgical action."

140. Cooke, *Sacraments and Sacramentality*, 96–97.

THE ASPECT OF JUSTIFICATION IN ROMAN CATHOLICISM

participation in the sacraments. The point here is that the monergists were able to provide more convincing proof that one's union with Christ is, in fact, a firm relationship that entails indwelling and incorporation. Indeed, this appears to be the Scriptural stance that one is actually *in Christ* through vital union (Rom 3:21–26, 6:11, 8:1 et al.) rather than only being in Christ whenever sacraments are partaken of.

Moreover, proof that the Roman Catholic Church holds (contrary to its admissions) that the efficient cause of justification is synergistic can be found in its belief that one can lose one's justification (and salvation). As stated above, continual faithfulness (and acquisition of merit) is required in order to be justified, and should there be a lapse into sin an individual will certainly lose salvation.[141] When an individual ceases to work (cooperate) with God, God ceases to work meaning there is no more infusion of righteousness. While what happens to the merit already acquired by an individual when one was working together with God is unclear, what is clear is that the cooperation (synergism) of an individual is so important that should it cease one will lose one's salvation. If God were the sole efficient cause, if God were the sole worker who effects justification, then such would not be the case. As has already been shown throughout, antinomianism is not a monergistic position; however, neither is a conditional justification based upon human cooperation. As such, the efficient cause, once again, can be viewed (in the Catholic view) as synergistic.[142]

Vatican II, while it by no means dealt with the doctrine of justification like the Council of Trent, still addressed the issue of justification in the Roman Catholic view providing a helpful, modern treatment of the issue. Therein, it states: "The followers of Christ, called by God not for what they had done but by his design and grace, and justified in Jesus, have been made sons and daughters of God by the Baptism of faith and partakers of the

---

141. Council of Trent, "Decree on Justification," Session VI.15, in Tanner, *Decrees of the Ecumenical Councils,* 677, and "On Justification," Session VI, canon XV, 680, Canon XXIII, 680; *Catechism of the Catholic Church,* §2005; Kenrick, *The Catholic Doctrine on Justification,* 113, see also 111–22. For Trent, there was a so-called second justification found in sections 10–13. While sections 1–9 stress the inability of one to save himself or herself, and section 7–9 particularly stress that God, not the human, is the justifier by grace, the second part of the decree (relating to second justification) stresses the duty laid upon individuals by God to increase in justification. Should this fail to be achieved due to sin, one's salvation would be lost. See Jedin, *A History of the Council of Trent,* 2:308.

142. This is not to imply that monergists affirm that one will be saved regardless of the life lived after conversion. Calvin clearly held to an assurance of salvation for those who are in Christ (*Institutes,* II.X.VIII), but this was never meant to imply a license for licentiousness. This is seen well in *Institutes,* III.VII. For Luther, see also Cunningham *The Reformers,* 105–6, 113, 117.

divine nature, and so are truly sanctified."[143] With such a clear statement that justification is not by what one has done but by God's design and grace, one may question why this study questions a dual efficient cause. The reason one must question all these claims of justification by grace can be seen in the very next sentence in this dogmatic constitution: "They must therefore hold on to and perfect in their lives that holiness which they have received from God."[144] As has been shown throughout this study, there is a continual mention of the essential necessity for an individual to cooperate (synergistically) with God in this regard for justification to occur. Here, Vatican II states that one "*must* therefore hold on to and perfect in their lives that holiness . . . " The reason this is a "must" is because it is up to an individual to perfect (through works of the sacraments) oneself unto justification, and if this is not done one will forfeit justification. When something has a conditional "must" which must be performed in order to receive something, one may very well question how this fits the definition of grace—a free gift.[145]

Recently, an attempt has been made to find common ground between the Lutheran World Federation and the Roman Catholic Church. These once very opposing parties were able to formulate a common statement that both sides could agree to regarding the doctrine of justification in a publication called *Joint Declaration on the Doctrine of Justification*. In this statement, both traditions affirmed that salvation is by grace through faith alone.[146] While this statement appears to end the divide between Protestants and Catholics, the two traditions were not able to agree on the issue of monergism and synergism. In 4.1 n. 20 of the *Joint Declaration*, Catholics still uphold human cooperation for preparing for and accepting justification (though it is important to note that they see this "personal consent" as an effect of grace and not arising from innate human ability). Lutherans, however, still reject human cooperation in justification claiming that a person can only receive justification and not contribute to it in any way.[147]

---

143. Vatican II, "Lumen Gentium," 5.40, 59.

144. Ibid.

145. Naturally, in the Protestant tradition, grace is freely given with the condition that it is received in faith. This, as has been shown, is very different from what the Roman Catholic Church claims. In the Catholic sense, it is not simply that one must receive something by faith. Instead, one must work the sacraments in faith. When one operates the sacraments, God operates the infusion. The difference between the Catholics and Protestants at this point is that (for Protestants) faith is the condition of being justified, and one must receive justification by faith. The Catholics, on the other hand, believe one must perform certain acts in order to be justified. The difference is significant and is at the heart of the Protestant Reformation.

146. *Joint Declaration*, 15, 45.

147. Ibid, 17, 30–31. Alister McGrath has highlighted the areas of common

All of this is to say that despite notions of "merit" and "acquisition" and "reward" being deemed as mere acts of grace and not the result of human works, these claims (despite denial to the contrary) show that the efficient cause of justification is synergistic—being the work both of God and the individual.[148] The effect of justification will not occur without two causes—one divine and the other human. This goes against the teachings of Scripture as affirmed both by Protestants and Catholics.[149]

EVALUATION OF THE INSTRUMENTALITY OF JUSTIFICATION IN ROMAN CATHOLIC THEOLOGY

As mentioned above, the instrumental cause of justification in Roman Catholic dogma is repentance and faith. What was also shown, however, was the meaning of repentance and faith. Repentance is not merely sorrow for and a turning away from sin as the Protestant tradition affirms, and faith is not simply belief in the saving promises of God. Rather, repentance is understood as acts of penance, and faith is understood as partaking of the sacraments.

---

agreement between Protestants and Catholics in a general way acceptable to many (though not all) in *Justification By Faith*, 71–72 that reflects much of the commonality found in the *Joint Declaration*. He rightly notes that justification both to Protestants and Catholics is attributed to grace and not for human works (though he also rightly observes that Trent taught that individuals acquire condign merit after, not before, justification, 69). However, noticeably missing from this list is the notion of synergism in the acquisition of merit in Catholicism of which the two major traditions retain significant disagreements.

148. Again, this is not just the conclusion of this author only but the express claim of many notable Roman Catholic theologians. Erasmus of Rotterdam spoke of synergism in this area more than anyone else during his time (and debated with Martin Luther). He states: "[W]e have received to the divine grace . . . which gave us this gift, that our will might be *synergos* ("fellow-worker") with grace . . . a good will cooperates with the action of grace . . . both man and God work (in salvation)" (*On the Freedom of the Will*, 81).

149. Jüngel claims that the Roman Catholic tradition ultimately holds on to a belief that faith-filled works leads to one's justification, forgetting the sinful nature bound within an individual, and that there can be no means of human cooperation and contribution to this aspect. He even goes so far as to say that the Roman Catholic Church needs to revise either certain proceedings from the Council of Trent or revise its claim to infallibility, for even the apostle Paul (in Jüngel's opinion) would be anathema. See Eberhard Jüngel, *Justification*, 246–51.

Sacrament of Penance

Beginning with penance as repentance, an important point to note upfront is that the notion of doing acts of penance as means to repent was not systematically developed as a sacrament until the Middle Ages (between AD 1050–1240), and the Catholic Church admits grounds for doing such were embedded in practical, pastoral concerns (rather than Scripture).[150] The concern was to make sure that people were truly sorry for their sins, and since the belief was (at least at the time) that there is no salvation outside of the Roman Catholic Church (and that the Church had authority over excommunication and restoration), formalized acts of penance were created to restore individuals into a right relationship not only with God but also the Church.[151] The significance of this is that over 1,000 years passed where people were able to be righteous before God without acts of penance. The Catholic Church, to date, has spent as much time not doing acts of penance (as a formalized, conscious meritorious activity) as it has doing acts of penance making one question the necessity of such acts as an instrumental cause to be justified.[152]

Because formalized acts of penance developed out of pastoral concerns for people's dealings with sin, it is safe to say that the origin and basis of this belief comes from the Catholic Church and not from the Scriptures themselves.[153] It has already been stated that the primary verse used to sup-

---

150. McGrath, *Iustitia Dei*, 117, and Osborne, *Reconciliation and Justification*, 19–20. Hans Küng makes a similar observation stating that it was in the middle of the twelfth century when the seven sacraments were more established; however, he also observes that around the seventh century, "[T]he idea of *recurrent* penance and at the same time of *private penance* developed" (*The Church*, 333–34).

151. One may question how Roman Catholic theology actually permits "separated brethren" per Vatican II based upon their sacramentology. As modern Catholic scholars state, the church is the dispenser of the sacraments and is, in fact, a sacrament (agent of grace) itself. The sacrament of baptism initiates the individual into the community, and the Eucharist is not just the manifestation or rite of the community but the communion itself. Jesus is physically present in the transubstantiated elements, so the sacraments (which may only be issued by the Catholic Church) are the means of grace by which one encounters Christ for the increase of righteousness. See Jenson, "The Church and the Sacraments," 207–23. As one is removed from the church (by excommunication or by other affiliation), the means to acquire merit is strictly impossible.

152. Loraine Boettner makes this observation as well, highlighting that the Catholic Church did not define the seven sacraments until Peter Lombard (1100–1164) published his famous work *Sentences*. Boettner then states, "It is important to notice that no author for more than a thousand years after Christ taught that there were seven sacraments" (*Roman Catholicism*, 189).

153. See ibid. who states, "Rome can give no proof for the additional five sacraments (confirmation, penance, extreme unction, marriage, and holy orders), except that tradition holds them to be such."

THE ASPECT OF JUSTIFICATION IN ROMAN CATHOLICISM

port the doctrine of penance (John 20:22–23) is admitted by Catholics to be a case of *eisegesis*.[154] However, Catholic exegetes claim that though there is no clear textual support for penance, the doctrine itself does not contradict Scripture. Still, one should note that the New Testament, nowhere, defines repentance (Gk. μετάνοια) as *acts of penitence*.[155]

A thorough analysis of how μετάνοια, used in the New Testament, cannot mean acts of penance is warranted though it will be spared for a sake of focus.[156] Still, one should note that Karl Rahner, a notable twentieth-century Catholic theologian, observed that the sacraments of Baptism and the Lord's Supper are the only sacraments that have any direct ties to Jesus (and thus the Scriptures). This does not mean that Rahner invalidates the other sacraments. He merely claims that the sacraments have indirect ties to Jesus because the Church originates with Jesus (and the Church originated the other sacraments).[157] This claim does not provide firm support for the sacraments (including penance), for it shows that this is the invention of God's community and not of God himself.

The notion of acts of penance as an instrumental cause creates a further problem, however. Again, let it be restated that penance as administered through the Church via the priests is essential for justification to occur. One will recall this quote mentioned above:

> The manifold mercy of God so assists men when they fall, that not only by the grace of baptism but also by the remedy of penitence is the hope of eternal life revived, in order that they who have violated the gifts of the second birth (i.e., baptism), condemning themselves by their own judgment, may attain to remission of their crimes, the provisions of the Divine Goodness having so ordained that God's indulgence cannot be obtained without the supplications of priests.[158]

Justification begins with baptism, yet it is maintained through continual acts of penance.[159] One can lose one's salvation, and the way one gains it back again is through acts of penance. The problem this creates is that it shows penance is a synergistic, cooperative work that must be done by an individual in order to be (and remain) justified.

154. Osborne, *Reconciliation and Justification*, 19–21.

155. See Bauer, *A Greek-English Lexicon of the New Testament*, s.v. μετάνοια.

156. For such a study, see Kittel, *Theological Dictionary of the New Testament*, vol. 9 Λ–Ν, s.v. νοῦς, esp. 999–1008.

157. Rahner, "What is a Sacrament," 282. See also Rahner, "Open Questions," 214.

158. Leo I, "Letters of Leo the Great," 80.

159. McGrath, *Iustitia Dei*, 118.

Monergism or Synergism

On their treatise on penance, the *Catechism of the Catholic Church* states that it is only Jesus Christ who expiates sins once for all, and penance is merely a tool to help an individual conform to the likeness of Christ.[160] However, in that same section, it also says, "They (acts of penance) allow us to become co-heirs with the risen Christ, 'Provided we suffer with him.'"[161] Notice the cause and effect relationship. Acts of penance (the cause) allows (effects) one to become co-heirs with Christ by means of (instrumentality) suffering with him. In the preceding section in the *Catechism*, it also makes a comparative analogy of how one may sin against one's neighbor. While the individual may forgive his neighbor for acts of wrongdoing, "[H]e (the offender) must 'make satisfaction for' or 'expiate' his sins. This satisfaction is also called 'penance.'"[162] This serves as the basis for penance before God. One *must* do acts of penance in order to bring satisfaction for and expiation of one's sins. These acts of penance, as was quoted above, allow individuals to become co-heirs with Christ. They are necessary, mandatory works which must be done.

What should one then make of the claims that forgiveness of sin is done by God (or Christ) alone? What should one do with the constant claims from the Catholic Church that says this is all of grace and not by works? Here, one must understand both what is said and what is not said.

What is said by the Catholic Church is that God forgives sins. What this group also says (though not always in the same sentence) is that God forgives sin by means of penance and sacraments. What the Catholic Church does not say as articulately is that God will not forgive sins without human cooperation. Yes, he is the Forgiver since the offence of sin was done against him; however, he will not forgive apart from human cooperation. As Trent makes clear, "These are called parts of penance, in that, by God's institution, they are required in the penitent for the integrity of the sacrament, and for the full and complete forgiveness of sins."[163]

While this may not sound contrary to the Protestant tradition (for many therein would claim that God would not forgive someone who does not show genuine remorse and a desire for holiness), it in fact differs in many ways. The Catholic tradition says one must make satisfaction for one's sins. One must be a part of the expiation process. One must do certain acts in order for God to forgive. One will not become co-heirs with Christ

---

160. *Catechism of the Catholic Church*, §1460.
161. Ibid.
162. Ibid., §1459.
163. Council of Trent, "On the Most Holy Sacrament of Penance and Extreme Unction," Session XIV.III, in Tanner, *Decrees of the Ecumenical Councils*, 704.

without observing formalized acts, yet when they are observed (in addition to other sacramental acts) then one becomes co-heirs. Seeing penance as a work is not difficult when one observes that it is up to the acts of an individual in order to regain one's standing within the Church and before God for justification. Indeed, Trent affirms them as such when it says, "Nor has any path ever been considered more secure in the church of God for removing the threat of punishment by the Lord than that people should make regular use of these works of penance with genuine sorrow of mind."[164]

There are three primary problems with such a view. First, contrary to claims of the alternative, human works are required for the remission of sins and the attainment of one's justification. One must do works of penance in order to be justified. The works, as mentioned above, include prayer, offerings, acts of mercy, and charity, though historically they have also included such things as buying paper indulgences, inflicting self-harm, and carrying signs in public arenas that confess one's sin. These are the instrumental causes by which an individual is justified. The problem with this is (as shown in chapter 1 and throughout this study) that works do not lead to one's justification, even if they are religious and grace-assisted works. Scripture, as has been shown above, does not define repentance as acts of penance; rather, it is a remorse, sorrow, and turning away from sin. This is the view of the monergistic tradition of chapter 5, and it most clearly shows how salvation is the result of God's grace and not works.

A second problem with mandating acts of penance for the remission of sins is that it implies that Christ did not ultimately atone for (make satisfaction for) sin on the cross. As mentioned above, one must make satisfaction for one's sin through the sacrament of penance. Apparently (though this would never be claimed), there is something lacking in the work of Christ. This observation was made by John Calvin who said:

> Here we never hear such falsehoods: as that after the initial purgation each one of us feels the efficacy of Christ's sufferings solely in proportion to the measure of satisfying penance; but as often as we lapse we are recalled solely to the satisfaction of Christ. Now set before yourself their pestilent absurdities: that

164. Council of Trent, "Teaching Concerning the Most Holy Sacraments of Penance and Last Anointing," Session XIV.VIII, in ibid., 709. Tony Lane observes how eternal punishment for one's sin may be remitted through repentance and confession to a priest (according to Trent), but a temporal punishment is owed to the sinner of which things such as "fasting, good works, penances, indulgences" and more may pay off the debt. Should a debt remain, one will go to purgatory to pay off the rest of the punishment owed. See Lane, *A Concise History of Christian Thought*, 223–24. As such, one may see how works and actions of an individual cause a given effect which seems contrary to notions of justification by grace.

in the first forgiveness of sins only the grace of God operates, but if we have fallen afterward, our works co-operate in obtaining the second pardon ... What a vast difference there is between saying that our iniquities have been lodged with Christ in order that they be expiated in him and saying that they are expiated by our works; that Christ is the propitiation for our sins, and that God must be propitiated by works![165]

For Calvin, if human works must expiate (or propitiate) human sin, there must have been something lacking in the work of Christ (which he vehemently rejects). He sees a big difference between Christ as the expiator of sins and Christ as one who expects human works to expiate sins.

This, for Calvin as well as those in the monergistic tradition, relates to the third major problem which is a diminishing of the glorious work of Christ. God is robbed of glory in such a view because his work requires human work to accompany it.[166] Consider the following claim: "The temporal punishment due to sin can be satisfied for in this life by good works; that is, by Attendance at the Holy Sacrifice of the mass, Reception of the Sacraments, Indulgences, Almsgiving, Prayer, and Spiritual and Corporal Works of Mercy."[167] Notice that sin is "satisfied for" through human actions. This has the (perhaps unintended) result of diminishing the work of Jesus on the cross through which sin was "satisfied for," and it claims that it is within one's grace-assisted (synergistic) power to satisfy (i.e., atone for) sin.

Other Sacraments

Penance, itself, is a sacrament, yet there are six other sacraments which must be performed to acquire merit before God. They are baptism, confirmation, the Eucharist (or Mass), extreme unction, order, and marriage.[168] It will not be necessary to define and explore each of these sacraments (though this study will explore some of them), for general conclusions about the nature of sacraments and instrumentality may be made without defining each sacrament in detail.

However, the sacrament of baptism (though mentioned above) requires further exploration. It was said above that the Roman Catholic

---

165. Calvin, *Institutes*, III.IV.XXVII, 653.

166. This statement from Calvin comes from a section on how the Roman Catholic doctrine deprives Christ of his honor and glory.

167. Burbach, *The Catholic Religion*, 60.

168. Council of Trent, "Decree on the Sacraments," Session VII. Proem and Canon I, in Tanner, *Decrees of the Ecunemical Councils*, 684.

THE ASPECT OF JUSTIFICATION IN ROMAN CATHOLICISM

Church views baptism as the entry point into justification (and the Church).[169] Baptism is also the means through which one receives initial justification.[170] Here, it becomes important to remember that justification, in the Catholic notion, does not refer to a verdict or stature one has before God. Rather, justification and sanctification coincide where one is progressively made righteous. As such, baptism (as was mentioned above) is a means/cause through which sin is washed away and an individual is cleansed, progressing in righteousness.

Moreover, the Council of Trent affirmed transubstantiation in the Lord's Supper whereby (in the Mass) the bread and wine change substances to the actual body and blood of Jesus Christ. By partaking of the bread and wine, one partakes of the crucified Christ and the merits therein with the result that one increases in justification.[171]

There are many arguments that could be made about the nature of baptism and Lord's Supper (whether baptism is something that is done after one is a believer, whether it has any effect on original sin, and whether the Lord's Supper is symbolic only or has some type of real presence). This study, however, will not take this approach, for in the Protestant/monergistic tradition, there is a wide spectrum of beliefs on when baptism should occur and what the Lord's Supper represents.[172] Moreover, one could also expound the 95 *Theses* and bring to mention that these outward acts of the

---

169. *Catechism of the Catholic Church*, §1987. See also §1992, §1993, §1997, §1999, §2003. Leo I, "Letters of Leo the Great," CVIII.II, 80.

170. *Catechism of the Catholic Church*, §1987. The quoted reference therein is from Rom 3:22; see also 6:3-4.

171. Council of Trent, "Doctrine on the Sacrifice of the Mass," Session XXII, in Tanner, *Decrees of the Ecumenical Councils*, 732-41. See also Cooke, *Sacraments and Sacramentality*, 102 who speaks of the Eucharist as a divine action whereby God works "as source of life" through the transubstantiated elements, yet God only works through them when there is cooperation from the assembly (something Cooke calls "a human action"). Hence, one can see the synergistic nature of the Eucharist.

172. One might recall denominations such as the Presbyterians and Anglicans which support infant baptism much like the Catholics. Moreover, Lutherans claim (in their view of consubstantiation) that there is some type of presence of Christ in the Lord's Supper. It is the opinion of this author that baptism is a sign or symbol of one's death to sin and new life in Christ (i.e., regeneration) with no effect of remitting sin and that it is an act to be performed by those who have already made a personal decision to follow Christ. However, as this study is arguing from the point of view of monergists, it must be recognized that there are a variety of monergists (when it comes to the doctrine of justification) who hold views not dramatically different with regards to baptism and the Lord's Supper. How they construe and formulate their doctrines of baptism and Lord's Supper, however, are quite different from the Roman Catholic's position. The point is, for the sake of focus, this study will not explore whether baptism is to be done before or after conversion and what the Lord's Supper actually represents.

sacraments could be done by individuals who are unrepentant of sin, or if the pope had the authority to absolve sin why he should do so out of goodwill. There are many good ways in which the sacraments as means to acquire righteousness could be analyzed; however, this study has the intention of studying instrumentality as a cause to acquire justification.

The point is: Jesus Christ has acquired merit, and it is up to an individual to acquire it. When an individual partakes of the sacraments, merit increases. When an individual does not partake regularly of the sacraments (including the sacrament of Penance and the Eucharist), merit is lost. It is up to the individual to acquire merit from Christ through partaking of the sacraments, for inside of him or her is a deficiency of merit that must be filled. What Christ does is provide individuals the opportunity to acquire merit from him through the sacraments. Baptism (in the Catholic view) is a means by which an individual cooperates with God to have sin washed away. The Mass is the means by which an individual partakes of the suffering Christ. Other sacraments are given by which merit and justice are acquired.

What this means, then, is that Jesus Christ infuses righteousness only when the individual performs a sacrament. According to Aquinas and numerous official papal bulls and decrees since then, one receives the "reward." This should make clear that the other sacraments (like the sacrament of penance) are works. While they may be faith-filled works (that is works of sacraments done in faith), they are nonetheless works.[173] In fact, Trent does not shy away from calling sacraments, like the Eucharist, the most holy and divine "work" an individual may do to reconcile oneself to the Father.[174]

The implications should be obvious. The Efficient Cause (God—though it was observed above that he is not the only efficient cause) works by means of human synergy with the sacraments. One acquires merit from God by means of partaking of the sacraments. The sacraments (which the Catholic Church defines as works) acquire merit leading to the reward of

---

173. The Catholic Church (stemming from Aquinas himself) does not hold that the sacraments themselves operate like some kind of magic inside of an individual where an individual is passively changed by manipulating God. Rather, it says that the sacraments must be received and performed by faith. See Vaillancourt, *Toward a Renewal of Sacramental Theology*, 96–102. This, however, does not mean that the sacraments should not be considered as works because they involve faith. The faith that an individual shows must be through the "works" (as is the claim from Aquinas, Trent, and others) of the sacraments; hence, they are faith-filled works and should not be understood as the Reformation principle *sola fide*.

174. Council of Trent, "Decree Concerning the Things to be Observed, and to be Avoided, in the Celebration of the Mass," Session XXII, in Tanner, *Decrees of the Ecumenical Councils*, 736.

justification. It is the responsibility of an individual to purge and expiate sin through acts of penance (done in synergistic cooperation with Christ) and acquire merit (also done synergistically) leading one to question how this system understands grace. What becomes evident is that the Catholic Church does affirm salvation by grace, but it does not claim salvation by grace alone through faith alone. Works must be performed to expiate one's own sin and acquire justification, something that the Protestant tradition's understanding of Scripture (as shown in chapters 1 and 5) explicitly denies.

This leads one to recall the monergistic position. In that tradition, God is the Justifier (the sole efficient cause). He justifies individuals by his grace alone by means of (instrumentality) faith alone. Faith, as shown in chapter 1, is not a work. It is an action, but it is not a work because it is merely a reception of blessing and not the acquisition or working for blessing. It is the act of receiving a gift (something done actively in this aspect), but it need not be progressively attained through works which infuse merit. The Protestant/monergistic tradition lays hold of the better claim.

One further thing must be explored regarding instrumentality in the Roman Catholic position. It concerns the notion of purgatory. Again the *Catechism of the Catholic Church* gives the clearest definition of purgatory and its purpose: "All who die in God's grace and friendship, but still imperfectly purified, are indeed assured of their eternal salvation; but after death they undergo purification, so as to achieve the holiness necessary to enter the joy of heaven. The Church gives the name *Purgatory* to this final purification of the elect . . ."[175]

The idea is that for those who were faithful enough not to lose their own salvation yet still did not acquire enough merit to be just before God, these individuals must undergo Purgatory. The origin of and basis for this doctrine was explored above and need not be restated.

Three primary things are important to observe. First, Purgatory is, in actuality, an instrumental cause of acquiring righteousness. One will notice from the above quote from the *Catechism* that those who are "imperfectly purified" undergo purification "so as to (instrumentality) achieve (merit-theology again) the holiness necessary to enter the joy of heaven." Purgatory is a cause by which one can acquire the amount of holiness required to enter into heaven and be in the presence of God.

A second observation to make is that suffering in Purgatory, being purged of one's sins, is entirely passive (not active) on the part of the individual. This is an interesting observation, for as mentioned above God (in this tradition) desires all individuals to exercise free will for the acquisition

---

175. *Catechism of the Catholic Church*, §1030 and §1031; italics original.

of righteousness. God does not work passively (according to Küng) when it comes to justifying individuals for heaven.[176] All the other sacraments which allows individuals to "achieve the holiness necessary to enter the joy of heaven" were done actively (except for perhaps infant baptism, which itself has its faults). Aquinas mentioned there were four things necessary (or required) in order for God to justify, and they include active instrumentality on behalf of the individual. None of it is passive. The point is that this is inconsistent with other Roman Catholic dogma. An individual is purged in Purgatory, or as the *Catechism* states, they "undergo purification." This passive language shows the passive nature of justification, yet passivity as it relates to justification has been denied throughout by the Roman Catholic Church.

A third and final observation concerns the relationship between Purgatory and acquiring merit. Again, the *Catechism* states: "[A]fter death they undergo purification, so as to achieve the holiness necessary to enter the joy of heaven." As has been shown throughout this study, holiness/merit/justice must be acquired or achieved through active involvement and participation (in the sacraments). Because Purgatory is passive whereby an individual burns in hellfire until purged of sin, it is unclear (even questionable) how being purged of sin leads one to acquire merit. Said another way, the Catholic Church affirms that the remission of sin is not all there is to justification. One must be made like Jesus. One must conform to Christ in holiness. One must acquire righteousness. While burning in Purgatory can be understood as a purification process whereby the impurities in an individual are burned out (similar to the refinement process of gold), what is important to notice is that suffering the penalty for sin is not the totality of how the Catholic Church understands justification. One must acquire the merits of Christ. It is not just that the bad goes away; it is that an individual must grow, progress, and conform into the likeness of Christ. One must "achieve (notice the active tense of the verb) the holiness necessary" according to the *Catechism*, not just have the bad removed. It is unclear, even questionable, how suffering passively in Purgatory is an active means to "achieve holiness" in order to get into heaven.

CONCLUSION

This chapter has used comparative analysis between the traditional, monergistic, Protestant position of justification against the Roman Catholic doctrine of justification. While the history and development of the doctrine of

176. Küng, *Justification*, 272.

THE ASPECT OF JUSTIFICATION IN ROMAN CATHOLICISM

justification was explored in chapters 1 and 5, what this chapter attempted to do was show how the Catholic Church defines and understands the doctrine of justification.

It was shown that the Catholic Church affirms justification as the activity of infusing the merits of Christ into an individual. This infusion is done progressively, over the course of a lifetime, and should not be conceived as a status one has before God in this view. It was also observed how Thomas Aquinas and the official Roman Catholic councils and publications made after him affirmed that God is the efficient cause of justification whereby he infuses the righteousness of Christ to individuals through the instrumental means of repentance and faith.

What was also observed, however, is that God does not infuse such righteousness into an individual without cooperation. He requires a free-will response in order to make (not declare) an individual righteous. God will not effect justification without the cause of collaboration. As such, it was shown above how the efficient cause of justification, in the Roman Catholic view, is synergistic. There must be two causes (one human and one divine) for the effect of justification to occur.

What was also observed was instrumentality. Though the Church affirms repentance and faith are the means to achieve, merit, and acquire justification, what is meant by repentance and faith is acts of penance and active participation in the sacraments. The Catholic Church continually refers to the sacraments as works, and when one understands that these works "acquire" and "achieve" the "reward" of "merit," the difference in definitions between the monergists and the Catholics becomes evident.

What was concluded is that synergism is embedded in the Roman Catholic theology of justification. This synergism requires human works in the efficient cause, for God will not work without the human also working. It was also shown that the agency by which God infuses righteousness is through the works of an individual under the auspices of the Church. Therefore, in Roman Catholicism, the grounds of justification should not be understood as being based upon human works, but human works (through the sacraments) are the cause by which one is justified.

What makes the monergistic position more coherent is the textual support they gave to show justification is by God's grace (unmerited favor) through the means of faith (belief and acceptance of the saving work of Christ) alone. Their view best illustrates how justification can be an active aspect of salvation (for it has to be received actively in faith) yet does not succumb to a merit-based salvation.

The Roman Catholic Church, moreover, has shown numerous inconsistencies and/or shown a lack of solid biblical and philosophical support with their doctrines of Purgatory and progressive justification as was shown above. The result is that the monergistic party holds the more coherent claim when it comes to the doctrine of justification.

Chapter 7

A Constructive Defense of Monergistic Soteriology

INTRODUCTION AND APPROACH

THE FOCUS OF THIS study has been to explore the views of monergists and synergists in the doctrine of salvation to determine which view better illustrates how salvation can be by grace through faith. The approach for analyzing such has been through presentation of the monergistic and synergistic views of each respective aspect of salvation, analysis of how each respective party and tradition views the efficient cause and instrumental means in that given aspect, and then using comparative analysis to determine which one better supports the affirmation that salvation is by grace through faith alone and not through works.

The conclusion and thesis reached is that the synergistic traditions (in their various forms) include human works in the efficient cause and/or the instrumental causes of salvation. Sometimes this comes from personal admission, and other times it comes from logical inference. Nevertheless, when claiming that a given aspect is cooperative or synergistic, the claim is that one must *work together* with God for the specific aspect to occur. The precise means of how one works together with God differs by aspect and tradition. Most often, the work an individual is asked to do to cooperate with God is faith. Faith, however, is not a work according to Scripture. Faith is an action, but it is not productive in the sense of it producing or achieving a given aspect.

Monergism, on the other hand, believes that any given aspect of salvation is entirely the work of God alone. Human depravity makes one incapable of self-justification or doing works which would be acceptable in a salvific way before God. The efficient cause and instrumental means were explored in each specific aspect, and it was shown that the monergists view God as the efficient cause (the agent that brings about a change) and that the instrumental cause (a secondary cause that produces the effect which owes its efficacy to the efficient cause) does not require human works. The conclusion of this study is that the monergists have the more coherent claim than the synergists in accordance with the biblical witness of salvation being by grace through faith (an instrumental means but not instrumental cause) alone and not by works.

However, if one were to propose monergism as the more coherent view in soteriology, it must provide reasonable defenses against the criticisms raised against it. That is to say that in order to uphold a claim that salvation is monergistic, the monergistic tradition must be able to defend its view against the major criticisms levelled against it. If it cannot, then synergists may have the more coherent claim. If, however, the monergistic party can defend its views against major criticisms, monergists may lay claim to the more coherent view of soteriology.

What this chapter will attempt to do is show whether or not monergists can defend their point of view from the criticisms of the traditions it has examined thus far. There will be no rigid outline in the ordering of these criticisms, though as far as possible they will be presented in the order as already presented in this study. Some of the criticisms mentioned here are articulated by synergists, and others will be anticipated criticisms.

SYNERGISM AND SEMANTICS

A stated criticism coming from synergists is to the effect that: by claiming that an individual "works" together with God by faith, one does not mean that one is contributing to one's salvation, denying the role of grace, or puts oneself on equal footing with God. Every major synergistic tradition examined in this study rejects outright any notions of Pelagianism or Semi-Pelagianism whether they are Wesleyan-Arminian or Roman Catholic. Each of these traditions, as was shown, believes in some type of prevenient grace that God must extend to an individual before he or she can cooperate with God. When the Wesleyan-Arminian tradition affirms synergism, it claims that synergism simply means to be active in the salvation process, to respond actively with one's will, and not be passive in salvation.[1] Roman

---

1. Olson, *Arminian Theology*, 17–18, 95, 159–61; Walls and Dongell, *Why I Am Not A Calvinist*, 77–78.

A CONSTRUCTIVE DEFENSE OF MONERGISTIC SOTERIOLOGY

Catholicism, while holding to synergism, also claims that synergism does not mean that salvation is by works but rather that God wants humans to freely love him without coercion or force.[2]

The implication, then, is that this is merely a debate about semantics. By saying one "works together" with God, or claiming that salvation requires cooperation, one merely is stating that an agent is active in the salvation process and must respond to the Gospel (and thus not be passive). Thus, it is merely semantics that one works with God in salvation, though the activity an individual does is not actual works.

Before one examines whether this is simply a matter of semantics, it must again be restated that each of these traditions does not shy away from using the term "works" in their definitions and theology. As such, if works as a means to acquire an aspect of salvation is not a part of their belief, it goes against their expressed claims. Consider the Wesleyan-Arminian claim coming from Roger Olson (who is commenting upon John Wesley): "For him (Wesley), as for all true Arminians, "God works; therefore you *can* work ... God works; therefore you must work."[3] Canon XXIV in the Council of Trent anathematized anyone who claimed that good works do not increase justice before God while also in chapter 10 of that same council affirming that faith must cooperate with good works to increase justice before God.[4]

This is to point out the fact that synergists consistently use phrases such as "work together" in their writings. This is not an accidental or one time occurrence, for it remains the norm in their historic and modern publications. This is not even to mention the fact that the term *synergism* is a Greek word which combines the prefix (συν—meaning "with") with the suffix (εργέω—meaning "to work") which translated means "to engage in cooperative endeavor, *work together with, assist, help*."[5]

Still, these claims of "work" may be a simple semantic mistake where "activity" or "faith involvement" would be the preferred term. However,

---

2. Baker, *Fundamentals of Catholicism*, 3:14–16.

3. Olson, *Arminian Theology*, 170. The "work" an individual does, according to Olson, is not resisting. The validity of this claim was questioned in chapter 3. The point is, for Olson and all other Arminians, they claim there is a co-working activity between the human and the Divine. See also Thomas Oden's claim: "It [Conviction] is a gift with which recipients are enabled to work cooperatively" (*Systematic Theology*, 3:91). The point is that this tradition does not shy away from using the word "work" in response to the human's activity in salvation.

4. Council of Trent, "On Justification," *Decrees of the Ecumenical Councils*, vol. II, Session VI, canon XXIV, in Tanner, *Decrees of the Ecunemical Councils*, 680, and "On Justification," Session VI.X, 675.

5. Bauer, *A Greek-English Lexicon of the New Testament*, s.v. συνεργέω.

what this study has shown is that it is not only the language (and definitions) of synergism that lead one to suppose that actual work is to be done by the individual to effect a given aspect of salvation. Rather, through examination of the efficient cause along with the instrumental cause, it becomes clear that the activity that synergists promote succumbs to a work in actuality.

The best way to determine whether something constitutes a work or not is to examine the cause/effect relationship with intentional examination of the efficient cause and the instrumentality of a given aspect. The efficient cause will show who or what brings about a given effect. The instrumental means will explore the agency or vessel through which the efficient cause operates. The *effect* (as shown in typical cause/effect relationships) will show the result of the efficient *cause* working through the instrumental means. As was shown in chapter 1, if the efficient cause requires God and the human to function together to effect an aspect, there is actual synergism (cooperation, a working together) in the efficient cause. Said another way, if an efficient cause requires activity from another source, two sources are working together to effect a given product or aspect. It takes the efforts of both to bring about the effect. Because something is actually being produced, it can rightly be thought of as a work. Similarly, in the instrumental cause, if one must do some activity to merit, acquire, or achieve a specific end, then it may rightly be thought of as a "work" according to all traditions surveyed here. This is to be contrasted with something that is merely received as a gift, for in that case there is no acquisition through contributing action or achieving that is required. It is a response, but it is not a contribution that effects (produces, awards) a given end. As discussed in chapter 1, all instrumental causes fall within instrumental means, but not all instrumental means are instrumental causes. This was supported by the major traditions examined.[6] Faith is necessary for salvation, but it need not be considered a *cause* that leads to an effect. To do so (by all definitions of all the parties surveyed here) would be to make faith a work.

While a thorough review of each tradition and soteriological aspect is not necessary at this point, what can be affirmed is that when two or more individuals must come together and perform an activity to cause or produce a given effect, there is actual working together (or synergism) in the efficient cause. The two actually cooperate in working together to cause a soteriological aspect. The synergistic traditions examined in this study (as was shown) believe that God will not operate a given aspect without the individual exercising one's will. That is to say, it is not as though God works

---

6. Aquinas, *Summa Theologica*, I, q. 45, a. 5. Arminius, "Disputation XLVIII On Justification," in *The Works of James Arminius*, 2:84. George, *Theology of the Reformers*, 70–71.

an aspect in an individual and the person merely receives the aspect. This, as was shown, is a violation of the human will in their view. Instead, the synergists examined in this study state that an individual must act at the same time God acts, and when both act together, there is a specific outcome (effect, result) from this combined activity which may rightly be defined as a work. As was shown in the Wesleyan-Arminian tradition, God's work of prevenient grace matched with human faith effect (produce) aspects (such as election, regeneration, and conversion). It is not only affirmed through the writings of this tradition that faith is the work which an individual does in cooperation; it is embedded in their system. God does his work, and humans do their work (i.e., faith) which produces a result of a soteriological aspect. In Roman Catholicism, it was shown how an individual participates in the sacraments with the product (effect) of such being an increased infusion of righteousness. As one can see, human actions produce a designated outcome. While one may wish to shy away from the word "work," this is exactly what it amounts to because human activity produces a given result (albeit with divine assistance and grace).

This is far different from the monergists' claim. Within this tradition, God is the sole agent who causes a given effect. He is the only efficient cause of a soteriological aspect. He works through various means (some are passive and some are active requiring faith). When an aspect is active (meaning one must exercise faith), this cannot be considered a work for two reasons: first, Scripture clearly states faith is not a work, and secondly, faith is the conditional act of receiving (not acquiring) a given aspect. Said another way, one receives the bestowed gift of a given aspect through faith, but this faith did not cause (or produce) the grace.

What has been shown throughout this study is that each tradition that holds to synergism in a given soteriological aspect succumbs to synergism in the efficient cause and/or instrumental cause. The activity of the synergist is to act in such a way so as to cause and/or acquire a given outcome. To cause an outcome is not the same thing as to receive the effects from an efficient cause. Moreover, as with both Arminianism and Catholicism, if an individual ceases to do the "work" (whatever action that may be) one will oftentimes lose one's salvation making it clear that the human activity performed in some way is responsible for producing the given aspect. As such, this is no mere matter of semantics. It is embedded within their theological and philosophical system.

Interestingly, Norman Geisler (a self-proclaimed synergist) makes the following accusation against monergists, "[T]he monergist confuses an *action* (faith) with a *work*. All works are actions, but not all actions are works. *The act of faith*, by which we acknowledge that we cannot work for or merit our salvation, *is not a work*."⁷ The monergist could not agree more with this statement except for the first sentence, namely that it is the "*monergist*" who confuses actions with works. It has been Norman Geisler (and other synergists) who inevitably make faith a work.⁸ It was Geisler who says, "God is the cause of the fact of freedom, and humans are the causes of the acts of freedom."⁹ Over and again, Geisler claims that faith is productive (not receptive) of soteriological aspects. Faith must work together with God's work to produce (or cause, as he stated above) a given aspect. As such, it is not the monergist who confuses what is an action and what is a work; it is the synergist.

A very interesting claim, likewise, was made by J. Matthew Pinson. He states, "Arminius was not a synergist; he did not believe that individuals share with God in their salvation."¹⁰ While it is hard to see how Arminius was not a synergist, Pinson's observation implies that if one holds to synergism, one *does* believe that an individual works together with God in their salvation. He goes on to state in a footnote: "Arminius would not have been comfortable with the term synergist or the idea of humans cooperating or working together with God in any way in their salvation."¹¹ A review of Arminius's theology at this point is not necessary. It has to do with how individuals understand the term *synergism*. There seems to be even amongst Arminians (based upon the definition of synergism itself) an implication that one works together with God in the effecting of salvation, something some of them strive to avoid.

SYNERGISM AND THE CLAIMS OF GRACE

The aforementioned critique draws a related concern. Each tradition examined within this study affirms that any activity (or work) done by an individual is solely by grace. Some, including the Wesleyan-Arminian tradition, affirm that God is the sole efficient cause, and faith is the sole instrumental means.¹² Despite the Thomistic notions of merit, Roman Catholics (it was shown in chapter 6) believe that human works do not actually merit (in terms of indebting God) justification. All is attributed to grace by these tra-

---

7. Geisler, *Systematic Theology*, 3:198; italics original.
8. Ibid., 192, 193–94; Geisler, *Chosen But Free*, 241–43.
9. Geisler, "God Knows All Things," 79.
10. Pinson, "Jacobus Arminius," 169.
11. Ibid., 169 n. 83.
12. Olson, *Arminian Theology*, 95. Notice he calls it an "instrumental cause" which is the point being made here. Faith is made to be a cause which leads to an effect.

ditions with full rejection of Pelagianism and Semi-Pelagianism.[13] As such, how can the monergistic tradition accuse synergists of attributing the effects of salvation to cooperative works given such affirmations of grace?

First, this study has never claimed that any of the traditions examined herein are Pelagian or Semi-Pelagian in any regard. In some form or fashion, each tradition upholds some notion of prevenient grace which dismisses any accusations of Pelagianism or Semi-Pelagianism. While the validity of their affirmations of prevenient grace is questioned in chapters 3 and 4, it is nevertheless incorrect to suggest that these traditions believe that salvation is by works.[14]

However, what this study has attempted to do is examine if the activities of an individual amount to works which effect a given aspect in these traditions. Despite claims to the contrary, an individual must do some type of action (which, again, is often claimed to be a "work") which produces a given result. It has been shown that monergists deny that faith (the activity of a believer) produces a given aspect; however, synergists (whether they claim so or not) ultimately affirm that faith produces (effects) a given aspect in cooperation with God and his grace. Grace is never denied. Credit and glory is never attributed to the human in these traditions. However, the actions of individuals produce and cause a given aspect. If such is the case, it cannot fully be understood as grace. Though God (by his grace) may supply an individual with the resources necessary to work out a specific aspect, it is nonetheless the activity of an individual that effects a given aspect as has been shown. Grace assisted works are still works. Grace assisted activity that produces a given aspect with cooperation from God is still work. As such, though grace is affirmed and Pelagianism (and Semi-Pelagianism) is denied, monergists show better how salvation is by grace through faith and not by works making it the more coherent view in soteriology.

MONERGISM AS COMPLETE PASSIVITY AND A DENIAL OF FREE-WILL

A common critique against monergism is that it affirms complete passivity on the part of an individual. The accusation is that God's love and salvation are forced upon an individual apart from consent. After all, monergism is

---

13. Osborne, *Reconciliation and Justification*, 129–30.

14. To restate the thesis of this study again, it is affirmed that monergists best articulate the case that salvation is by grace through faith alone and not by works. It is not that these other traditions deny this but that the monergistic tradition best articulates this.

the belief that God is the sole worker of salvation apart from any work of an individual. Some claim that monergists believe that humans are entirely passive in salvation (with the exception of sanctification).[15] Another critic claims that monergism "excludes free human participation."[16] As was shown in the chapter on Roman Catholicism, the *imago Dei* still belongs to people, and God desires to work with his creatures without violation of their will. The implication is that monergists deny any involvement of the human will since they reject synergism. Finally, because monergists believe that the human does not cooperate with God in salvation, one author has claimed that such passivity and forced work upon an individual is a violation against humanity making God into "[A] divine rapist!"[17] As such, the character of God is put into question.

Yet are such accusations merit-worthy? Do monergists affirm complete passivity and deny any active part in the salvation event? This study has already showed how monergists do not claim such. It has been shown how affirmations of monergism do not assume complete passivity or a denial of human involvement.

First, it is too broad of a statement to say that salvation is *either* active *or* passive. To say that everything in salvation rests upon the free will and choice of an individual is to ignore the aspectual nature of salvation. As was shown in chapter 1, salvation is complex by God's design. There are various aspects within because God completed a complex (multi-faceted) salvation for a very complex human problem (sin). Justification is not the same thing as regeneration just as election is not the same thing as sanctification, though it is beyond question that these aspects are inseparably related (though distinct).

This is to say that there are some aspects of salvation which are passive by nature and active by nature. To say that certain salvific aspects are passive by nature, it is meant that God is the efficient cause and that he works this given aspect solely by his own activity and accord. Passive aspects (as were shown) include election, regeneration, and conversion. To assume passivity in certain aspects is not to assume passivity in all aspects, for monergists uphold certain aspects as active. That is to say, God is the efficient cause of certain aspects while working through active instrumentality from the believer. In aspects such as justification (for example), this aspect only comes by means of faith. It is not the cause of justification, but it is the instrument through which one receives the justifying work of God. Monergists, it was

15. Geisler, *Chosen But Free*, 241.
16. Olson, *Arminian Theology*, 13.
17. Geisler, "God Knows All Things," 69.

A CONSTRUCTIVE DEFENSE OF MONERGISTIC SOTERIOLOGY

shown, fully affirm the active role of an individual and the necessity for each individual to exercise active faith.[18]

Yet can the active aspects of salvation as defined by the monergists properly be understood as affirming human will and genuine response given their claim that regeneration precedes conversion as was shown in chapter 3? If God must regenerate the human heart so as to allow him or her to believe, and such regeneration is done passively upon an individual, how can monergists affirm that the active aspects of salvation are really genuine and not a violation of the human will?

It is true that (most) monergists affirm that regeneration precedes conversion and that God must liberate the will for faith to be expressed. Yet does this mean that the faith an individual shows after regeneration is not genuine? Perhaps this question could be answered with another question: Can the human will freely believe whenever it is still dead in its trespasses and sin? How "free" is the human "free-will" when it is still enslaved to the bondages of sin? If regeneration means "to make alive again" (as was shown to be the Arminian definition in chapter 3), what other implication can there be than that an individual is incapable of expressing faith without radical transformation?

As was shown in chapter 3, the Wesleyan-Arminian tradition fully affirms depravity from sin and the need for regeneration to undo the effects of sin. To maintain their view of free-will, however, they draw upon a notion of prevenient grace which allows them to place faith before regeneration. This, they claim, makes the choice truly free.

As was shown in chapters 3 and 4, this has numerous problems. First, the Wesleyan-Arminian notion of prevenient grace requires a violation of the human will itself. It requires God to undo the effects of sin so that an individual is able to believe. Their attempt to preserve unadulterated human freedom is not consistent. Second, Wesleyan-Arminians affirm that *regeneration* must undo the depraving effects of sin as was shown in chapter 3. The problems of sin must actually be overcome, which is done through regeneration by the Spirit. Their view does not remain consistent. Third, faith becomes an efficient cause of regeneration making faith a work.

Norman Geisler criticizes monergism at this point (claiming monergism is equivalent to irresistible grace) by stating that it goes against the "Protestant Principle" where salvation is by faith alone. Geisler claims that if salvation is by faith then faith must be prior to regeneration (logically speaking). He supports his claims with various verses that show salvation is

---

18. Monergists tend to shy away from using the term "free-will" but typically have no problem using the term "freed-will" to show how God must regenerate an individual's will so that active instrumentality will occur.

through faith with affirmations that faith must be logically prior to regeneration.[19] Monergists do not wish to deny salvation *by* faith. What they do wish to deny is salvation *because of* faith. According to Geisler, if salvation is to be *by* faith (instrumental means) then it must be that faith is prior to (efficient cause) regeneration. Geisler makes the mistake of making faith the cause of regeneration in this regard. Not only that, Geisler does not address the fundamental issue of how someone who is dead in trespasses and sin and in need of new life (i.e., regeneration) is able to believe and exercise such faith. Geisler, like many within his tradition, makes faith an efficient cause and work, something that is not only observed from his writings but also clearly stated in his works.[20]

When the monergists contend that an individual is active through faith in salvation, they mean that God has freed one's will. One is actually able to believe freely. Because God graciously changed the dead and rebellious heart of an individual, does this mean that the response of an individual is invalid? The monergist would deny such, for now one is enabled (finally) to believe freely. As such, monergists deny complete passivity in salvation, and because the human will is freely engaging God, God cannot and should not be thought of as violating his creatures or forcing his love upon them.[21]

MONERGISM AUTOMATICALLY ASSUMES FIVE-POINT CALVINISM

This study has not shied away from associating monergism with the Reformed tradition or contrasting itself against Arminianism (though Arminians do consider themselves *Reformed* in the broad sense).[22] Does this, therefore, mean that monergism assumes TULIP Calvinism, oftentimes called Five-Point Calvinism, that affirms Total Depravity, Unconditional Election, Limited Atonement, Irresistible Grace, and Perseverance of the Saints? This is indeed the claim of some.[23] Yet is this accusation merit-worthy?

19. Geisler, *Systematic Theology*, 193.

20. Ibid., 192–94.

21. Again, see the section below on Unconditional Election and Reprobation. Naturally, there are some who are self-proclaimed monergists who deny any role in the individual and that "human free will is a myth," per Storms, *The Grandeur of God*, 80. However, monergism need not necessitate complete passivity even if some proponents may affirm it.

22. Olson, *Against Calvinism*, 23.

23. Geisler, *Chosen But Free*, 241–43 and Geisler, *Systematic Theology*, 475–88. Kenneth Keathley does something similar with his doctrine of Molinism. He affirms that salvation is entirely the work of God but claims that others who affirm such are

Once again, it is important to recognize the parts that make up the whole, for monergists could fully affirm TULIP (as indeed some do) or affirm parts of TULP (as some do as well). This is to make the assertion that affirmation of monergism does not automatically affirm TULIP Calvinism.

No monergist denies Total Depravity, nor do most in the Wesleyan-Arminian tradition or Roman Catholicism for that matter. Monergists also affirm Perseverance of the Saints (as do some within the Arminian tradition, though Roman Catholicism denies this), for God completes the work of salvation and sees it through according to monergists.[24]

What becomes of significant debate and merits further consideration is Unconditional Election, Limited Atonement, and Irresistible Grace. Does affirmation of monergism automatically assume these other three aspects of Calvinism?

As was shown in chapter 2, monergists do affirm across the board Unconditional Election whereas synergists (commonly in the Wesleyan-Arminian tradition) reject such. In chapter 2, it was shown how election (both in the Reformed and Arminian traditions) falls within the divine decrees. God, in other areas of election (such as service, people, and means) makes his choice and carries it out efficaciously. This is not denied by the Arminian camp until it gets to election of specific people for salvation. While one need not rehash all the arguments mentioned in chapter 2, what can be stated here is that monergists do typically affirm Unconditional Election.

However, does affirming Unconditional Election assume that individuals are entirely passive and are saved without their will, assent, and acknowledgement? This study has already shown the monergists rejection of this. Though a decree was made in eternity past, it can come into its fullness in a moment in time when faith is actively expressed. As such, affirmation of Unconditional Election in monergism does not affirm complete passivity as was shown.[25] However, does monergism (in its affirmation of Unconditional Election) assume reprobation? This will be studied below.

Moving to Limited Atonement, it must be clearly stated that monergists fall on both sides of the issue and that affirmation of monergism does

---

Calvinists affirming TULIP. See Keathley, *Salvation and Sovereignty*, 1–3. Roger Olson rightly discerns a difference between the Reformed tradition and TULIP Calvinism in *Arminian Theology*, 16–19.

24. Again, this was a major point in showing how some synergistic traditions affirm faith and faithful works as an efficient cause and instrumental means because the cessation of such would forfeit salvation.

25. Some monergists, as mentioned above, affirm passivity because of Unconditional Election, though this not need be the case.

not necessitate affirmation of Limited Atonement.[26] What critics must understand regarding the monergistic tradition is how one can understand the *provision* of the atonement and the *application* of the atonement.[27] Christ can die sufficiently for the whole world (universally) while it will only be those who respond in faith to Jesus who will efficiently receive the atonement.[28] The point is, Limited Atonement is not central to the monergistic view. Monergism does not necessitate Limited Atonement, and many monergists are in favor of Universal Atonement.

Regarding Irresistible Grace, the concern mentioned by synergists is that God forces his will upon individuals, faith is not genuine, and it betrays God's goodness.[29] Roger Olson claims that this is the essence of monergism because it believes salvation requires no cooperation and is always irresistible.[30] Laurence M. Vance claims that salvation, then, does not come to people because they believed but because irresistible grace saved them apart from any choice.[31]

Many things are worthy of consideration regarding this criticism. First, one must recall what was mentioned in chapter 4 over the meaning and nature of grace. Is grace that which is merely presented as an offer or is it something that is actually bestowed? Though a gift may be resisted, it does not mean that what is given is not truly a gift, nor does it mean that it was not actually given and bestowed. The clearest example of this relates to John 1:11–12 and 3:16. God gave (as a gift) his Son into the world, and the world did not receive him. Christ was still the gift bestowed even though he was rejected. Those who did receive Jesus he gave (bestowed) the right to become children of God, but the gift of the incarnation was bestowed despite human resistance to it. In other words, the gift may very well be resisted! But as in the nature of the Arminian doctrine of prevenient grace, God does

---

26. This author rejects Limited Atonement in favor of Universal Atonement. Christ died for all people, satisfying the penalty for all sins for all time, though this atonement is made applicable only to those who respond in faith in Jesus Christ. For a historical examination on this matter (which questions if John Calvin himself held to Limited Atonement) see Kennedy, *Union with Christ*. See also Nicole, "John Calvin's View of the Extent of the Atonement," 212–17. Arminians have observed that not all within the Reformed tradition affirm Limited Atonement. See Walls and Dongell, *Why I Am Not a Calvinist*, 11–13.

27. Demarest, *The Cross and Salvation*, 193.

28. This is the view of Erickson (as well as many others) in *Christian Theology*, 849–52.

29. See Geisler, *Systematic Theology*, 192–94 who consistently calls monergism "irresistible grace." This accusation is not valid.

30. Olson, *Against Calvinism*, 50.

31. Vance, *The Other Side of Calvinism*, 527.

overcome human will and rebellion to enable an individual to believe in Jesus. Despite sinful resistance, God does overcome willful human rebellion (as the Arminians would agree). Second, and importantly, monergism does not mandate irresistible grace as affirmed by some Calvinists. Monergism does not affirm by default that an individual has no decision, response, or part to play in salvation as has been shown. Does God work upon the unwilling according to monergists? Yes, and Arminians claim as much. However, what God does is allow an individual to act willingly whereas before one was actually unable to do so. One's depravity leaves one hostile to God. God bestows grace (monergists affirm this is regenerating grace while Arminians claim it is prevenient grace apart from regeneration) upon individuals that overcome the depraving effects of sin allowing individuals to believe in Christ. Finally, Arminians such as Olson who criticize monergism for denying salvation as a cooperative affair do not fare better with this criticism, for in their claim an individual must work together with this grace to attain salvation. This questions (as has been shown throughout) the very nature of grace. As such, the criticisms associated with Irresistible Grace should not be attributed to monergism.

MONERGISM AS SUPRALAPSARIANISM

As mentioned above, there are close associations with monergism and Calvinism, many of which are unwarranted. In that association, there is the criticism against monergism that because salvation is not cooperative (in the sense of the human working with God) that it leads to supralapsarianism. Supralapsarianism (literally meaning "before the fall" and oftentimes referred to as Double Predestination) is found historically in the works of John Gill and in modern days in Herman Hoeksema. It concerns the issue of whether God decreed first to save some people and then permit the Fall thereby implying a foreordination of people to hell whereby their fate could not be otherwise.

For the sake of fairness, it must once again be affirmed that there are monergists who affirm such. R. C. Sproul would be an example of a proponent. For Sproul, there is a sense where predestination is double. Positively, God chooses to work belief into the hearts of the elect. Negatively, God sovereignly chooses to pass individuals by and withhold grace to them (which should not, according to Sproul, imply God is actively damning these individuals to hell.[32] Still, it is worth noting in Sproul's theology that their fate could not be otherwise. Arminians such as Roger Olson claim that this does

---

32. Sproul, *What is Reformed Theology?*, 158.

not raise an Arminian concern about God's justice (for God is perfectly just to do such) but rather with God's goodness.[33] This criticism is valid and must be addressed.

Again, one should not assume that monergism is the same thing as TULIP Calvinism.[34] Monergism is the belief that God is the sole worker (efficient cause) of salvation and that certain aspects must be received by faith and not by works. As such, monergism does not relate directly to the issue of supralapsarianism.

However, given the affirmation that salvation is entirely the work of God and cannot be caused by human beings, and affirming that not all people are saved, how does a monergist respond to the supralapsarian issue? Said another way, why is God the efficient cause of some coming to faith and others not? Here, Bruce Demarest gives a helpful and fairly standard reply for those in the Reformed tradition who reject Supralapsarianism. He claims that for reasons known only to God, he chooses to save some and permit others to stay in their willful rebellion. He states: "When we speak about damnation, we mean that God predestines persons not to sin and disobedience but to the *condemnation* that issues from sin."[35]

It would be helpful to reiterate what Arminius meant by reprobation and how he understood it:

> [W]e define reprobation to be the decree of God's anger or of his severe will, by which, from all eternity, he determined to condemn to eternal death all unbelievers and impenitent persons, for the declaration of his power and anger; yet so, that unbelievers are visited with this punishment, not only on account of unbelief, but likewise on account of other sins from which they might have been delivered through faith in Christ.[36]

33. Olson, *Against Calvinism*, 62–64.

34. This author rejects supralapsarianism. Michael D. Williams also provides a case that Calvinism does not assume supralapsarianism in "The Five Points of Arminianism," 15. See also Cowan, "Common Misconceptions," 191–92.

35. Demarest, *The Cross and Salvation*, 138; italics original.

36. Arminius, "Disputation XL On the Predestination of Believers," in *The Works of James Arminius*, 2:72. It would be helpful to consider what William Cunningham said regarding Arminius's treatment of Supralapsarianism in *The Reformers*, 426–27. There, Cunningham observes that Arminius made an unfair representation of the view, devoted four-fifths of his treatise on predestination to the "highest Supralapsarianism" thus leaving a small portion to consider Sublapsarianism and a modified version of Supralapsarianism, and, finally, wrote most lengthily and vehemently against the "highest Supralapsarianism" which is professed by few Calvinists. Indeed, as Sell in *The Great Debate*, 1, 7–10 aptly notes, the Calvinism that received protest from Arminius was the high supralapsarianism found in Theodore Beza, not in Calvin himself. As such, according to Cunningham, the Supralapsarianism that Calvinists (or one might say monergists) are accused of is often unwarranted.

A CONSTRUCTIVE DEFENSE OF MONERGISTIC SOTERIOLOGY

When considering that God is the efficient cause of salvation and does not engage in synergistic activity with individuals, the claim is that monergism succumbs to supralapsarianism (or reprobation as defined by Arminius). However, there is nothing in monergism itself which states this position. Rather, one may be a monergist while also believing that God allows certain individuals to stay in their willful rebellion and suffer the consequences for their actions. As for why God regenerates some and not others (allowing some to receive salvation and others not), monergists contend that this lies in the hidden mysteries of God. When opponents claim that this is merely an evasive reply, the monergist responds with the question: Then why do you believe God purposefully creates individuals whom he knows will reject him and thus go to hell?[37] No answer to these very difficult questions will be fully satisfactory to all persons involved, yet what may safely be affirmed is that the belief that God is the sole worker of salvation does not mandate reprobation.

Moreover, when Arminians question the character of God on why he extends the ability for some to be saved and not others, one may draw upon this reflection. Reformed and non-Reformed alike typically affirm that there was some type of rebellion from angels in accordance with Jude 6. Naturally, the views concerning this verse and the doctrine of demons vary widely. Nevertheless, there is a wide understanding in Christian circles that believes that angels are moral beings with a free will and have a capacity to be faithful or disobedient to God. Assuming that rebellious angels (including Satan) became demons (which is not the view of all but will be assumed for the sake of argument), one may pose this question: Why did God not permit fallen angels to be saved? Why did God decree that Satan be eternally damned in hell (Revelation 20:10) with no hope of redemption? Why did the cross not atone for demonic sin? How can God be a good God when he does not extend the possibility for demons to be saved yet leaves them in their sin? A typical monergist would likely contend that he or she does not have the answers to these questions, but he or she would likely observe that there is not a large outcry from the Arminian tradition accusing God of injustice.

As such, the monergist cannot provide a clear explanation on why God serves as the efficient cause of some but not others. The best response is that God (for reasons known only to him) regenerates some and leaves others

---

37. See Welty, "Election and Calling," 230. See also Muller, "Grace, Election, and Contingent Choice" 2:277 where Muller concludes that Arminians are locked into a belief where God genuinely wills the salvation of all while at the same time binds himself to a plan of salvation where he foreknows with certainty that salvation will not be effected. As such, the very thing the Arminian tradition wishes to avoid is the very thing they assume.

in their own willful rebellion (which is what these individuals in their depravity prefer) in the monergistic party's understanding. Still, the claim that God is the sole worker of salvation does not directly relate to the issue of supralapsarianism, and as such, these criticisms are not applicable.

DEPRAVITY, THE IMAGE OF GOD, AND UNIVERSAL GRACE

Another criticism against monergism worth mentioning is a criticism from Arminians and Roman Catholicism. It has to do with the issue of total depravity and the retention of the *imago Dei*.

Classical Arminians do not reject the "T" in the TULIP system (namely Total Depravity), though they wish to affirm that things are not as bleak and corrupt as monergists (they would say "Calvinists") admit.[38] As was shown in chapter 6, the Roman Catholic Church has continually rejected any forms of Pelagianism since the Council of Orange.[39]

Nevertheless, there is stark criticism from each of these traditions regarding the effects (and in some cases the extent) of depravity, the image of God, and universal prevenient grace. Beginning with the Arminian position, it was shown in chapter 3 that the major proponents in this tradition (including Arminius and Wesley) hold to a universal prevenient grace that overcomes the depraving effects of sins. Consider John Wesley again on this matter:

> "[P]reventing grace" (is) all the drawings of the Father; the desires after God, which, if we yield to them, increase more and more;—all that light wherewith the Son of God "enlighteneth every one that cometh into the world"; showing every man "to do justly, to love mercy, and to walk humbly with his God";—all the convictions which His Spirit, from time to time, works in every child of man—although it is true, the generality of men stifle them as soon as possible, and after a while forget, or at least deny, that they ever had them at all.[40]

The specific criticism levelled against monergism is that this universal prevenient grace permits individuals to work together with God by faith

---

38. Olson, *Against Calvinism*, 42–43, 62.

39. "The Council of Orange," in Leith, *Creeds of the Church*, 38–45.

40. Wesley, "On Working Out Our Own Salvation," in *The Essential Works of John Wesley*, 148; italics added. See also Olson, *Against Calvinism*, 129–31 who affirms universal prevenient grace as well as Wynkoop, *Foundations of Wesleyan-Arminian Theology*, 99.

A CONSTRUCTIVE DEFENSE OF MONERGISTIC SOTERIOLOGY

leading to regeneration.[41] God has so overcome the depraving effects of sin through prevenient grace (hence there is no Pelagianism) that all persons are now able to believe freely.

It should be concerning to the reader that the effects of sin (in this view) are applicable but not affective (as in carrying no affect). This point was observed in chapter 3 but requires further exploration. Sin does deprave, but one is not in that depraved state because of a universal prevenient grace. The penalty for sin remains, but the effects of it do not.[42] Prevenient grace does not take away the penalty of sin, but it does allow an individual to freely believe in Jesus for salvation. There are numerous concerns over such affirmations. As has been stated, there is no Scriptural support for some "in-between" state between death and life, bondage and free, darkness and light, etc. as would be the case in the Arminian notion of prevenient grace.

The Reformed Presbyterian scholar R. L. Dabney accuses Arminians of Semi-Pelagianism at this point. While this accusation is too strong (for their doctrine of prevenient grace does dismiss direct association with Semi-Pelagianism), he does make a helpful observation:

> The essential idea and argument of the Arminian (arguing for universal prevenient grace) is, that God could not punish man justly for unbelief, unless He conferred on him both natural and moral ability to believe or not... Man, then, decides the whole remaining difference, as to believing or not believing, by his use of this precedent grace, according to his own free will... Hence, the operations of grace are at every stage vincible (sic) by man's will; to be otherwise, they must violate the conditions of

---

41. Olson, *Arminian Theology*, 159–66.

42. This view was condemned at the Synod of Dort. For a discussion on this, see Heick, *A History of Christian Thought*, 2:70. Specifically, what was rejected was that in general prevenient grace God does not infuse new qualities, gifts, or faith (though Arminians see faith as a gift of God, the Synod saw otherwise because God, in the Arminian view, merely provides the opportunity to express faith). The Reformed monergists, here, did not do such. While they would claim that faith is an activity performed by the individual, they claim (perhaps more consistently) that faith is a gift of God given upon regeneration and is thereby able to be expressed. See Peterson, *The Canons of Dort*, 64–71. There appears to be a conflict with the Arminian notion that faith is a gift of God but that the gift of faith is not given until faith is shown leading to regeneration. The Synod also rejected (in Art. VIII) that one can resist grace and choose not to become regenerate. This seems understandable given that both agree that individuals are dead in their trespasses and sin and in need of new life (regeneration, not just prevenient grace as defined by Arminians). They finally rejected, in article 9, that the cause of conversion is cooperative between grace and free will. This makes grace dependent upon free will rather than the will of God. See Schaff and Schaff, "The Canons of the Synod of Dort," 3:581–95.

Monergism or Synergism

> moral agency. Even after regeneration, grace may be so resisted by free will, as to be dethroned from the soul, which then again becomes unrenewed.[43]

While much is ascribed to initial grace, it becomes clear that the Arminian tradition places significant weight on the ability of an individual who is still unregenerate. While trying to protect the integrity of God's justice, one may rightly question the ability of unregenerate wills in this regard.

Second, prevenient grace amounts to regenerating grace in Arminian theology, though that tradition does not wish to affirm such (see chapters 3 and 4). All of these statements (and more) have already been made. But consider one final argument—if God prevenes upon the whole human race, overcoming the effects of depravation to allow all persons the ability to express faith, and that faith cooperates (synergistically) with God so that both work together, one is making faith (as has been shown throughout this study) a work. If the point of prevenient grace (as expressed by the Arminians) is that it allows an individual to work together with God by exercising faith which has the end result of producing regeneration, faith has been reduced to a work despite claims to the contrary. The premise to this criticism against monergism is wrong, for it claims that universal prevenient grace overcomes the depravation of humanity and allows individuals to work together with God by faith leading to regeneration. The premise is wrong, and thus so is the criticism.

In the section regarding Catholicism, the Roman Catholic Church (though it rejects Pelagianism) affirmed at the Council of Trent (and continues to affirm to this day) that there was not an utter corruption on the part of the person as a result of Adam's sin. The image of God, though tainted, was not destroyed.[44] Canon 5 of Trent made this clear. It anathematized anyone who claimed that human free-will is lost or extinguished through Adam's sin. Humans still retain the *imago Dei* and possess freedom of the will which God moves to himself.[45] The accusation against monergists, then, is that the human must cooperate with God (synergistically) through involvement with the sacraments as a means to be justified. The Roman Catholic Church rejects the monergistic belief that God must be the sole

---

43. Dabney, *Systematic Theology*, 581–82.

44. O'Collins and Rafferty, "Roman Catholic View," 267–68. This is affirmed by monergists as well. See Hoekema, *Created in God's Image*, 83–91. Monergists do not criticize Catholic dogma on these grounds. Rather, they would deny that the image of God allows one to cooperate synergistically with God to effect justification.

45. O'Collins and Rafferty, "Roman Catholic View," 267–68.

worker in this aspect because it violates the human will and image of God residing within an individual.[46]

The aforementioned responses from Arminianism are applicable here in many regards. Two points will be reiterated. First, sin is that which violates the human will, not God. God is the liberator of the will. He is the one who regenerates the will whereby an individual may respond freely. This erroneous view of freedom does not account for the need for regeneration as expressed in chapter 4. Second, and importantly, Roman Catholics make human activity a meritorious work in salvation. Monergists would agree with other traditions that humans are still made in the image of God and do not criticize them on these grounds. Rather, the cooperation (the act of working together) puts human actions together with divine actions effecting a given aspect (in this case *justification*). This again shows that monergists lay hold to the more coherent claim that salvation is by grace through faith alone.

MONERGISM IS A DENIAL OF SCRIPTURAL SYNERGISM

A common criticism against monergism is that Scripture clearly teaches synergism in salvation. The foundational verse is Philippians 2:12–13: "Work out your own salvation with fear and trembling; for it is God who is at work in you, enabling you both to will and to work for his good pleasure." Here, synergists claim they have biblical support for their doctrine of synergism, namely that an individual must work in salvation too with repentance and faith. They also affirm that this "work out" which they perform only comes from a God who is at "work in" the individual meaning that no credit or glory should be given for the human's role of repentance and faith.[47]

What is of first importance is to note that Philippians 2:12–13 is addressing the church at Philippi who are already saved, converted believers as even synergist Norman Geisler observes.[48] The apostle Paul is not claiming that an individual must do works of repentance and faith in order to be saved. This would contradict his whole theology of salvation by grace

---

46. This point was made by Erasmus of Rotterdam against Martin Luther. Arminians praise Erasmus as an early leader in synergism. See Erasmus, *On the Freedom of the Will*, 50–51.

47. Walls and Dongell, *Why I Am Not a Calvinist*, 11; Oden, *The Transforming Power of Grace*, 53; Wesley, "On Working Out Our Own Salvation," in *The Essential Works of John Wesley*, 323–30.

48. Geisler, *Chosen But Free*, 130, 134.

through faith alone. Rather, he is speaking to Christians, calling them to experience the fullness of the salvation that they already have while being faithful to the calling of God upon their lives.[49] In other words, this is a call to sanctification, the ongoing pursuit of holiness after the event of salvation has already occurred.[50] This is why the verse states, "Work out *your own salvation.*" The idea is that the salvation is already one's own. They are already saved. They have already repented of their sin and placed their faith in Jesus; now, they must experience the fullness of this through the work that God does within them.

It was already stated in chapter 1, salvation has a past, present, and future dynamic. There is a sense in which one has been saved at the moment of conversion (past), is being saved as one who has been justified and is pursuing sanctification (present), and will be saved in final redemption (future). It was also mentioned in chapter 1 that monergists do not (typically) reject all notions of synergism. While the standard definition of synergism is "the belief that salvation is a cooperative work between God and a human" (implying the activity done before the event of salvation), there must be an understanding that salvation is both an event and a process. There is a continuous element of salvation that progresses into the future. This is called sanctification. Monergists do not deny that there is cooperation (even synergism) in sanctification, though this should not be understood as equal work or that this is because of one's own natural ability.[51] Wayne Grudem even defines sanctification as, "[A] *progressive work of God and man that makes us more and more free from sin and like Christ in our actual lives.*"[52] For this monergist, he can claim that sanctification (an aspect of salvation) is a "work of God and man." This is synergism, and Grudem (supporting this notion with Philippians 2:12–13) calls this combined activity "work" and "cooperation."[53] The reason for this is that the event of salvation has already occurred, and now the individual (with a newfound relationship with God) has the ability to effect holiness in cooperation with God. This ongoing holiness in sanctification points to the heart of synergism found in Philippians 2:12–13, namely that one is working out one's own salvation unto eternal life.

What this does not mean, however, is that repentance and faith are the works of an individual prior to a true, saving relationship with Jesus Christ.

---

49. See Hawthorne, *Philippians*, 106–7.
50. Ladd, *A Theology of the New Testament*, 563.
51. Hoekema, "The Reformed Perspective," 71–72.
52. Grudem, *Systematic Theology*, 746; italics original.
53. Ibid., 753–56.

Philippians 2:12–13 is not addressing non-believers yet to be converted but a church of regenerate believers who need to realize the fullness of their salvation through activity (works) brought about through the power of God.

As such, the monergists do not deny Philippians 2:12. Moreover, as was observed in chapter 1, of the thirteen times where the Greek word συνεργός is used, all thirteen uses of the noun refer to the fellow workers who partner with the apostles in the work of evangelism and ministry.[54] This is not a reference to individuals working synergistically with God by means of faith and repentance to receive salvation. Regenerate Christians are aided by the supernatural work of God to assist them in their work of evangelization. Synergism is causing evangelism through the work of God and the evangelists. This is not a reference to non-believers working together with God for salvation. Indeed, as was shown in chapter 1, there is not a single verse that supports that notion in all the New Testament.

JUSTIFICATION AS MAKING JUST

As was observed in chapter 6, an important feature of the synergistic doctrine Roman Catholicism is that justification means "making just" rather than the Protestant perspective of "declaring just." As was shown in chapter 6, Catholics believe there must be continuous change wrought within an individual to conform to the divine (though they construe these concepts very differently). For the Protestant who affirms justification is a monergistic activity (something agreed to by both the Reformed and Wesleyan-Arminian traditions), this is an erroneous blending of justification with sanctification. Yet which perspective lays hold to the better claim?

Answering this question with the attention it deserves would warrant an entire chapter (or chapters) itself which cannot be done here. What one can do is provide major supporting arguments that will show the rationale for the monergistic perspective. Many of these arguments were made in chapters 5–6, though they will be restated for emphasis.

Both Protestantism and Roman Catholicism understand justification in different ways. Protestants view justification in primarily a judicial framework while Roman Catholicism views justification in terms of progressive merit.

Protestants admit that there are uses of the δικ- roots that are non-forensic, and Roman Catholics admit that there are uses of δικ- in a judicial context. Both can supply impressive amounts of support for their

---

54. Rom 16:3, 9, 21; 1 Cor 3:9, 2 Cor 1:24, 8:23; Phil 2:25, 4:3; Col 4:11; 1 Thess 3:2; Phlm 1, 24; 3 John 8.

perspective and what they view as the primary meaning of δίκ-. At this point in this study, there will be no attempt to restate all of this debate.

There are numerous things that make the monergistic perspective the more coherent alternative, particularly in the shortcomings of *infused righteousness* observed in chapters 6. First, in traditions where righteousness is progressive, it is important to note that this third state of being (somewhere in between being unrighteousness and righteous) is nowhere found in Scripture. As was stated throughout, one is either a child of God or is not, bound to sin or redeemed from sin, in favor with God or at enmity with God, etc. One is either righteous or unrighteous according to Scripture, and to use a Christological term, there is no *tertium quid*. Second, the means through which one becomes righteous or divine surmount to works. Indeed, both of these traditions call the activity of an individual to become more righteous or divine as "works." This clearly contrasts the notion of faith alone by grace alone. Third, it shows there was some type of deficiency in the work of Jesus on the cross if sin must be undone and covered up by synergistic activity. All of these conclusions (as well as many others) were made in their respective chapters showing the monergistic tradition to lay hold of the more coherent claim.

However, there is a further element, which must be restated, which shows that righteousness refers to the declaration of righteousness rather than the progressive making of one righteous. This has to do with the nature of union with Christ. All three of these major Christian traditions hold to some notion of union with Christ. The question is: does one actually have union with Christ or does one partake of it gradually and progressively? Protestants affirm the former while Catholics affirm the latter.

As was shown in chapter 5, monergists lay hold to a very well-articulated and scripturally supported claim that an individual actually has union with Christ through faith. It was shown that there are numerous Scriptural references of believers being buried and raised *with him* through faith (Gal 2:20, 5:24, Col 2:12, Rom 6:4, 11, 2 Tim 1:1 et.al.) just as there are supporting verses of being saved *in Christ* (2 Tim 2:10) and being reconciled *through Christ* (Rom 5:11). Romans 12:5 and 1 Corinthians 12:27 speak of being members in Christ's body while John 15:5 speaks of abiding *in Christ* for showing spiritual fruit. As D. A. Carson observed, in one's union with Christ, there is a death of the old self, salvation of the new self, reconciliation, ability to do works that are pleasing to God, and more.[55]

---

55. Clowney, "The Biblical Doctrine," 46–50. See also Carson, "The Vindication of Imputation," 73.

The point is that there is actual union that an individual has when one believes in Jesus Christ. This union leads to a variety of effects including righteousness in Christ. While monergists deny that one shares in Christ's essential righteousness bound within the divine character, they find numerous sources of biblical support for claiming that sin is actually done away with and righteousness is found in individuals because of one's union with Christ.[56] Just as sin is imputed to Christ, so is righteousness imputed to believers.

Simon Gathercole observes this point observing the converse of righteousness (namely unrighteousness and sin). He argues that sin reckons a status that one has before God. It is the basis for judgment and condemnation. Citing David as an example that proves the point of Paul, Gathercole states that God can only justify the sinner by not reckoning one's sin towards the individual. The flip side of that, claims Gathercole, is that God can reckon one to be righteous, as a status, on the basis of union in Christ.[57]

As such, justification should be thought of as the declaring of one as just because of the union one has with Christ. Though justification does admittedly have non-forensic associations, its primary meaning (as was shown) is forensic.[58] Overlooking debates on primary meaning and prooftexts (which are supplied amply by all parties), one may merely look to the overwhelming support that one has (by faith) union with Christ which serves as the basis for one's right standing with God. Despite the fact that the notions of infused righteousness have numerous difficulties (which have been mentioned throughout chapter 6), it is clear that actual union that one has in Christ (along with its numerous benefits) is not properly accounted for.

CONCLUSION

This chapter has sought to answer criticisms against monergism that were not addressed in their respective chapters. Particularly, this chapter explored the more common accusations that monergism denies human free will, assumes TULIP Calvinism (especially Irresistible Grace), that monergism is synonymous with reprobation, and that justification is the making of one righteous rather than the declaration of one as righteous. For further responses to the criticisms against monergism, see each respective chapter.

56. See chapter 5 for full support, though Scriptural support is found in Rom 5:17, 21; 1 Cor 6:9–11; 2 Cor 5:21. See also Horton, "Traditional Reformed View," 95.

57. Gathercole, *Where Then Is Boasting?*, 247.

58. Buchanan, *The Doctrine of Justification*, 226.

With the responses to criticisms made here, one returns a final time to the thesis of this study. Which perspective (synergistic or monergistic) best portrays salvation as being by grace through faith in accordance with the Scriptures? This study has surveyed two primary traditions that advocate synergism in the various aspects of salvation. The Wesleyan-Arminian tradition affirms synergism in election, conversion, and regeneration, though not justification (generally speaking). Roman Catholicism, as was shown in chapter 6, advocates for synergism in the aspect of justification.

The approach of this study was to examine each of these aspects as set forth by proponents of synergism to determine whether the given aspect should be considered monergistic or synergistic. Through comparative analysis of each tradition's view of the efficient cause and instrumental means, it was shown how each party views the worker(s) of an aspect and the means of acquisition. The conclusion reached in each chapter is that synergists hold to (whether by their own admission or not) a dual efficient cause and/or a works-related instrumental cause. By claiming that one must work together with God through faith, one is making the claim that faith is a work (which it has been shown not to be). By claiming that one works together with God through religious activities (as was shown to be the case in Roman Catholicism), the works which one does merit, acquire, and effect a given aspect.

This was contrasted against the monergistic perspective which states that God is the sole efficient cause of salvation. He alone causes a given outcome. While he may cause this outcome by active instrumental means as expressed through volitional faith, the faith does not cause the effect but is a means by which it is freely received. It is not as though faith is cooperative with God's work, though it is in accordance with it. The faith is still real, genuine, and shown volitionally by the individual, but it is not the cause of (or the producing agent of) the aspect.

With the aforementioned considerations in mind, one may conclude that, on balance, monergists hold to the more coherent view that salvation is by grace through faith alone. They best articulate this statement against all others. Moreover, this tradition also has valid responses to the criticisms levelled against it. Salvation, then, should rightly be understood as monergistic.

Bibliography

Ahlstrom, Sydney E. *A Religious History of the American People*. New Haven: Yale University Press, 1972.
Anselm of Canterbury. *De Concordia*. In *Anselm of Canterbury: The Major Works*, edited by Brian Davies and G. R. Evans, 435–74. New York: Oxford University Press, 2008.
———. *Why God Became Man*. In *Anselm of Canterbury: The Major Works*, edited by Brian Davies and G. R. Evans, 260–356. New York: Oxford University Press, 2008.
Aquinas, Thomas. *Summa Theologica*. 5 vols. Translated by Fathers of the English Dominican Province. Notre Dame: Christian Classics, 1948.
Aristotle. *The Basic Works of Aristotle*. Edited by Richard McKeon. New York: Random House, 1941.
———. *De Anima*. In *The Basic Works of Aristotle*, edited by Richard McKeon, 535–603. New York: Random House, 1941.
———. *Metaphysics*. In *The Basic Works of Aristotle*, edited by Richard McKeon, 689–934. New York: Random House, 1941.
Arminius, James. *The Works of James Arminius*. 3 vols. Translated by James Nichols and W. R. Bangle. Spring Valley, CA: Lamp Post, 2009.
Augustine. *Augustin: Anti-Pelagian Writings*. Edited by Philip Schaff. Nicene and Post-Nicene Fathers 5. Peabody, MA: Hendrickson, 2012.
———. *Homilies on the Gospel of John*. Edited by Philip Schaff. Nicene and Post-Nicene Fathers 7. Peabody, MA: Hendrickson, 2012.
———. *On Christian Doctrine*. Edited by Philip Schaff. Nicene and Post-Nicene Fathers 2. Peabody, MA: Hendrickson, 2012.
Ayer, Joseph Cullen, Jr., ed. *A Source Book for Ancient Church History*. New York: Scribner's, 1939.
Baker, Kenneth. *Fundamentals of Catholicism*. Vol. 3. San Francisco: Ignatius, 1983.
Baillie, Donald M. *The Theology of the Sacraments and Other Papers*. New York: Scribner's, 1957.
Balthasar, Hans Urs von. *Engagement with God*. Translated by R. John Halliburton. San Francisco: Ignatius, 2008.
Barrett, Matthew. *Salvation by Grace*. Phillipsburg, NJ: P&R, 2013.

BIBLIOGRAPHY

Barth, Karl. *Church Dogmatics*. Edited by G. W. Bromiley and T. F. Torrance. Peabody, MA: Hendrickson, 2010.

———. *The Faith of the Church: A Commentary on the Apostle's Creed according to Calvin's Catechism*. Edited by Jean-Louis Leuba. Translated by Gabriel Vahanian. New York: Meridian, 1958.

———. *The Theology of John Calvin*. Translated by Geoffrey W. Bromiley. Grand Rapids: Eerdmans, 1995.

Bartholomew, Craig G., and Michael W. Goheen. *The Drama of Scripture*. Grand Rapids: Baker Academic, 2004.

Basil. "The First Canonical Epistle of Our Holy Father Basil, Arch-Bishop of Caesarea in Cappadocia to Amphilochius, Bishop of Iconium." In *The Seven Ecumenical Councils of the Undivided Church*. Edited by Philip Schaff and Henry Wace. Nicene and Post-Nicene Fathers, Second Series 14. Peabody, MA: Hendrickson, 2012.

Bauer, Walter. *A Greek-English Lexicon of the New Testament*. Edited and translated by William F. Arndt, F. Wilber Gingrich, and Frederick W. Danker. 3rd ed. Chicago: University of Chicago Press, 2000.

Bavinck, Herman. *Reformed Dogmatics*. Vols. 3–4. Edited by John Bolt. Translated by John Vriend. Grand Rapids: Baker Academic, 2006.

———. *Saved by Grace*. Edited by J. Mark Beach. Translated by Nelson D. Kloosterman. Grand Rapids: Reformation Heritage, 2008.

Bayer, Oswald. "Justification: Basis and Boundary of Theology." In *By Faith Alone*, edited by Joseph A. Burgess and Marc Kolden, 67–85. Grand Rapids: Eerdmans, 2004.

Beasley-Murray George R. *John*. Word Biblical Commentary 36. Waco, TX: Word, 1987.

Benedict XVI. *Jesus of Nazareth*. San Francisco: Ignatius, 2011.

Berkhof, Louis. *The History of Christian Doctrines*. Carlisle, PA: Banner of Truth Trust, 2009.

———. *Systematic Theology*. Grand Rapids: Eerdmans, 1976.

Berkouwer, G. C. *Faith and Justification*. Grand Rapids: Eerdmans, 1954.

———. *Studies in Dogmatics: The Sacraments*. Grand Rapids: Eerdmans, 1969.

Best, W. E. *Studies in the Person and Work of Jesus Christ*. Houston: W. E. Best Book Missionary Trust, 1975.

Bird, Michael. "Progressive Reformed Response." In *Justification: Five Views*, edited by James K. Beilby and Paul Rhodes Eddy, 131–57. Downers Grove, IL: IVP Academic, 2011.

Boettner, Loraine. *Roman Catholicism*. Phillipsburg, NJ: Presbyterian and Reformed, 1962.

Bokenkotter, Thomas. *Dynamic Catholicism: A Historical Catechism*. New York: Image, 1986.

Bordwine, James E. *A Guide to the Westminster Confession of Faith and Larger Catechism*. Jefferson, MD: Trinity Foundation, 1991.

Bouwsma, William J. *John Calvin*. New York: Oxford University Press, 1988.

Boyce, James Petigru. *Abstract of Systematic Theology*. Philadelphia: American Baptist, 1887.

Brantl, George, ed. *Catholicism*. New York: George Braziller, 1962.

Brown, Colin, ed. *The New International Dictionary of New Testament Theology*. 3 vols. Grand Rapids: Zondervan, 1979.

BIBLIOGRAPHY

Brown, Francis, S. R. Driver, and Charles A. Briggs. *A Hebrew and English Lexicon of the Old Testament*. Oxford: Clarendon, 1996.

Buchanan, James. *The Doctrine of Justification: An Outline of Its History in the Church and of Its Exposition From Scripture*. Birmingham, AL: Solid Ground Christian, 2006.

Bultmann, Rudolf. *Jesus and the Word*. Translated by Louise P. Smith and Erminie H. Lantero. New York: Scribner's, 1958.

———. *Jesus Christ and Mythology*. New York: Scribner's, 1958.

Burbach, J. H. *The Catholic Religion*. Rockford: Tan, 1993.

Burkhill, T. A. *The Evolution of Christian Thought*. Ithaca: Cornell University Press, 1971.

Burtner, Robert W., and Robert E. Chiles, eds. *John Wesley's Theology*. Nashville: Abingdon, 1982.

Calvin, John. *The Bondage and Liberation of the Will*. Edited by A. N. S. Lane. Translated by G. I. Davies. Grand Rapids: Baker, 1996.

———. *Concerning the Eternal Predestination of God*. Translated by J. K. S. Reid. Louisville: Westminster John Knox, 1961.

———. *Institutes of the Christian Religion*. Edited by John T. McNeil. Translated by Ford Lewis Battles. Louisville: Westminster John Knox, 1960.

Campbell, Constantine R. *Paul and Union With Christ*. Grand Rapids: Zondervan, 2012.

Carson, D. A. *Divine Sovereignty and Human Responsibility: Biblical Perspectives in Tension*. Eugene: Wipf & Stock, 2002.

———. *Exegetical Fallacies*. 2nd ed. Grand Rapids: Baker Academic, 1996.

———. *The Gospel According to John*. Grand Rapids: Eerdmans, 1991.

———. "The Vindication of Imputation." In *Justification*, edited by Mark Husbands and Daniel J. Treier, 46–80 Downers Grove, IL: InterVarsity, 2004.

Cassian, John. *The Works of John Cassian*. Edited by Philip Schaff and Henry Wace. Translated by Edgar C. S. Gibson. Peabody, MA: Hendrickson, 2012.

Catechism of the Catholic Church. Liguori: Liguori, 1994.

Chafer, Lewis Sperry. "Biblical Theism: Divine Decrees." *Bibliotheca sacra* 96/382 (April–June 1939) 138–63.

———. *Systematic Theology*. Grand Rapids: Kregel, 1976.

Charles, David. *Aristotle on Meaning and Essence*. New York: Clarendon, 2000.

Chemnitz, Martin. *Examination of the Council of Trent, 3 Parts*. Translated by Fred Kramer. St. Louis: Concordia, 1971.

Clark, Gordon H. *Ephesians*. Jefferson, MD: Trinity Foundation, 1985.

———. *Faith and Saving Faith*. Jefferson, MD: Trinity Foundation, 1990.

———. *First Corinthians*. Jefferson, MD: Trinity Foundation, 1991.

Clarke, F. Stuart, *The Ground of Election: Jacobus Arminius' Doctrine of the Work and Person of Christ*. Eugene: Wipf & Stock, 2006.

Clowney, Edmund P. "The Biblical Doctrine of Justification by Faith." In *Right With God*, edited by D. A. Carson, 17–50. Grand Rapids: Baker, 1992.

Cobb, John B., Jr. *Grace and Responsibility: A Wesleyan Theology for Today*. Nashville: Abingdon, 1995.

Code, Alan. "Aristotle's Logic and Metaphysics." In *Routledge History of Philosophy: From Aristotle to Augustine*, edited by David Furley, 2:40–75. New York: Routledge, 1999.

BIBLIOGRAPHY

Cole, Graham A. *He Who Gives Life*. Wheaton, IL: Crossway, 2007.
Collins, Kenneth J. *The Theology of John Wesley*. Nashville: Abingdon, 2007.
The Companion to the Catechism of the Catholic Church. San Francisco: Ignatius, 1994.
Conner, W. T. *Christian Doctrine*. Nashville: Broadman, 1937.
Cooke, Bernard. *Sacraments and Sacramentality*. Mystic, CT: Twenty-Third, 1997.
Cottrell, Jack W. "Conditional Election." In *Grace Unlimited*, edited by Clark H. Pinnock, 51–73. Minneapolis: Bethany, 1975.
Cowan, Steven B. "Common Misconceptions of Evangelicals Regarding Calvinism." *Journal of the Evangelical Theological Society* 33/2 (June 1990) 189–95.
Cox, Leo G. "Prevenient Grace—A Wesleyan View." *Journal of the Evangelical Theological Society* 12/3 (Summer 1969) 143–49.
Craig, William L. "Middle Knowledge, A Calvinist-Arminian Rapprochement?" In *The Grace of God and the Will of Man*, edited by Clark H. Pinnock, 141–64. Minneapolis: Bethany, 1989.
Crampton, W. Gary. *What Calvin Says*. Jefferson, MD: Trinity Foundation, 1992.
Crisp, Oliver D. "The Letter and the Spirit of Barth's Doctrine of Election: A Response to Michael O'Neil." In *Evangelical Quarterly* 79/1 (January 2007) 53–67.
Cunliffe-Jones, Hubert. *A History of Christian Doctrine*. Philadelphia: Fortress, 1978.
Cunningham, Robert L. "The Call of All Nations by Saint Prosper of Aquitaine." In *Masterpieces of Catholic Literature*, edited by Frank M. Magill, 204–7. New York: Harper & Row, 1964.
Cunningham, William. *The Reformers and the Theology of the Reformation*. Carlisle, PA: Banner of Truth Trust, 1979.
Curran, Charles E. *Moral Theology: A Continuing Journey*. Notre Dame: Notre Dame Press, 1982.
Dabney, R. L. *Systematic Theology*. Carlisle, PA: Banner of Truth Trust, 1985.
Demarest, Bruce. *The Cross and Salvation*. Wheaton, IL: Crossway, 1997.
Denney, James. *The Death of Christ*. Eugene: Wipf & Stock, 2005.
Dibelius, Martin. *James*. Translated by Michael A. Williams. Philadelphia: Fortress, 1975.
Dunn, James D. G. *Romans 1–8*. Word Biblical Commentary 38A. Dallas: Word, 1988.
———. *Romans 9–16*. Word Biblical Commentary 38B. Dallas: Word, 1988.
Ebeling, Gerhard. *Luther: An Introduction to His Thought*. Philadelphia: Fortress, 1977.
Edwards, Jonathan. *The Freedom of the Will*. Lafayette, IN: Sovereign Grace, 2001.
Ehring, Douglas. "Contemporary Efficient Causation." In *Efficient Causation*, edited by Tad M. Schmaltz, 285–310. New York: Oxford University Press, 2014.
Ellis, E. Earle. *The Sovereignty of God in Salvation*. New York: T. & T. Clark, 2009.
The Encyclopedia of Philosophy. New York: Macmillan & The Free Press, 1967.
Erasmus, Desiderius. *On the Freedom of the Will*. In *Luther and Erasmus: Free Will and Salvation*. Edited and translated by E. Gordon Rupp. Louisville: Westminster John Knox, 2006.
Erickson, Millard J. *Christian Theology*. Grand Rapids: Baker, 2003.
Feinberg, John. "God Ordains All Things." In *Predestination and Free Will: Four Views of Divine Sovereignty and Human Freedom*, edited by David Basinger and Randall Basinger, 17–43. Downers Grove, IL: InterVarsity, 1986.
Ferguson, Sinclair B. "Ordo Salutis." In *New Dictionary of Theology*, edited by Sinclair B. Ferguson, David F. Wright, and J. I. Packer, 480–81. Downers Grove, IL: InterVarsity, 1988.

BIBLIOGRAPHY

Fesko, J. V. *Justification*. Phillipsburg, NK: P&R, 2008.

Fiddes, Paul S. *Past Event and Present Salvation: The Christian Idea of Atonement*. Louisville: Westminster/John Knox, 1989.

Finney, Charles. *Lectures on Systematic Theology*. Edited by J. H. Fairchild. New York: George H. Doran, 1878.

———. *Revivals of Religion*. Virginia Beach: CBN University Press, 1978.

First Vatican Council. *Decrees of the Ecumenical Councils*. Vol. 2. Edited by Norman P. Tanner. Washington, DC: Georgetown University Press, 1990.

Fletcher, John. *On Perfection* in *Christian Perfection: A Compilation of Six Holiness Classics*. Vol. 1. Salem: H. E. Schmul, 1974.

Forde, Gerhard O. *On Being A Theologian of the Cross: Reflections on Luther's Heidelberg Disputation, 1518*. Grand Rapids: Eerdmans, 1997.

Forlines, F. Leroy. *Classical Arminianism*. Nashville: Randall, 2011.

Forrester, F. J. *A Righteousness of God For Unrighteous Men: Being an Exposition of the Epistle to the Romans*. Nashville: Sunday School Board of the SBC, 1926.

Garcia, Mark A. *Life in Christ: Union with Christ and Twofold Grace in Calvin's Theology*. Eugene: Wipf & Stock, 2008.

Garrett, James Leo, Jr. *Systematic Theology*. Vol. 2. N. Richland Hills, TX: BIBAL, 2001.

Gathercole, Simon. *Where Then Is Boasting? Early Jewish Soteriology and Paul's Response in Romans 1–5*. Grand Rapids: Eerdmans, 2002.

Geisler, Norman. *Chosen But Free: A Balanced View of Divine Election*. Minneapolis: Bethany, 2001.

———. "God Knows All Things." In *Predestination and Free Will: Four Views of Divine Sovereignty and Human Freedom*, edited by David Basinger and Randall Basinger, 61–84. Downers Grove, IL: InterVarsity, 1986.

———. *A Popular Survey of the Old Testament*. Grand Rapids: Baker Academic, 2006.

———. *Systematic Theology*. Vol. 3. Minneapolis: Bethany, 2004.

George, Timothy. *Amazing Grace: God's Initiative—Our Response*. Nashville: Lifeway, 2000.

———. *Theology of the Reformers*. Nashville: Broadman, 1988.

Gerrish, Brian A. *Grace and Reason: A Study in the Theology of Luther*. Chicago: University of Chicago Press, 1979.

———. *Saving and Secular Faith*. Minneapolis: Fortress, 1999.

Gilson, Etienne. *The Christian Philosophy of St. Thomas Aquinas*. Translated by L. K. Shook. Notre Dame: University of Notre Dame Press, 1994.

Godwin, Johnnie C. *What It Means to Be Born Again*. Nashville: Broadman, 1977.

González, Justo L. *A History of Christian Thought*. 3 vols. Nashville: Abingdon, 1975.

Gossett, Earl Fowler, Jr. *The Doctrine of Justification in the Theology of John Calvin, Albrecht Ritschl, and Reinhold Niebuhr*. Ann Arbor: University Microfilms, 1961.

Graesser, Carl, Jr. "Righteousness, Human And Divine." *Currents in Theology and Mission* 10/3 (June 1983) 134–41.

Green, Joel B. *Salvation*. St. Louis: Chalice, 2003.

Grenz, Stanley J. *Theology for the Community of God*. Grand Rapids: Eerdmans, 1994.

Grosheide, F. W. *Commentary on the First Epistle to the Corinthians*. The New International Commentary on the New Testament. Grand Rapids: Eerdmans, 1968.

Grounds, Vernon C. "God's Universal Salvific Grace." In *Grace Unlimited*, edited by Clark H. Pinnock, 21–30. Minneapolis: Bethany, 1975.

BIBLIOGRAPHY

Grudem, Wayne. *Systematic Theology*. Grand Rapids: Zondervan, 1994.
Guthrie, Donald. *New Testament Theology*. Downers Grove, IL: InterVarsity, 1981.
———. *The Pastoral Epistles*. Tyndale New Testament Commentaries 14. Grand Rapids: Eerdmans,1989.
Gutierrez, Gustavo. *A Theology of Liberation: History, Politics and Salvation*. Translated by Caridad Inda and John Eagleson. Maryknoll, NY: Orbis, 1973.
Hägglund, Bengt. *History of Theology*. Translated by Gene J. Lund. Saint Louis: CPH, 1968.
Hagner, Donald A. *Matthew 1–13*. Word Biblical Commentary 33B. Nashville: Thomas Nelson, 1993.
———. *Matthew 14–28*. Word Biblical Commentary 33B. Nashville: Thomas Nelson, 1995.
Harnack, Adolf. *History of Dogma*. Vol. 5. New York: Dover, 1961.
Harper, Steve. *The Way to Heaven: The Gospel According to John Wesley*. Grand Rapids: Zondervan, 1983.
Hart, Trevor. "Redemption and Fall." In *The Cambridge Companion to Christian Doctrine*, edited by Colin E. Gunton, 189–206. New York: Cambridge University Press, 1997.
Hawthorne, Gerald F. *Philippians*. Word Biblical Commentary 43. Waco, TX: Word, 1983.
Heick, Otto W. *A History of Christian Thought*. Vol. 2. Philadelphia: Fortress, 1966.
Helm, Paul. *The Beginnings: Word and Spirit in Conversion*. Carlisle, PA: Banner of Truth Trust, 1986.
Hill, Jonathan. *The History of Christian Thought*. Downers Grove, IL: InterVarsity, 2003.
Hodge, A. A. *Evangelical Theology*. Carlisle, PA: Banner of Truth Trust, 1990.
Hodge, Charles. *Systematic Theology*. Peabody, MA: Hendrickson, 2013.
Hoekema, Anthony A. "The Covenant of Grace in Calvin's Teaching." In *Articles on Calvin and Calvinism*, edited by Richard C. Gamble, 8:45–73. New York: Garland, 1992.
———. *Created in God's Image*. Grand Rapids: Eerdmans, 1986.
———. "The Reformed Perspective." In *Five Views on Sanctification*, edited by Melvin Dieter et al., 59–90. Grand Rapids: Zondervan, 1987.
———. *Saved by Grace*. Grand Rapids: Eerdmans, 1989.
Hoitenga, Dewey J., Jr. *John Calvin and the Will*. Grand Rapids: Baker, 1997.
Horton, Michael S. *The Christian Faith: A Systematic Theology for Pilgrims on the Way*. Grand Rapids: Zondervan, 2011.
———. "Evangelical Arminians." *Modern Reformation* 1/3 (1992) 15–19.
———. *For Calvinism*. Grand Rapids: Zondervan, 2011.
———. "Traditional Reformed View." *Justification: Five Views*m edited by James K. Beilby and Paul Rhodes Eddy, 83–111. Downers Grove, IL: IVP Academic, 2011.
Hume, David. *The Letters of David Hume*. Edited by J. Y. T. Greig. Oxford: Clarendon, 1969.
Hunt, Dave, and James White. *Debating Calvinism: Five Points, Two Views*. Sisters, OR: Multnomah, 2004.
———. *What Love Is This?* Sisters, OR: Loyal, 2002.
Hunter, A. Mitchell. *The Teaching of Calvin*. London: James Clarke, 1950.
Jedin, Hubert. *A History of the Council of Trent*. 2 vols. Translated by Dom Ernest Graf. New York: Thomas Nelson, 1961.

BIBLIOGRAPHY

Jenson, Robert W. "The Church and the Sacraments." In *The Cambridge Companion to Christian Doctrine*, edited by Colin E. Gunton, 207–25. New York: Cambridge University Press, 1997.

Jeremias, Joachim. *New Testament Theology*. New York: Scribner's, 1971.

Johnson, Kevin Orlin. *Why Do Catholics Do That?* New York: Ballantine, 1994.

Joint Declaration on the Doctrine of Justification. Grand Rapids: Eerdmans, 1999.

Jones, E. Stanley. *Conversion*. New York: Abingdon, 1959.

Jüngel, Eberhard. *Justification: The Heart of the Christian Faith*. New York: T. & T. Clark, 2001.

Kearsley, Roy. "Grace." In *New Dictionary of Theology*, edited by Sinclair B. Ferguson, David F. Wright, and J. I. Packer. Downers Grove, IL: InterVarsity, 1988.

Keathley, Kenneth. "The Doctrine of Salvation." In *A Theology for the Church*, edited by Daniel L. Akin, 686–765. Nashville: Broadman & Holman Academic, 2007.

———. *Salvation and Sovereignty: A Molinist Approach*. Nashville: Broadman & Holman Academic, 2010.

Kelly, J. N. D. *Early Christian Doctrines*. 2nd ed. New York: Harper & Row, 1960.

Kennedy, Kevin Dixon. *Union with Christ and the Extent of the Atonement*. New York: Peter Lang, 2002.

Kenrick, Francis Patrick. *The Catholic Doctrine on Justification: Explained and Vindicated*. San Bernardino, CA: St. Pius X, 2014.

Kittel, Gerhard, ed. *Theological Dictionary of the New Testament*. Grand Rapids: Eerdmans, 1964.

Klein, William W. *The New Chosen People*. Eugene, OR: Wipf & Stock, 2001.

Klotsche, E. H. *The History of Christian Doctrine*. Rev. ed. Grand Rapids: Baker, 1979.

Knight, Henry H., III. "Love and Freedom 'by Grace Alone' in Wesley's Soteriology: A Proposal for Evangelicals." *PNEUMA: The Journal of the Society for Pentecostal Studies* 24/1 (Spring 2002) 57–67.

Koehler, Ludwig, and Walter Baumgartner. *The Hebrew and Aramaic Lexicon of the Old Testament*. Vol. 2. Edited by M. E. J. Richardson. Leiden: Brill, 1995.

Köstlin, Julius. *The Theology of Luther in its Historical Development and Inner Harmony*. Vol. 2. Translated by Charles E. Hay. Philadelphia: Lutheran Publication Society, 1897.

Küng, Hans. *The Church*. Translated by Ray Ockenden and Rosaleen Ockenden. New York: Sheed and Ward, 1967.

———. *Justification: The Doctrine of Karl Barth and a Catholic Reflection*. Translated by Thomas Collins, Edmund E. Tolk, and David Granskou. Louisville: Westminster John Knox, 2004.

Ladd, George Eldon. *A Theology of the New Testament*. Grand Rapids: Eerdmans, 1993.

Lake, Donald M. "Jacob Arminius' Contribution to a Theology of Grace." In *Grace Unlimited*, edited by Clark H. Pinnock, 223–42. Minneapolis: Bethany, 1975.

Lane, Anthony N. S. *A Concise History of Christian Thought*. Rev. ed. Grand Rapids: Baker Academic, 2006.

———. *Justification by Faith in Catholic-Protestant Dialogue*. New York: T. & T. Clark, 2006.

Lemke, Steve. "A Biblical and Theological Critique of Irresistible Grace." In *Whosoever Will*, edited by David L. Allen and Steve W. Lemke, 109–62. Nashville: B&H Academic 2010.

BIBLIOGRAPHY

Lockwood, Gregory J. *1 Corinthians*. Concordia Commentary. Saint Louis: Concordia, 2000.

Leith, John H., ed. *Creeds of the Church*. Richmond, VA: John Knox, 1973.

Leo I. "Letters of Leo the Great." In *Leo the Great, Gregory the Great*. Edited by Philip Schaff and Henry Wace. Translated by Charles Lett Feltoe. Nicene and Post-Nicene Fathers, Second Series, 12. Peabody, MA: Hendrickson, 2012.

Luther, Martin. "The Babylonian Captivity of the Church." In *Three Treatises*, translated by A. T. W. Steinhäuser et al., 115–260. Philadelphia: Fortress, 1960.

———. "The Freedom of the Christian." In *Three Treatises*, translated by W. A. Lambert and revised by Harold J. Grimm, 265–316. Philadelphia: Fortress, 1960.

———. "Luther's Small Catechism." In *The Creeds of Christendom*, edited by Philip Schaff and David S. Schaff, 3:74–92. Grand Rapids: Baker, 1998.

———. *On Christian Liberty*. Minneapolis: Fortress, 2003.

———. *On the Bondage of the Will*. In *Luther and Erasmus: Free Will and Salvation*, edited and translated by E. Gordon Rupp. Louisville: Westminster John Knox, 2006.

———. *Three Treatises*. Translated by W. A. Lambert and revised by Harold J. Grimm. Philadelphia: Fortress, 1960.

———. *Two Kinds of Righteousness*. Edited by Timothy F. Lull. Minneapolis: Fortress, 2005.

MacDonald, William G. "The Spirit of Grace." In *Grace Unlimited*, edited by Clark H. Pinnock, 74–94. Minneapolis: Bethany Fellowship, 1975.

Machen, J. Gresham. *What is Faith?* Carlisle, PA: Banner of Truth, 1991.

Mackinnon, James. *Calvin and the Reformation*. New York: Russell & Russell, 1962.

Marshall, I. Howard. *New Testament Theology*. Downers Grove, IL: InterVarsity, 2004.

Martin, Ralph P. *James*. Word Biblical Commentary 48. Nashville: Thomas Nelson, 1988.

Maurer, Armand A. *A History of Philosophy*. New York: Random House, 1969.

McCartney, Dan G. "Atonement in James, Peter, and Jude." In *The Glory of the Atonement*, edited by Charles E. Hill and Frank A. James III, 176–89. Downers Grove, IL: InterVarsity, 2004.

McGonigle, Herbert Boyd. *Sufficient Saving Grace: John Wesley's Evangelical Arminianism*. Waynesboro, GA: Paternoster, 2001.

McGrath, Alister E. *Iustitia Dei: A History of the Christian Doctrine of Justification*. 3rd ed. New York: Cambridge University Press, 2005.

———. *Justification By Faith*. Grand Rapids: Academie, 1988.

———. *Luther's Theology of the Cross*. Cambridge: Blackwell, 1985.

Miley, John. *Systematic Theology*. Vol. 2. New York: Eaton & Mains, 1894.

Moo, Douglas. *The Epistle to the Romans*. The New International Commentary on the New Testament. Grand Rapids: Eerdmans, 1996.

Moody, Dale. *The Word of Truth*. Grand Rapids: Eerdmans, 1981.

Morris, Leon. *The Apostolic Preaching of the Cross*. Grand Rapids: Eerdmans, 1965.

Mounce, William D. *Pastoral Epistles*. Word Biblical Commentary 46. Nashville: Thomas Nelson, 2000.

Muller, Richard A. "Grace, Election, and Contingent Choice: Arminius's Gambit and the Reformed Response." In *The Grace of God, the Bondage of the Will*, edited by Thomas R. Schreiner and Bruce A. Ware, 2:251–78. Grand Rapids: Baker, 1995.

———. *The Unaccommodated Calvin*. New York: Oxford University Press, 2000.

Mullins, E. Y. *The Axioms of Religion*. Philadelphia: Judson, 1908.
Nettles, Thomas. *By His Grace and For His Glory*. Grand Rapids: Baker, 1986.
———. *The Grace of God, The Bondage of the Will*. Vol. 2. Edited by Thomas R. Schreiner and Bruce A. Ware. Grand Rapids: Baker, 1995.
Newell, William R. *Romans*. Chicago: Moody, 1938.
Nicole, Roger. "John Calvin's View of the Extent of the Atonement." In *Articles on Calvin and Calvinism*, edited by Richard C. Gamble, 197–225. New York: Garland, 1992.
Noll, Mark A. "John Wesley and the Doctrine of Assurance." *Bibliotheca Sacra* 132/526 (April–June 1975) 161–77.
Oberman, Heiko Augustinus. *The Harvest of Medieval Theology: Gabriel Biel and Late Medieval Nominalism*. Durham: Labyrinth, 1983.
O'Collins, Gerald, and Oliver P. Rafferty. "Roman Catholic View." In *Justification: Five Views*, edited by James K. Beilby and Paul Rhodes Eddy, 265–90. Downers Grove, IL: IVP Academic, 2011.
Oden, Thomas. *Systematic Theology: The Word of Live*. Vol. 2. San Francisco: HarperSanFrancisco, 1992.
———. *Systematic Theology: Life in the Spirit*. Vol. 3. Peabody, MA: Hendrickson, 2008.
———. *The Transforming Power of Grace*. Nashville: Abingdon, 1993.
Olson, C. Gordon *Getting the Gospel Right*. Lynchburg, VA: Global Gospel, 2005.
Olson, Roger. *Against Calvinism*. Grand Rapids: Zondervan, 2011.
———. *Arminian Theology: Myths and Realities*. Downers Grove, IL: IVP Academic, 2006.
———. *The Mosaic of Christian Belief*. Downers Grove, IL: InterVarsity, 2002.
Osborne, Grant R. "Exegetical Notes on Calvinist Texts." In *Grace Unlimited*, edited by Clark H. Pinnock, 167–89. Minneapolis: Bethany Fellowship, 1975.
Osborne, Kenan B. *Reconciliation and Justification: The Sacraments and Its Theology*. New York: Paulist, 1990.
Owen, John. "The Doctrine of Justification By Faith, Chapter XVIII." In *The Works of John Owen*, edited by William H. Goold, 5:356–63. Carlisle, PA: The Banner of Truth Trust, 1981.
Packer, James I. *Evangelism and The Sovereignty of God*. Downers Grove, IL: IVP Academic, 1961.
———. "The Love of God: Universal and Particular." In *The Grace of God, The Bondage of the Will*, edited by Thomas R. Schreiner and Bruce A. Ware, 2:413–27. Grand Rapids: Baker, 1995.
———. "The Way of Salvation Part III: Problems with Universalism." *Bibliotheca Sacra* 130/517 (January–March 1973) 3–11.
Packer, James I., and O. R. Johnston. "Historical and Theological Introduction." In *The Bondage of the Will*, by Martin Luther, 13–61. Grand Rapids: Fleming H. Revell, 1999.
Page, Frank S. *Trouble with the Tulip*. 2nd ed. Canton, OH: Riverstone, 2006.
Pasnau, Robert. *Thomas Aquinas on Human Nature*. New York: Cambridge University Press, 2002.
Patterson, Paige. "Total Depravity." In *Whosoever Will*, edited by David L. Allen and Steve W. Lemke, 29–44. Nashville: B&H Academic 2010.
Pelagius. *The Letters of Pelagius*. Edited by Robert Van de Weyer. Worcestershire: Arthur James, 1995.
———. *Pelagius's Commentary on St Paul's Epistle to the Romans*. Translated by Theodore De Bruyn. Oxford: Clarendon, 1993.

Peters, George William. "The Meaning of Conversion." *Bibliotheca Sacra* 120 (July–September 1963) 234–42.

Peters, John L. *Christian Perfection and American Methodism*. New York: Abingdon, 1956.

Peterson, Henry. *The Canons of Dort: A Study Guide*. Grand Rapids: Baker, 1968.

Pfeiffer, August. *Anti-Calvinism*. Columbus: Joint Synod of Ohio, 1881.

Pfurtner, Stephen. *Luther and Aquinas on Salvation*. Translated by Edward Quinn. New York: Sheed and Ward, 1964.

Picirilli, Robert E. *Grace, Faith, Free Will*. Nashville: Randall, 2002.

Pinson, J. Matthew. "Jacobus Arminius: Reformed and Always Reforming." In *Grace for All: The Arminian Dynamics of Salvation*, edited by Clark H. Pinnock and John D. Wagner, 146–76. Eugene, OR: Resource, 2015.

Polhill, John B. *Paul and His Letters*. Nashville: Broadman & Holman, 1999.

Pope, William Burt. *A Compendium of Christian Theology*. Vol. 2. 2nd ed. New York: Hunt & Eaton, 1889.

Rahner, Karl. "Open Questions in Dogma Considered by the Institutional Church as Definitively Answered." *Journal of Ecumenical Studies* 15/2 (Spring 1978) 211–26.

———. "What Is a Sacrament." *Worship* 47/5 (1973) 274–84.

Rahner, Karl, and Herbert Vorgrimler. *Dictionary of Theology*. 2nd ed. New York: Crossroad, 1985.

Rainbow, Jonathan H. *The Will of God and the Cross: An Historical and Theological Study of John Calvin's Doctrine of Limited Redemption*. Eugene, OR: Pickwick, 1990.

Reasoner, Vic. "John Wesley's Doctrines on the Theology of Grace." In *Grace for All: The Arminian Dynamics of Salvation*, edited by Clark H. Pinnock and John D. Wagner, 177–96. Eugene, OR: Resource, 2015.

Reist, Irwin W. "John Wesley's View of Man: A Study in Free Grace Versus Free Will." *Wesleyan Theological Journal* 7 (1972) 25–35.

Robertson, A. T. *Word Pictures in the New Testament*. Nashville: Broadman, 1931.

Robertson, O. Palmer. "The Holy Spirit in the Westminster Confession of Faith." In *The Westminster Confession into the 21st Century*, edited by Ligon Duncan, 1:57–100. Ross-shire, UK: Christian Focus, 2004.

Rogers, Charles Allen. "The Concept of Prevenient Grace in the Theology of John Wesley." PhD diss., Duke University, 1968.

Ropes, James Hardy. "'Righteousness' and 'The Righteousness of God' in the Old Testament and in St. Paul." *Journal of Biblical Literature* 22/2 (January 1, 1903) 211–20.

Ross, David. *Aristotle*. New York: Routledge, 1995.

Schmaltz, Tad M. "Efficient Causation From Suárez to Descartes." In *Efficient Causation*, edited by Tad M. Schmaltz, 139–64. New York: Oxford University Press, 2014.

———. "Introduction to Efficient Causation." In *Efficient Causation*, edited by Tad M. Schmaltz, 3–19. New York: Oxford University Press, 2014.

Schreiner, Thomas. *40 Questions About Christians and Biblical Law*. Grand Rapids: Kregel, 2010.

———. "Does Scripture Teach Prevenient Grace in the Wesleyan Sense?" In *The Grace of God, The Bondage of the Will*, edited by Thomas R. Schreiner and Bruce A. Ware, 2:365–82. Grand Rapids: Baker, 1995.

Seifrid, Mark A. *Christ, Our Righteousness: Paul's Theology of Justification*. Downers Grove, IL: InterVarsity, 2000.

BIBLIOGRAPHY

Sell, Alan P. F. *The Great Debate: Calvinism, Arminianism, and Salvation*. Grand Rapids: Baker, 1983.

Schaff, Philip, and David Schaff, eds. "The Canons of the Synod of Dort." In *The Creeds of Christendom*, 3:581–95. Grand Rapids: Baker, 1993.

———. "The Formula of Concord." In *The Creeds of Christendom*, 3:93–180. Grand Rapids: Baker, 1993.

Shedd, Russell. "Justification and Personal Christian Living." In *Right With God*, edited by D. A. Carson, 163–77. Grand Rapids: Paternoster and Baker, 1992.

Shedd, William G. T. *Dogmatic Theology*. Grand Rapids: Zondervan, 1969.

———. *A History of Christian Doctrine*. Vol. 2. Scribner's, 1889.

Shelton, R. Larry. "Initial Salvation: The Redemptive Grace of God in Christ." In *A Contemporary Wesleyan Theology*, edited by Charles W. Carter, 1:469–516. Grand Rapids: Francis Asbury, 1983.

Shelton, W. Brian. *Prevenient Grace: God's Provision for Fallen Humanity*. Anderson, IN: Francis Asbury, 2014.

Slaatte, Howard A. *The Arminian Arm of Theology*. Washington, DC: University Press of America, 1977.

Smeaton, George. *Christ's Doctrine of the Atonement*. Carlisle, PA: The Banner of Truth Trust, 1991.

———. *The Doctrine of the Atonement According to the Apostles*. Peabody, MA: Hendrickson, 1988.

Smith, David. *The Life and Letters of St. Paul*. New York: Harper, n.d.

Sproul, R. C. *Faith Alone: The Evangelical Doctrine of Justification*. Grand Rapids: Baker, 1995.

———. *The Glory of Christ*. Wheaton, IL: Tyndale, 1990.

———. *The Holiness of God*. Wheaton, IL: Tyndale, 1985.

———. *What is Reformed Theology?* Grand Rapids: Baker, 1997.

———. *Willing to Believe*. Grand Rapids: Baker, 2008.

Spurgeon, Charles. *All of Grace*. Chicago: Moody, n.d.

Stagg, Frank. *New Testament Theology*. Nashville: Broadman, 1962.

Stanglin, Keith D. *Arminius on the Assurance of Salvation*. Boston: Brill, 2007.

Staples, Rob L. "John Wesley's Doctrine of the Holy Spirit." *Wesleyan Theological Journal* 21/1–2 (Spring–Fall 1986) 91–115.

Stasiak, Kurt. *Sacramental Theology: Means of Grace, Ways of Life*. Chicago: Loyola, 2002.

Storms, C. Samuel. *Chosen for Life*. Grand Rapids: Baker, 1987.

———. *The Grandeur of God*. Grand Rapids: Baker, 1984.

Stott, John R. W. *The Cross of Christ*. Downers Grove, IL: InterVarsity, 1986.

Strong, Augustus H. *Systematic Theology*. Valley Forge, PA: Judson, 1969.

Stuhlmacher Peter. *Revisiting Paul's Doctrine of Justification: A Challenge to the New Perspective*. Downers Grove, IL: InterVarsity, 2001.

Sullivan, Francis A. *Salvation Outside the Church? Tracing the History of the Catholic Response*. New York: Paulist, 1992.

Summers, Thos O. *Systematic Theology: A Complete Body of Wesleyan Arminian Divinity*. Nashville: Methodist Episcopal Church, South, 1888.

Sunday, William, and Arthur C. Headlam. *A Critical and Exegetical Commentary on the Epistle to the Romans*. 5th ed. Edinburgh: T. & T. Clark, 1958.

Sungenis, Robert A. *Not By Faith Alone: The Biblical Evidence for the Catholic Doctrine of Justification*. Goleta, CA: Queenship, 1997.

BIBLIOGRAPHY

Tanner, Norman P., ed. *Decrees of the Ecumenical Councils*. Washington, DC: Georgetown University Press, 1990.

Taylor, Richard S. "Historical and Modern Significance of Wesleyan Theology." In *A Contemporary Wesleyan Theology*, edited by Charles W. Carter, 55–71. Grand Rapids: Francis Asbury, 1983.

Tertullian. "On Repentance." In *Latin Christianity: Its Founder, Tertullian*, edited by Alexander Roberts and James Donaldson. Ante-Nicene Fathers 3. Peabody, MA: Hendrickson, 2012.

Thielman, Frank. *Ephesians*. Baker Exegetical Commentary on the New Testament. Grand Rapids: Baker Academic, 2010.

Tillich, Paul. *Dynamics of Faith*. New York: Harper, 1957.

Tucker, William Jewett. "Progressive Orthodoxy, Pt. 5: The Work of the Holy Spirit." *Andover Review* 4/21 (1885) 256–64.

Tuozzo, Thomas M. "Aristotle and the Discovery of Efficient Causation." In *Efficient Causation*, edited by Tad M. Schmaltz, 23–47. New York: Oxford University Press, 2014.

Turretin, Francis. *Justification*. Edited by James T. Dennison Jr. Translated by George Musgrave Giger. Phillipsburg, NJ: P&R, 1994.

Tyerman, L. *The Life and Times of the Rev. John Wesley*. New York: Burt Franklin, 1973.

Vaillancourt, Raymond. *Toward a Renewal of Sacramental Theology*. Translated by Matthew J. O'Connell. Collegeville, MN: Liturgical, 1979.

Van Asselt, Willem J., J. Martin Bac, and Roelf T. te Velde, eds. *Reformed Thought on Freedom: The Concept of Free Choice in Early Modern Reformed Theology*. Grand Rapids: Baker Academic, 2010.

Vance, Laurence M. *The Other Side of Calvinism*. Rev. ed. Pensacola, FL: Vance, 1999.

VanGemeren, Willem A., ed. *New International Dictionary of Old Testament Theology and Exegesis*. 5 vols. Grand Rapids: Zondervan, 1997.

Van Mastricht, Peter. *A Treatise on Regeneration*. Morgan, PA: Soli Deo Gloria, 2002.

Vatican Council II: Constitutions, Decrees, Declarations. Northport, NY: Costello, 1996.

Vaughan, W. Curtis. *The Letter to the Ephesians*. Nashville: Convention, 1963.

Venema, Cornells P. "Covenant and Election in the Theology of Herman Bavinck." *Mid-America Journal of Theology* 19 (2008) 69–115.

Vos, Johannes G. *The Westminster Larger Catechism: A Commentary*. Edited by G. I. Williamson. Phillipsburg, NJ: P&R, 2002.

Walker, Williston. *John Calvin*. New York: Putnam's, 1906.

Walls, Jerry L., and Joseph R. Dongell. *Why I Am Not a Calvinist*. Downers Grove, IL: InterVarsity, 2004.

Walsh, Liam G. "Sacraments." In *The Theology of Thomas Aquinas*, edited by Rik Van Nieuwenhove and Joseph Wawrykow, 326–64. Notre Dame: University of Notre Dame Press, 2005.

Waltke, Bruce. *An Old Testament Theology*. Grand Rapids: Zondervan, 2007.

Warfield, Benjamin B. *Benjamin B. Warfield: Selected Shorter Writings*. Vol. 2. Edited by John E. Meeter. Phillipsburg, NJ: Presbyterian and Reformed, 1980.

———. *Biblical and Theological Studies*. Philadelphia: Presbyterian and Reformed, 1968.

———. *Calvin and Augustine*. Philadelphia: Presbyterian and Reformed, 1956.

———. *The Person and Work of Christ*. Philadelphia: Presbyterian and Reformed, 1950.

———. *The Plan of Salvation*. Eugene, OR: Wipf & Stock, 2000.

Waterhouse, Steven W. *What Must I Do To Be Saved? The Bible's Definition of Saving Faith*. Amarillo, TX: Westcliff, 2004.

Waters, Guy Prentiss. *Justification and the New Perspective on Paul: A Review and Response*. Phillipsburg, NJ: P&R, 2004.

Webster, John. "Rector et iudex super Omnia genera doctrinarum? The Place of the Doctrine of Justification." In *What is Justification About? Reformed Contributions to an Ecumenical Theme*, edited by Michael Weinrich and John P. Burgess, 35–56. Grand Rapids: Eerdmans, 2009.

Wells, David F. *Turning to God*. Grand Rapids: Baker, 2012.

Welty, Greg. "Election and Calling: A Biblical Theological Study." *Calvinism: A Southern Baptist Dialogue*, edited by E. Ray Clendenen and Brad J. Waggoner, 216–43. Nashville: B&H Academic, 2008.

Wendel, François. *Calvin: Origins and Developments of His Religious Thought*. Translated by Philip Mairet. Grand Rapids: Baker, 1997.

Wesley, John. *Calvinism Calmly Considered: Predestination, Sovereignty, and Free Choice*. Salem, OH: Schmul, 2001.

———. *The Complete Sermons: John Wesley*. San Bernardino, CA: CreateSpace, 2013.

———. *The Essential Works of John Wesley*. Edited by Alice Russie. Uhrichsville, OH: Barbour, 2011.

Wetzel, James. "Snares of Truth: Augustine on Free Will and Predestination." In *Augustine and His Critics*, edited by Robert Dodaro and George Lawless, 124–41. New York: Routledge, 2000.

White, James R. *The God Who Justifies*. Minneapolis: Bethany, 2001.

———. *The Potter's Freedom*. Amityville, NY: Calvary, 2009.

Whyte, Alexander. *An Exposition on the Shorter Catechism*. Ross-shire, UK: Christian Focus, 2004.

Williams, Michael D. "The Five Points of Arminianism." *Presbyterion* 30/1 (Spring 2004) 11–36.

Williamson, G. I. *The Westminster Confession of Faith for Study Classes*. Philadelphia: Presbyterian and Reformed, 1964.

Witherington, Ben, III. *The Problem with Evangelical Theology*. Waco, TX: Baylor University Press, 2005.

Wood, Susan K. "Catholic Reception of the Joint Declaration on the Doctrine of Justification." In *Rereading Paul Together: Protestant and Catholic Perspectives on Justification*, edited by David E. Aune, 43–59. Grand Rapids: Baker Academic, 2006.

Wright, N. T. *Justification: God's Plan and Paul's Vision*. Downers Grove, IL: IVP Academic, 2009.

Wynkoop, Mildred Bangs. *Foundations of Wesleyan-Arminian Theology*. Kansas City: Beacon Hill, 1967.

Yarbrough, Robert W. "Divine Election in the Gospel of John." In *The Grace of God, the Bondage of the Will*, edited by Thomas R. Schreiner and Bruce A. Ware, 1:47–62. Grand Rapids: Baker, 1995.

Zemek, George J. *A Biblical Theology of the Doctrines of Sovereign Grace*. Little Rock: BTDSG, 2002.

Ziesler, John A. *The Meaning of Righteousness in Paul*. New York: Cambridge University Press, 1972.

———. *Pauline Christianity*. Oxford: Oxford University Press, 1990.

Index

Abraham (Abram), 2–3, 57
active, defined, 17
active obedience, 182–83, 190–91
active powers, 22n62, 44–45, 135–36
actual, defined, 17
actual justification, 204, 207
actuality, of righteousness, 177–79, 192
Adam
    election of people, 57, 59
    sin of, 6, 6n13, 23–24n64, 177, 200–201, 205
angels, 265
Anselm of Canterbury, 202, 205, 220
Anti-Pelagian Writings (Augustine), 140
apostasy, 81–82, 140–41n45
Aquinas
    on causation, 23–24n64
    on creation, 57
    on divine justice, 208n40
    on divine motion, 229, 229n116
    on efficient or principal cause, 20, 21n60
    on faith as a work, 40
    on grace and merit, 8–9
    on justification, 203, 205, 211, 216, 226–27, 227n109, 227n110
    on merit, 8–9, 198–99, 209, 231, 231n122, 232n126
    on preparation of the soul, 202
    principal agent and, 52
    principal cause and, 198, 214–15
    Purgatory doctrine, 212–13
    on regeneration, 103
    on repentance, 222
    on sacraments, 167–68, 167n7, 246
    on sanctifying grace, 52
    twofold efficient agency, 18n49
    on work, 26–27
Aristotelian Causation, 24, 74
Aristotle
    active and passive powers, 22n62
    aspects of causation, 19n53, 20n57
    causation theory, 19–20, 22n61
    instrumental causation, 20n59, 22n22
    moral agents, 22
    perception of proper sensibles, 19n54
The Arminian Articles, 138
Arminian tradition
    on conditional election, 54–55
    criticism of, 132
    divine decrees, 68n61, 70n67, 71, 84
    on efficient cause, 74–75, 111–14, 160–61
    on election, 61–68
    on faith, 39–40, 159, 163
    on grace, 33–34, 155–57
    human-centered view of salvation, 132–33
    on instrumental means, 40n136, 161–62
    on prevenient grace, 100–101, 116–125, 137–38n34, 150–53, 150n85, 162, 227n109
    on regeneration, 87n9, 88, 127–28
    on salvation, 46–47
    soteriological synergism and, 50
    on total depravity, 89n17, 90n19
    unconditional love and conditional election, 82, 82n121
    on works, 25, 253, 253n3

INDEX

Arminius, Jacob (James)
  Arminian tradition, 54
  on assurance of salvation, 80–81n112
  on conversion, 143–44
  on cooperating grace, 115
  on divine decrees, 64n42
  on divine grace, 132
  on efficient cause, 104–5
  on election, 63–64
  on free will, 86n6
  on God's love, 82
  on prevenient grace, 137, 152
  on regeneration, 89, 97, 97n44, 113, 144–45
  on seeking after God, 93, 93n31
  on sin effects on disposition, 98
  on unregenerate, 115
aspects of causation
  Aristotle, 19n53, 20n57
  causation theory, 19n53, 20n57
  Hume, David, 19n53
aspectual, defined, 17, 44
aspectual nature of salvation
  justification, 175–76, 176n40
  ordering of aspects, 15–16n44, 16–17
  overview, 13–15, 14n40
Athanasius, Bishop of Alexandria, 92n27
atonement, 157–58, 214, 261–62
Augustine of Hippo
  on grace, 169n11
  grace, priority of, 7
  on justification, 166–67n6
  Luther and, 168–69
  on merit, 208
  monergism belief, 5, 6, 52, 52n187
  predestinarian theology, 6–7, 130–31
  on prevenient grace, 137, 140, 140–41n45, 140n44
  on Purgatory, 213
  on spiritual good, 92n28
  synergistic views, 52, 52n187
  on total depravity, 12
  on unconditional election, 72
Aulén, Gustav, 14

"The Babylonian Captivity of the Church" (Luther), 169
Baker, Kenneth, 212, 212n61
Balthasar, Hans Urs von, 207
baptism
  Aquinas on, 168
  Catholic Catechism on, 223–24
  Catholic tradition on, 244–45
  infant baptism, 227n109, 245n172
  Leo the Great on, 221
  Luther on, 108–9n101
  Vatican II on, 41
Barth, Karl, 56n10, 206, 210, 217
Bavinck, Herman, 60n26, 109, 149n82
belief, term usage, 43
Benedict XVI, Pope, 224
Berkhof, Louis, 70–71n69, 71, 99, 110, 114, 182–83, 195
Berkouwer, G. C., 194–95
Beza, Theodore, 137
Bird, Michael, 191, 191n100
Boettner, Loraine, 240n152
Bokenkotter, Thomas, 228n113
The Bondage and Liberation of the Will (Calvin), 9, 87
The Bondage of the Will (Luther), 85, 86
"born again." *See* regeneration
Boyce, James P., 34–35, 71
Buchanan, James, 190
Bultmann, Rudolf, 13

The Call of All Nations (Prosper Tyro), 7n17
calling, 32, 152
Calvin, John
  on aspectual nature of salvation, 15–16n44, 16–17, 176
  on benefits of faith, 181
  on conversion, 133, 141, 148n79
  on depravity, 90–91, 91n23
  on double justification, 181
  on faith, 148, 148n80
  on grace, 34
  on instrumental cause, 23–24n64, 170n18
  on justification, 41, 169–170, 206
  on Osiander, 180

on passivity of the human will, 109, 109n103
on penance, 242–43
on prevenient grace, 137
on rewards, 231–31n125
on righteousness, 177, 177n43, 177n46
on salvation, 9, 47–48, 47n168
on sin effects on disposition, 99
on Spirit of God, 32
on works, 31, 206
Calvinists. *See* Reformed tradition
Campbell, Constantine, 191–92
Canon laws, 29–30
Canons of Basil, 220
Canons of Dort, 54, 108, 267n42
Carson, D. A., 79, 272
Cassian, John, 7, 129–130
Catechism of the Catholic Church
on Eucharist, 236n139
on forgiveness of sin, 219, 219n83
on grace, 34
on incarnation of Christ, 46
on justification, 205, 212, 223–24
on merit, 207–8
on penance, 242
on preparation of man, 201–2
on purgatory, 213–14, 247
on rewards, 231
on salvation, 46n164
on works, 28–29
The Catholic Doctrine on Justification Explained and Vindicated (Kenrick), 204
Catholic tradition. *See* Roman Catholic Church
causation theory
Aristotle, 19–20, 22n61
aspects of causation, 19n53, 20n57
cause/effect relationship of work, 32–33
examples, 21–23
Hume on, 19n53
instrumental causation, 20n59
Thomist doctrine, 199
Christ
cooperation with, 207, 233–34
as the last Adam, 182

second coming of, 29
union with, 189–192, 272–73
Clark, Gordon H., 43, 157
community, God's work through, 207–8, 207n37
Condign merit, 208n40
conditional election, 54–55, 67–68, 71, 71n73, 72, 78–80, 84
congruous merit, 208n40
Conner, W. T., 16n45
conversion
active and passive aspects, 135–36
Arminian view, 129–132
definition of, 133–35
efficient cause, 146–48, 159–160
faith and, 158–59
grace and, 153–58
instrumental cause, 149–150, 160–62
prevenient grace, 136–144, 150–53
as progressive in nature, 206–7n34
Reformed view, 133
regeneration order of, 144–46
synergism's perspectives, 141–44
Conversion (Jones), 134
conversion experience
Jesus' response to the rich ruler, 4
Paul's response to the jailer, 4
Paul's teaching to the Ephesians, 5
Peter's four-fold response to, 4, 4n8
cooperating grace, 9, 18n50, 51, 114–15
cooperation with Christ, 207, 233–34
Cottrell, Jack W., 90n19
Council of Carthage (417), 6, 92n28
Council of Florence (1439), 213
Council of Orange (529), 7–8, 92n28, 131, 200, 226–27, 266
Council of Trent (1545)
on actual justification, 204, 207
on certainty of justification, 212
on corruption of the person, 268
on efficient cause, 217
on imputed righteousness, 210–11
on justification, 229
justification, definition of, 202, 204
on justification by faith alone, 223
on justification doctrine, 199, 203–4, 208–9, 235, 237n141
on merit, 209

INDEX

Council of Trent *(cont.)*
  on original sin, 200
  on penance, 221, 242
  on prevenient grace, 201
  on Purgatory doctrine, 213
  on sacraments, 224, 246
  on transubstantiation concept, 245
  work, definition of, 29
  on works, 253
covenant of grace, 60n26
covenant people versus covenant persons, 59–60
covenant with Abraham (Abram), 2–3, 57, 58
Cox, Leo G., 112n113
Craig, William Lane, 147
Cunningham, William, 81n118, 264n36
Cur Deus Homo (Anselm), 205

Dabney, R. L., 267–68
Demarest, Bruce, 89, 89n16, 148, 183–84, 264
demons. *See* Satan
Denney, James, 188
depravity, 90–91, 91n23, 266–69
  . *See also* total depravity
disposition, regeneration of, 98–99
divine decrees and election, 64–65, 68–72, 70–71n69, 70n67, 84
divine justice, 64, 201, 208n40
divine motion, 229, 229n116
divine wisdom, 64, 72
divorce, 140–41n45
Dongell, Joseph R., 115–16, 143, 158
double justification, 181
double predestination, 263–66
Dunn, James D. G., 42, 150, 164
Dyrness, William, 2–3

early church, 5–8
Edwards, Jonathan, 9–10, 87, 93n31
effectual calling, 32
efficacious grace, 100
efficient cause
  Arminian perspective, 74–75, 111–14, 160–61

Catholic tradition perspective, 214–18, 225–239
of conversion, 146–48, 159–160
defined, 17
election and, 74–76, 75n86, 80
instrumentality and, 19–24, 128–29
of justification, 192–94
monergism perspective, 75, 75n86, 109–10
principal efficient cause and, 18n49, 20, 21n60
Reformed perspective, 160–61
regeneration and, 103–5, 109–14
of righteousness, 181–83, 182n66
synergist perspective, 74–75, 75n86
twofold efficient agency and, 18n49
Wesleyan perspective, 111–14, 160–61
work and, 25
election
  conditional election, 54–55, 67–68, 71, 71n73, 72, 78–80, 84
  covenant versus, 60
  critique of synergists' view, 77–83
  divine decrees and, 64–65, 68–72, 70–71n69, 70n67, 84
  efficient cause of, 74–76, 75n86, 80
  election of means, 58, 62
  monergists and synergists divide, 58–60, 60n25, 60n26, 62–63
  in Old Testament, 55–60
  of people, 56–57, 61
  to service, 57–58, 61–62
  synergists' perspective, 63–68
  types of, 56n10
  unconditional election, 54, 72–74, 261
  underlying issue, 54–55
  . *See also* predestination
Ellis, E. Earle, 117, 157
enabling grace, 124, 124n159, 152
enlightening, 152
Erasmus, Desiderius
  on cooperative salvation, 9
  on debate on salvation, 199
  on justification, 30n87, 30n88
  on merit, 209
  on prevenient grace, 86n3, 106, 137

INDEX

on regeneration, 99n51
on sin, effects of, 85–86
on synergism, 239n148
Erickson, Millard, 93n31, 134, 176n40, 184, 188
Eucharist, 213, 224, 236n139, 240n151, 245, 245n171
evangelism, 51
Existential Theology, 13

faith
  as action, not work, 251, 255–56
  Arminian tradition on, 39–40
  conversion and, 158–59
  expression of, 3
  free will and, 216
  justification and, 195–96, 195n119
  preceding regeneration, 100–103, 107–11, 113, 144–45
  Protestant understanding, 218–19
  religious traditions, understanding of, 33n100
  repentance and, 216–19
  scriptural meaning, 36–38
  as work or instrumental cause, 39–44, 81–82, 84, 113, 114–16
  works and, 222
Faustus, of Rhegium, 130
Feinberg, John, 68n61
final cause, 19–20, 20n58
Finney, Charles, 34, 136n30
first grace, 202
five-point Calvinism, 260–63
Fletcher, John, 121
Forde, Gerhard O., 169n11
foreseen faith/foreknowledge, 65–66, 73, 78, 81n118, 84
forgiveness, 219
Forlines, F. Leroy, 25n70, 54, 55, 67, 105–6, 132, 143
formal cause, 19
Formula of Concord, 136
Four Causes (Aristotle), 19
four-fold conversion experience, 4, 5–8
fourfold prevenient work of God, 142
free will
  Aquinas on, 199, 214–16, 227
  Augustine on, 166–68

Ellis on, 117
Luther on, 85–86, 199
monergism on, 257–260
Olson on, 12
Pelagius on, 5–6
The Freedom of the Will (Edwards), 87
The Freedom of the Will (Locke), 9

Gathercole, Simon, 273
Geisler, Norman
  on conditional election, 55, 71n73
  on conversion, 143
  on efficient cause, 74–75, 147
  on election, 67, 77–78, 78n99
  on irresistible grace, 259–260
  on justification, 269–271
  on means of regeneration, 105
  on meritorious work, 25
  on predestination, 65–66, 68n61
  on regeneration, 88, 103
  on seeking after God, 93
  on spiritual deadness, 94–95
  as synergists, 12
  on works, 255–56, 269–270
general calling, 32
George, Timothy, 41–42, 91n23, 108–9n101
Gerrish, B. A., 43
Gill, John, 263
God
  hostility before, 94
  love of, 82
  omni-benevolence of, 67–68, 73, 84
  pleasing of, 91–92
  seeking after, 93
  spirit of, 32
Godwin, Johnnie C., 100n54
grace
  Aquinas on, 8–9
  Arminian tradition on, 33–34
  Augustine on, 7
  conversion and, 153–58
  cooperating grace, 9, 18n50, 51, 114–15
  efficacious grace, 100
  enabling grace, 124, 124n159, 152
  first grace, 202
  habitual grace, 202

grace *(cont.)*
   infused grace, 205
   irresistible grace, 137–38n34, 145, 262
   of justification, 6
   prevenient (*See* prevenient grace)
   sanctifying grace, 52
   saving grace, 137–38n34, 138
   scriptural meaning, 35–39
   universal grace, 102–3
   works and, 33–35
The Grace of God (Arminius), 137
Green, Joel B., 134–35
Grenz, Stanley, 142, 144n62
Grounds, Vernon C., 102–3, 103n71, 121
Grudem, Wayne, 52n191, 133–34, 178, 186, 270
guilt and punishment, 223
Guthrie, Donald, 44, 154, 187–88
Gutierrez, Gustavo, 14

habitual grace, 202
Hägglund, Bengt, 130n2
Hagner, Donald, 187, 187n87
Harnack, Adolf, 130–31
Hart, Trevor, 14n40
Hawthorne, Gerald F., 51
Helm, Paul, 110, 160
historical survey
   biblical tensions, 2–5
   considerations, 10–11
   early church tensions, 5–8
   grace and merit, 8–9
   overview, 1
   reformation debate, 9–10
Hodge, A. A., 48
Hodge, Charles, 32
Hoekema, Anthony, 52, 109, 144n62, 154n99, 183, 263
Holy Trinity, work of, 28, 32
Horton, Michael
   on conversion, 132–33n12, 135
   on effectual calling, 32
   on election, 54, 67, 73
   on justification, 186
   on regeneration, 148
   on righteousness, 178, 190

human depravity, 251–52
   . *See also* total depravity
human-based monergism, 6
Hume, David, 19n53
Hunt, Dave, 90n22

image of God, 266, 268–69
imputed righteousness, 210
indulgences, 9, 9n24, 168
infant baptism, 227n109, 245n172
infused grace, 205
infused righteousness, 272
instrumental means/instrumentality
   active and passive powers, 44–45
   Aquinas on, 8
   Calvin on, 170n18
   Catholic tradition perspective, 218–224, 239–248
   causation theory and, 20n59, 22n22, 40n136
   causes versus means, 23–24n64
   of conversion, 149–150, 160–62
   defined, 17, 18, 18n49
   efficient cause and, 19–24, 128–29
   faith as, 39–44, 81–82, 84, 113, 114–16
   of justification, 194–95
   monergism perspective, 75–76, 82, 110–11
   righteousness and, 183–84
   synergism's perspectives, 82, 105–7
intermediary cause, 24
irresistible grace, 137–38n34, 145, 262

Jeremias, Joachim, 162n125
John Paul II, Pope, 200n5, 205
Johnson, Kevin, 219n84
Joint Declaration on the Doctrine of Justification (Catholic Church), 34, 228, 235–36, 238
Jones, E. Stanley, 134
Jüngel, Eberhard, 239n149
Junius, Franciscus, 91n23
justice
   Liberation Theology and, 14
   repentance and, 220
   works and, 29

INDEX

justification
　Catholic tradition on, 199–206
　definitions, 165–66, 166n4, 202–3
　efficient cause of, 192–94
　faith and, 195–96, 195n119
　good works and, 195–96
　instrumentality of, 194–95
　making just vs. declaring just,
　　271–72
　Middle Ages, 167–68, 208
　Modern Period, 170–71
　Patristic Era, 166–67, 166n5
　Reformation Era, 168–170
　righteousness and, 168–69, 169n15,
　　185–86
　traditions understanding of, 164–65,
　　185n81

Keathley, Kenneth, 91n23, 133–34,
　260–61n23
Kelly, J.N.D., 130n3
Kenrick, Francis Patrick, 204, 212
Kittel, Gerhard, 187
Klein, William, 77
Klein, William W., 65
Küng, Hans, 41, 210, 217–18, 232,
　233–35

Ladd, George, 42–43, 173
Lane, A.N.S., 208n40
Lane, Tony, 243n164
Lemke, Steve, 100, 106, 125–26, 145–46
Leo I, (the Great), Pope, 220–21
Leo X, Pope, 9n24
Liberation Theology, 14
Limited Atonement, 261–62
Locke, John, 9
Lombard, Peter, 168, 240n152
Luther, Martin
　Augustine and, 168–69
　on causation, 199
　on conversion, 136, 141
　on faith preceding regeneration,
　　108–9, 108–9n101
　on free will, 85–86
　on instrumental cause, 110
　on justification, 169

　on justification doctrine, 30–31,
　　41–42
　on merit, 209–10
　on merit-based salvation, 9
　monergistic and synergistic views, 52
　on operative grace, 194n116
　on regeneration, 97, 97n45, 114
　on righteousness, 177–78, 177–
　　78n53, 180n59
　on sacraments, 180, 192
　on sin effects on disposition, 99
　works, term usage, 30–31, 30n87,
　　30n88, 180
Lutheran World Federation, 238

MacDonald, William G., 151n88
Machen, J. Gresham, 110–11, 111n111
marriage and divorce, 140–41n45
Marshall, Howard, 94n36
Martin, Ralph P., 44
Massilians, 7
material cause, 19
McCartney, Dan, 184
McGonigle, Herbert Boyd,
　119–120n141
McGrath, Alister, 180n59, 208, 208n40,
　210, 238–39n147
medication, as example of causation,
　21–22
merit
　Aquinas on, 8–9, 198–99
　attaining, 207–8, 208n40
　Calvin on, 31
　definition, 207
　on instrumental cause, 195
　Luther on, 9, 31
　reformation debate, 9–10
meritorious work, 25, 25n70, 43, 78,
　269
Methodism, 64
　. See also Wesleyan tradition
Middle Ages
　justification, 167–68, 208
　penance as sacrament, 240
"Middle Knowledge" (Molina & Craig),
　147
Miley, John, 10, 113
Molina, Luis, 147

295

INDEX

monergist and monergism
- activity of individuals, 24
- biblical portrayal of divine decrees, 69–72
- defined, 18, 18n50
- efficient cause, view of, 75, 75n86, 109–10
- on election, 58–60, 60n25, 62–66, 68–74, 80n109
- on free will, 257–260
- on instrumental means, 75–76
- on regeneration perspectives, 107–11, 128
- on rewards, 231–31n125
- on righteousness in scripture, 172–75, 183
- righteousness position on, 183–85
- salvation, with God alone, 251–52
- salvation, more coherent view of, 274
- scriptural synergism, 269–271
- significance of, 11–12
- as supralapsarianism, 263–66
- variant positions amongst, 52–53
- works, term usage, 30, 255

Moody, Dale, 66, 86, 100
moral agents, 22
Morris, Leon, 43, 183
mortal sin, 27
Muller, Richard A., 265n37
Mullins, E. Y., 100

Nettles, Thomas, 164–65n1
new life, regeneration and, 99
New Perspective on Paul, 164, 185
non-believers, 49, 50, 271
non-Reformed traditions. *See* Arminian tradition; Wesleyan tradition
Not By Faith Alone (Sungenis), 222

obedience, 174n34, 182–83, 190–91, 222
Oden, Thomas
- on conversion, 133, 142–43, 149
- on cooperating grace, 51, 114–15
- on divine decrees, 68n61
- on efficient cause, 103, 104, 107
- on faith, 158

- on prevenient grace, 117, 147, 149
- on regeneration, 88, 113, 146
- on sacrifice, 60
- on salvation, 47

Olson, C. Gordon, 65, 77–78
Olson, Roger
- on conversion, 142, 147
- on double predestination, 263–64
- on efficient cause, 74
- on election, 54–55, 65
- on faith, 159n113
- on free will, 12
- on instrumental cause, 77
- on instrumental means, 75, 161
- on irresistible grace, 262
- on justification, 164n1
- on prevenient grace, 67, 105, 126, 140, 152
- on regeneration, 146
- on total depravity, 90
- on TULIP Calvinism, 260–61n23
- on works, 253, 253n3

omni-benevolence of God, 67–68, 73, 84
"On Conscience" (Wesley), 119
On Working Out Our Own Salvation (Wesley), 114, 115
operative grace, 18n50, 194n116
ordo salutis, 16–17
Origen, 14
original sin, 200
Osborne, Grant, 82
Osiander, Andreas, 177n46, 180
Owen, John, 34

Page, Frank S., 121n146
passive, defined, 18
passive obedience, 182–83, 190–91
passivity, 22n62, 44–45, 109, 109n103, 135–36, 157, 257–260
Patterson, Paige, 92, 94
Pelagianism, 6, 6n13, 10, 257
Pelagius
- on free will, 5–6, 6n13
- sin, effects of, 90, 130, 200

penance, 168, 217, 219–222, 219n84
Picirilli, Robert E., 67n57, 72
Pighius, Albert, 9

296

INDEX

Pinson, J. Matthew, 256
pleasing God, 91–92
Polhill, John, 188
Pope, William Burt, 101, 102n69, 120
predestination, 6–7, 63–64, 63n40, 65n50, 66, 68n61, 69, 145
. See also election
predestination, double, 263–66
"preparation of man," 201–2
prevenient grace
    Aquinas on, 227n109
    Arminian view, 100–101, 116–125, 137–38n34, 150–53, 150n85, 162, 227n109
    Catholic tradition on, 150n85, 201–2
    in conversion, 136–141, 150–53
    definition of, 18, 112, 112n112, 112n113, 151–52
    Erasmus on, 86
    Forlines on, 132
    need for, 10
    Olson, on, 67
    Semi-Pelagianism and, 7n17
    universal coverage of, 137–38n34, 137–38n36, 266–68
    Wesley on, 51, 138–39n36
principal agent, 52
principal cause, 8, 18n49, 20, 21n60, 198, 214–16
    . See also efficient cause; instrumental means/instrumentality
progressive conversion, 206–7n34
Prosper of Aquitaine, 6–7, 7n17
Protestant Reformation
    debate on salvation, 9–10
    on justification, 168–170
    on merit and free will, 199
    on regeneration, 85–87
    works, term usage, 30
punishment, 223, 243n164
purgatory doctrine
    Aquinas' proposal of, 8–9
    righteousness and, 168
    Roman Catholic Church on, 212–14, 247

radical depravity, 91n23
Rahner, Karl, 233n130, 241

Rainbow, Jonathan H., 170n18
Ratzinger, Joseph, 224
Reasoner, Vic, 156n102
reconciliation, sacrament of. See penance
redemption, regeneration versus, 89n16
reformation, historical survey, 9–10
Reformed tradition
    Arminians as, 47n165
    on divine decrees, 70n67, 71
    on efficient cause, 160–61
    on election, 61–62, 63
    on faith as a work, 41–42, 42n147
    five-point Calvinism, 260–63
    God-centered view of salvation, 133
    on grace, 34–35, 156–57, 162–63
    on instrumental means, 161–62
    monergistic and synergistic views, 52n191
    in the Netherlands, 60n26
    on prevenient grace, 151–53
    on regeneration, 87n9, 88, 146
    on salvation, 46–48, 47n168
    on sin, effects of, 91n23
    unconditional election, 54
regeneration
    analysis and critique of views, 111–127
    Augustine on, 5
    conversion and, 144–46
    of disposition, 98–99
    efficient cause and, 103–5, 109–14
    faith preceding, 100–103, 108–9
    grammatical and lexical examination, 87–88
    hostility before God, 94
    inability to please God, 91–92
    inability to seek after God, 93
    instrumental cause and, 114–16
    instrumentality and, 105–7, 110–11
    MacDonald on, 151n88
    monergists perspectives, 107–11
    nature of, 95–99
    need for, 88–91
    new life and, 99
    overview, 85–86
    pleasing life and, 96–97
    prevenient grace and, 116–125

regeneration *(cont.)*
  of senses, 97–98
  spiritual deadness, 94–95
  synergism's perspectives, 99–107
  theological definition, 88–95
Remonstrance, 138
repentance, 64, 135–36, 162n125, 216–19, 222, 241
Replacement Theology, 61n29
reprobation, 264
response, defined, 18
rewards, 29–31, 231–31n125
righteousness
  actuality of, 177–79, 192
  as aspects of the aspect, 175–76
  biblical definition, 186–88
  efficient cause of, 181–83, 182n66
  extent of, 179–181
  imputed righteousness, 210–11
  infused righteousness, 272
  instrumental cause, 183–84
  judicial aspect of, 172–74, 187–88, 192, 196, 203–4
  justification and, 168–69, 169n15, 185–86
  sacraments and, 167–68, 167n7
  theological definition, 175–181, 188–192
  union with Christ and, 189–192
Robertson, A. T., 44n157
Rogers, Charles Allen, 119–120n141, 156n103
Roman Catholic Church
  abuse of merit-based salvation, 9, 168
  baptism and, 41, 168, 221, 223–24, 227n109, 244–45
  beliefs of (*See Catechism of the Catholic Church*)
  Canon laws, 29–30
  conversion as progressive, 206–7n34
  councils (*See* Council of Carthage; Council of Florence; Council of Orange; Council of Trent; Vatican Council I; Vatican Council II)
  on efficient cause, 214–18, 225–239
  on faith as a work, 40–41
  on forgiveness, 219
  on grace, 34, 169n11
  historic and modern issue, 198–99
  on image of God, 268–69
  on instrumental cause, 218–224, 239–248
  on instrumentality, 170n18
  Joint Declaration on the Doctrine of Justification, 34, 228, 235–36, 238
  on justification, 199–206, 206–10, 271–72
  justification as a "state," 211
  on merit, 206–10, 256, 269
  penance and, 168, 217, 219–222, 219n84
  on prevenient grace, 150n85, 201–2
  on purgatory doctrine, 212–14, 247
  on regeneration, 202
  on repentance and faith, 219
  on righteousness, 167–68, 167n7, 171
  sacraments and, 167–68, 224, 244–48
  on salvation, 46
  salvation outside the church, 224–25
  separated brethren and, 225n106, 240n151
  on sin, 46, 46n164
  soteriological synergism and, 50, 253
  transubstantiation concept, 236, 240n151, 245
  work, term usage, 25–30, 28n80, 255

sacraments
  Augustine on, 213
  baptism (*See* baptism)
  Catholic tradition on, 167–68, 224, 244–48
  Eucharist, 213, 224, 236n139, 240n151, 245, 245n171
  instrumental grace, 17
  penance, 219–220, 219n84, 240–44
  in Reformed tradition, 195n120
  righteousness and, 167–68, 167n7
  seven sacraments defined, 240–41, 240n150, 240n152, 240n153
  as symbols and causes of grace, 228

INDEX

sacrifice, 60
salvation
  abuse of merit-based salvation, 9, 168
  aspects of (*See* aspectual nature of salvation)
  assurance of, 80–81n112
  as a gift, church emphasis on, 8
  grace and, 47n168
  loss of, 237
  meaning of, 45–49
  ordering of aspects, 16–17
  outside the church, 224–25
  past, present, and future dynamic,, 48–49, 48n170, 70, 270
  principal efficient cause of, 18n49, 20, 21n60
  Reformation debate on, 9–10
  scriptural debate on, 2–5
  sin and, 46, 46n164, 48
sanctification, 180, 235, 270
sanctifying grace, 52
Sanders, E. P., 164
Satan
  power of, 14
  salvation not extended to, 265
  temptation, 23–24n64
  works of, 28
saving grace, 137–38n34, 138
Scholastic formula, 228
Schreiner, Thomas, 122–23, 122n150, 172
"Scriptural Depiction of Prevenient Grace" (Shelton), 124
scriptural synergism, 269–271
scripture references
  atonement, 158
  born again terminology, 88, 88n15
  conversion, 134
  covenant with Abraham, 2–3, 57, 58
  creation and works, 33, 33n99
  debate on salvation, 2–5
  divine decrees, 69–72
  election, lexical meaning, 56
  election in New Testament, 61–63, 78, 83
  election in Old Testament, 55–60, 83
  election of means, 58

election to service, 57–58, 83
faith, lexical meaning, 36–38
faith, role of, 42–44
faith alone, 222
grace, 35–39, 153–54, 155n101, 160, 262
hostility before God, 94
instrumental means, 76
justification, 186–88
penance, 220
prevenient grace, 101–3, 118–124, 119–120n141
righteousness, 172–76, 179
seeking after God, 93
sin, effects of, 91
spiritual deadness, 94–95
synergism used in, 49–51
work, lexical meaning, 38–39
second coming of Christ, 29
Semi-Pelagianism, 7–8, 7n17, 10, 130–31, 257
senses, regeneration of, 97–98
Shedd, William G. T., 94, 135
Shelton, W. Brian, 123–24, 124–25n159, 156n102
sin
  of Adam, 6, 6n13, 23–24n64, 177, 200–201, 205
  Arminian belief, 47
  Catholic perspective, 46, 200
  cause of, 14
  depraving effects of, 10, 259
  disposition, effects of, 98
  effects of, 10, 15, 86–87, 89, 89n16
  mortal sin, 27
  original sin, 200
  penalty of, 267
  salvation and, 48
  unrighteousness and, 181, 273
  violation of human will, 269
Slaatte, Howard, 121
Smeaton, George, 157n107
soul, nature of, 92n27
spiritual deadness, 94–95
spiritual good, 92n28, 92n29
Sproul, R. C., 94, 155n101, 263
Spurgeon, Charles, 110, 148, 184
Stagg, Frank, 88

INDEX

Stanglin, Keith D., 120–21
Staples, Rob L., 159n112
Storms, C. Samuel, 80
Stott, John R. W., 160
Strong, Augustus H., 68
Summers, Thos, 157–58
Sungenis, Robert A., 222–23
supralapsarianism, 263–66
synergist and synergism
    defined, 18, 18–19n52, 19, 252, 256
    efficient cause, view of, 74–75, 75n86, 254
    on election, 60, 63–68, 77–83
    forms of, 11n32
    on grace, 256–57
    on instrumental means, 75, 254
    in the New Testament, 49–51
    on prevenient grace, 141–44, 252
    regeneration perspectives, 99–107, 127–28
    salvation, in cooperation with God, 251, 253–54
    significance of, 11–12
    variant positions amongst, 52–53
    work, term usage, 24, 253–54
Synod of Dort, 54, 108, 267n42

telephone, as example of causation, 22–23
Tertullian, 219–220
Tetzel, John, 9n24
Thomas of Aquinas. *See* Aquinas
Thomist. *See* Aquinas
Tillich, Paul, 43–44, 44n156
Tilly, William, 119–120n141
total depravity, 12, 89–90, 89n17, 90n22, 261, 266–69
transubstantiation concept, 236, 240n151, 245
A Treatise on the Predestination of the Saints (Augustine), 7
Treatise on the Sacraments (Aquinas), 8
trust, term usage, 43
TULIP Calvinism, 260–63
Turretin, Francis, 186–87

Unconditional Election, 261
unconditional election, 54, 72–74
unconditional love and conditional election, 82, 82n121
Universal Atonement, 262, 262n26
universal grace, 102–3, 137–38n34, 138–39n36, 266–69
universal law, 138–39n36
unrighteousness, 181, 273

Van Mastricht, Peter, 95, 95n38, 109–10
Vance, Laurence M., 262
Vatican Council I, 230
Vatican Council II
    on faith, 41
    on justification, 237–38
    on sacraments and justification, 171, 171n20
    on salvation outside the church, 225, 225n106
    on separated brethren, 225n106, 240n151
Vincent of Lérins, 7
virtuous works, 27

Walls, Jerry L., 115–16, 143, 158
Walsch, Liam G., 229n116
Waltke, Bruce, 172
Warfield, B. B., 9–10, 87, 125, 132–33n12, 161n121, 169n11
Waterhouse, Steven W., 135
Waters, Guy Prentiss, 179
Wells, David, 150–51
Welty, Greg, 73, 78
Wesley, John
    on assurance of salvation, 80–81n112
    on conversion, 144
    on cooperating grace, 114
    on divine decrees, 69, 132
    on efficient cause, 104, 105
    on faith as a work, 40, 158–59
    founder of Methodism, 64
    monergistic and synergistic views, 52
    on predestination, 145
    on prevenient grace, 51, 101–2, 137, 137–38n34, 138–39, 138–39n36, 266
    on regeneration, 90, 99, 145

INDEX

synergism's role, 66
on works, 25n70
Wesleyan tradition
   on assurance of salvation,
      80–81n112
   on divine decrees, 64–65
   on efficient cause, 111–14, 160–61
   on election, 63n37
   on faith, 159, 163
   on God's love, 82
   on grace, 155–56, 156n102
   on instrumental means, 161–62
   on prevenient grace, 150–52, 162, 227n109
   on regeneration, 87n9, 88, 127–28
   on total depravity, 90
Westminster Catechism, 42, 69
Westminster Confession of Faith, 54, 72–73, 108, 108n100, 189
Westminster Shorter Catechism, 68
White, James, 191, 196
Why God Became Man (Anselm), 220
Williams, Michael D., 264n34
Witherington, Ben, 118
work
   action and, 251, 255–56
   Arminian tradition on, 25
   Calvin on, 31
   Catholic belief, 25–30, 28n80, 255
   cause/effect relationship, 32–33
   common consensus, 24–33
   contrasts of work and grace, 33–35
   defined, 19, 33
   efficient cause, 25
   grace and, 33–35
   as instrumental cause of faith, 39–44, 81–82, 84
   Luther on, 30–31, 30n87, 30n88, 41
   obligate, as description of, 25n70
   as sanctification, 270
   scriptural meaning, 38–39
works of the law
   covenant with Abraham and, 2n4
   early Christian understanding, 3–4, 5, 184, 187, 194
   faith alone and, 222
   faith as antithesis to, 42
   Luther on, 30n87
   sin of Adam, 200
works-based-righteousness, 224, 225
Wright, N. T., 164
Wynkoop, Mildred, 106, 140

Ziesler, J. A., 187

www.ingramcontent.com/pod-product-compliance
Lightning Source LLC
Chambersburg PA
CBHW050623300426

44112CB00012B/1632